MW00597696

Bernabé at 29, holding Mary

Miguel, Guadalupe, Carlota, and Pascual (ca. 1945)

We Became Mexican American

How Our Immigrant Family Survived to Pursue the American Dream

Revised Edition

By Carlos B. Gil

The GilDeane Group Inc.
Seattle, Washington

Copyright © 2014 by Carlos B. Gil

First published by XLibris 2012

Re-printing and distribution of this edition is by
Lightning Source/Ingram Inc. U.S.A.
2014

Publisher:
The GilDeane Group Inc.
6015 NE 205th Street
Kenmore WA
U.S.A.
www.diversitycentral.com

Map and cover by Serena C. Tsang

Library of Congress Control Number: 2012911773

ISBN: Hard 978-0-9899519-06
Soft 978-0-9899519-1-3
E-book 978-0-9899519-2-0

All rights reserved. No part of this book may be reproduced or transmitted in any form or by any means, electronic or mechanical, including photocopying, recording, or by any information storage and retreival system, without permission in writing from the copyright owner.

This book was printed in the United States of America

To order additional copies of this book, contact:
The GilDeane Group Inc.
1-206-362-0336
www.diversitycentral.com
Orders@diversitycentral.com

Dedication

To my children, grandchildren, my great-grandchildren,
and to the rest of my relatives
across the various lines of our extended family,
today and tomorrow.
May they all reach for the stars.

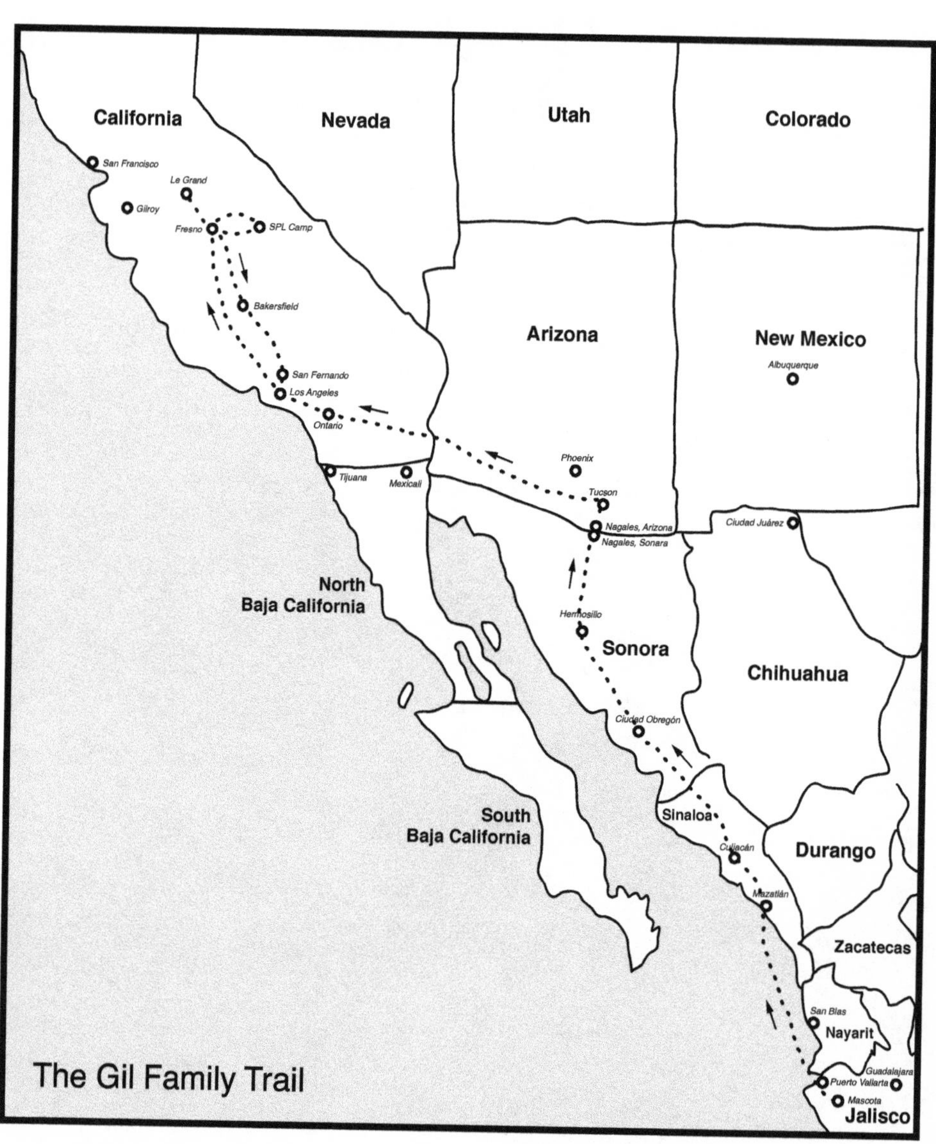
California
Nevada
Utah
Colorado
San Francisco
Le Grand
Gilroy
Fresno
SPL Camp
Bakersfield
Arizona
New Mexico
Albuquerque
San Fernando
Los Angeles
Ontario
Phoenix
Tijuana
Mexicali
Tucson
Nagales, Arizona
Nagales, Sonara
Ciudad Juárez
North
Baja California
Hermosillo
Sonora
Chihuahua
Ciudad Obregón
Sinaloa
South
Baja California
Culiacán
Durango
Mazatlán
Zacatecas
San Blas
Nayarit
Guadalajara
Puerto Vallarta
Mascota
Jalisco
The Gil Family Trail

Table of Contents

Introduction ix

Part I: The Push and Pulls

Chapter 1: Peasants One and All (1880–1914 1
Chapter 2: The Young Rebel Goes North (1914–1921) 27
Chapter 3: The Family Follows (1919–1922) 45
Chapter 4: Arriving in the United States (1922–1923) 67
Chapter 5: The First Years in the United States (1919–1923) 89
Chapter 6: Shuttling between Sunland and the Logging Camp (1924–1927) 101

Part II: Putting Down Roots

Chapter 7: Settling in San Fernando (1874–1927) 113
Chapter 8: Life Becomes Ever more Challenging (1927–1938) 131
Chapter 9: We Stumble Forward (1938–1942) 157
Chapter 10: Our Toughest Years (1942–1972) 171
Chapter 11: Looking Back at Our Toughest Years 205
Chapter 12: Connecting and Celebrating 223
Chapter 13: Good-bye to the First Generation 265

Part III: The Second and Third Generations

Chapter 14: The Second Generation 289
Chapter 15: A Glimpse at the Third Generation 323
A Word About Discrimination and Racism 335

Part IV: Additional Materials

Appendix I: Searching for My Father's Story 351

Appendix II: The Gil Family Tree (a partial view) 373

Appendix III: The Boys and One Girl in the Santa Rosa Band (ca. 1950) 375

Appendix IV: The Sources 377

Glossary 385

Index 389

End notes 397

Introduction

This is a story of my ancestors emigrating from Mexico in the first decade of the twentieth century and settling in San Fernando, California, on the northern edge of Los Angeles. In this story you, the reader, will learn that despite their unprivileged background and utter poverty, they were propelled to leave Mexico in order to keep the family together as one of them had already gone north on his own, driven by the political instability of those years. They all traveled in stages in order to earn money at each stop and thus be able to push on to the next locale, and then finally cross the border and step onto American soil.

The chronicle laid out in these pages leans on several key ideas concerning Latinos in the United States, Mexican Americans constituting the largest and oldest component. One of them is that migrating from Mexico to California began over a hundred years ago; it is not a contemporary phenomenon. Despite the fact that Mexico and the United States share a contiguous border, this exodus was no easy feat and my folks' experience bears this out quite clearly. Moreover, reaching the border and crossing over were not ends in themselves. They constituted only the beginning of a long battle to survive in America because my folks knew neither the language nor the culture and had little schooling. The two countries may be long-standing neighbors, but they are vastly different from one another and this is why immigrating to the United States is no walk in the park. Another component of my story is that my folks arrived in the United States at the worst of economic times—the beginning of the Great Depression. The reader will discover that my ancestors managed to survive and multiply despite the staggering challenges that over came them because of this economic turn of events.

But surviving the Depression to pursue the American dream was only the beginning. They also came face-to-face with the vexing decisions that immigrants worldwide have to make: how much of the new culture to accept and how much to reject. Which cultural rules were going to guide my parents in their child-rearing? Lastly, what would the impact of all these contradictions be on my parents' and *our* lives, the lives of the children born in America?

The story in these pages may also offer an opportunity for the reader who possesses prior knowledge of the immigration experience either through personal experience or through study. If so, my chronicle offers the possibility of comparing immigration experiences, although a comparative view is not the objective here. Still, what we, the Gils,[1] lived through, may offer an insight into the formation of a Mexican American family, one that immigrated to the United States in the 1920s. Considering the significant growth of the Latino population in the United States in the second half of the twentieth century and the consequent arrival of countless other Mexican families, our experience may serve as a contrast with those who arrived more recently. Only the informed reader and the interested student can make the ultimate judgment on this question.

Be that as it may, the story in these pages shows that my folks experienced a fair amount of anguish when they gave up their own country and took up a new one. Their distress was at least twofold.

On the one hand, my old folks felt the sorrow of loss when they left the only home they had ever known. Informed hindsight tempts me to say that while they may have left an archaic and unfair world behind, it was still theirs nevertheless. It was all they knew despite its outdated and antiquated way of doing things even as it gave primacy to the close human bonds that defined them up to the point of their departure. Archaic or not, my ancestors were near to weeping when they left their world behind. The reader may appreciate the words that my mother used to describe the moment when she and her mother and brother took one last look at the plantation where they spent all their lives. I believe they adequately convey the sorrow that overcame them. The words were heartrending when I first heard them, and then again when I wrote them down and looked at them again. Other moments described elsewhere in part I reveal this regret to part ways with the old. My grandmother, who led the way, was older and therefore must have felt the pangs of distress once they left home more than her children. Not surprisingly, she was often described as not feeling well for many years after. These early chapters will also show that my maternal uncle Miguel left Mazatlán quite reluctantly but not his rebel brother, Pascual. My ancestors stopped at this western port on the migrant trail in order to work and save money to be able to move on to the next stopover. Miguel's feelings clearly inform us that after settling in Mazatlán he no longer desired to reach the United States.

On the other hand, the distress my ancestors felt didn't magically disappear by simply arriving in "the land of the free." All indications are that the bewilderment they must have felt once arriving in California was soon taken over by a sense of growing apprehension not only because they found themselves in a foreign environment but also because they arrived just a few years before the American economy plummeted to the historical depths we know as the Great Depression.

In fact, a paradox arose from my family's experience during the Depression. My ancestors not only survived these years of despair, they also managed to lay down the foundation for an old-age pension of sorts. Mom and Dad found themselves scratching and saving at the cost of great pain and stress in order to buy a small home, very small, as we'll learn below. Still, no one expected it, but it became the starting point for rental income half a century later, helping Mom to assure modest retirement income.

Be that as it may, our family grew in numbers as the economy tumbled, making things quite desperate. Life became so difficult for my parents in the depth of the Depression and even afterward, that I believe my mother, at least, looked back wistfully to her time as a teen ager in Mexico. We know she reminisced more than once on the rosy days she spent strolling the *malecón* in Mazatlán, arm in arm with her friends, enraptured by the sea mist blowing in from the ocean, so different from the places where she grew up and, oh, so distant from the responsibilities of being a wife and mother of so many children in Southern California, and not having a penny to spare.

Composing the chapters for part III "Taking Root" were the most challenging for me. Seeking to understand how my family evolved after settling in San Fernando was far from easy. I concluded there were several reasons for this.

On the one hand, my mother's memory, serving as a strong support for this book, seems to have favored the details about the migrant journey itself and remembered less or chose to remember less about the years after she married and began having children. It's as if the singularity of their decision to emigrate (my mother's, my grandmother Carlota's, and my uncle Miguel's) and the actual migration itself —to abandon everything in Mexico and throw themselves into the journey, having to face daunting tests, undergo strange experiences, and having to meet new friends—came to a close when they arrived in San Fernando, where they finally settled. It seems that in her mind the uniqueness of the immigrant experience, no matter how trying or risky, outshined the more shadowed and sobering familiarity of raising a family in a new country and in the most daunting of times. It's also fair to speculate that Mother's limited recall of the settled years may have also simply been her choice in omitting details about her married life. The fact is that her notes and reminiscences about the settled years became devoid of enthusiasm, no longer crisp, abrupt, turning even sorrowful as the reader will see. My father's experiences, memories, and feelings are absent here because he died before I was old and sensible enough to interview him; I greatly missed his involvement for this story. What I attribute to him comes via our mother, my siblings, and my own remembrances.

Taking root in another culture is a very complicated and painfully frustrating process, but doing so in the middle of the Great Depression could only add to the many predicaments that my family encountered. Had my parents remained childless after they came together, their trials might not have been so difficult but launching a family in those needy years definitely raised the bar for them—they had more mouths to feed as a result and this only added to their burden.

The other complications involved in this rooting process began to emerge when we, the Gil children, started arriving and growing up. In comparison to the home country, things were done differently in Southern California, where my folks chose to settle, and one of the many variances in this anchoring process was linked to how we, as Mexican American children, were to be raised (the term *Mexican American* didn't exist at the time). Stumbling upon this question gave me some pause when writing these chapters. I discovered that my siblings associated conflict more than I did with the way our parents raised us, especially with regard to our mother; I was especially slow in grasping this hurtful dimension of our family life. The reader will also discover that this sense of discord was raised with some forcefulness by my older siblings when I started asking certain questions. It seems I had overlooked this friction, as I explain in chapters 10 and 11—and so I had to grapple with why I had been remiss, blithely musing on books and other things.

¤

One of the deeper insights that gradually penetrated my mind as I prepared to complete this volume is that coming to America remains a complicated experience. There is more to the idea of arriving to simply fill a job that most native-born Americans may prefer to shun. While I might have appreciated this at one level, I believe I gained a new understanding when I applied it to my own family. I concluded that taking up a new life in a completely different land is akin to reforging one's personality or one's sense of self, at least for an adult immigrant, and it demands a process that is highly complex in itself.

I am convinced the immigrant experience is worth retelling because in our case it served as an opportunity to chronicle to the younger ones how our patrimony was built up slowly and painfully. Patrimony may be defined in financial or cultural terms.

The reader may appreciate how my folks shared their hopes and joys openly along with their anguish and despair. Their remembrances are stated in simple, everyday language, confirming in my mind the universal need for self-esteem so essential for human survival no matter how impoverished a person might be. I exult in having been able to understand this and record it opportunely not only because these were my *viejos*, my own ancestors, but because their testimony reminded me of our tendency to overlook the humanity in the people who pick our fruits and vegetables, clean our yards, and build our houses. Immigrating to the United States, or to any country for that matter, is no joyride, and the experience of all immigrants is vastly under appreciated by those of us who don't migrate.

The precursors in our family, the subjects of this story, were like most of the men and women who have walked across the southern border over the last one hundred years. They never got into politics, and they never entertained the idea of forming a labor union or even joining one, even though I believe they commanded every reason to do so. Nonetheless, I hold that their lives possess an important meaning for the rest of us. I stress this idea more than once in these pages.

The apolitical past of my ancestors alone makes this account different from most explanations about Mexicans in the United States because much of what has been written about them tends to highlight an organized struggle usually against bad Anglo farmers and/or politicians. My folks in this story fought silently on their own, rarely searching for a larger solution to their specific condition. Like most of their compatriots who crossed the border in their time and afterward, my kinfolk shunned politically oriented leaders of any skin color and set themselves down to do the job that had to be done, to begin setting down roots in a land that offered them more than what they could find back home. Go to work, do it well, and come home and rest—if you can. And, as we'll see, they found a formula that allowed them to nudge forward despite many painful setbacks. I hope my own children, grandchildren, and great-grandchildren grow to appreciate this past.

¤

I have woven the memorials of my old folks with other sources including the remembrances of my own siblings, all of whose voices were machine-recorded. The transcriptions of these recordings in English and in Spanish served as a foundation for the content written into the pages of this book. "Tell me what you remember about Mom and Dad and about when we were all growing up!" I pleaded many times with recording tools at the ready. I also include bits and pieces of my own memory although the premier sibling recollections naturally lie with my older *hermanos*, my sister Mary, and my brother Manuel (there were eight of us, three dying before I could put my questions to them). Mary and Manuel witnessed more because they were older. I too discovered that they inevitably honed a perspective different than my own, something that surprised me at the beginning—"how could this be?" I asked myself. "How could we have different angles of memory within one closely knit family?" But, of course, my older siblings *would* have a distinct view. And so would the rest of us who were younger; we would obviously preserve fewer reminiscences of our parents, in comparison, certainly different ones, and would remember shorter spans of the years we spent inside the family circle and these would conform to our own unique position in the family, to our own special point of view, to the way we reacted individually to our parents, and so on. I was amazed at how we all remembered different things! Yet they all added up.

Here are the names of my ancestors who play as the main characters in this story:

Carlota Hernández, my grandmother,[2]
Pascual Naranjo, my uncle and my mother's elder half-brother,
Miguel Naranjo, my uncle and my mother's younger half-brother,
Guadalupe (Lupe) B. Gil, my mother, and
Bernabé Gil, my father.

With the exception of my grandmother and father, the above named persons served as the main sources for this book. I interviewed them in the years 1978–1979 at their places of domicile in San Fernando when I was a Ford Foundation Fellow at UCLA in the History Department, eagerly learning and anxious to apply the tools of oral history provided to me by Dr. James W. Wilkie, an appreciated mentor. It took me more than thirty years, however, to finally work on these interviews leading to the preparation of this book because I had given priority to other kinds of historical work in the interim.

Here is an introductory statement about each of my interviewees.

Carlota Hernández, my grandmother. She is one of three key individuals whose decisions helped create our Mexican American family as we know it today. Born to a family of semi-indentured peasants (*peones acasillados*) tied to a *hacienda* in west central Mexico in 1880, and a full blooded Indian, as we like to say in the United States, she made the initial determination to leave the world she knew in order to follow her ungovernable son, Pascual, to the United States taking her other children in tow, son Miguel and daughter Guadalupe. A stalwart and self-reliant woman, she finally settled in San Fernando and established a micro business that kept her afloat economically for the rest of her life. Needless to say, she etched a durable impression on the family she left behind when she died in 1953.

Pascual Naranjo, my uncle. My *tío* (uncle) Pascual is the second of the three individuals whose actions led to the founding of our family in Southern California. Born in 1900, he is clearly our first precursor in this story because his restlessness goaded him out of his mother's adobe hut at the age of fourteen and cast him all the way to California by the time he was eighteen. He thus led the way on my mother's side of the family. He worked hard in the United States and was savvy enough to become foreman on many jobs but he returned to Mexico at age 31 at the height of the Great Depression. His return coincided with Mexico's implementing socialist-oriented policies which generated considerable controversy and turmoil. Being politically minded and supportive of the rights of workers and land reform programs he took part in various labor-related encounters that put him at risk. This encouraged him to rejoin his family in California where he took employment in construction work for most his life. He had a handful of girlfriends but no children and he passed away in 1985 near his extended Mexican American family.

Miguel Naranjo, my uncle. No one could have been a better contrast to Pascual than his younger brother, Miguel. Although they were both *morenos* (dark-skinned) and shared the same Mexican dark eyes and straight black hair pushed back by long receding hairlines in their older years, they were complete opposites in behavior. Where one was brash and willing to confront, the other tended toward politeness and civility. In chapter 4, I surmise that my uncle Miguel's personality may have taken on a softer quality because, as the youngest in the family, he spent more time with his mother and sister than did his elder brother, and he didn't live with his silver mining father like Pascual. My *tío* Miguel founded a large family in San Fernando, and his most significant job was helping to landscape the numerous freeways that crisscross Los Angeles. After retiring, he died in 1995.

My mother, Guadalupe B. Gil. The reader will discover in these pages that my mother occupies a prominent position. Her remembrances and her later role as a full-fledged matriarch help explain the part she plays here. First of all, she outlived all the persons named above by at least twelve years. Dad died quite young, relatively speaking, a loss that permitted Mom the opportunity to cast her mark over the rest of us Gils because she outlived him by fifty-one years. Her influence on us was thus great to say the least. Moreover, she wrote a lot about her life in comparison to her brothers, who could write but with difficulty even though they were first-rate conversationalists. In 1999, eight years before she took her last breath, mother sent me her slim manuscripts in the US Mail, and she wrote on the back of the envelope, "*Aquí está mi historia y mi testamento.*" (Here is my history and testament.) She was always keen on sharing with us stories about her growing up in Jalisco and her initial journey to the United States. This repeated exposé of her experience, drummed into our memories, lasted right to her final days. She valued her story so much that she actually wrote three drafts of her memoirs and numerous letters where she repeated tales of her early life. The reader will learn that, like her brothers, she received no more than two or three years of grammar school education although this didn't stop her from writing her *memorias*. The narrative in these pages also profits from the innumerable conversations she and I held until about 1998, more or less, when her memory and mind began to weaken. She died in November 2007, a few days before her 102nd birthday.

My father, Bernabé Gil. Despite the regrettable absence of biographical information about Dad, he nevertheless constitutes the third key person responsible for our family taking root in Southern California. We grew up knowing that Dad was born in 1899 and became an orphan in a small farming town in Michoacán. Unlike Mother, he was reluctant to share information about his early life, so she became the vehicle to pass down to us the few fragments we inherited about him. While he didn't live as long as Mother, Dad nonetheless bequeathed a clear legacy of fatherhood to us, the Gil children. He suffered a tragic accident at age thirty-eight, but this didn't weaken his responsibility to his family. Because he avoided looking back on his home country, I felt compelled to go searching for information about him half a century after his death, and I write about my experiences in appendix I, a story within a story. In the end, Dad's tale confirms that Mexican immigrant workers have been contributing their labor and lives to the United States for at least a hundred years. He died relatively young on Christmas Eve of 1955.

¤

As stated already, some of my siblings came to my aid in helping me gather information and analyzing it. They gladly shared from their store of memories, and they also helped me fill in the gaps and fissures in the remembrances my mother and my uncles provided. Excluding the three siblings who died before I could interview them,[3] my *hermanos* who helped me are as follows:

María de Jesús Gil Valdez (Mary Gil Valdez), my eldest sister,
Manuel Gil, my eldest brother,
Soledad Gil Ruitenbach (Sally), my younger sister, and
Emily Gil Countryman (Country), the youngest of us all.

Mary and Soledad lived in Southern California at the time of this writing not far from where we all grew up. When I interviewed them, Manuel lived at the intersection of Arizona, California, and Nevada, and Emily held residence in Southern Arizona.

A third group of interviewees provided me with background information about my father who passed away when I was seventeen. In this respect, I owe important advise from his cousin, Francisco Negrete García (my *tío* Pancho), who in his last years resided with his very large family, my cousins, in Fillmore, California—many of them Mormons. I also appreciate the critical insights I gained about my father's family from his niece, my second cousin, Eloisa Gil Barragán, who I found when I went searching for my father's origins. She resided in Ario de Rosales, Michoacán, when I wrote this book. Their contributions to my understanding of my father's origins are amplified in appendix I.

Paranthetically, I offer a brief examination of us, the Gil children, who gave shape to the second generation within the Gil clan. In doing so I discuss the ways we differed from our immigrant parents especially in sensing that we were no longer Mexican like them, that we were becoming, and in the end, became Mexican American. I offer a brief assessment of the third generation on similar grounds.

¤

My role as storyteller gave me certain privileges as it also assigned responsibilities. It required me to interlace the individual accounts of immigration and settlement into a chronology that hopefully makes sense to the reader; it also necessitated that I lend perspective to specific claims and statements made by my main interviewees in order to make them more understandable. I did this by inserting brief summaries of the larger events and trends that lay behind a statement or claim made by my interviewees. For example, in Part I my mother refers cryptically to "the revolution" that nudged them all into emigrating from Mexico. As an honest storyteller and professional historian, I felt obliged to explain that she was referring to the great Mexican Rebellion of 1910, nearly unparalleled in world history, and so I lay down a context for the reader's fuller comprehension.

As author and narrator it is my place to regulate language matters too. This became critical because most of the interviews were conducted in Spanish, of course, and so as author, editor, narrator, and translator, I took the liberty of rendering their words and idioms into everyday American English using appropriate turns of a phrase when necessary. My old folk may have employed words or phrases that might now be antiquated or they may have chosen a regional or colloquial term, of the many in Mexico. This obliged me to restate what they said for greater clarity and understanding. When I believed their choice of words rang in a unique, rural, and working class sort of way I preserved the Spanish words they used, always italicizing them and including an English equivalent. This was particularly true of the male interviewees who at times preferred a rough vocabulary except my uncle Miguel, who never employed rough language that I can recall.

The technique I use to refer to my ancestors in these pages is a simple one. For the sake of clarity, I use their proper names as needed in part I. In parts II and III, wherein I discuss the time when we, Gil children, lived side by side with them, I set their proper names aside and call them by the terms we used daily at the time: Grandma, Mother or Mom, Uncle or *tío*, and Father or Dad.

¤

So why did I really write this book? One part of the answer is that I owed it to my old folks, my interviewees. They graciously allowed me to interrogate them and they generously shared from their memories in order to help me understand the world in which they lived. They wanted to transmit their experiences. Another reason is that I came to the realization, in my teaching career, that my family and I had in fact lived through the major periods that constitute the bullet points in any outline of Mexican American history (distinct from Mexican history) as taught in most American colleges and universities between 1970 and 2005. Our family founders were "pushed" out of Mexico because of revolutionary turmoil; they were "pulled" by the labor-hungry farmers and railroad engineers in the United States; they traveled the migrant trail, they settled in an American community before World War II, they lived through the days of repatriation; they toiled in the fields, and so on. I finally understood that we, Gil family members, could describe each phase in Mexican American history based on our own angle of vision and experience, and perhaps in this way could help others comprehend the complexity involved even when a simple working-class family is concerned.

Another part is my wish to express my admiration for the sacrifices that our *viejitos* made for us, their children, often under discouraging circumstances. In the autumn of my own life, I can look back and appreciate the gauntlets they faced and the counter responses they chose. I am willing to recognize their failures and be proud of their accomplishments at the same time, nothing more, and nothing less. Their progress may appear turtle-like to my grandchildren and grandnephews, but they too will appreciate sooner than later that moving forward an inch at a time is meritorious, especially when it is costly. My forebearers were willing to pay the price; we, their descendents, stand on their shoulders, and this is the most important reflection that I can pass on to my own lineage.

Lastly, a caveat is in order here. While the following pages draw in the themes of Latino immigration, acculturation, and assimilation, the reader needs to keep in mind that this is not an academic study. It is mostly based on the testimony of my old folks and so I keep theory to a minimum. My purpose as author is to tell you their story about crossing the United States-Mexican border for the sake of family unity, settling in Southern California, and proceeding to raise a family that became Mexican American. And while this is a chronicle of just one family, an extended one to be sure, it contains, nevertheless, many details and insights that may inform the interested reader about America's current immigration challenge which defies an easy solution. The interested reader may peruse my "Afterword" now retitled "A Word About Discrimination and Racism" as it offers some brief comments about Latinos in the United States today.

"All the past we leave behind,
We debouch upon a newer, mightier world, varied world,
Fresh and strong the world we seize, world of labor and the march,
Pioneers! O Pioneers . . ."

(Walter Whitman, Leaves of Grass,"Pioneers! O Pioneers!"
[Mount Vernon: Peter Pauper Press], 168–169)

Part I

The Push and Pulls

Chapter 1

Peasants One and All
(1880–1914)

The Hacienda Santa Rosa • Registering Grandma Carlota's Birth • Mascota in the Late 1800s • Grandma Carlota Growing Up • Pascual Naranjo, Her First Son • Miguel Naranjo, Her Second Son • Guadalupe Gil, Her Daughter • A Time of Revolution • Pascual Gets into Trouble

OUR TALE STARTS in the late summer of 1922 when a young woman carried a new suitcase as she hiked in the hot sun toward a large opening in a low fence. Along the wide city street they were walking on, an older female trudged behind her with thoughtful deliberation. The two were walking away from Nogales, Sonora, Mexico, the younger one springing ahead, letting her strides announce her excitement about walking across that opening which marked the Mexican-US border. This gap in the fence was the entrance to the United States at Nogales, Arizona, two sister cities separated by a simple barrier and a lone guard. After traveling by train from the interior, the two women had stayed in the Mexican Nogales a handful of weeks getting their papers in order, and now they were actually crossing. They would show their papers to the guard who would give them a cursory inspection, cross the wire barrier that represented the line separating the two countries, and they would keep going north.

The older woman was my grandmother and the younger one my mother. Grandma Carlota, age forty-two, wore a simple shift dress made of plain cotton cloth that nearly touched the ground, combined with a dark handwoven shawl wrapped around her shoulders. The wrap, also called a rebozo, contrasted with the plain pale dress in a fashion typical of Mexican peasant women of the time. Long, thick braids or *trenzas* gathered her straight black hair, adding a touch of severity to what was already a strong-looking face. My mother, Guadalupe, seventeen years old, had put on that day a wrinkly piqué skirt trimmed with a simple cotton top that complimented her slightly fuller body. A pair of dark boots buttoned up on the side sharply accented her outfit. Miguel, one of mother's two older brothers, had already gone ahead crossing the border impatiently a few days earlier without documents. The three of them were eager to join Carlota's eldest son, Pascual, who was already working somewhere in a place called California. These four individuals, plus my father who entered the United States separately, comprise the immigrants in our family, and, as we can see, they arrived on foot from Mexico.

While my mother, the eager stepping teenager, might have been wearing new clothes packed inside a recently purchased suitcase, they didn't have too much else to their name. They walked across the border because they owned no automobile and could not afford to hire a taxi, having already spent a big part of their savings on their simple suitcases and their new clothes. What little money they possessed they carried in cash as they held no credit cards, of course, and retained no bank accounts. We'll learn later that they didn't pay for their train tickets in order to ride to Nogales all the way from the port city of Mazatlán in the south. In any case, they were walking onto American soil facing many challenges. Not only did they not speak the language, they also didn't know anyone locally, and they were running out of money with no idea of how to replenish the little they had.

One of the purposes of this story is to lay out my family's Mexican origins. So in order to do this, we need to look back a few years in order to learn what Grandma Carlota and her children were leaving behind. Where were they coming from? What kind of community did they surrender? We'll answer these questions in this chapter and the next before rejoining their journey into the United States in Chapter 3.

The Hacienda Santa Rosa

Three and a half years before arriving in Nogales, Grandma and her two children were living on a plantation called Hacienda Santa Rosa (the word hacienda refers to an agricultural estate) located about nine hundred miles south of the US border, in the state of Jalisco.[4] The hacienda was lodged in the high mountains just east of Puerto Las Peñas, a sultry port village that you could almost see from a mountain perch half a day's walk away if you knew the back trails surrounding the hacienda. The tiny seaport later became known as Puerto Vallarta which grew by leaps and bounds in the 1970s serving as a Shangri-la for many Americans. When referring to this port, however, we'll only use its newer name for the sake of clarity.

Even though the sun shined brightly on the hacienda and its rugged surroundings, the air always blew cool. It still does because the hacienda sits at 5,500 feet above sea level, free of the heat and humidity that hovers over the coast. While Puerto Vallarta is trimmed in jungle green, especially during the rainy season, Santa Rosa was painted in the darker colors of the Mexican savanna that encourages *ocote* pine trees and wide leaf holm oaks to cover the encircling mountains, allowing at the same time a blend of shrubs to grow on the grassy floor which the locals call *raspa viejo* (rough leaf tree), *estafiate* (silver sagebrush), and golden *nanche* berries. In the 1910s, the hacienda held several pastures bordered by woodlands intersected with noisy creeks that traversed the narrow valley. In summertime, much of the farmland was covered with corn and wheat with beans rooted in between the corn rows according to a timeworn tradition. Lime-green bushy sugarcane reached for the sky, as well, in the distant corners of the property. Scores of cattle roamed the many *potreros* or open pastures that filled up the property, including the plentiful burros that also left their organic trace wherever they went. This was the land Grandma Carlota and her children left behind when they traveled north.

Santa Rosa was a place of work. The people who lived on the hacienda included the owner and his wife, Don Manuel Merino and Doña Victoria, his family, and the folks who actually did the work. (In the early 1900s, the words *don* and *doña* were used in front of a man or woman's first name to denote upper-class membership and therefore special status.) This is where our folks come into this story—or at least my maternal ancestors. The workers on the estate included Grandma and her children and numerous other family members, plus many other campesinos or peasants who tilled the soil and cared for the animals. The wives and daughters of these families helped out in the owner's house. They did the cleaning, cooking, and looking after the owner's children. Peasants who lived on the plantation were known locally as *peones acasillados*, which means live-in peasants. This is what my ancestors were, and they had lived on the Hacienda Santa Rosa for many generations.

Campesinos had little say about their lives. Our family lore includes assertions by our relatives that young peasant girls in those days were raped by the hacienda owner, their fathers, not being able to do anything about it without getting killed or losing their jobs if they were lucky. What we know for certainty is that when a plantation was sold from one landowner to another in this region, the peasants were listed as assets in the local land records. In other words, when a property was sold, the number of cattle on the property was noted in the local land office along with the number of peasants who lived on it, all listed as part and parcel of the possessions being transferred. They were all viewed as mere enhancements to the value of the property. In more ways than one, the peasants belonged to the hacienda and to its owners who prevailed over them easily.

The two-room adobe hut that Grandma Carlota's family lived in didn't belong to them given this situation. In fact, they could only live there if they worked for Don Manuel and did his bidding. Their chances of moving on to find better opportunities were, at best, extremely challenging because it required, among other things, saving money, a next to impossible task. The necessities they needed to live on, like beans and corn, cloth to make clothes, candles to light up the night, and so on, could only be bought at Don Manuel's hacienda "store," a simple storeroom. Also called *tienda de raya*, in the old days, this is where their purchases were deducted from a monetary value assigned to their labor. Essentially, the price of the goods they purchased was deducted from the "pay" they received although they were never paid in cash. What's more, they were never paid more than they could buy, and so this is why they lived in endless debt to the hacienda owner. The concept of saving for a better future was simply unthinkable. It was next to impossible to be ambitious and beat the system. Most *peones* lived like slaves, and millions of Mexican campesinos toiled in a similar situation.

Most of the campesinos of the Hacienda Santa Rosa lived in scattered shelters on the farm property. Grandma and her children lived immediately behind the owners' large home, at the foot of a tall, craggy bluff. I remember visiting this site for the first time in 1984 when I accompanied my mother there because she wanted to revisit her birthplace. When we spotted a creek that ran by the foot of a bluff, she yelled excitedly at me, "Look, *mijo*, there's the *acequia* (a water ditch) that ran by our house moving water to a grain mill that was located right over there," pointing down yonder. The mill was gone but the memory remained.

The life of a peasant might appear simple to our eyes but nothing could be further from the truth. For example, Grandma's father, Francisco Hernández, arose before dawn in his dark two-room adobe hut in order to trek to the fields to begin the day's work. His job included planting corn, cutting wheat, feeding the animals, or whatever Don Manuel ordered him to do. He was always on call.

Of course, growing corn was central to Don Manuel and nearly every other Mexican hacienda owner at the time. But for men like my great-grandfather, Francisco, it meant even more because he actually did the work. He had to ready the oxen that pulled the plow to furrow the rich earth where the corn seeds were sown by dropping them and stepping on them as he goaded and guided the big animal. Diana Kennedy, a close observer of life in rural Mexico, aptly described the toil that occupied my ancestors for the most part of their lives:

> [The] planting [of corn] . . . begins just before the rain starts toward the end of May. [This is when] the first longed-for rain eventually falls and the corn sprouts and grows; there is first the weeding, *la descarda*, to be done. As the rain continues and the corn grows apace, new weeds spring up and thicken around the base of the corn, and the *segundando*, the second weeding takes place. It is a backbreaking job for the laborer, who squats with his knees almost up to his chin, coaxing out the weeds with the tip of his curved machete so as not to hurt the young corn plant. Then there is the fertilizing and afterward the anxious watch for mealybugs that burrow through the heart of the sprouting ears, until the first tender *elotes* (ears of corn) begin to form.[5]

The *tiempo de los elotes* (time for corn on the cob) would take place in October when the rain began to thin and the harvesting was completed. By December, when the rain was gone, the dried-up corn ears were removed from the stalk and stored in "rustic bins made of reeds," as Kennedy carefully notes, in the *trojes*, the hacienda barns. Lastly, around the New Year, the final task was carried out when the dried cornstalks were cut and chopped up as fodder for the animals.

Francisco would sometimes be assigned to assist the hacienda mule drivers who, in the absence of automobiles or trucks, prodded their animals over mountain trails and valleys to deliver grain poured into gunnysacks loaded on the mules. In some cases, they traveled in a southwesterly direction for four or five days to the outskirts of the big city of Guadalajara to deliver a shipment of corn or wheat to buyers there. At other times, the mule drivers pulled their animals westward and down the mountains to the coast to deliver their goods. Although trains could be found in other parts of Mexico at the time, the highlands of Mascota and Santa Rosa were too remote and too rugged for train access.

Nepomucena Ponce, Francisco's wife and my great-grandmother, also rose early in the dark to prepare breakfast for her husband. In the absence of electricity, she would light an *ocote*, a sap-filled kindling, or, if lucky a kerosene lamp, and prepare the early morning meal of beans and tortillas for her husband to enjoy a bite before his long workday. Prepared foods were not a viable option for my great-grandparents because they couldn't afford them and those that were available for purchase from a regular commercial store required a long walk into town. All the victuals on the hacienda had to be made from scratch every day, and Nepomucena was responsible for all of the family's meals, of course, when she wasn't helping out at the hacienda owner's house. Everyone ate corn tortillas (flour tortillas were unknown in this region at this time), and making these by hand alone took many long hours beginning before daybreak. Francisco and Nepomucena lived almost entirely on beans and tortillas spiced with some hot chiles and meat on occasion. The diet was limited, and making tortillas was backaching work unto itself.

This was the life Grandma and her children left behind. And, as we've seen, they broke away from it to begin a new life in an alien land.

Registering Grandma Carlota's Birth

Like her own children, Grandma Carlota was born on the Hacienda Santa Rosa which stood inside the legal jurisdiction of the nearby city of Mascota, a *cabecera*. This words means that Mascota functioned like a county seat with its authority extended far beyond the thousand or so dwellings that made up the town. Every important life event including death had to be registered at the *cabecera*. This is why Grandma's parents knew what was expected of them even though they lived on a backcountry plantation. So early on a September day in 1880, Nepomucena wrapped Carlota's newborn body in a rebozo and, tying it to her shoulders, proceeded to march alongside her husband about four hours over hill and vale to Mascota. There is no doubt they informed their *patrón* about their plans. The new parents also understood they not only had to register Carlota's birth but to baptize her at the same time which meant presenting the newborn child to the parish priest so that he could inscribe her into the parish books along with their own names as parents, plus the godparents and two witnesses. All this took place on September 25, 1880.

Barefoot, most probably, and dressed in simple untinted cotton peasant clothes, Francisco and Nepomucena crossed the plaza from the church and entered the city offices also known as the *palacio municipal*. With whispered reverence, they asked to see the *presidente municipal* or mayor, Don Pedro Bermúdez. When he finally admitted them, they requested that their daughter be registered according to the law, to which he agreed after asking details about her birth. He then dictated to one of his secretaries the customary language, including the answers to his questions. Dressed in a long-sleeved cotton shirt fastened by sculpted bone buttons, tight riding pants trimmed with gaiters, and low-cut riding boots, Don Pedro dictated aloud. He declared under oath that Carlota was born two days earlier at five o'clock in the afternoon to her parents, whom he identified by name, plus two witnesses gathered from people standing nearby. This is how my grandmother's birth registration was thus entered in the records books and made official.[6] It's worth noting too that the mayor also identified Carlota's race because the birth entry indicates that the child's parents were *indígenas* or "Indians."

This detail informs us that Carlota's skin color or race, and everybody else's for that matter, was considered an important fact to record at the time. There is little doubt that our grandmother was a full-blooded Indian though culturally speaking she was mestizo, meaning that the life her family led was now a blending of Spanish and Indian ways.[7] The mayor's assertion about their racial origin probably hinged on the prevailing knowledge of who did the work in the region's haciendas, so noting their general appearance and what their livelihood was, he must have said to himself, "These people are Indians and so is the child." I came across these details in the original civil registry records in Mascota.

Mascota in the Late 1800s

When my siblings and I were growing up in California in the 1950s, we came to view Mascota as my mother's hometown even though she too, like her own mother, was born on the Hacienda Santa Rosa a few miles away. Mascota, as we've seen, acted as the cultural urban hub of the region where the most important activities affecting the entire *cabecera* took place, like the recording of vital statistics. Mascota played a vital role in other ways.

For my siblings and I, Mascota and the region around it became our first mental window into Mexico. Thanks to the lore that Mom built up about it over the years, any discussion about Mexico prompted us to try to understand it in terms of whatever images of Mascota and its hinterland we might have held. Any references to Mascota also included Puerto Vallarta—down the mountain trails to the coast, as we'll see below, mother always visiting both places during her travels to Mexico. So let us examine Mascota some more since it meant so much to mother, and consequently to me and my brothers and sisters. My own children spent many hours playing in its parks and plazas in the 1970s, so maybe someday it will mean something to them too—and hopefully to their own children as well.

In the late 1800s, Mascota was the largest and most important community in the high mountain valleys east of Puerto Vallarta. As a *cabecera*, government officials in Mascota were responsible for law and order not only in the town itself but also beyond the city limits—past the Hacienda Santa Rosa, all the way down to sandy beaches of Puerto Vallarta and even south to Tomatlán. All the little hamlets, haciendas, and ranchos in between, up and down the mountains owed jurisdiction to the officials in Mascota. Pedro Bermúdez, the man who registered Carlota's birth, was more than just the town's mayor; he was also the *Jefe Político* (political chief) of the entire county zone, and his word was law throughout. For example, the court archives in Mascota were filled with criminal cases, written on fading and cracking paper, revealing details about how the Mascotan policemen apprehended delinquents or criminals throughout the large area even if it took weeks or months and a lot of horseback riding. The population living in the town itself was reported at about six thousand when Carlota was born, and if you include the people living in the jurisdiction of the *cabecera*, or the surrounding villages, ranchos, and haciendas, the total population more than doubled.

Although no rail lines led to Mascota, tucked away in the mountains as it was, and no major highway lay nearby, evidence tells us that the town nonetheless reflected a strong connection to Guadalajara, the state capital, and to the rest of the world as well. In the late 1800s, for example, Mascota boasted a mayor and a city council all of whom held court in the local city hall where Carlota was registered and constructed with a certain provincial elegance. The important role of the *cabecera* was demonstrated by the fact alone that campesino families like Carlota's, living on haciendas, tucked away in the surrounding mountain glens, felt it their civic and religious duty to walk for hours to register a child in Mascota as Francisco and Nepomucena did.

Mascota hosted other government officers. For example, it prided itself with a chief of police who was responsible for keeping the peace and applying the law, which included administering the local jail. State and federal tax collectors kept their respective offices in Mascota, and the local judge, representing the judicial power of the state, also retained his office there as his authority extended about a hundred miles down to the coast. Mascota also prided itself with having a full-time priest, the very one who baptized tiny Carlota, who was in charge of the spiritual health of the community and maintaining the integrity of the local church.

Mascota was also home to numerous professionals and many simple employees. The professional class included lawyers and doctors who studied for their licenses and obtained degrees in the state capital, Guadalajara, but also elsewhere in Mexico. They carried out their various professional duties in a manner consistent with the time. Schoolteachers were also assigned by the state office of education to bring enlightenment to young, mostly the well-to-do children of hacienda owners, professionals, or government employees. Campesino children and other "low-class" citizens were not so fortunate and did not attend school. My mother, for instance, didn't go to school beyond second grade for this very reason. The rest of the population worked either as store employees or, for the most part, as agricultural workers or as peons like my ancestors, factory jobs being nonexistent in Mascota for the most part.

As in most other towns, merchants, big and small, played an important role, even in a mountain-fast community like Mascota. They imported wares from the outside and sold them to local buyers who could afford them. Ponciano Guzmán, a notable resident of Mascota who owned several haciendas, also owned *El Transvaal,* a store named after a region in South Africa whose shelves were stocked with Spanish Madeira wine and Canadian Club whiskey. If a local townsman required fine crystal glasses, he could also buy them there.

Despite the fact that Mascota was surrounded by farms and mountains, one could say it held its head high because its inhabitants felt connected to Guadalajara. They also felt linked to the rest of Mexico and even Europe in some cases.

When I visited in the 1970s, I climbed a low mountain nearest the city to look down on the collage of whitewashed buildings covered with earthy red-tiled roofs. Cobblestoned streets crisscrossed the urban patchwork interspersed by trees that bore avocados, lemons, and bananas, and a rich green undergrowth in open lots. A shiny white spire surrounded by leafy plazas marked the tallest building—the church dedicated to *La Purísima Concepción,* the Immaculate Conception, one of the many versions of Mary in the Catholic world. Beyond these buildings and streets, the furry green mountains undulated out to the high-peaked horizon. As I peered from the mountaintop, I conjectured that Nepomucena must have observed very nearly the same vista that I did as she walked alongside Francisco back to Santa Rosa in 1880, lugging newly christened and duly registered Carlota on her back.

Grandma Carlota Growing Up

We only know a few facts about my grandmother's life growing up on the hacienda in the early 1900s. This is due to the fact that she didn't write any letters or memoirs nor was she written about in the newspapers. Except for a birth record or a death notice, a personal paper trail of this sort was nonexistent for my relatives because they were too poor to know how to write. When they died, they didn't leave a will behind because there were no possessions to pass on. Traditional history tends to ignore poor folk for these reasons. However, drawing bits and pieces from her children, my mother and my two uncles, and from other background information, I offer a portrait of her, albeit a sketchy one at best.[8]

Our family lore informs us that Carlota grew up surrounded by family members—two brothers and three sisters in her immediate family. It seems her parents died when she was a child. We know for sure that Nepomucena died in 1884[9] when Carlota was four years old, and this is why my mother often recalled that Grandma Carlota referred to her eldest sister, Rafaela, as *Mamá Rafaela.* This confirms that Carlota had little or no memory of her own mother. She was the youngest child, and so Rafaela, her eldest sister, ten years her senior, became a mother substitute, thus *Mamá Rafaela.* If Nepomucena gave birth to a child on an average of every two years, then Rafaela, her first child, would have been born approximately in 1870, then Sotero in 1872, Sabino in 1874, Estanislao in 1876, Soledad[10] in 1878, and Carlota in 1880, more or less. Nepomucena mostly likely maintained poor health throughout her life and could have easily been worn-out by the time Carlota came along.

Our family lore tells us that Carlota was raised on the Hacienda Santa Rosa by her older siblings for the most part, once Nepomucena died, especially by "Mamá Rafaela." As the youngest, she was probably taken care of by all of her siblings in one way or another and influenced by their backcountry ways. It is safe to assume she grew up as a young campesino woman just like her elder sisters and became familiar with city life only after she abandoned the hacienda in her late thirties. She thus grew up in a rural area filled by mountains, small rivers, and creeks, and extensive fields of corn and wheat. It can be affirmed that about three-quarters of all Mexicans at this time mostly knew about farmland and farm animals the way Carlota did, not of city life.

For Carlota and others in her family, the margin between being healthy and ill was always slim. If she got sick, there were no clinics or doctors to rely on because of the remote location coupled with the fact that they were only mere peasants. When ill, Rafaela and Carlota's other aunts would care for her by employing herbal medicines and other home remedies just as their Indian ancestors had done. It's possible that in dire emergencies, they might have turned to the hacienda owner's wife, Doña Victoria, for special assistance, but they too probably relied on home remedies most of the time. This hard experience in early life may explain why Carlota's grandchildren would remember her, many decades later in the United States, as a crusty and determined woman who lived by simply defined values and insisted on strict behavior—and getting her way. Grandma probably never traveled beyond the mountainous district of Santa Rosa-Mascota until she started her own family.

Although she hailed from a long line of *peones* who worked as resident day laborers on the hacienda working in the fields or with animals, they enjoyed moments of pleasure nonetheless. Their heavy work week was occasionally sweetened with the music they themselves created. Grandma recounted stories to her daughter about their love of music and the importance that music played in their lives. Family lore informs us, for example, that Sabino played the violin, Sotero strummed the guitar, and Carlota sang. Her cousins Lupe and Aurelio Peña, who would also venture to work in California years later as we'll see, played musical instruments and sang passionately as well. In their free time, when celebrating birthdays, weddings, or even at funerals, they dusted off their rustic instruments and played and sang to bring some measure of joy into their hardworking lives, or, in some cases, mark a moment of sadness. My mother liked to recall the day when her own mother sang at a local cockfight accompanied by musicians like her uncles, a type of event that supposedly attracted scores of gamblers and fans alike.

The memory always elicited pride because while my ancestors may have been mere peasants, they could also punctuate a community event like this artistically. When I lived in Mascota in the 1970s, I attended several cockfights myself and witnessed the very special nature of these events that continued to attract scores of gamblers, musicians, and aficionados alike.

The first thirty years of Grandma's life, 1880 –1910, coincided with one of the most dynamic periods in Mexican history. The country was governed by a man who forced the economy to boom as never before; this was Porfirio Díaz. His economic policies brought about the growth of commerce, agriculture, and new industries in a way not seen before. Many new textile factories appeared in different parts of Mexico, and old haciendas began growing new products at the same time that cities grew at a rapid pace. Between the time Grandma was born and the time she left Mascota for the US border, railroads sprouted across the country, they were spiked into the Mexican soil for thousands of miles. This included the rail line that would eventually take Grandma north to Nogales in the company of her two youngest children, where we first caught sight of them walking across the border at the start of this story.

These changes, however, occurred far away from Mascota. The ruggedness of the land enfolding the Hacienda Santa Rosa and nearby Mascota filtered out most of the progress mentioned above which I describe elsewhere.[11] Grandma probably first heard of the new jobs that were being created and of the new railroads being built from the traveling salesmen who drifted into the backcountry ranchos and haciendas like Santa Rosa. Leading two or three mules packed with bags filled with brightly colored cloth, the newest buttons or mirrors, and other consumer goods that might have been for sale in the rustic stores of Mascota but not in Santa Rosa, these peddlers drifted in and out of mountain-fast communities introducing new-fangled products and stirring dreams of wonderful places far away.

Grandma began relating to men and having her own children during the Díaz years. In 1900, when she was twenty years old, she gave birth to Pascual Naranjo, the first of her three children. In 1902, she had her second son, Miguel Naranjo, and then my mother (Guadalupe) in 1905, when she was twenty-five years old. Indications are that my mother's father (my grandfather) was a backcountry peddler. It never ceased to cause us to scratch our heads and wonder what was going on when Mom would remind us that Grandma "was married to an older man [who lived on the hacienda]. He is the one who raised us," my mother wrote, "His name was Leonides Ponce," she would add. Mother also wrote this into her memoirs: mainly that in the days before they abandoned the Hacienda Santa Rosa to travel north to the US border, Leonides refused to join them because he was too old, he was supposed to have said.

This conjunction of men in Grandma's early life requires some examination. Let's pause to examine what we know about Grandma's "marriages" or relationships that produced her children. Why was my mother surnamed Brambila while her two brothers, my two maternal uncles, Naranjo? Why did my mother describe Grandma as being "married" on the eve of her departure from Santa Rosa to a man named Leonides Ponce whom she left behind? Was Grandma a promiscuous woman?

While this book is not about the institution of matrimony, the information in the preceding paragraph requires an explanation of marriage in the context that my family faced in these early years and a closer look at my grandmother specifically.

My view is that there is much to suggest that marriage differs from culture to culture and era to era. Most modern-day Americans view marriage as a relatively stable relationship between a man and a woman who profess to love each other and whose union is blessed by the church or at least recognized by the government for the purpose of procreating a family. This at least has been a majority view although obtaining such a relationship has not always been within everybody's reach. My view is that this romantic outlook on marriage became more of a reality as the world modernized slowly. Not all families enjoyed the stability required to make marriage work over a lifetime. In the sweep of time, the well-to-do most likely enjoyed marriage as described above and the poorer people enjoyed it less.

This ideal view of marriage was not to be for Grandma Carlota. She was too poor. Her life, and that of her brothers and sisters, depended too much on the people who owned the land they lived on and controlled the jobs necessary to survive. The lords of the land dictated nearly everything, and our peasant ancestors enjoyed little control over their lives.

It stands to reason that when my grandmother was a young woman, she looked for a decent man with whom to share her life. Being part of a family of workers who lived on a plantation owned by others, she undoubtedly began looking for a man who might not only respond to her need for affection but also pull her up from the bottom, up the social scale at least a peg, and perhaps even out from poverty. Like all parents, she wanted a better life for her children, and what better way when you're a poor peasant woman than to have a child by a man who is not a peasant so that he might help that child?

Cecilio Naranjo, Pascual and Miguel's father, represented this kind of man and so did the itinerant salesman, Concepción Brambila, my mother's biological father whose blurred photographic portrait she kept all her adult life, one revealing European features, Brambila being an Italian surname. Men of this kind enjoyed a great advantage over a peasant woman like Grandma because they possessed economic independence, comparatively speaking. They were not peasants beholden to the lord of the land. My mother's explanation of her own mother's situation fits into the thoughts I provide above:

> I heard my mother say that when the boys' father [Cecilio Naranjo] left her (I don't believe they ever married), he got a hold of another woman named Rosa who gave him eight to ten children. This didn't satisfy him, so he had an affair with Rosa's sister who gave birth to a son named Camilo who now lives in Richmond, California. My mother was

> so distressed about this that when a stranger arrived on the hacienda, my father, Concepción Brambila, she lost out with him too. The least she could get out of it all was to work as a servant for the man who raised us, Leonides Ponce. He married her properly. He was a supervisor on the farm—I remember he was a plowman and a tenant farmer.[12]

As stated already, my mother remembered seeing her biological father only once and a pivotal experience at that. She remembered him asking Grandma Carlota for her so he could raise my mother and give her a better life. We don't know what discussion they had, if any, leading up to this moment. We can only imagine. My mother told us about this moment in her life many times as if she sensed that it represented a potentially important "if," a possible turning point in her life.

Without engaging in a discussion of the culture of machismo here, which polluted almost all men in Mexico in these days, I believe it is evident that the relationship between Grandma and the fathers of her children were always an uphill battle due to the considerable class differences between them. Not being impoverished *peones* tied to a hacienda, these men took advantage of her need for affection and support and left her with the children that resulted from the brief liaisons that ended in tortured frustration.

The hardships of a single peasant woman raising three children on the hacienda under the conditions described in these pages demanded extraordinary measures, and Grandma did not hesitate. My mother recounted the story many times of how Grandma was forced to leave Mom by herself at the age of five because she had to serve in the owner's house. This long-lasting neglect created "sores that covered my body," Mother wrote, including "big bumps on my neck." A pharmacist advised Grandma Carlota to feed her daughter properly, so she aimed at two birds at the same time. Somehow she bought a cow one day not only to provide milk for my mother but also to give her the opportunity to sell milk and cheese and presumably earn a few pennies. However, this grab at micro-commerce did not go over well with Don Manuel, the hacienda owner, because in his eyes, the cow was destructive. He claimed that it got loose too often and into places that caused a lot of trouble. Because of his accusations, Grandma felt forced to place the cow in a dairy ranch that required a long walk to get there, including crossing streams that ran high in the rainy season.

Another example of Grandma trying to assure her own income or a smidgen of it involved her son Pascual. He remembered his mother sending him as a child to buy liquor so she could resell it on the plantation, a story that my mother included in her memoirs. Country liquor, probably *aguardiente* or mescal, was not bottled in those days; it was sold in clay jars (*jarros*) instead, and selling to minors was no problem. "This was the reason why he learned to drink early," my mother explained. "He got thirsty [and opened the jar to drink], and sometimes he would fall asleep as a result. But I don't personally remember these incidents at all," she added. On other occasions, Grandma would make *gorditas de horno* (baked corn dough treats) and *semitas* (baked semisweet bread) to sell. Having scraped a few coins together, she was later able to order fresh baked bread from the nearby village of Cimarrón and sold it on the hacienda on pay days. Guadalupe wrote that she could also sew and make clothes, *calzones blancos* and *cotones*—simple ones no doubt.[13]

They lived from day to day with little aid; if the corn harvests suffered because of some pestilential blight, there was no social welfare agency that would send food to their table. There were many bad harvests in the backlands of Mexico, and the peasants would simply suffer and often die from starvation or malnutrition. My book *Life in Provincial Mexico* examines the frequent epidemics that swept Mexican communities before World War II, carrying away countless husbands and wives and other members of the families. People like my grandmother were lucky to share their life with another adult because they didn't control their lives as much as we'd like to imagine.

Pascual Naranjo, Her First Son

My uncle is important to us not only because he was Grandma's eldest son but also because his indomitable character pulled her and his sister and brother out of Mexico and into the United States. The three persons who are described as crossing the US-Mexico border in 1922 did so because they were drawn out by Pascual. He was born on August 5, 1900; he always used to say, "I am as old as the [twentieth] century."

Pascual's father, Cecilio, lived near Santa Rosa in a mineral gulch known as Los Jiménez near the mountain village of Santo Domingo, a larger mining community nestled in the western sierras of Jalisco. This part of Mexico encloses many mining communities or *minerales* like Santo Domingo, where silver was dug out of the ground for hundreds of years. In the company of some of my children, I visited Copala, Sinaloa, a small *mineral* near Mazatlán in 2004 which I propose must have looked a lot like Los Jiménez. It was a village formed by twenty or thirty adobe dwellings held together by cobblestoned pathways leading to a small chapel and a tiny plaza and beyond the urban patch to dozens of small mine holes in the nearby mountains. Hanging from a mountainside, it hummed busily with men digging for silver. These villages attracted the tough guys who were willing to dig tunnels inside the earth in search of precious ores in order to make a living. This is where my uncle Pascual, already a headstrong boy at fourteen, started taking life lessons from his father. This was the "school" he attended because there weren't any others for boys like him. Otherwise, my uncle's destiny would have been to work with the other youngsters in the fields helping their families do the agricultural labor necessary to earn their keep as hacienda peons. Pascual didn't quite fit this role.

He went to Santo Domingo long enough for my mother to remember visiting him there, the earliest memory she had of her brother. Did Grandma Carlota and Cecilio ever live together? Probably not. Did they fight with each other enough to lead to a separation? We don't know what circumstances sent Pascual to his father at this time. On yet another occasion, Guadalupe recalled a trip to the town of Cocula, farther to the southwest, to retrieve Pascual once again because he had traveled there with his father. My mother mentioned this trip many times as we were growing up, reminding us of how frightened she became about having to stop at night on the way to and fro and how they had to light bonfires to keep the wild animals away. She must have been no older than five years old.

Pascual seemed to have realized quite early that he didn't want to remain very long on the hacienda where he was born. He made a mental note, for instance, that there were men who didn't have to work as hard as his peasant uncles and their hacienda friends. His aunt Estanislao's[14] husband, Bernabé, "didn't like to do farmwork," Pascual remarked to me. "He became one of those individuals who bought and sold things . . . He actually made money that way during Lent," he said with a little awe.[15] That was quite different from the hacienda peons!

In any case, Pascual's mobility as a boy, made possible by his father's mining interests, foreshadowed the historic trip to the north that Grandma would make in search of her son.

Miguel Naranjo, Her Second Son

Grandma gave birth to a second son by Cecilio Naranjo and that was my uncle Miguel Naranjo. He was born on July 5, 1902 and, like his sister, also grew up on the hacienda within the family circle that provided human warmth to Grandma despite the poverty that hung over them all. As in the case of Pascual, Miguel's uncles (Sotero and Sabino) undoubtedly took it upon themselves to teach him how to become a farmworker and eventually develop into a country peasant or a *peón acasillado* in the age of Porfirio Díaz. Miguel did not seem to outwardly resist this lifestyle. It was expected that, at about the age of nine or so, he too would begin donning the simple peasant wardrobe: white cotton shirt and trousers with a sash to keep them up, and, if lucky, wear sandals instead of going barefoot. Guadalupe remembered the derisive comments upper-class look-down-their-nose people would say to someone like her being *Indios de pata rajada* (Indians with cracked feet) employing the word *pata* used only for animals. My ancestors on this farm fell into this category even though they weren't complete *indios* as such. In this uniform, Miguel would assist in the planting of corn, or harvesting wheat, or even helping out with the farm animals. As he grew older, he had no choice but to work. Looking back on his childhood at age seventy-six, sitting in his comfortable middle-class home in San Fernando, California, he acknowledged these dire circumstances by simply saying that "my mother did not have the means to support us [and so] we lived quite poorly," and he was always ready to do his part. He always did all he could do to support the family.

Miguel Naranjo didn't experience life in the mineral gulches the way his elder brother did. This may have been due, in part, to the fact that in those days, my tío Miguel was too young to be away from his mother, and so he consequently lived with her and his sister in Santa Rosa most of the time with some exceptions.

Miguel remembered going to school and that many of his friends did not. "My mother became enthused with the idea that we learn how to read, and so she enrolled us into the school in El Cimarrón [near the hacienda]. My sister and I went to school there." He then added, "But soon the teacher went away and they closed the school."[16] As if to make up for this loss, Grandma placed them in school again—in Mascota with her elder sister Estanislao (my mother referred to her as "*tía* Lau"). They never had any children, and so they insisted on helping Carlota out with her children, recognizing that her life on the hacienda was much tougher. Miguel was about six years old at the time and took notice of the fact that "[his] mother sacrificed a lot to keep us there." She walked between Santa Rosa and Mascota "every Sunday, a distance of about ten miles, to bring us food and in that way helped our aunt [by lessening the load of keeping us]. This lasted about a year and a half." Naturally, Aunt Lau developed a relationship with the children, especially Miguel. At one point, Aunt Lau didn't want to give up Miguel, and she and her sister argued over it, consequently. As if to side with his Aunt Lau, Pascual observed that there just wasn't enough food in his mother's house in Santa Rosa. He remembered the struggle his mother went through with Aunt Lau over who would raise Miguel, but eventually Carlota got her way and Miguel returned to live with his mother on the hacienda, while Pascual and Guadalupe stayed a little longer with their aunt Lau in Mascota. Miguel was distraught over the fact that he was taken away from school. Even though he was expected to become a *peón*, Miguel liked school nevertheless. He remembered details about school with a certain fondness:

> In school, we learned to spell using the *silabario* [a spelling book] that taught us to identify the letters and then to put them together. We also studied numbers. The teacher would also instruct us on how to make silk and then teach us a little bit of the history of Mexico. It wasn't a whole lot because it was just first grade. On Thursdays, we had to take lessons in Catholic doctrine at church which was nearby. Our teacher was a young woman who was very smart. At ten in the morning we went out for recess . . . We played games like putting a boy on his hands and knees, and we would jump over him. We also played a game known as *la roña*, in which somebody touched you and you were "it," then you had to touch somebody else, and so on. There were no sports. It was too small there.

Even if Miguel had been older, he still might not have chosen to leave his mother to live with his father, the way Pascual did, for two reasons. One reason was that of the three children, Miguel seemed to have been the most concerned about his mother's dire situation and wanting to help out. Pascual openly recognized the poverty that surrounded them, but this only spurred him to get away quickly and find his own way, especially after he got into trouble. Guadalupe was too young and overtaken by her own growing up and discovery about the world. Despite Miguel's tender age, he began working to help his mother and family quite willingly.

He was assigned by the plantation owner to help get the hacienda's milled flour to market. He was told to assist the hacienda mule drivers, leading a team of fifteen to twenty mules, to make deliveries to designated transshipment points down in the big valley or out on the coast. They customarily made such deliveries traveling west over mountain trails to Puerto Vallarta and Salina Cruz just farther north on the coast. From there the flour was placed on small ships to be sold in Tepic, in the neighboring state to the north. They also made deliveries eastward through the wooded sierras to Ameca, where the sacks of flour were loaded onto trains headed to Guadalajara. The muleteers would bring sugar, salt, or clothing on the way back to the hacienda.

Little Miguel's main task was to help load the animals and walk in front of the lead mule to make sure it kept moving forward at all times. The muleteers, friends of the family, would keep an eye on him and make sure he didn't have to lift heavy loads or get hurt in any way. Still, it was a big experience and responsibility for nine-year-old Miguel on these trips that easily lasted three to four days one way. As an old man looking back on his childhood experiences, he marveled at the fact this is the way he began discovering the world outside the hacienda.

No matter what, Miguel's delivery trips were filled with their ups and downs. For example, he remembered arriving in Ameca one day, located about fifty miles southeast of Santa Rosa, when a community celebration was in progress. Ameca, at 23, 457 inhabitants in 1910,[17] was considered a giant city in comparison to the Hacienda Santa Rosa. The fact was that the Ameca festival attracted lots of people and,

> . . . there were many booths selling fresh drinks, fruit, and so on—and they also had music. I remember seeing a tarima [a wooden dance floor] where people danced sones [regional music] which were very popular. One day I saw a man and woman get on the tarima and do a zapateado together [a quick dance step]. The man would really get into it with a lot of verve and then stop, and the woman would continue stamping her feet with the music and then the man would take over. I thought it was such a special thing because I had never seen anything like that in Santa Rosa when they laid down the tarima because it was just this one fellow who would dance. But the guy in Ameca, he really knew how to move! Ameca was quite a place!

On the other hand, Miguel also remembered being robbed on one of these mule driving trips. The hacienda muleteers, including the owner's brother, had just made a delivery of flour in Tepic and were on their way back through a wooded mountain trail carrying the money from the sale. Miguel was out in front of the mule team, coaxing the lead mule ahead, when two men suddenly appeared through the brush, pointing a rifle at him and barking at him to stop and get down from his mount. When several of the muleteers caught up with little Miguel, three more robbers appeared and demanded the mule drivers to put up their hands and reveal the location of the money. "We know you're carrying money! Which bag do you have it in?" they shouted. Young Miguel was terrified by this time, especially when one of the bandits threatened to hang him from a tree if he didn't tell them where the money was. When the hacienda owner's brother finally showed up, he too was pistol-whipped. Succumbing to the threats and physical abuse, the owner's brother handed the cash over to the outlaws. The bandits then tied up all of the muleteers, including the owner's brother and our little Miguel, against some nearby trees and fled. Six hours went by without a single sign of help or rescue. Finally, Chencho, one of the muleteers, untied himself and then freed Miguel who helped unfasten the rest of the men.

My uncle never forgot this incident. Miguel remembered asking Don Manuel for a different kind of job and got rebuffed. His mother must have petitioned that he be relieved of these duties, and after much coaxing, the landowner relented. He assigned young Miguel to help the field hands plow the land with oxen. Miguel spent several years doing field work. "I worked on the hacienda for a long time," he remembered, "weekdays and weekends and the boss never raised my pay." He felt he did the work of a grown man, but the landlord never paid him what he expected and this discrimination rubbed him wrong. He noted that "This ended when we left the hacienda to come here [the United States]." Even though Miguel was a gentle soul, a stark contrast from his impulsive elder brother, he still knew he deserved better in life.

Miguel's gentleness marked him even as an older man when I knew him. My siblings and I remember him as a good-hearted, soft-spoken family man to the very last day of his life in San Fernando. His mother adored him, and his sister favored him for his gentility, the opposite of Pascual's testy gruffness. We don't know the relationship that Miguel had with his father; he never mentioned him in his interviews.

Guadalupe Gil, Her Daughter

My mother was Grandma's third child, born on November 22, 1905, also on the Hacienda Santa Rosa, when Grandma was twenty-five years old. She was registered as Francisca which her birth records confirm, and why she was called Guadalupe for her entire life was never fully explained to us. Nevertheless, we know that the local priest, Rev. Salvador Palafox, filled out the baptismal register on December 10 of that year, noting at the same time that she was the illegitimate daughter of Carlota and Concepción Brambila, and for this reason her birth inscription was entered into a register for "natural children," meaning illegitimate. The church kept track of such distinctions.[18]

As we've noted already, Mother's father was a traveling merchant pulling a pack of mules who supplied the backcountry villages and hacienda communities like Santa Rosa with cloth and trinkets from the outside world. He also asked to take Mother so that he could raise her properly "because he was a man of commerce and had the wherewithal to do [so]." These words were burnt into Mom's memory as well as the fact that Grandma refused.

Like her brothers, Miguel especially, Guadalupe also guarded fond experiences living with her aunt Lau. As stated above, she and her two brothers were able to leave the hacienda to go live in Mascota for a time to attend school when she was about seven, or about 1912. Mom later recognized how lucky she was to be able to attend classes, and this is why she remembered her student days in Mascota with great tenderness. Her brief time in school helped her establish a reading habit that stayed with her most of her adult life. I remember her putting on her glasses to read the Sunday supplements of *La Opinión*, the leading Spanish-language newspaper published in Los Angeles, and when she visited me in Seattle, she often asked for a book written in Spanish containing interviews of famous men who took part in the Mexican Revolution.[19] She would sit and read quietly for long periods of time and then fall asleep.

Like her brother Miguel, Guadalupe clearly remembered that it was better living with her aunt Lau in Mascota than on the plantation. At age eighty-seven, she noted that Aunt Lau, who lived with her husband, was comfortable enough to own beds and other furniture. "[She] had everything," my mother recalled with a mixture of pride and amazement. The word *everything* in this context reveals more about the bareness in Grandma's peasant adobe home in Santa Rosa than whatever meager furniture her aunt Lau might have possessed jointly with her husband. In her memoirs, written at her kitchen table in San Fernando about seventy-five years later after leaving Mascota, Mom noted that her aunt, whom she also called Nina Lau, died in 1914 and, consequently, she had to return to the hacienda. We can presume that she left reluctantly and probably complained about not being able to attend school because her mother soon placed her in a one-room schoolhouse in a village called Cimarrón Chico near the hacienda. The boys, who didn't attend school for as long as Mom did, returned to Santa Rosa, and Pascual eventually went to live with his father in the mining town Santo Domingo already mentioned. Miguel stayed with his mother and presumably helped his uncles do their farm work.

While Mother learned to read and write in school, she also began learning the ways of men early on. One day the boys' father, Cecilio, sent a message to Grandma Carlota advising her to take Pascual back to Mascota because "he was in danger." Though a mere lad, Pascual had been seeing a girl in Los Jiménez, the mining village. According to our family lore, he found out that she had some kind of an affair with Cecilio's boss and so this enraged my teenage uncle. He apparently beat her in a way that led to her death later and this alarmed his father enough to dispatch a note to Carlota. Obviously, Cecilio feared his boss would get even with young Pascual.

The trip to Los Jiménez taught Mom some early lessons about macho men. One was that an older man could engage a much younger, moneyless woman especially if the man had power and influence. Another is that a young man's jealousy could lead to a lot of trouble. Whatever the details might have been, my mother never forgot going to Los Jiménez with her mother and Sotero, Grandma's elder brother. She also remembered having to stay a week in the mining town because Pascual refused to leave.

A Time of Revolution

Mother also notes in her memoirs that the journey back to Mascota was unforgettably frightening. They ran across some of the many armed men who roamed the countryside as a result of the revolution unleashed in 1910. At one point, they were stopped by a squad of armed men who, at a distance, shouted at them, "*Quién vive* (who's there)?" Sotero, my mother's uncle, yelled back, "*Es gente buena*! (We are friendly folks)." They were thereupon allowed to pass according to our family lore. As they descended into a valley, they again met up with more horsemen carrying weapons, one of whom yelled at Pascual, "Put her on my horse. She's tired of walking already," referring to my twelve-year-old mother. Mom wrote that her elder brother either dismissed the horseman or somehow talked him out of the idea, and my mother's group kept on marching along the country path they were following. Hours later, they arrived at a hut also surrounded by armed fighters on horseback. They stopped to try to get a meal, but a man quietly warned them against it, and so my mother and her relatives fled into the night. About five in the morning, they arrived at another town where they finally slept, but not before learning that some of the soldiers they had seen earlier belonged to a mounted squadron of armed revolutionaries known as the Zamoras. The next day, my relatives finally arrived in Santa Rosa, safe and sound. My mother also recalled that on another occasion, when her brother Miguel traveled with them, they came across dead men hanging from trees. We heard these stories many times when we were growing up in San Fernando.

The Mexican Revolution of 1910 endured until about 1920, more or less, depending on where you were living in the country. In the briefest terms, the revolution came about because Mexico was beginning to modernize, albeit in a very simple way, but enough to reveal many backward practices most noticeable in the rural areas, as we've seen regarding the farmworkers or *peones* in Mascota who were sold, along with the machinery, buildings, and cattle as part of an estate. The rich lived well, and the workers were condemned to laboring, practically to death. Many revolutionary leaders wanted to change this among other things, and so they rose up against the established order. The Catholic Church and its scores of priests and bishops across the Mexican landscape supported the old ways and generally preached against revolutionary change. While the conditions in Mascota may have been quite poor, the situation in southern Mexico was worse.

When revolutionary leaders like Francisco Madero and Pancho Villa demonstrated in 1910 that ordinary people could rise up against Diaz and his ruling class and resist their oppression, many loutish and vulgar men also arose like dry leaves in a windstorm. This made it very difficult to distinguish between the good and the bad. In the fight for power, the poor suffered the most because they were oppressed by the ruling class as well as by the revolutionists, who used scare tactics to force people into submission. This is why my mother never viewed revolutionaries in a positive way even though some history books heaped praise on them.

Was the Mexican Revolution good or bad? The question is debatable, but one clear result was the end of the big haciendas filled with *peones* like our ancestors. The Hacienda Santa Rosa, for example, was taken over by the government in the 1930s, broken up into small plots known as *ejidos*, and these were given to landless individuals who became known as *ejido* holders or *ejidatarios*.[20] In essence, they could now farm their own land and profit from their hard work or lose from their mistakes or ignorance.

Our Santa Rosa relatives who stayed behind, or did not emigrate, received farmland near Mascota, though not from Santa Rosa itself. They received land parcels from the Hacienda de Galope now called ex-Hacienda Galope. This is why Mom began her visits there decades after she left Santa Rosa as a little girl; our relatives possessed *ejidos* there. I visited Galope many times in the 1970s and so did my children. Breaking up the old haciendas turned out to be one of the unmistakable results of the Mexican Revolution. Advocates of dismembering haciendas were known as *agraristas* (agrarians) and they raised a national storm with their militancy in the 1920s and 1930s. My uncle Pascual became an *agrarista* as we'll see in

Chapter 13. How the small farmers who received this land fared decades later and how the government treated them is another story entirely.[21]

Another controversial outcome of the revolution of 1910 was the beginning of a government-backed effort to strip the Catholic Church of its power. This process reached an alarming intensity in the late 1920s when many religious conservatives organized antigovernment rebellions. The tension slowly receded as time went by, culminating in a severe reduction of church power in Mexico.[22]

The revolution affected most everyone in the country. It certainly upset my mother whose earliest memories were colored with frightening images. The revolution cast my Pascual adrift as well. Mother wrote the following:

> There was a lot of revolution at this time. There were men who belonged to Pancho Villa and those who belonged to Venustiano Carranza . . . The revolutionaries would come to a farm and . . . take young girls with them against their wills. In the meantime, they would seize a granary, where corn was stored, and feed their horses. They would even throw it on the ground! They were always hungry and demanded food. My mother would sell it to them. Sometimes we would have to hide in the woods at the foot of a mountain [to avoid the armed men].

Pascual Gets into Trouble

Pascual's return to Santa Rosa from the mining towns was not well received in these troubled times because Don Manuel, the hacienda owner, didn't trust him, young as he was. How can we better understand this lack of trust between a man of means like Don Manuel and a teenager like Pascual, a son of the boss's peons?

The answer to this question lies hidden in the complex relationship between peasants, like my ancestors, and their lord of the manor. If he didn't like one of his farmworkers, then that worker found himself at great risk. Campesinos couldn't appeal to a policeman because lawmen at this time only enforced the interests of the land owners. For all practical purposes, there was no law campesinos could appeal to at this time.

Pascual, about fourteen years, served as an apprentice farmhand when he wasn't living with his father. In 1974, he recalled some of the skills he brought to the table in those days: "I knew the trails and pathways because I had already helped lead mule teams belonging to *el señor* Merino." As we've seen already, in the absence of roads, cars, and trucks, all merchandise, big and small, was transported on mule back from big cities or railroad stations to backcountry towns and farms like Mascota and the Hacienda Santa Rosa. "I knew these trails like I knew the creases of my hand," he added. He had seen mules, loaded with bags of silver ore, trekking along narrow mountain paths overstepping the edge and losing their footing. Loaded with bags of ore, their bodies would break rolling down the mountainside as they somersaulted with their heavy load crushing them on the way down. Young as he was, Pascual grew up around farm work, but what made him different was that he already knew what life was like away from the farm—he knew the life of independent miners who toiled in mountain communities like his father.

The hacienda owner had greater reason to distrust my uncle. He had joined up with a local military brigade near his father's mining town on a whim. He did this to get back at his father who whipped him for drinking with a buddy and not reporting for work on a Monday morning. He recalled getting up the next day and enlisting and never laying eyes on his father again.

How could Pascual, a mere lad, join the military just like that? At about the time that Pascual joined up, 1914, the people who had risen in revolt led by Madero and Villa, as already mentioned, were bearing down on the government, and it needed every warm body that came its way. This probably explains why Pascual was able to join and get assigned to the cavalry, as he claims, even though he was just a mere teenager. He quickly learned about guns, a skill that would prove to be quite relevant.

Prior to his departure from the hacienda for good, Don Manuel asked Pascual to accompany him on a special assignment to a nearby hacienda called El Rincón de Mirandilla, which he also owned. Before the trip, Don Manuel quizzed Pascual about his familiarity with firearms. Pascual remembered many years later that the plantation owner asked him to break down a German-made Mauser rifle, which Pascual did quickly without question. Don Manuel might have rubbed his chin with growing concern, but whether his trust in Pascual was affected or not, he took out two Winchester.30-30s and gave one to Pascual and they both rode off to El Rincón. Upon arrival, Don Manuel ferreted out a local worker who was giving him a lot of trouble. The owner thereupon threw a rope over a tree branch and placed a noose around the man's neck. He instructed Pascual, who held the end of the rope, to slowly raise the man off the ground in order to force him to disclose certain information. My uncle never forgot the power that Don Manuel possessed over that poor and helpless man.

In my interview, my uncle summarized the situation with the land owner:

> He had come to dislike me a lot. He thought I would turn his peasants against him. He thought that I was an *agrarista* even though I didn't know anything about that stuff at the time. And, that was it! He came to hate me, and I didn't know how to patch things up!

Coupled with the fact that there was "little to eat" at home and that he simply "wanted to roam freely," Pascual decided to go away on his own. "I was too big [to be hanging around the hacienda]. I didn't have an alternative!" Thus, he left his father behind in the mineral gulch and walked away from his family and the hacienda as well.

Chapter 2

The Young Rebel Goes North
(1914–1921)

Pascual Becomes a Soldier • Pascual Crosses into the United States • Pascual Begins Work on the Railroad

AT ABOUT SEVEN in the morning of May 2, 1914, young Pascual stepped out from the adobe shack on the hacienda that he had long known as his mother's house and walked away with a heavy heart. He was leaving and not coming back. He hiked about two hours down to his aunt Lau's home in Mascota, where he had spent pleasurable days as a boy, to bid her good-bye, he remembered. He also stopped at his cousin Felipa's home to eat a snack, "*unos tacos*," he said, and bid them farewell too. Felipa was Grandma Carlota's grandniece, and as an adult, she would move down to Puerto Vallarta, where her son Leonardo the singing baker, would take residence and host me and my siblings many times.

Knowing the mountain pathways, Pascual climbed down all day from the cool pine forests of the Mascota valley toward the sea, descending as the rising heat of the tropical coast covered him with perspiration. At the end of the day and after constantly trekking down slopes and stepping over rills, he came upon a house whose occupants were preparing the evening meal. "I only had seven cents in my pocket," he recalled, but after introducing himself and explaining where he was headed, they fed him and let him sleep in one of the corners of the property. He woke up early the next day and continued stepping downhill, finally strolling into Puerto Vallarta by way of the cemetery at about nine in the morning. "Vallarta was a scrawny village in those days," Pascual brought to mind. "It might have had approximately five hundred houses at the most," he added. And, as he would soon be reminded, Puerto Vallarta might not have been anything more than a seaside village at this time, but it also functioned as a regional port. Agricultural products like corn and tobacco were brought down to it from the surrounding ranchos and haciendas and placed on small ships to be transported and sold up and down the coast, at various ports including Manzanillo and Mazatlán. As a mule driver's assistant, he knew all this well.

The first thing Pascual did in Puerto Vallarta was look for one of his uncles, Rafael Ramos, married to Emilia, one of his aunt Rafaela's daughters. Even in those days people from Mascota and the surrounding area traveled down to Vallarta in search of adventure or opportunity even as they do today. Pascual, however, was unable to find his uncle but remained in Vallarta nonetheless, sleeping on the beach about a block or two away from the main plaza. "If the night was cold, I would cover myself with sand and stay warm that way," he recalled.

About a week later, Pascual noticed a man leading a herd of burros over the cobblestoned streets of Vallarta, all carrying a load of one thing or another. Having had ample experience helping out with mule teams, young Pascual approached the man and asked if he could be of help to him. The man warned him about getting hurt by the animals, but Pascual explained that he knew how to work with draft animals—he knew how to load them, tie them, and lead them anywhere, he told the man. Convinced that this lad knew what he was talking about, the man offered Pascual seventy-five Mexican cents per day, plus meals, to transport tobacco for him. The tobacco leaves could be picked up at a place called La Boquita at a nearby river, and they were to be unloaded in town. Our dark-skinned teenager from Santa Rosa thus got the job of transporting tobacco on the backs of burros, and if he didn't move tobacco from one place to another, he transferred beans or corn. This went on for about a week or so.

When a medium-sized ship docked offshore to take a load of beans and corn, Pascual managed to talk with the captain and ask him to take him as a passenger to Mazatlán. He told the captain that he had left his mother in Mazatlán and was now trying to return to her. Pascual had overheard residents of Navidad, a mining community near Santa Rosa, talking about their travel north to work: some near Mazatlán, and other places like El Tigre, farther up north near Los Mochis. People who worked in the mines carried money in their pockets, and he wanted to be one of them.

The captain consented to take Pascual to Mazatlán but only as an apprentice seaman. My uncle learned to work on a hundred-feet-long cargo ship named *Maria de la Luz* (Mary of the Light). Alongside eleven other seamen, he helped load sacks of corn and beans on board, carrying them on his back from dockside up to the boat and walking on wooden planks and down a ladder to the hold where the sacks were stacked. When unloading, Pascual helped carry the bags up the ladder and onto the docks. In between ports, out at sea, he was responsible for pumping water out of the hold and making sure that the cargo remained dry. He also helped open and close sails, and when time permitted, he played cards and engaged in other betting games. The world was quickly opening up to him.

Pascual worked this way for several weeks, including some time spent rudderless at sea. The coaster ship sailed south to Manzanillo to deliver goods from Puerto Vallarta, and then returned to Vallarta to deliver products from the southern port. Afterward, the ship sailed north to the one of the oldest Mexican ports on the Pacific, San Blas, Nayarit, and made a delivery there. The *Maria de la Luz* then sailed north to Mazatlán, but its engine conked out, and the men on board couldn't fix it. So they unfolded the sails, and the wind blew them out to sea for about fifteen days. "A northerly wind dragged us far out, very far! Only God knows how far we went out to sea! Normally, it took about three days to sail from Vallarta to Mazatlán," Pascual remembered. But after much work and worry, they finally regained control of their direction and sailed back to Mazatlán.

As they were coming into port, the ship's captain reassured Pascual that he would now be able to rejoin his mother. The runaway teenager replied, "Well, yes, but look at me! I don't have any clothes!" Indeed, young Pascual probably wore most of the clothes he owned when he left the hacienda, and if he packed anything, he could probably fold it into a knapsack carried on his shoulders. By the time he arrived in Mazatlán, he may have been dressed in rags, which might have been fine while working at sea, but wouldn't do in this well-known port town. He remembered that the captain surprised him by offering him a pair of pants and a shirt. When he told me this, he searched his memory some more and said that the captain might have offered him a few coins, too, as payment for his work aboard the ship.

The port city of Mazatlán was still small and relatively young when my uncle discovered it in 1914, walking off the cargo boat with a new shirt and pants and a couple of coins in his pocket. Unlike the cities of interior Mexico, Mazatlán grew up much later—later than Mascota, and at least 150 years later than the cities around Guadalajara. Except for a bedraggled community of Indians and *pardos* or mulattoes who lived in a handful of wooden shacks and served whatever ship happened to stop, it was a wild outpost in the early 1700s, when Mascota was supposedly founded.

Mazatlán didn't begin to look like a civilized town until the early 1800s.[23] Much of northern Mexico was practically empty at this time except for numerous bands of semi sedentary Indians constantly threatening scattered Spanish outposts.

When my uncle arrived in Mazatlán in 1914, it probably reminded him of Mascota except for the fact that it was somewhat bigger and it stood on a small peninsula buffeted by the ocean breeze. Its population was just slightly larger, about ten thousand, and its urban footprint appeared to be the size of Mascota's. Old maps reveal that Mazatlán's town extension in the late 1800s was no greater than the small peninsula on which the port began, so I surmise that when Pascual arrived, wearing his new pants and shirts, the limits of the city had not extended much more.[24] The two bluffs that shielded the old center now known as the Olas Altas district are still visible today, and they continue to separate what is now the core of the old city from the pounding surf that crashes on the western side—Pascual's coaster loaded with staples from the south probably disembarked on the southern edge of the peninsula as other vessels continue to do so at the present time. The modern hotel district that now fills up with American tourists on the beaches north of the peninsula was populated at this time only by swaying palm trees and lizards of many stripes.

The couple of coins that young Pascual put in his pocket after he landed in Mazatlán didn't last long. He took stock of his new situation once again and proceeded to make the most of it by looking for a job and soon found one at the *mercado*, the open market in Mazatlán. The energy of the place and the allure of fruits and vegetables piled high amidst stalls filled with freshly butchered meat convinced him to hang around long enough to observe where the food came from and where it went. And so he noticed that horse-drawn carts brought it from the nearby rail station where boxcars arrived loaded with foodstuffs and other provisions. He placed himself first at the station and then at the *mercado* and quickly began to help one man here or another there with the loading and unloading of crates and boxes. This eventually earned him a nickel from one fellow and a dime from another. "There was always something to do. One guy left and another arrived, and I would offer to help. I did pretty well, actually. This helped me stick around Mazatlán for about five or six months."

Pascual worked hard in Mazatlán, and he lived hard too, apparently. This is where he contracted syphilis, a sexually transmitted disease that can make a man sterile. He admitted flat-out in one of our interviews that he was syphilitic and that he had been admitted into a hospital in Mazatlán where he was treated by a "Chinese" doctor; he also remembered that

"Chinese" vendors were very active in the city. This explanation throws light on the fact that despite having had several women, who each in turn shared his home for many years at a time, he never had children.

Pascual Becomes a Soldier

After leaving the hospital, my uncle decided it was time to go north to the US border, and so he joined a soldier's family in order to do this. In the middle of the great revolution discussed in the previous chapter, Mazatlán was constantly in flux because it was a major railroad hub and an important transit point between Guadalajara and the US border. Hundreds of thousands of people traveled by train at this time, especially federal soldiers and their families who were often obligated, when there was no other room, to ride atop of the railroad cars—on the roofs! As previously explained, significant battles took place in the northern states. Amidst this hustle and bustle that came to Mazatlán due to the fighting, Pascual conceived another plan to keep on traveling. He approached a soldier traveling with his family and, explaining that he might be taken off the train because he was a single male, asked the soldier if he could join them posing as a family member and thus travel north. The soldier ultimately accepted the young man's proposition, and, climbing to the rooftop of one of the railroad cars, they all rode out of Mazatlán together. Miguel, his younger brother, would do the same a handful of years later and my father too.

Soon after the train left the city station, a band of revolutionary Yaqui Indians attacked it much like in the old Western movies. Many of the leaders of the revolution were men of the north—often miners and owners of big haciendas—who had learned to share the region with important Indian communities that had lived there from time immemorial, including the fierce and hardy Yaquis. These Indians played an important role in the revolution because they allied themselves with leaders like Pancho Villa. Thus, we find that my uncle's train chugged to a stop because the tracks had been burned red-hot and bent out of shape to effectively halt any movement. This provided the horse-riding Yaquis an opportunity to make good with an attack on the train filled with federal soldiers whom Villa was fighting including our young Pascual.

As the bullets began flying through the air and smashing into the walls of the railroad cars, an army lieutenant approached my teen age uncle and his "family" offering weapons. He gave Pascual a rifle and a canvas bag filled with a 150 cartridges. He advised Pascual and his family, "Don't let them kill you without defending yourselves!" My uncle enjoyed himself bringing these old memories to the forefront of his mind.

The battle continued, and the Indian horsemen kept shooting at the train. Many men and women were killed. "As it turned out," Pascual recalled, "we didn't defeat them, but they didn't wipe us out, either." The soldiers on the train managed to mount machine guns on the railroad cars and soon began mowing down many attackers, ultimately defending the train and fending off the Yaqui revolutionaries who began retreating. Taking advantage of this lull, the soldiers reheated and straightened out the rails, and eventually, the train was able to continue on its way to the desert city of Hermosillo, many hours north of Mazatlán. Young Pascual had become a soldier by default. This battle took place sometime in 1915 or early 1916.

When they arrived in Hermosillo, at an old barracks building, he and the others were fed and given some money and a blue uniform to wear. My *tío* remembered that blue was the color of the *carrancistas*, the name given to the soldiers loyal to Venustiano Carranza who had proclaimed himself first chief of the constitutionalist forces which my uncle mislabels "government troops."[25] According to him, no one bothered to write down any details about boyish recruits like Pascual other than their name. Nothing was recorded about who the parents were or where anyone came from.

My uncle also dredged up recollections about the officer in charge. He said he might have been a colonel but he was sure his name was Joaquín Amaro, "whom they used to call *el rajado* or 'the guy with a scar' because he had a long scar on one of his ears." Worthy of note is the fact that this officer's name didn't mean anything else to my uncle, not at this time nor later. As it turns out, a full-blooded Indian from Michoacán by that name did in fact become famous for fighting fearless Pancho Villa like few other military commanders could, even orchestrating his assassination many years later. And, he "perforated his earlobe," writes one of his biographers, "in order to wear a gold earring" as a way of standing out from everybody else.[26] Amaro would later rise to become a famous general who not only survived the revolution but also became a very influential secretary of war. My uncle never learned this.

In these campsites, Pascual learned that women, wives, or girlfriends traveled with their men, the soldiers. "Some men traveled with their wives—some traveled with women who were not their wives! They were called *galletas* or *soldaderas*,[27] and if their man was killed, they would continue marching along with the troops and band up with some other guy!" If the chance arose, he added, they would advance to the next town to scrounge for food and make tortillas to have a meal ready when their man arrived. "And the ball would keep on rolling!"

My uncle found a friend in these days. Circulating amidst the hordes of men, women, and children, and soldiers on horseback or on foot, Pascual crossed paths with an older man who asked him for his name. He explained that he reminded him of his son who had been killed in a recent fracas. Perhaps looking for protection and guidance, our teenager kept close to this man who acted paternally toward him amidst the chaos of war, looking after him and advising him about the ways of a soldier. They spent many weeks together in the camp and out in the shooting fields. They were sent together on special assignments. "I came to feel close to him," Pascual admitted, he who had become averse to close relationships, "because he took care of me." But in an attack against Villa, the old man was killed in action. Sixteen-year-old Pascual didn't see this but later learned what had happened from a buddy who did. "I felt very sad," he admitted. But he also expressed comfort from the fact that many other people looked out for him as well—after all, he was just a kid.

Colonel Joaquín Amaro apparently kept most of his soldiers quartered in Hermosillo for many weeks, including our teenager from Mascota. Pancho Villa had pulled his troops out of that area and Pascual's fighting group was not chosen to chase after them. Originally from Chihuahua, a nearby state, Villa had decided to take refuge in its high mountains. And so, Amaro sent soldiers after him—but not Pascual. He was assigned to form part of a clique of apprentice fighters who didn't get to go chase Villa and they became restless.

Slightly older than our pathfinder, they informed Pascual that they were going to disappear—they planned to desert. They had all been assigned to guarding the horses placed in a large corral at night. One of them told Pascual that they were going to slip away in the darkness and head north to the US border—and take the saddles and other mountings they were using with them as well—and that he should go ahead and move the horses in the morning according to previous instructions. In this way no one would suspect they were missing right away. "You think I'm going to stay here? I'm going, too!" Pascual protested, and he sneaked off as well that night.

He may have decided to go to the United States while still in Mascota because he had already heard talk about how you could earn money "up north." "I knew that people from Navidad and Cimarrón traveled to the United States to work in the mines up there," Pascual remembered as an old man, referring to some small towns near Santa Rosa. People in Mascota also knew there were jobs in the Miami copper mines of Arizona in the early 1900s. "This is why I said 'Heck no, I'm not staying' when the guys said 'We're leaving.' I answered 'I'm going too!'" His fellow soldiers retorted, "You're too young! No one is going to give you a job! Besides, they'll catch you, so you'd better stay!" Pascual didn't stay, and he tagged along with his older fellow soldiers. They all crossed the border into the United States without realizing it. It was 1917.

Pascual Crosses into the United States

The small band of young, ragtag militiamen came upon scattered houses in an arid spot known locally as Calabazas, south of Tucson. This is desert country accented by tall organ-pipe cactus, fiery ocotillo, greenish paloverde trees, and other arid shrubbery. In telling me his story, my uncle remembered that a Mexican woman intercepted them and called out, "Hey, where do you think you're going? There's a detachment of American soldiers around the bend, and they're going to catch you and send you back! Don't go any further!"

The runaway fighters took her advice and then explained to her that they didn't want to continue fighting any more, and so she invited them to take cover in her corral behind the house. While they were resting, her husband showed up and learned what was going on and agreed, "They could have shot at you." This Spanish-speaking couple seems to have been well aware of what was going on south of the nearby border and may have seen other men running away from the conflict and seeking places to hide on American soil. The man advised them to bury their uniforms, guns, and ammunition and continue heading north. Pascual's companions apparently took the man's advice about hiding their military equipment and kept going north from the border while my uncle managed to stay behind with the couple who had intercepted them in the first place. His traveling alone and being younger than the others may have contributed to this arrangement.

They helped him find a job in a nearby farming area called Amadoville (probably present-day Amado, Arizona, thirty miles north of Nogales), and soon he found himself sitting at the dining table with the family that sharecropped corn, watermelon, and beans for the Nogales market. My uncle became impressed at the fact that they ate three regular meals a day at appointed times—and they ate plenty, too. "So different from back home!" he mused. It was here that he also discovered the giant-sized northern flour tortillas which came hot off the griddle with every meal as opposed to the smaller corn tortillas from Santa Rosa and Mascota. Like so many other Mexican immigrants to the United States, young Pascual also took a crash course doing farmwork on a commercial scale here when he accompanied

Pedro, one of the farmer's sons, to remove a high weed from the growing cornstalks the next day. Pascual didn't mind the hard work, and he stayed here about three and a half months.

While residing on the edges of Tucson, our young migrant from Santa Rosa went from one job to another. On one occasion, he became an assistant to a firewood merchant whose wife was blind. Getting paid a dollar a day, he first spent most of his time caring for the small farm or rancho where they all lived and soon after began driving a wagon pulled by five horses loaded with firewood to sell in Nogales. His job as a teamster involved driving the firewood load to the border town, dumping it there, and returning the next day for a new load. His route paralleled the main highway out of Nogales, and he recalled taking extra care not to get in the way of the new-fangled horseless carriages that sped back and forth on the highway. Pascual grew restless within a short time. He also felt that the blind woman was beginning to feel "romantic" about him. Instead of getting into trouble with her husband, Pascual decided to move on. "I'd better get out of here! Enough with this situation!" he swore as he marched away.

He found a job about twenty miles away, clearing the desert of mesquite trees in order to plant guayule, a shrub native to this area whose bark contained latex rubber. Using a plow and even a Caterpillar tractor to dig out the desert plants and trees, he and other workers would clear city block–sized sections in order to plant guayule bushes. His fellow army renegades had found a job there too, and so it must have been a pleasant surprise to come upon them if for no other reason than that they were fellow compatriots in a foreign land. Pascual may not have known it at the time, but he and his fellow deserters were taking part in an experiment to end US dependence on expensive foreign rubber.[28]

Pascual met his first significant mistress, Rosario, at the guayule plantation, and she merits a mention here not only because she hung around with him for about a year or two, but also because he never really forgot her even though he enjoyed about five long-term relationships with other women during the course of his lifetime. I personally knew his last two life-mates, Salvadora and Ester, both *güeras* (light-skinned Mexicans) who happened to look very much alike. Fifty-seven years later, he labeled Rosario a "tough and wicked woman." In his recorded memoirs, he never used her surname. His characterization of Rosario is difficult to interpret by hindsight since I didn't ask why he called her "wicked." It is clear that she was not a shrinking violet beholden to her man's every whim. Single immigrant women had to be tough indeed. "She was one of those who always got what she needed, knew how to go to the commissary and stock up. She knew her way around," he added. Mentioning his first significant female partner here also reminds us that Mexican immigration to the United States, which began in earnest when my uncle arrived, always included both men and women from the start.

Pascual Begins Work on the Railroad

Our itinerant young worker didn't stay long tearing chaparral and mesquite trees from the water-thirsty ground because he soon discovered the great need for railroad workers in America in those days.

Traveling by train in 1917 was the principal mode for covering long distances because stagecoaches pulled by horses had long given way to the "iron horse," and it was too early for the mass production of automobiles—cars were still in their infancy. Henry Ford's Model T was only nine years old when Pascual planted guayule plants in Southern Arizona, and Ford's managers were still tinkering with the best way to manufacture the biggest number of cars without sacrificing quality.

Trains, on the other hand, were time-tested. American railroads had spread from east to west forty years earlier, in the 1870s, and thus constituted the most civilized form of long-distance transportation for people and the most efficient way to ship goods. By the time my uncle began looking for work in Southern Arizona, the US railroad network was about forty-five years old and had spread from the East Coast all the way to Arizona, California, Oregon, and Washington State. More than a hundred railroad companies had consolidated through the late 1800s into a handful of the most important ones, and by 1900 the Southern Pacific Railroad Company was "the world's largest transportation company with ten thousand miles of railroad line."[29] It linked New Orleans to Tucson to Los Angeles to Portland.

Collis P. Huntington, the infamous owner of the Southern Pacific, needed workers to keep his trains moving. Strong men were needed not only to move the heavy rails but also to pound them with giant hammers into the ground, and then later maintain them because they would wear out or loosen or, in certain cases, they would need to be extended to new corners of the country. The need to perform this work made it vital to have plenty of recruits. While much of the track laying was done earlier by Chinese, Irish, Italians, and Greeks, as early as 1907, Mexican workers began to command respect for their ability to work long hours laying down track and otherwise help keep trains flowing steadily. A well-known investigator of the time wrote that "there was not a single instance in which the men in actual touch with railroad labor did not give the Mexican preference over either Japanese or Greeks." They worked hard and didn't create as much trouble as the others.[30] When Pascual and thousands of other Mexicans were cast about by the Mexican Revolution, landing in distant places like the US-Mexican border, the railroad system was thirsty for men like him. In fact, Mexicans from Jalisco were among the leading suppliers of workers when Pascual arrived in the United States.[31]

Pascual's first railroad job in the Tucson area was to work as an *aguador*, the person who refills the steam engines with water. Although it was one of the less grueling and less complicated positions, it provided him the opportunity to inquire about other jobs available in connection to the railroad and to learn how the entire railroad system worked. He discovered, for instance, that he could keep an eye on a certain blackboard in one of the railroad offices near his work that announced the *renganches* of Mexicans who were hauled away from the border to places up north where they were needed (*renganche* is a term used at this time for gangs of Mexican workers contracted and transported by railroad companies to do track work). One day, he saw an announcement of a *renganche* coming to Tucson from El Paso, Texas, which acted as a funnel for Mexicans displaced by the tumult of the revolution. In old age, Pascual looked back on this scene and concluded that, "These men appeared dazed to me. They didn't know where to turn or where to go. They were hungry and lacked many things."

"I inquired about the next *renganche*," Pascual remembered, and learned that one was headed to California and Oregon at the very moment he deciphered the scrawl on the chalkboard. He didn't need to know English because every train official he had met so far spoke Spanish, some were Anglos others were Mexican Americans—they were contracted by the railroad company to gather the workers and ship them where they were needed. He thus hurried home and announced to Rosario that a train was headed their way, and he wanted to be on it. "I just learned about a *renganche* that's on its way, and I know we are going to join it. I want you to be ready so we can go! I'm going to get the details now." He soon learned all he had to do was board the train, speak with the man in charge, and get on the *renganche* list.

When the train arrived from El Paso, he noticed that it was pulling about eight cars filled with workers. As a result of his inquiries, he and about thirty other men were placed on the *renganche* list and told they would soon ship out. He went home one more time and exclaimed to Rosario, "We've done it! We're in for it! Let's see where in the hell we windup!" Within hours, they clambered aboard and took their seats, and the train bolted forward, gaining speed and heading northwest over the sandy desert. My uncle had thus become a *renganchado*.

The steam-driven locomotive pulling Pascual and his fellow Mexicans traveled for four days with occasional stops in the Arizona wilderness until they reached Los Angeles. At these stopovers, if more workers were not brought on board, vans loaded with food would arrive to be distributed to the dazzled and hungry train passengers. "At mealtime, I saw two vans arrive with food, one with five legs of beef. From another we got potatoes, beans, and all kinds of food! They had coffee, pies—all the stuff! We filled our plates and walked back to where we were seated."

In Los Angeles, a city of half a million in 1917,[32] they stopped for about half a day and then, without waiting for any stragglers who might have gone out to explore, resumed north until they reached Northern California. Here they began dropping off groups of recruits in the middle of the forested mountains. Our young vagabond and his girlfriend knew the train was headed for Oregon and recalled being dropped off in Truckee, at almost six thousand feet above sea level, which he mistakenly placed in Oregon. The presence of timber-covered ridges with snowy peaks in this part of Sierra Nevada, so different from home, may have induced him to believe he was a farther north. It was May, and the daytime temperatures were still quite cold in comparison to Santa Rosa.

The recruiters for the Southern Pacific dropped Pascual and his girlfriend off at the railroad section station in Truckee, California, along with eight other men. Truckee had become a rail town by this time, a remote one to be sure, later described as a "a major operations center in the High Sierra" in part because millions of dollars had already been invested about fifty years earlier in this area to connect a rail line linking Sacramento with Omaha. Truckee became part of the historic transcontinental rail line laid down in 1869 with the Last Spike being driven on May 10 of that year in Promontory, Utah. The rails were laid over the Sierra Nevada across Truckee linking up with Reno and the rest of Nevada, thus joining the eastern half of the nation with the western half.[33]

Pascual arrived in Truckee in 1917 with Rosario just a few weeks after the United States declared war against Germany. The country was beginning to prepare for what would turn out to be a major global war, and so the government immediately asked the nation's railroad companies to help it coordinate rail operations in order to insure that the war effort could be launched as soon as possible. This may explain the frenzied need for railroad workers that year and why Pascual saw so many Mexicans being loaded aboard trains in Nogales and taken into the interior. To be sure, millions of dollars were spent "for road extensions, additions, and betterments" at this time, including "double tracking," and this meant a lot of work for laborers like my uncle. Railroad company officials allegedly endowed the Truckee railroad center not only with the latest in railroad construction materials but also with industry-setting health facilities for its officers and employees, including a clinic and a pharmacy. All of this was part of the Southern Pacific Company's "early expansion and systematization of employee health care . . . to reduce employee turnover and cope with severe injuries common in railroad work."[34]

On the personal level, Pascual had some serious problems with his girlfriend here. They arose in part due to the fact that the ratio between men and women at the work camp was woefully off-balance—Pascual claims that he was one of two men in the work camp who brought a woman as part of the family, and although Pascual and Rosario were not married, they were apparently viewed as a couple. This contributed to one of many violent moments in Pascual's life. He and his girlfriend lived in a one-room apartment near the work site in the midst of other units filled with single men. On a morning that Rosario claimed she was not feeling well, Pascual stepped into the cooking corner of their room to fix his lunch when he suddenly heard a scratching noise on the nearest window which happened to be painted over. Not being able to see clearly through the windowpane, he went outside and found a young man standing by it. An intuitive understanding of what might have been going on seems to have been instantaneous in our Pascual. The young fellow was stalking Rosario, and she may not have been resisting his advances too much.

Still able to recall the details of this incident decades later, my uncle flashed back on the fact that the young fellow told Pascual right off, "Come out of there." Pascual didn't hesitate, remembering that his opponent was ready with a brickbat in hand which he arced over Pascual's head, knocking him to the ground. Feeling dazed from the blow, my uncle couldn't get up right away since the assailant, who was wearing heavy work boots, began kicking him. Pascual recalled that the attacker shouted furiously at him while he merely kept quiet guarding himself against the blows that rained down upon him. Finally, a neighbor, who also had a woman in the house, came out with a gun, threatening to shoot the young attacker who then ceased the assault and paced away. Rosario, who had come out of the room to witness the violence, went back in.

Pascual claims he told her, "Look at what you've gotten us into! We're not part of the revolutionary bands anymore! Things are very different here. We have to behave differently here!" He inferred that Rosario may have been a *soldadera*.

She replied by saying, "He's been doing that for a long time. He comes and calls for me, but I don't respond. There've been times he even wanted to barge in, but I put a bolt on the door or I just don't go out!"

"That's what you say," Pascual answered. "But I don't believe you. I know you very well already."

Pascual remembered her sassy reply: "Well, whatever!" Upon hearing these words and still enraged from the fight, he knocked her onto the bed then took a knife and walked out in search of his aggressor—but didn't find him. Although later in the day, the two men worked near each other; they didn't fight again; still the incident burned into my uncle's psyche. He decided he was nearly finished with doing railroad work in Truckee, but there was one more important incident that affected his stay in the sierras this time around.

This one put him over the edge, ready to move to Fresno which somebody recommended to him. "This bizarre thing happened to me there," he said, referring to Truckee. "I don't know whether it was the change of scenery or perhaps I was already getting sick. I'll be damned if I know what it was!" His work in Truckee required the use of self-propelled rail cart which inexplicably turned over, accidentally knocking him into an adjacent ravine. The machine hit him hard enough to put him out cold. "I believe I was unconscious for about a minute—maybe even less—before I came to. I got back on my feet, climbed back to where I was, and discovered the guys [his fellow workers] were all looking at me. I told them, 'You should have come to help me.'" His sense of self-composure prevented him from demanding to know more about why no one rushed down to attend to him. He may have instantly reminded himself that he was all alone in a foreign country and occupied the bottom rung of the social totem pole, and appealing for help was too much to ask. In all fairness, the supervisor and his fellow workers may have been either stupefied or confused about what to do but Pascual seems to have interpreted their inaction as a sign of disregard. If Truckee had been invested by the railroad company with special facilities to reduce injuries or deaths to the hundreds of men who worked on the rail lines, Pascual's experience didn't seem to profit by it.

The Anglo supervisor who spoke some Spanish finally asked him whether he was all right and whether anything hurt. Pascual pointed to his lower abdomen and, in fact, later concluded he had hurt his appendix somehow. The boss told him that if he wanted to, he would write a report and then send him to a nearby company "hospital" to be looked over. But his girlfriend would not be able to accompany him, he added. She would have to stay.

Pascual seems to have reached a turning point upon hearing this. "I'll be goddamned!" he said to himself. He dismissed the offer to get checked and walked to a nearby creek. Sitting down, he took his shoes off and cooled his feet in the mountain water. "I threw water on my face and that was the moment I began to think about my mother." It had been about four years since he had left and not seen her. Pascual wrote to his mother that evening.

A few days later, our young immigrant informed his supervisor that he wasn't feeling good and wanted to change jobs. The boss replied that it was against the rules for a contracted *renganche* worker to leave his job before it was finished, but Pascual pressed him by stating that he wanted to go to Fresno to look for work—he had heard that there were jobs there and doctors to attend to him if something should develop from the fall. The boss relented, saying that he would send an order for Pascual to pick up his check at the Fresno railroad office, and this is the way Pascual and Rosario landed in Fresno, California, for the first time.

Arriving there in at the beginning of 1918 without a job seems to have become unsettling to Pascual. First of all, his relationship with Rosario came to an end, finally. Within a couple of weeks of their arrival from the camps in the sierra, she reconnected with some people she knew and obtained a job in a restaurant where men like Pascual congregated for a meal. This facilitated their eventual split, which further threw Pascual into a spin. These were lean days for him, too, because he remembers having to hock a woolen mackinaw jacket which he wore up in the mountain encampments and held dear. He also found it necessary to avoid running into Rosario, so he went searching for a job in Bakersfield, later returned to Fresno, and subsequently got in touch with another railroad supervisor who ultimately gave him a job with the Santa Fe Railroad, once again. The winter months thus gave way to spring as he worked to lay railroad ties on the main line between Fresno and Bakersfield.

Not feeling obligated to return home to a girlfriend as before, he spent many of his evenings and weekends at the gambling tables that came alive in the railroad camps and in the taverns nearby. He remembers losing so much sometimes that he bet his clothes and blankets. At times, our young émigré couldn't even take a girl on a date because he had no money. *Era el vicio de jugar*, he recalled calmly many years later in order to explain his penury at this time. He meant it was the gambling vice that brought him woes. He would even borrow from friends to be able to place a bet. A friend from El Paso who occasionally counseled him got angry one time about his addiction to gambling. It didn't help at all that his luck would sometimes change. One weekend, he won about $600, and "it allowed [him] to get even with things." He went to Fresno, where he bought some new clothes.

On this trip, he met the woman who would become his next significant partner and, in this way, provide us with a name that would become part of our family lore: Cleofas. My uncle remembered that they met at a Fresno laundry shop where she worked. One aspect of her singularity in our family memory is that she was older than my uncle by about twenty years. "She was a big woman," he remembered, and she had a family with her. "She loved life," he added with appreciation—*estaba llena de vida*. She may have helped to wean Pascual away from his gambling ways to some extent because his wantonness seemed to have reached a high point up at about the time he met her. Her own manner suggests she was cut from the same traditional cloth as Carlota and Guadalupe. Obviously a Mexican immigrant just like Pascual, we don't know the story of how she turned up in Fresno at this time. My mother and grandmother usually referred to her with a certain touch of respect. Was she a mother substitute for young Pascual, especially after a difficult relationship with Rosario?

In one of two photographs fastened into one of our family photo albums, she stands tall in her whitish dress with an ankle-length hem as she pauses next to my grandmother, Carlota, and holds on to a ten-year-old girl while someone takes the photograph (the girl was identified as her granddaughter). In both photos, she wears a turban-style hat that reflects a touch of dignity as she looks straight at the camera. Summoning his memory, Pascual said that they agreed to create a new life together (*hacer una vida nueva*) on New Year's Day of 1921, approximately.

This is about the time that my father, Bernabé Gil, entered the picture. He and Pascual met in the Fresno area perhaps as early as 1919, the year Bernabé was supposed to have entered the United States. How my dad turned up in Fresno is unknown, but surely the story was like Pascual's and the others on my mother's side of the family: he left his hometown in Michoacán, as we'll see below, looking for a job—and the railroad lines led the way. Fresno was already one of the central destinations for workers seeking agricultural employment at this time. Pascual told me that he met my father in *blaqueston* (Blackston?) near Fresno and that they worked together many times even before he met my mother.

In summary, the reader may now come to appreciate my uncle's path finding trajectory. Young as he was, he broke away from an atmosphere of subjugation in Santa Rosa. Fearing that Don Manuel, the owner of the hacienda, would hurt him if not kill him for demonstrating a sense of self-reliance considered by the plantation owner to be menacing and which my uncle didn't even realize he was projecting, Pascual abandoned his family and took flight. He inevitably headed north where opportunities beckoned. Despite the flame of revolution that was exerting a pull on other young men, he ultimately ended up in California working in projects designed to unleash the economic capacity of the Golden State. My father would follow a similar and independent path as we'll see later in these pages. In any case, Pascual's flight from Santa Rosa to Fresno in its various stages represents the first step that would introduce the rest of my family to California and ultimately settle in San Fernando.

Chapter 3

The Family Follows
(1919–1922)

Carlota and Her Children Leave the Hacienda • They Arrive in the Port of Mazatlán • Miguel Works for the Railroad • Living and Working in Mazatlán • Saying Good-bye to Mazatlán • They Arrive at the Border

THE LETTER THAT Pascual wrote to his mother after getting hurt on the job eventually reached the Jalisco backlands. Live-in peasants like our ancestors didn't ordinarily receive letters because most of them were illiterate, so the arrival of Pascual's correspondence in the hacienda had to be a special event. That it was delivered at all is a curious fact on its own because few of us historians know how mail delivery really worked in the backlands of Mexico at this time. It probably created considerable gossip not only among the other *peones* on the hacienda but also in the owner's house, although there is no recording of this fact in our family lore. Had the letter survived, it would probably reveal an elementary scrawl punctuated in an unconventional way, similar to the memoirs my mother wrote in the 1970s in which words starting with the letter h would be missing the letter and three or four dots or a dash would indicate a new thought or a new paragraph. I neglected to ask my uncle about that letter.

In any case, Miguel, his younger brother, remembered that Pascual "had written to us asking us to join him and saying he would send us the money for it." His sister Guadalupe's hopeful-minded memory identified more than one letter reaching her mother. She asserts that Pascual wrote from Arizona urging her to make the trip to which Carlota responded, "No. No. I won't." That even his boss got into the act by encouraging Carlota to go ahead and make the trip because "by water and by train it really wasn't that far at all." My siblings and I remember this phrase because Mother used it often enough. In any case, Pascual's letter must have said something like "Come join me and keep Lupe away from the land owner too." In other words, he urged his mother and siblings to leave the hacienda, mother's memoirs recording the fact that Pascual warned his mother to beware of Don Manuel because he might want to rape or otherwise take advantage of Guadalupe and this should be reason enough to leave. He must have also affirmed that work was easily available in America.

Whether it was one or more letters, Pascual's message nevertheless hit the mark. Carlota began to talk openly about her son's invitation to join him. Guadalupe recalled that she implored her stepfather, "Güicho," to go with them—but since he was an older man, he repeatedly rebuffed her by saying, "Why should I go? I'm too old!" Carlota apparently insisted on his joining them many times as well, but he refused. We don't know anything else about Güicho other than that my mother called him "stepfather."

Miguel and Guadalupe, young as they might have been, coincidently remembered that the hacienda owner found out about the letter and Pascual's attempt to lure his family to the United States. They also remember that he made fun of them. Both Miguel and Guadalupe committed the hacienda owner's words to memory: "I know you folks want to go to the United States, so when you get there, whistle at me," he chided mockingly, as if to say, "You have as much as a chance to get there as I do to hear you whistle at me from that far away." My siblings and I remembered that phrase during most of our lives. Like many hacendados or hacienda owners of his time and place, he couldn't envision peasants having a mind of their own. Miguel added the following words somewhat wistfully:

> He never believed we would leave. We didn't have money, but we did everything we could to get away. We had a milk cow that fed on Don Manuel's land and this had always brought us a lot of problems—he would always reproach us because the cow got into this and that. He didn't want us to have anything. He wanted us to depend on him alone. So we sold the cow [to help pay for our trip], and I don't know what else we might have sold—we didn't have much else.

This is how they scraped a few coins together to be able to prepare to walk away and never return.

Guadalupe recorded on paper that before they left, on March 19, 1919, her mother took her to the nearby town of Talpa, where pilgrims venerate a richly garbed statue of Mary (known locally as Our Lady of Talpa) to say good-bye to "her aunt Tomasa," her father's sister, who lived there. This note tells us that Grandma Carlota kept up a relationship with Guadalupe's father's family even when he disregarded her. Grandma rented a donkey to carry Mother because she was too young to walk all the way. They followed a trail that winds for about ten miles through rugged, semi-forested mountains connecting Santa Rosa and Talpa. They had walked this path as pilgrims before, so they knew the way. My mother believed that Carlota also wanted to catch her old boyfriend, Concepción Brambila, at his sister's home—but to no avail. She never saw him again. They did find Tomasa, however, and after a tearful reunion, they said good-bye never to see each other again.

"My mother decided we would leave in the month of April," Guadalupe jotted down, and I speculate that Carlota might have decided this on the rigorous walk back to Santa Rosa from Talpa. Grandma may have chosen the month of April for walking long hours because the sun heats up considerably in May in this part of the world and the rainy season gets started with lots of electrical storms in late June. Packing for the trip was probably the easiest thing to do because they had so little, but saying good-bye to their numerous family members and friends was easier said than done. Nevertheless, we know that once she decided, Carlota was steadfast.

Carlota and Her Children Leave the Hacienda

Guadalupe wrote the following in her memoirs about the day they left:

> I remember the day we left Santa Rosa with a broken heart. Everybody gathered the night before to say good-bye. It was unforgettable because they made a bonfire and stayed with us until very late.
>
> We left before dawn. We passed the village of El Cimarrón while it was still dark and, as we climbed away from it, the glimmer of the morning light began to grow. We all stopped to look back, to take our last look at Santa Rosa as if we wanted to stamp on our memory that piece of earth that saw our birth, that we'd never forget, and that we grieved to leave behind.

A few hours later, they stopped downhill in Mascota and stayed overnight with their relatives, Rafaela, Leovi, and Chon, just as Pascual had done five years earlier. This is when Carlota would say good-bye to her brother and elder sisters, regretting it bitterly in the years to come. To Miguel and Guadalupe, however, this visit was probably distressing but it must have been exciting as well. After all, they were youngsters looking forward to a strange new future. They had youth on their side.

The next morning, they bid adieu. They walked out of Mascota in a westerly direction, traveling the length of the green Mascota valley and heading toward the wooded sierras that slope down from the coolness of the valleys into the hot and sticky jungly warmth of Puerto Vallarta.

After leaving, Carlota's heart must have been stricken with anguish as she trudged down the trail. Although traveling on horseback in those days took about three days, Guadalupe remembers it took them a day and a half on foot, about the same time that it took Pascual to traverse the same distance. They pressed forward down the familiar mountain trails carrying a handful of clothes and bean-filled tacos, plus the coins from the sale of the cow that the hacienda owner could not tolerate. A twisting asphalt road was installed roughly along the same route about ten years before the writing of this book.

My folks finally approached the seaside community. Much like today, Puerto Vallarta held many people who had moved down from the upper-mountain communities like Mascota in search of nonagricultural work, so our brand-new refugees carried with them the names of friends and relatives who would put them up for a night, and this is how it went. Miguel remembered, "We looked up a family we knew—the man was married to one of my cousins." Mother merely recalled that Carlota carried someone's name but could not remember any more details about it.

Carlota, Miguel, and Guadalupe, peon refugees, stayed in Puerto Vallarta for about three months, living with their kin from upland Mascota. If they arrived in April, as Guadalupe recalled, they must have sweltered in the tropical sun that beats down on the jungle coast unmercifully at this time of the year—so different from the cooler weather of the forested valleys they left behind up top.

Thirty-nine-year-old Carlota began to feel the pull of home, the homesickness of leaving her loved ones. Bereft of a social support system, including her aunts and uncles, she began crying and saying she wanted to turn back. Seventeen-year-old Miguel pleaded with her many times, and Guadalupe, who was fourteen, supported her brother in refusing to go back to the hacienda. Their arguments must have been bitter. Miguel brought to mind the many times he and his sister had to tell Carlota they would not return: "If you want to stay here, we'll stay, but we won't go back!" Guadalupe noted that her mother sent Güicho a note advising him that she didn't want to go on any more, but he replied that if they came back, the landlord "would laugh at us" and they would lose face with everybody else. Perhaps another reason that Carlota's determination weakened in these early days of their flight from the past was that they had written to Pascual to inform him they had already made their break from Santa Rosa, but he never answered. They went to the post office so often that they felt they were bothering the mailman, who would often say that revolutionary soldiers had interrupted the mail. This was about the time that Emiliano Zapata, Mexico's most famous revolutionary, was ambushed in faraway Morelos, a bloody episode that nevertheless began to lessen the turmoil. Miguel remembered they even spent money of the precious little that they had on a telegram to communicate with Pascual, but to no avail. He didn't reply, and this disheartened his mother even more.

Young Miguel didn't falter, however. It also seems he was able to instill a sense of optimism and common cause in his mother and sister. He paid attention to the rhythm of the seaside port the way his brother had done five years earlier, and he too discovered that the *mercado* beat like the economic heart of the community, so he visited it enough times to finally land a job the way that his brother had done. Miguel remembered he landed a job in construction where he worked for a time and then later helped on a fishing boat, pulling in *huachinango* (red snapper) and *garlopa* (grouper) out of the ocean to sell in the market. Guadalupe wrote that her brother earned a peso and ten cents a day, whereas older men in Santa Rosa earned only fifty cents a day. Her memory is supported by historians who studied this period in Mexican history many years later and discovered similar wage patterns. Agricultural jobs always paid less.

Guadalupe brought to mind feeling comforted by her brother's willingness to work hard and give them purpose. Consequently, she too found a job, but on the beach, serving grilled snapper, hot sauce of some kind, and tortillas served under a palm thatch roof held up by four poles. As a teenager, my mother was already showing her willingness to work hard in the face of uncertainty and pitch in to help the family. She proudly noted that she earned eight pesos per week doing this work, more than she had ever expected and more than her uncles received, working up on the hacienda. She must have cut quite a profile in any case. Unfortunately, we have no photographs of her in Puerto Vallarta, but she did stand in front of a camera when she reached Mazatlán, revealing the fact that she was becoming an attractive, young, dark-eyed woman with plenty of energy. Carlota, on the other hand, shook off the blues and found a way to buy *masa* (corn dough) to make tortillas by hand and discovered she could sit on the beach in the evening—probably a stone's throw from where her daughter worked so she could keep an eye on her—and sell her tortillas. Customers probably used them to wrap the fish her daughter grilled on an open fire. Mom and Grandma saw many sunsets darken the blue horizon this way. Our ancestors thus survived and kept going in Puerto Vallarta by the skin of their teeth.

Guadalupe recalled that "the days went by this way when one evening, one of the mule teams from the hacienda, led by their old friends and hacienda neighbors, came by, and when my mother saw them, she stood up and cried out, 'There they are, children! Let's go back [to the hacienda] with them!'" Mom didn't mention anything about the painful bickering that this outburst must have triggered. Miguel did. He remembered that Carlota couldn't convince her children to go back. They steadfastly said they would not go back. They didn't mind embracing an uncertain prospect but Carlota's heart was shredded with regret.

The *tiempo de aguas* or monsoons come to this part of Mexico in June, bringing relief to the very hot sun that bakes everything in sight in April and May. Getting through to October, when the rainy season comes to an end, is always a test of human resistance, even now with electric fans and air conditioners. Our self-exiles must have thanked the saints in heaven when the rainy season began in 1919 because it meant periods of cooling. The clouds would build up on the horizon for several days in June, billowing bigger and higher each time until they released their moisture with powerful lightning and deafening thunder, giant bolts illuminating the darkened clouds and melting into the ocean. The hard rain would chill everyone and everything. The heat would be defeated for an afternoon and evening, and the brightness of a new day would only help the high temperatures settle the next day when the cycle would begin anew. Like today, the people then would just pulse their fans rapidly and perspire silently in the shade and look relieved when they would see the clouds reappear in the sky and build up for another tropical rainstorm, another cooling down. Our ancestors, however, didn't see the end of the monsoons in Puerto Vallarta that year. They left before the rain moved on.

Mother seems to have a fuller but more troublesome memory than my uncle Miguel about how they were able to leave Puerto Vallarta and move up the coast to Mazatlán, leaving behind all traces of their familiar world. This is the following explanation we children heard countless times:

> Since we lived on a hillside where we could look out on the sea quite well, I saw a ship one day and I told my mother, "Look, Mother, we're going to go to Mazatlán on that boat.

> Do you see?" She replied, "But how?" I said, "You dictate a letter to me," and sure as can be, I ran down [with the note in my hand] to meet the captain when the ship arrived and asked, "How much will you charge to take us to Mazatlán in order to attend our sick grandmother there [just as the note says]?"

Here is one of the best examples of my mother's far too sunny memory regarding a period that by all intents and purposes had to come to an end—their leaving Puerto Vallarta behind and all links to Santa Rosa. Is it hard to believe that a fourteen-year-old girl raised on a plantation with a minimal education could quickly conjure a plan involving a lie, to be sure, which would enable her and her mother and brother to board a ship to travel to Mazatlán, clearly the next step on their agenda? Thinking about it, two scenarios had probably already taken place when my mother and her own mother saw a ship appear on the horizon. One was that they had already learned by observation that Puerto Vallarta was an intermediate point in a series of ports that enabled local products and people to be transported up and down the coast, as we learned from Pascual's experience. In other words, they had a good idea about where the ship was headed. The second possibility is that all three of them had probably discussed options that they would have to take advantage of in order to travel north in pursuit of their dream to rejoin Pascual. This reflection makes it easier to accept that when Guadalupe sighted the ship, probably coming to port from the south—perhaps one that might have already stopped by before—the plan then clicked in her mind the way she remembered it, and the same way she repeated it to us many times as we were growing up.

In any case, Guadalupe writes in her hand-scrawled memoirs that after she presented the dubious note to the ship's captain, Carlota showed up to push the negotiations to the next stage. Guadalupe's notes and my uncle Miguel's memory do not dwell on the talking and negotiating that might have gone on at this point. The palaver might have been minimal because it's not far-fetched to surmise that travel along the Pacific coast on these cargo schooners was probably very common. What is clear, however, is that both parties finally agreed on thirty pesos as a fair fee—but only for two people. Miguel would have to travel down in the cargo hold where tobacco leaves plucked from the nearby plantations were stacked high. In order to complete the thirty pesos, Guadalupe wrote that they had to resort to selling Miguel's poncho which he had taken an entire year to pay off—not that it was fashioned from expensive materials, but it's just that he earned so little to begin with. She repeated this story to us many times.

Miguel is a bit more tight-lipped about these circumstances. He merely said the following to me:

> We had some money because I had worked for about a week, and then the fishing that I did, plus the cow we had sold up in Santa Rosa. He [the captain] didn't charge for me—I rode aboard as contraband.

His sister recorded that on May 3, 1919, the captain announced they would leave Puerto Vallarta the next day, "and that was what happened." Their thirty pesos gave Carlota and her daughter the right to share a cabin with another lady and her son about Guadalupe's age. "And my poor brother!" Guadalupe lamented. "We hardly saw him because he had to travel sunken in the pile of tobacco!" She added that "it took us forty-eight hours [to reach Mazatlán] or the next day in the afternoon." Miguel simply said to me, "We sailed out about 5:00 p.m. and navigated all night and all of the next day. We ate cahuama or turtle meat. I got seasick and remained so all the way."

They Arrive in the Port of Mazatlán

Being careful to dodge any port inspectors who might have had to check the cargo hold and find a stowaway, Miguel was able to leave the ship on time and join his mother and sister on land. Once reunited, all three of them walked into the small port and undoubtedly stood out when they began gaping at the stir and bustle of the local people who seemed to speak more loudly and more rapidly than folks back home. They surely had to be caught staring at those who dressed in simple cotton garments like themselves and at others who wore more colorful and refined clothing. It was like Mascota on special holidays. Little did they know that the Mazatlán would grow many years later into one of the major seaside resorts on Mexico's west coast. In 1919, it held a little more than ten thousand inhabitants approximately, in comparison to the four hundred thousand and then some at the time of this writing. They also didn't realize that they were retracing Pascual's footsteps even to the point of heading straightaway to the *mercado* and purchasing some squash with the last six pennies they could put together in order to enjoy their first meal there.

Miguel observed that the two families who had accompanied them from Puerto Vallarta claimed to have jobs waiting for them in Mazatlán working in private homes as domestic employees or servants. This may be a clue to the distinct possibility that in addition to transporting staple products, like tobacco or flour, from one Pacific coast port to another, workers and others also traveled back and forth along the coast in the early 1900s and possibly much earlier, thereby contributing to the formation of a Mexican west coast economy.

Our wandering ancestors found a *mesón* or an inn that would let them take shelter in exchange for Carlota working in the kitchen. Miguel remembered that the inn was a big one: "It occupied the size of a city block [and it included spaces] where animals also boarded—people from [farms and] ranchos came by and stayed—like a hotel with a stable." *Mesones* were common everywhere in Mexico.

Miguel Works for the Railroad

Feeling evermore the primary earner in the family, seventeen-year-old Miguel went out to look for a job right away—and found one. The *mesón* manager had suggested to him that he might get a job delivering newspapers, but this idea didn't appeal to Miguel. "Can you imagine," he laughed as he told me, "born and raised on a rancho [and me selling newspapers! The idea was so far removed for me that I felt] it was impossible for me, but I told her that I would try it out, but I didn't get the job." Instead, he found employment at the roundhouse[35] with the Sur Pacífico, the Southern Pacific Railroad Company of Mexico.

Indeed, both my uncles came face-to-face with the ever growing importance of the railroads themselves as well as the labor demands of the railroad industry in Mexico as well as in the United States. We may recall that pretending to be a member of a military family, Pascual climbed onto the roof of a railcar and rode north from Mazatlán alongside many soldiers and their families. Railroads became vital prizes well worth fighting for during the revolution. Five years later, here was his brother arriving in the same city and finding a job at the railroad center where trains were repaired and maintained. And he too would ride on top of a railroad car.

> I learned about a job possibility at the *casa redonda* [the roundhouse] where they hired people to fix the rail lines. So I went there and I got it! I asked the supervisor if he had any jobs, and he looked at me and said, "You're looking for work? You should be in school!"

Miguel explained to the supervisor that he and his family had just arrived from the south, and that he was the main breadwinner, and that getting a job was critical all the way around. The railroad manager, a Mexican, rubbed his chin, trying to evaluate this amiable young man, and then asked Miguel to come back the next day. He would see if a job was possible. "I was so happy," Miguel exclaimed. "I ran all the way back to tell my mother!" His prideful enthusiasm about this moment endured nearly sixty years later.

The next day, Miguel got a job as an *aguador*, different from Pascual's position by the same name. Here, Miguel was in charge of providing water to the workers, paying the huge sum of two dollars a day, in US currency, no less, because it was a US company. Miguel must have walked on clouds at that moment, but in retrospect, he interpreted the decision as a socially conscious one. "[The supervisor obviously] did it to help out, not because I was going to do the work of an adult male. Their jobs required heavy lifting. My job was to carry a water can." Miguel's remembrances suggest that his fellow workers looked out for him too, given the fact that he was just a young fellow. They did this by making sure he didn't overdo it for his size and age. "They might have felt sorry for me too [had I had to do any heavy lifting]," he added.

Though hard to believe in our time, my uncle also obtained lodging with the railroad company. He learned from his coworkers after having worked a few days that the company made lodging available to its workmen. So he asked his supervisor if a house or an apartment was available to him, and lo and behold, within a few days, Miguel got word that he could, indeed, occupy one of the workers' houses. This must have astonished our former teenage mule driver from the Hacienda Santa Rosa, but he was nonetheless able to provide shelter for his entire family. Outside of the adobe hut they had lived in, in Santa Rosa, and the rooms they borrowed or rented in Puerto Vallarta and Mazatlán, they had never lived in their own apartment or house. All three of them must have jumped for joy. To know that he, as a seventeen-year-old, was providing shelter for his loved ones must have made my uncle Miguel dizzy with self-accomplishment. In the end, they lived in company housing in Mazatlán for about three years. Indeed, many foreign companies at this time, including US firms, offered housing to their workers, especially in the mining and railroad sectors.

Young Miguel thrived while working for the railroad company not only because he became a principal wage earner for his family but also because industrial work appealed to him. He continued working as an *aguador* for several weeks, and then his supervisor assigned him to clean the latrines in the houses occupied by the company managers. "I didn't like that job very much, but I did it anyway," he remembered. His duties, however, allowed him to meet the wife of one of the mechanics who worked in the *casa redonda* who, after talking with Miguel and getting to like him, as most everyone did, discovered his longing to get a job there. The mechanic, also a Mexican, talked to him and said he would get him a job in the roundhouse as long as he promised to go to school and get some education.

> "Do you know how to read and write?" he asked me. I said I didn't know very much. "Do you know how to add and subtract?" I replied that I didn't know very much—"*en cuentas estoy muy atrasado*! [I'm not very good with numbers!]" He said, "Look, there are schools here where you can learn those things. You'll have a future if you do that!" And I said of course I would go to school. Then he asked me to show up at the *casa redonda*, and I was thrilled!

Miguel's job at the *casa redonda* was to clean the locomotives when they came into the roundhouse for repair. This required him to climb aboard the iron giants, inspect them, and clean them, and no doubt wonder with awe what it would feel like to drive them. Cleaning the cab, which was hard to climb into because the steps are high and you have to pull yourself up entirely, and discovering a door that opened up into the sweltering furnace must have been bewildering at first. How on earth did the train move? How did the engine work? What did this lever do? What did that gauge mean? Here was a real man's job, so different from coaxing a pair of oxen to plow the earth! Instead of wearing sandals and the peasant's loose white cotton pants and shirts, he now wore boots and *mezclilla* or blue jeans, the uniform of the industrial workers who were being recognized as important for the nation by the new revolutionary government. He must have felt so proud. Soon his boss also taught him about the levers and how to pull them in order to make the engine go forward and backward. "The engineers would stop them outside and someone had to drive them into the roundhouse, and so he taught me [how to run them] and I learned! I was absolutely overjoyed!"

Moving the railroad engines that came in for cleaning and repair provided Miguel with a broader vision of railroad work. He met other *ferrocarrileros* or railroad workers but was particularly impressed by the *garroteros* who signaled the engineers to make the train stop or go. "I would help them and learn from them too," he remembered.

> I noticed that the *garroteros* dressed well—some even wore a tie! They'd travel on the job all the way north to Culiacán—to the Estación Ruiz, where the line ended. But the rails had been wrecked on account of the revolution. The

> line didn't reach [south to] Guadalajara yet [either]. There were good patches and bad ones on account of the destruction by the revolution.

My uncle's job allowed him to compare work assignments. One day, for instance, he was asked to help staff a train that was transporting troops in pursuit of a "General Carrasco who had rebelled [against the government and joined the revolutionary forces]." His job on the train for this assignment was that of a firewood assistant or a *pasaleña*. This meant that while the train was moving, he rode in the firewood car directly behind the engineer's cab and passed firewood to the stoker, who in turn threw it into the hot furnace in order to keep the steam going. This had to be most exciting for a young man like my uncle.

Assignments like this also allowed him to become familiar with the cities and towns connected by the railroad line. When they went chasing after General Carrasco, Miguel helped feed the steam engine all the way to Culiacán, the state capital of Sinaloa, a day's trip north. The next day, he boarded the train back to Mazatlán and was given the choice of riding in the caboose or accompanying the *fogoneros*. He chose the latter and met a young *fogonero* who invited him to ride atop one of the railroad cars, like his elder brother had done along the same track years earlier. With the dry desert wind whistling past them, the two rode all the way back to the seaport this way, past dusty little towns like the Villa de Costa Rica, La Cruz de Elota, and others. Miguel's enjoyment could not have been greater. He loved working with trains and the men who made them run.

Living and Working in Mazatlán

Guadalupe, my mom, who arrived in the port city at the age of fourteen, remembered that she too got a job in an inn as soon as they arrived. "I had to clean the rooms when they became vacant, wash dishes, and clean chickens and fish [in the kitchen]," she wrote. Working from seven in the morning till eight at night, she had to sleep with the other female employees: "Maria Angulo, the fry cook, and Mariquita, who made tortillas. [They protected me by] making me sleep in between them as a way to keep a close eye on me." One night, however, she recalled, "I felt someone squeezing my arm, and I woke up and screamed!" The two Marias jumped out of bed and discovered a man who ran away; they chased after him but didn't catch him.

As a result of this disturbing event, young Guadalupe was made to sleep with the inn owner's niece, a girl about the same age whom she befriended, but says little about her in her handwritten notes other than identifying her family as the Santiagos. As it turns out, they became close friends and kept in touch with one another for many years.

Guadalupe's mind at this time seems to have started focusing on clothes. She became quite conscious of how poor she and her family appeared when they first arrived in Mazatlán and how she needed some better attire: "Since I didn't have many clothes, they [the Santiagos] bought me a change of clothing which I had to pay back [eventually]."

Her mother, Carlota, thirty-nine at this time, tried her best to keep her chin up. She worked at the inn for a short while and then, one day, according to Guadalupe, "she found work with a doctor." She doesn't say anything further about this, but the probability is high that Grandma worked as a servant of some kind. Miguel's memory, as we have seen above, was focused on his work accomplishments and consequently says little about what his mother did, work-wise. Perhaps more sympathetic to her mother, Guadalupe notes that while they lived in Mazatlán she noticed that her mother "cried often because she had not heard anything about Pascual." Indeed, it must have been challenging for Grandma Carlota to be at ease in a strange city, and she undoubtedly missed her close-knit family back home on the hacienda. Life in Santa Rosa may have seemed more like a dream at this point. Guadalupe writes that her mother "was often sick and had to see the doctor regularly."

If Carlota worried about Pascual, she also worried about her other two children as well. This is exemplified in the following notes her daughter jotted down about their first days in Mazatlán when Miguel disappeared for about two weeks:

> "My mother looked for him all over with the help of my boss [the inn owner]. They even searched for him at the local jail and didn't find him. She cried so much! But one day, he showed up looking like a Negrito [a black man] because he had gone to work for a charcoal maker" [on the edge of town and he was all covered with soot]. Afterward, he found a job in the roundhouse where the trains came in from the north and south. He was so happy because they gave him the job of an *aguador de trenes*. They also gave him a house to live in, and my mother could even go to the commissary to buy everything we needed!

Life in Mazatlán was not entirely toil and unredeemed hardship—at least not for our young voyagers. Since all three family members were working, Carlota perhaps less consistently, they must have had the most money ever up to this point in their lives—at least enough to buy the necessary food and clothing, and perhaps even spend a little bit for pleasure now and then. While Carlota might have spent her time pining for the world she left behind and working hard in somebody else's house, her two teenagers were undoubtedly trying to have the best time of their lives every chance they got.

This probably helps explain why Guadalupe wrote that community dances were organized every so often, probably in the center of old Mazatlán across from Olas Altas. Working alongside other young women, she undoubtedly learned about social life in this maritime community, including the municipally sponsored *tardeadas* or afternoon dances where young men and women were allowed to mix and even dance together if their parents approved. This must have been why she wrote in her memoirs that on Sunday afternoons, she and her brother Miguel, and possibly Carlota too, would join their friends from the inn, the members of the Santiago family, and "walk about a mile and a half to the brewery fronting the sea to attend the *tardeadas* where two musical groups took turns playing in front of a dancing platform. 'We enjoyed ourselves very much,'" Guadalupe remembered fondly. In these outings, she met Pedro, who belonged to the Santiago family, one of her first beaus who mentioned in her memoirs.

The city fathers also organized dances at night under the watchful eye of the local leading families. My mother wanted to attend these too, so, with Miguel in tow, she asked her mother permission to attend some of them, and so Carlota probably resisted at first but eventually relented, Guadalupe recalled. They could go but with the requirement that they "Not be out too late. You need to be home by eleven o'clock at night." Like Cinderella, my mother had to arrive at home when the clock struck the eleventh hour; otherwise, her life would be dire for a few days. "When the moment arrived that we had to go home, my brother would ask me to dance and [while we were dancing] we would go out the back door without letting our friends know and that way they wouldn't delay us." Orders were orders. Despite the restrictions imposed by her mother, days like this probably became unforgettable for Guadalupe.

It was at this time that she took one of her first photographs. In the photo, she stands beside one of her Mazatlán friends, Susana Santarín (Mother wrote her friend's name on the photograph itself) who is sitting, and each is clasping a handheld flower bouquet. Looking somewhat stiffly at the photographer, they each wear what appears to be a soft whitish pastel cotton one-piece dress with short sleeves, each accented with small pearl necklaces. Susana wears her hair in the close-cropped wave style, popular in the 1920s, while Guadalupe wears her black hair pulled back in a bun.[36] Mother is thus dressed in an upper-class style in this photograph. She probably felt like she walked on clouds in those days.

By the time she was sixteen, Guadalupe worked as a maid away from the inn too—"I worked for three different families," she recalled, and this is how she met her best friend yet, Conchita. Her new friend was the young wife of an American railroad engineer named Elmer Alvis—they had a baby boy, and Guadalupe helped care for him. They became such friends that wherever Conchita went, Guadalupe would go too. "They treated me like I was part of the family," she wrote. They would often go on picnics because Elmer's job took him away from home, so the two young women would spend time outdoors together and undoubtedly talk about what young women like to talk about.

She met Conchita's family. "Her mother was a very large woman," Guadalupe recalled. She also noted that her friend's mother "looked [Mexican] Indian, although her children were good-looking, like Conchita, who was olive-skinned and had green eyes—her brothers had the same look [as hers]." The family also comprised "about five brothers, including the eldest, a mechanic, and another one named Miguel, who worked in the telegraph office in Culiacán," the state capital to the north. Miguel, the young *telégrafo*, showed a romantic interest in her. "He would talk with me when he came to visit her [Conchita's] house," she remembered and then added, "He told me that they too were planning to move to the United States."

Good-bye to Mazatlán

While at work one day, my uncle Miguel learned that the mechanic who had gotten him the roundhouse job was being transferred. He was taking a work assignment in Navolato, near Culiacán to the north, and asked Miguel whether he wanted to join him. My uncle must have been tempted but could not decide by himself because of his attachment to and responsibility toward his family, so he consulted with his mother that evening. She said no. The discussion must have been heated and painful. Grandma defended her decision: "I want to go see my son Pascual. We must go [sooner or later]." Miguel didn't take this lightly because he remembered pleading with his mother, but to no avail. Carlota was determined to join Pascual in the United States, and leaving Miguel behind was not an option. Mother didn't record this discussion.

Miguel must have felt very torn because the mechanic also mentioned that if he could not join him in Navolato, he, Miguel, would do well staying at the *casa redonda*. "[Here] you could become a *maquinista* [a regular engineer in charge of driving the trains long distances] and do well because they [the railroad officials] were extending the line south to Guadalajara." This meant that once Mazatlán was connected to Guadalajara, it would also be connected to Mexico City. The importance of the Pacific coast railroad would grow by leaps and bounds, as it eventually did. The words of the mechanic must have burned inside Miguel.

God, how he had come a long way from being a mere peasant farmhand in Santa Rosa! When the mechanic heard of Miguel's mother's refusal to allow him to stay and find better prospects, he pressed my uncle: "Stay here! Don't go to the United States! They treat Mexicans very badly there, they kick them! There's discrimination there! [Don't go there.] You have a future here!" The mechanic, whose name my uncle never mentioned, might have been influenced by the first labor unions in Mexico under the new revolutionary, President Álvaro Obregón, who was known to have been friendly to workers; many of these unions encouraged Mexican nationalism and the promotion of young people like my uncle. In any case, try as he might, Miguel couldn't turn his mother around.

It seems that part of Carlota's intransigence was that she had received a letter from her son in the United States at about this time, according to Guadalupe. "My mother heard from Pascual who had been working in Arizona. He [wrote to us] asking us to come to the United States. Thus, my mother identified a date of departure."

Having set the date they would leave Mazatlán, they began to prepare for the trip north to the US border. They went shopping and purchased some clothes and shoes for themselves—especially for Guadalupe and Miguel, who had worked hard. This is why the introduction in this book describes them dressed smartly at the moment they crossed the border into the United States—she in her new, wrinkly piqué skirt and cotton top accented by a pair of shiny dark boots buttoned up on one side, and he in dark pants and a fine, light-colored shirt. All were toting a new suitcase.

"I was forced to say good-bye to my dear Conchita—we were such good friends!" wrote my mother, recalling yet another heart-wrenching departure. She never forgot Conchita's words to her: "If you didn't have your mother, you would stay and live with us." It helped that Conchita's young brother, the *telégrafo* named Miguel, was also leaving Mazatlán on the train with my mother and her family.

My uncle Miguel's memory of his separation from this northern Pacific port was haunted by the sting of the heated argument with his mother in order to convince her to stay. In the end, he admitted, "I had to leave my job." He might as well have said, "I had to leave a great opportunity, an entire life that stood within my reach!" Different from his elder brother, however, he remained faithful to his mother and sister, as he would most of his adult life, and he began thinking about traveling north. Although several more weeks went by and he continued going out on overnight train-work assignments to the north and south as before, still the day of departure finally arrived. Leaving Mazatlán was made a tad easier by the fact that the railroad company allowed him and his family free passage north as part of a liberal compensation policy for employees wanting to travel to other cities served by its railroad line. They were able to save some travel money this way, not having to pay to reach Nogales.

They left Mazatlán in mid-July 1922, headed for the US border—my grandmother, my mother, and my uncle. Guadalupe recalled that she had "mixed feelings" on their way to the train station. On the one hand, she felt sad because they were leaving friends behind once more, but on the other, she felt elated because they were joining Pascual in the great country to the north—and Guadalupe's admirer, the young telegraph clerk, was also on board the train because he was going home to Culiacán, on the way.

Nevertheless, the excitement of leaving the port city by train that day was enlivened by music and cheer. They happened to board a car where a guitar trio was playing and singing songs to a couple of lovers who were riding north as well. The man had hired the musicians to play to his girlfriend as they rode away from Mazatlán. Everyone in the car, including our relatives, undoubtedly enjoyed the music and the singing.

Ya se va la embarcación,	(Look, our ship is leaving,)
Ya se va por vía ligera,	(It's going along the short route,)
Ya se va, ya se le llevan	(They are going, they're taking her,)
A la dueña de mi amor . . . [37]	(She's the one who owns my heart . . .)

Miguel, the telegraph clerk, who was obviously smitten by Cupid over my mother, got into the act and paid the musicians to sing and play for my mother too—as well as to her family, of course.

As they galloped on the rails to Culiacán, the telegraph clerk asked Carlota permission to take Guadalupe to the dining car and treat her to a snack. My grandmother granted it. This is, in itself, quite surprising because Carlota was dreadfully strict about how young women should act in public, especially her own daughter. Normally, she would have denied permission. That she granted it may reflect the high degree of earnestness that the young telegrapher was able to muster. Did he declare his love to my teenage mother? Did he propose? We don't know because Guadalupe chose not to describe her feelings about this episode; she merely jotted it down. But what she did allow us to know is that when they arrived in

Culiacán, the telegraph clerk asked Carlota if they could all get off and visit with his family—he went that far! Would he have requested this if he wasn't love-struck by my mother? We can't answer this question either, but we do know that Carlota said no; they would not stop. My mother recorded in her notes somewhat dryly, "Thus we said good-bye [in Culiacán], and he begged me to write to him. But I never did." Then she added with some cautious embarrassment, "and I didn't even write to Conchita, who rewarded me with such fine moments to remember her by, to this day—along with the memories that I continue to have from all of them," she admitted seventy years later.

My uncle Miguel recalled that after chugging through the sage-scented night, the train pulled into the town of Guamúchil at about two o'clock in the morning, and lo and behold, a scraggy but cheerful oompah band greeted them with loud and brassy tones.[38] Bare electric light bulbs and lanterns lit up the station where the band performed, whose members played to the top of their lungs as if the morning sun would rise sooner if they played louder.

> This struck us as very sad because we had just left a place where we had lived for about five years. We were missing it, and hearing the band almost made us cry. The music sounded so joyous yet at the same time we [felt so sad because we] had left everything behind [and found ourselves] amidst people who were getting on and others getting off [unaware of our feelings] . . .

Guamúchil and all of the other towns north of Mazatlán contrasted vividly from their home in Santa Rosa and Mascota. Back home, the land was draped with many shades of evergreen, where some mountains rose softly while others climbed abruptly. Here in the arid north, the land was not only flat, dusty, rock-strewn, and sandy, but also dotted with cacti of many shapes and sizes when it wasn't barren. And a lot of the people were boisterous and abrupt more often than not, except for the Indians who were easy to spot. "Indians would get on board [at one place] and then [they would get] off [at another place]. It was just so different! We [felt like we] were leaving something familiar and going to places [totally] unknown," Miguel said as he flashed back to this trip. Coming from Santa Rosa, all this gave you butterflies in the stomach.

They Arrive at the Border

My grandmother and her grown children arrived in Nogales, Sonora, a small city of about thirteen thousand inhabitants that sits at the US border.[39] They held a recommendation for a place to stay here, making it quite likely that Conchita gave it to them. Miguel doesn't give great importance to this minor but critical arrangement since he merely notes, "I think we were recommended to go to a certain house—and we began to live there."

Guadalupe, more attuned to social relationships, reserved more detail regarding this moment in her memory. She wrote that they stayed with "a very fine family that included an older woman, a young woman schoolteacher, three youngsters, and two [other] women of advanced age. I became very fond of these two women," she observed. "We stayed with them a month and a half while we made arrangements to immigrate. May God repay them!" she added. Mother does not say anything else about these good people, and of course, Uncle Miguel hardly nods to them.

Making arrangements to immigrate into the United States in 1922 included paying a "head tax" or border processing fee, and this was at least one more reason why they had to look for jobs anew. Carlota obtained a job working in a laundry that paid too little, at least in the eyes of Guadalupe—"She worked two weeks, and they paid her one miserable dollar!" she exclaimed. She herself found work as a live-in housemaid with a doctor's wife living across the border, in Nogales, Arizona. After a few days, the woman accused my mother of stealing a necklace and even threatened her with the police, but apologized when she discovered she possessed the jewelry piece all along. Guadalupe couldn't wait to see that job come to an end.

And so the day for which they had long been preparing finally came. Carlota and her daughter saved enough money from their meager chores to be able to report to the US Immigration Service office at the port of Nogales and request official entry. Guadalupe writes that on or about September 2, 1922, they paid "sixteen dollars" each for their documents, and the archival record supports her claim almost completely. The files in fact show that on August 31, "Carlota Hernández, thirty-six, a widow," and her daughter "Guadalupe Hernández, sixteen," received permission to enter the United States as immigrants even though they indicated they were not interested in becoming citizens. They declared Nogales, Sonora, as their "last residence" and Nogales, Arizona, as their "final destination." Their sole purpose in crossing the border was to work, they declared. It seems they didn't tell the immigration officials that they were really looking to connect with my uncle Pascual, probably to avoid complications.

The immigration official also noted that Carlota appeared to have "good" health, measured 4'11½", had a "dark" complexion, wore "black" hair, possessed "brown" eyes, and that her face was "pitted." She declared she could read but not write, and considered herself Mexican. The US official also had to indicate where she was born, and he wrote "Mazatlán." He also had to classify her race, so he jotted down "Mexican race." Her daughter, my mother, was also judged to possess "good" health, measured 5'1", also revealed a "dark" complexion (although Mom was not of dark complexion), and had the same color hair and eyes as her mother. Although she was registered as a Mexican knowing how to read and write, she was noted as having been born in Mazatlán as well. She revealed no physical markings or other shortcomings. To complete the procedure, my grandmother signed her manifest with a deliberate "X" that looked more like a cross, whereas my mother signed with a dignified signature, revealing her schooling in Mascota. When I was a boy, I saw the Xs my grandmother signed many times, and when I moved away, I appreciated my mother's venerable signature in her many letters to me.[40]

Now they were free to cross the border into the United States and continue their journey! Guadalupe wrote that Miguel didn't go with them to the immigration office because he couldn't wait. As we'll see, he became impatient and crossed the border into the United States on his own. Guadalupe simply noted, "He went in illegally."

Hence, another leg in our family's immigration process was now nearly complete. It not only involved the physical motion of crossing a political border laid across an arid geography but also the molding of the mind and the psyche to leave a familiar cultural system behind and accept a new one including new surroundings, more difficult for Grandma being as old as she was and easier for her children as we've seen. Supported by them, Grandma had taken a major step in breaking away from the foundation that supported her including her beloved *Mamá Rafaela*, her aging friend, Güicho, and her other sisters and her brothers. Stepping across the border into Arizona and into the United States must have clinched the reality of what she was doing. There was no going back now. She must have made the sign of the cross silently to herself as she took her first step onto American soil looking up at the same time to see her daughter prancing ahead of her.

Guadalupe on right, age 16, with Susana Santarín, in Mazatlán

Chapter 4

Arriving in the United States
(1922–1923)

Miguel Pushes on to Fresno • Carlota and Guadalupe Enter the United States • A Word about "Juárez" • Early Courting Issues Involving Mother • They finally Arrive in California

MY UNCLE MIGUEL had, in fact, gone ahead. After arriving in Nogales and, no doubt wanting to get out of a stranger's house filled with women, he spent a lot of time in the town's main square like many undocumented Mexicans do nowadays when planning to skip across the border. A border town plaza serves many purposes even to this day. For a would-be immigrant it's where you go when you're looking for a *pollero* or someone who will escort and guide you across the border, or in the absence of one, where you go for advice about the route to take, what to look for, learn how tough it might be, and so on. Miguel was not looking for *polleros* because there weren't any in 1922.

> I sat on a bench in the *plazita*[41] and began to talk with a young guy very much like me. We agreed we would cross the line; we agreed to plan things out and cross the next afternoon—they allowed people to cross.

Miguel talked it over with his mother. He told her, "Once on the other side, I'm going to get a job and I'll send you some money." He remembered that she reluctantly agreed. "I decided to cross the border. I don't know whether that was good or bad to cross illegally," he said, looking back across decades of time from his comfortable California home.

He and his friend crossed the border at night by staying away from the main road. There were few if any fences marking the border in those days, and the US border guards tended to stay posted inside their office cubicles at the official border crossing. Miguel searched his memory and explained the following:

> We guided ourselves by watching for automobile traffic part of the time and watching [for] the trains too. We walked half the night and then slept under a bridge. The next day, we arose and continued following the track. The ground was full of brush and trees in some areas and bare in others.

Indeed, walking north on the desert floor, flanking the railroad track that partly parallels the old Nogales–Tucson road and now the new Interstate 19, they stepped past groves of gnarly mesquite. They also walked around the clumps of spiny ocotillo and cylindrical cholla cactus as many scaly and luminous reptiles must have slithered away from our intruders as they trudged north. Unknowingly, they ambled past the crumbling Tumacacori missions built in the 1690s by the Pimas under the direction of the unforgettable Father Kino and paced not too far away from the ruins of the old Spanish fort known as the Presidio de Tubac, now decaying having been erected to ward off unfriendly Indians 170 years earlier.

In the coolness of the morning, about thirty-five miles south of Tucson, near present-day Green Valley, someone offered to give them a ride. A Mexican man in a truck stopped and asked them, "You're coming in from Nogales, right?" My uncle and his friend said yes, and the truck driver replied, "You're lucky. You've gone past the most dangerous part [of the road], so I'll take you into Tucson." Miguel recalled that he and his walking buddy thanked the man from the bottom of their hearts when he dropped them off right in the middle of Tucson. He would be the first of many Good Samaritans driving a vehicle along the immigrant trail and willing to help my pioneering ancestors.

Not having eaten a proper meal since Nogales, they were able to put together a few Mexican and American coins, and bravely entered a small café. Like many eating establishments in Tucson today, the waitresses spoke Spanish—lucky for our young explorers—but the fare was American. Consequently, my uncle and his fellow adventurer gulped down their first meal in the United States, and it turned out to be a plateful of the proverbial pancakes, a new type of breakfast for my uncle. "That's what we ate!" he affirmed. "[It was] our first American meal! It was good too!" he said with a measure of glee.

Like so much of northern Mexico, Tucson also looked and felt different to Miguel. Its dry, sunny climate and its diverse blend of desert-hardened people stimulated Miguel in a way he never forgot. He tried putting it into words: "We noted a different atmosphere [even] from Nogales. There were a lot of people [on the street]—Mexicans and Americans—and the town looked different in my eyes."

The opportunity to work did not wait long, however. My uncle said it clearly:

> Afterward, we went to the *plazita* [town square], and a Mexican man came to us and said, "I need about thirty-five men to work on the railroad! I need to take them to the state of Oregon, so anyone wanting to go only has to provide me [with] their name." I talked with my friend, and we decided to get on the list. The man didn't ask for documents, just our names. He told us to go to a certain hotel while he finished getting the rest of the men, and from there we would leave at night.

Like Pascual had done five years earlier, my uncle and his vagabond friend joined the legions of men contracted on the spot. These were the *enganchados*, true testimony of the great thirst for railroad workers in the American West in these years. My uncle Miguel and his buddy helped fill the need that day for thirty-five more railroad laborers—part of the thousands enlisted in these years. So, he and his buddy gathered at the appointed Tucson hotel at 6:00 p.m. where they met the contractor who had jotted down their names at the plaza. He directed them to the train where chow was waiting and it wasn't very long before my uncle and his friend and the others made a beeline for the food tables loaded with canned tuna and other kinds of fish, bread, and a variety of other rations. "They fed us," Miguel observed in a satisfied way, and the *enganchados* were soon on their way into the interior of the United States. They knew little about the path they followed, and even less about what they would find once arriving at their destination.

Miguel Pushes on to Fresno

As his brother had done five years earlier, Miguel and his buddy boarded the Southern Pacific coming in from Texas heading west to Los Angeles. They traveled all night across the desert, reaching Los Angeles at two o'clock in the morning.

On the way, they began to "learn the ropes" by sitting next to a veteran immigrant, someone like themselves but older. His name was Lázaro. Perhaps not as dark-skinned as my uncle, he wore a self-assurance that quickly impressed Miguel. He asked them where they were headed and they both answered "Los Angeles," forgetting that the labor contractor had enlisted them to work in Oregon. Lázaro informed them that he had made this trip before, and he was now headed to Fresno, but not to Portland where the train would complete its journey. "It's too cold over there! It snows there!" he added scornfully, and mentioned that he would stop off in Los Angeles. The idea of cold and snow must have jolted our intrepid explorers, so this bit of information immediately provided my uncle and his companion a perspective they had not considered. "We began to think, 'well, maybe we should get off in Los Angeles too,' but we didn't tell him this."

When the train stopped in Los Angeles, the labor contractor told the *enganchados* not to leave the train. "Don't get out," he yelled over the din of excited men, "I'm going to bring you some *pan dulce* (Mexican sweet bread), some milk, and other things you can eat, but don't go out!" He locked the doors to underscore his point.

Well, little did he know! Minutes after the contractor disappeared, Lázaro carefully secured his backpack and, coolly unlatching the window seat beside him, pulling it down, nimbly jumped out of the railcar and walked away waving good-bye to our young Mexican nomads who couldn't believe their eyes. They looked at each other as if to say "why not?" and quickly decided to do the same! They jumped out the window too and soon caught up with their riding companion who was somewhat surprised when he found them at his heels: "So you jumped out, too!" The impromptu guide walked my uncle and his friend to the nearby *plazita*, the old town square that marks the heart of old Los Angeles right off Main Street. They didn't know where else to go.

Sharing his memory enthusiastically with me in 1978, my uncle said, "You should've seen it! [The city] was so busy [at this early hour] you'd think it was daytime! People were going up and down [the street]. Don't these people sleep?" he asked rhetorically, laughing to himself because, in hindsight, he saw himself as a country bumpkin in a big town. Los Angeles was home to about half a million people at this time, the largest city he had seen so far.

Lázaro wanted to rent a room because he needed to sleep. My uncle and his friend didn't offer an alternative and simply followed him to a nearby hotel like boys stepping behind their dad. After registering at the desk, he said to them, "Go ahead and register too," but our young adventurers confessed to having no money, "not even a dime." Lázaro must have expected this. "How can that be?" he asked rhetorically, perhaps even feeling a bit put-upon. "You can't hang around [the street] because the police will catch you and throw you in jail!" Miguel recalled that after some awkward moments Lázaro talked it over with the hotel clerk who was reluctant to allow three men to gain entry into a single room, but he finally agreed. The two younger men realized upon entering the hotel room that there was only one bed, so they said they would sleep on the floor. Thanks to their more practiced guide, my uncle and his sidekick spent their first night in the United States in a cheap Los Angeles hotel room, a situation that probably struck them as quite commodious and comfortable; counting sheep on the floor was not a problem.

In the morning, Lázaro asked his younger traveling companions, "Well, what are you guys going to do? I'm going to Fresno." Miguel replied that he had a brother in Fresno and wanted to find him. Miguel's buddy explained that he was looking for an uncle in a place called El Cajon, but he didn't know where that was—he would later discover it was located south of Los Angeles, down near Tijuana, so at this point he was too far north. After some discussion, Miguel and his friend decided to follow their guide to Fresno. And so all three literally walked away from La Plazita, in the city center, and hiked north along Main Street and turned left onto San Fernando Road, known today as US 99, which Miguel would come to know like the palm of his hand many years later. When I was a boy, before the days of Interstate 5, the most convenient way to get to Los Angeles from San Fernando was in fact to follow San Fernando Road all the way south, reversing the direction that my uncle Miguel and the other two men took that day. Our three Mexicans thus marched all the way to Burbank on that same boulevard until a man with a truck offered them a lift—another Samaritan. He was going north on "US 99!"

My uncle and his friends were lucky once again. Not only was the Spanish-speaking truck driver kind enough to take them the entire twenty-mile length of the arid San Fernando Valley—which lay north of Los Angeles and where Miguel would make his home years later—he would also agree to transport them north of the valley to Newhall, a desert community. This home to ranchers and cowboys was surrounded by rugged brown mountains standing like a gateway to the high mountain passes leading north to Fresno in the fertile San Joaquin Valley. The truck driver shared his sandwiches with our three Mexican trekkers and advised them they'd have to eat plenty more because "they were going to be climbing the sierra" to get to where they wanted to go.

After the Good Samaritan with the truck dropped them off in Newhall,

Lázaro said to Miguel and his friend, "I have a dollar here," taking a bill out of his pocket. Pointing to a nearby wooden building, he asked, "Who will go to that little store there and buy some bread and cheese? We can eat by that arroyo over there," gesturing to one of many dry creeks in the area. Lázaro seemed to be assigning his charges small lessons on how to navigate and survive in a new culture. Miguel volunteered and entered the modest store with its cool, sun-protected interior packed high with groceries.

> I quickly identified the bread right away, so I picked out a loaf, but I couldn't see the cheese. So, in Spanish, I asked the lady store clerk for some cheese. Are you kidding! [She couldn't understand me] but there was an American man there who knew some Spanish, so he asked me what I wanted and I told him. He told the clerk, and so I paid with the dollar and even got some change back and returned to my friends. We walked to the arroyo and ate our lunch there.

After their simple repast by a rocky arroyo, the three wayfarers resumed their trek along US 99, still a two-lane road but now cutting across the desert and meandering higher into the mountains. Miguel recalled that it became very windy as they walked along the paved artery reaching another cluster of low wood and stucco buildings known as Castaic. Today a large part of this barren and windy area is known as Valencia and Santa Clarita now crowded with affluent track homes, shopping centers, and apartment buildings all linked together by a web of well-paved roads traversed by thousands of modern automobiles speeding hither and thither.

Just as Lázaro was reminding his two younger charges that they had no choice but to continue to climb ever higher above Castaic, a truck with an open cargo bed stopped and offered them a ride. This new Samaritan driver was an Anglo-American who motioned for the three men to jump aboard in the back and off they rode once again. Miguel said contentedly, "He took us all the way to Bakersfield where we slept." Indeed, the helpful gringo[42] with a truck took them for a total of about sixty miles across "the Grapevine," past the always blustery Tejon Pass (4,183 ft. above sea level) and down into Bakersfield, the first major city a traveler encounters going north into the San Joaquin Valley.

Tired from riding in the back of the truck, our travelers were dropped off on the edge of town where they quickly found a place to rest out in the open, probably under a tree or bridge. There they all fell asleep.

In the morning, they followed Lázaro's plan to catch a freight train that would take them another hundred miles north to Fresno. To this day, the city of Bakersfield is traversed by a railroad line that links with Los Angeles and runs east-west through the oldest part of town, paralleling Truxtun and California Avenues between Union Avenue and Oak Street. It must have been somewhere near this urban rectangle that my uncle and his adventurous friend got a tip on how to hop on a train. Their seasoned Lázaro told them how to board a moving rail freighter although it seems they already knew. He instructed them, "You have to catch the train in close" instead of trying to jump too far out, and you have to find a speed comfortable for you "because otherwise it would be rolling too fast" and climbing aboard would be the riskier. My uncle continued:

> Soon we heard the train coming, and it was coming fast. I was already accustomed to catching trains, so my buddy and I jumped aboard, but Lázaro didn't—he was about fifty-five years old [and he must have decided not to risk it because it was traveling too fast]. "What shall we do?" I said [to my friend when I noticed that Lázaro didn't get on board]. "He's our guide!" So [after a few seconds] we jumped off and rejoined him! He yelled at us, "Why did you get off?" I said "You're the guide!" And privately I realized he had money too although he never showed it [to us, and we had none]. We said, "No, you're our companion and we'll stick with you." He said, "OK, let's keep going."

It's possible that Lázaro was tiring of his role as a guide. He may have held off from jumping aboard the freight train because it was rolling too fast for him but he may also have felt overburdened from guiding our two novices. So he might have said to himself at that point, "I'll let them go on their own" although my uncle didn't admit this possibility in our interview. Obviously, Miguel and his friend were taking advantage of Lázaro's goodwill, but they also had little choice themselves. After all, they had to navigate a foreign culture, speak a different language, and live with the burning desire to connect with their relatives. If they didn't lean on him, they wouldn't reach their goal.

Later on that summer day, they all clambered aboard another freight train going north. Miguel remembers seeing many cultivated fields as they rolled along the broad valley already well known for its blazing July days and its agricultural bounty. My uncle described being impressed because he could see people picking watermelons and other fruits of the earth in a way that he hadn't seen before.

At one of the train stops, three guys jumped aboard their wooden rail boxcar. This could happen easily enough when a car was empty and its heavy sliding side door stood open, practically allowing anyone to jump in or out. The three strangers greeted our three travelers and sat in a corner, talking to each other loudly and openly. My uncle described them as "strong and cheerful" fellows who were most probably Mexican American or "from here" because they spoke English and Spanish.

They conversed loudly enough so that Miguel overheard one of them explaining that even though he had enough money, he may as well ride the trains because they were going in his direction anyway. "Yes, I have some money, but I have to save it. Why should I spend money when I can get a train and go where I want?" Miguel recalled. Here was yet another small lesson about America.

Engaging our young globe-trotters and their guide in a conversation, one of them asked where they were headed. Lázaro told them they were coming from Los Angeles and were headed for Fresno, at which point the interrogator offered a warning.

> We're going there too, but we have to get off early because the police there can be very hard with the *trampas* (tramps).[43] They'll throw you in jail!

Soon enough the train rolled into the outskirts of Fresno and Miguel noticed that Lázaro was already standing at the open door. Suddenly, and without warning, he jumped out, and my uncle and his buddy never saw him again! Obviously, he had decided that his role as a guide to our greenhorn travelers had worn thin, and so it came to an end without a word. Young Miguel felt both shaken and saddened by Lázaro's departure, but he also felt emboldened because he had arrived in Fresno, where he hoped to find his brother. After getting over the sudden disappearance of their friend, he and his partner bid the three rowdy but friendly fellow travelers good-bye and jumped off before the train got closer to town. "Night was coming and so we slept in a park near the baseball diamond," my uncle recalled. They hadn't eaten very much either.

Awakened by the rising sun, Miguel and his friend sauntered into the center of town and discovered that it was busy place indeed. They came upon a lot of men who carried lunch pails in their hand and gathered at certain city corners where farmers in trucks came by to pick them up, obviously to work that day. Suddenly, the three fellow train travelers appeared and greeted them warmly and loudly. In the early morning banter, the three acquaintances discovered that my uncle and his friend were hungry and had no money at all. Without further notice, one of them reached into his pocket and produced a five-dollar bill and said, "Here," extending it to Miguel. "Go to that café on the corner and get something to eat," pointing to a nearby eatery. He also said, "When you're finished, walk down that street to a canal and take a bath. Wash your clothes. And after the clothes have dried, come back here because this is where you'll get a job." As he said these words, he indicated one of the street corners where men milled about expectantly as they held on to their lunch boxes. "That's exactly what we did," Miguel noted with great satisfaction. "We ate, found the canal which was pretty isolated, away from the rancho homes, and [with] a lot of foliage [to give us privacy]. We took a bath as we had bought some soap, washed our clothes, dried them, and walked back to town."

After cleaning up, Miguel's first concern was to look for his brother, Pascual. As a result, he and his friend spent much of the first full day in Fresno searching for him. "I began looking for my brother," he explained, "and it was impossible to find him! I checked the local pool halls, and no one knew him. I didn't have an address for him. I asked around and looked in many places but didn't find a trace." Exhausted and disillusioned, they found an abandoned automobile on the edge of town and slept there for their second night in Fresno.

The next morning, bright and early, they stood on the street corners where Fresno farmers took their pick of Mexican workers. Nothing happened. No one offered them a job. By noon they were both crestfallen and getting hungry once again, and soon Miguel's sidekick gave up. "I'm going back," he told my uncle. Before disappearing, Lázaro had informed them that El Cajon lay considerably south of Los Angeles, so at this juncture Miguel's companion announced he was determined to find his own family down in the southland. Miguel tried to dissuade him: "Don't go yet. Help me look for my brother first!" But his friend said no; he was going to go—he *had* to go. As they were arguing, the tugging whistle of a train reinforced the young fellow's resolve, and he turned and ran toward the train heading south, jumping aboard when he caught up with it. The train rumbled on. "Suddenly I felt so alone!" Miguel remembered. "So I ran to catch up with him! And off we [both] went! It was so cold that night!"

It was a chilly night as desert nights can be even in summer. To this day, the main rail line connecting Fresno with Los Angeles runs south of the city. It parallels the Central Valley Highway (US 99) past the farming towns of Visalia and Tulare and on down to Wasco, where it turns east into

Bakersfield. From there the railroad tracks veer southeast up a gradual slope leading to the western edges of the Great Mojave Desert, skirting around the mountainous Grapevine crowned by Tejon Pass. As Miguel's train gradually climbed, it got colder. Rattling in the night, it rolled past the desert villages of Tehachapi and Mojave at nearly four thousand feet above sea level, groaning past the hefty mountains that brought shadows to scrubby Palmdale, wheeling south at Bouquet Canyon near Newhall, and then descending into the more open San Fernando Valley. Here it rolled side by side with San Fernando Road, past the city where Miguel would live most of his life and where he would eventually die, San Fernando itself. Many hours later the rolling stock on which my uncle rode began slowing down near Burbank, finally arriving in Los Angeles.

Miguel and his *paisano,* his fellow countryman, landed the following night in Los Angeles once again. As they walked the busy streets to calm the growling in their stomachs, a police officer approached them and stopped to talk with them. This patrolman was also the first black man that my uncle had ever laid eyes on—and he spoke Spanish to boot! Miguel and his buddy must have stammered and felt a mix of fear and awe at being confronted by a tall uniformed black man who asked them where they were going—all in Spanish. After a few awkward moments, the vagabonds admitted they were hungry and needed a place to sleep. The officer must have been familiar with this kind of situation because he drew out some recommendations.

> "Go down this street and you'll find a church. Go into the church and you'll find you'll have to do some singing. Go ahead and sing. But afterward, they'll take you to where you can sleep." Can you imagine! He helped us out just right! We found the church. We sang. They gave us dinner and then took us where we could sleep.

After a good night's rest followed by a satisfying breakfast, thanks to religious charity, the next morning the two young explorers set out to find work once again. They soon discovered which street corners contractors in need of day laborers used to pick up their workers. In order to stretch their luck, they agreed to wait for work on separate street corners—Miguel on one and his buddy on another, a few blocks away. "If you get a job, you wait for me here this evening, and I'll do the same," Miguel made it clear. His travel mate agreed and then marched off to find his corner.

Within the hour, a Mexican man approached my uncle Miguel saying he was a contractor and needed forty men who had experience doing tunnel work. My uncle said that he was interested and claimed he had worked in mines before. The contractor quizzed him: "Where have you worked inside a tunnel?" Miguel replied, "Sinaloa," the state in which Mazatlán is located. The contractor asked him to name some mines there, and my uncle, who had never worked in a mine but knew about them from his three years in Mazatlán, named two: El Tigre and El Rosario—mines that were well known even by the men from Santa Rosa and Mascota. The contractor replied that he knew about the mines and that he had worked in them too. "I concluded that he was lying," Miguel later reflected. "He had probably heard them mentioned but had not worked in them. The mines were indeed prominent, but they were not located in Sinaloa but located in northern Sonora in the mining district of Cananea.[44] "Anyway, he put my name on his list," my uncle continued, adding that while the contractor talked with Miguel several other Mexicans appeared on the scene looking for work, and they too were drafted.

It didn't take long for him to gather his forty men after which Miguel asked him, "Can you add another name to your list?" He explained about his buddy who would be returning soon, and the contractor said, "Sure enough." The supplier of workers led the newly contracted gang, including my uncle, to a hotel where they would sleep that night. Upon learning of this plan, Miguel returned to the corner where he was supposed to meet his traveling companion and waited for a long time, but his friend never showed up. "I never saw him again," Miguel said flatly. My uncle was alone again, and no doubt feeling deserted.

The next morning, the work contractor gathered the forty Mexican laborers and told them that he would only accept those men whose bags or luggage weighed at least seventy-five pounds. If anyone had any less, the contractor explained, it meant that person didn't have enough clothing to stay warm and thereby resist the cold weather where they were going. Miguel scratched his head a little bit because he didn't have any extra clothing, so, after a moment's reflection, he appealed to an older man standing nearby who was carrying a heavy coat and lots of baggage. He asked him to lend him his coat, and the man consented after looking closely at Miguel. He said that they were going to the same place so he could get his coat back later. Thanks to this ruse our clever Miguel passed the test and joined the rest of the men who were put on a train later that day—one which took them back to Fresno. In less than a week, he had traveled from Los Angeles to Fresno, back to Los Angeles, and then back to Fresno—a distance of 215 miles each way! My uncle chuckled at the irony of this effort.

From Fresno they traveled east into the high forested sierra, not far from Sequoia National Park, where they came upon a canyon holding thirty-five labor camps strung along its length. "We were about forty men who were contracted. We arrived, and I think they dropped me off with about three other guys at Camp 35, and the man who loaned me the coat was dropped off about three camps down." They were taken to some tents on a hill, "and gosh, they had plenty of blankets," my uncle recalled. Nobody was going to be cold! And "they had plenty of food too!" he added. He also remembered a building about thirty feet long called the "bull house" which served as a cafeteria, and so it seems he was positively impressed by the measures the company had taken to insure that workers like him were properly housed and fed.

In the morning, Miguel and his work gang were taken down into the earth—into mine shafts about three hundred feet below the surface. The work consisted of digging tunnels by blasting the rock with dynamite. With the aid of powerful air-driven machines, long, pointed steel bars or bits were driven into the rock to make holes into which dynamite sticks were inserted, and then blasted. The explosion expanded the tunnel producing rock that had to be removed. The men then placed the debris into carts on rails and this rubble was taken out. Miguel's job, working alongside Austrians, Italians, blacks, and white Americans, as he recalled decades later, was to even out the tunnel walls after the blasts in order to install heavy wooden buttresses to hold up the ceiling and keep the tunnels from caving in. "I said to myself, 'Goodness, this is easy enough—unless they put me to run these [drilling] machines!'" He added, "In the end, I liked the work a lot! And they fed us so well! I was very happy . . . Within two weeks I gained weight and felt very good."

Considering that my uncle Miguel was operating in a diverse environment that was new and different from all of his previous experiences thus far, I asked him whether he lived through any discrimination or treatment that was unfair. He replied, "I never saw any discrimination at these campsites. I never felt that I was mistreated due to my race. I did not detect any differences along those lines." He then added, "The only problem I can remember having is that sitting in the dining room, if I didn't have the food I wanted in front of me, I had to ask someone to pass this or that and I didn't know the words! [Thank goodness,] there were some Italians who spoke Spanish, so they helped me out."

> On weekends, I discovered that many men organized betting games, and many [of them] placed big bets on poker, dice, and so on. I liked to go watch on Saturdays. A group of Mexicans arrived in the camps, and I got to know them at the gambling tables. They told me that they were not

> really interested in the available jobs; they were really interested in gambling. They were good at it.

Once settled, restoring family ties took first priority. Miguel began to correspond with his mother and sister in Nogales: "I had their address. I told my mother where I was and that I was going to send her some money, but it turned out I didn't have to. They went out in a *reenganche* to pick cotton, and so they were earning their own money." In the meantime, Carlota wrote to Pascual telling him where Miguel was, and this is the way the two brothers finally began to communicate once more after five years of not seeing each other.

Pascual wrote to Miguel telling him to join him in Fresno, but Miguel was reluctant because he was so comfortable at the tunnel camps. "And they paid so well too," he sighed. "They paid me four dollars a day or fifty cents an hour and kept one dollar for room and board, so I got three dollars. I stayed there for about three months and wanted to stay longer in order to save some money, but Pascual insisted that I join him." Consequently, Miguel gave up a good-paying job once again to help keep the family together, and so he proceeded on to Fresno.

He found him. "I had his address," my uncle said, omitting in his mind whatever details were involved in finding the address. "We were so happy to see each other," he remembered adding that "so many years had gone by!" Miguel had not seen his elder brother since the day the two said good-bye at the door of their adobe hut on the Hacienda Santa Rosa just as Pascual was preparing to walk down to Puerto Vallarta. The two Naranjo brothers caught up on their lives, reminisced about life on the hacienda, and remembered the relatives they had left behind. "We talked frequently about where we had grown up," Miguel added. Having left his tunneling job for good, he moved in with his brother in Fresno and lived there about five or six months.

Carlota and Guadalupe Enter the United States

Shortly after acquiring their visa to enter the United States, Carlota and Guadalupe finally crossed the international line into Nogales, Arizona, and, within hours, were met by agents looking to hire cotton workers. Here was another *reenganche*, but the first for my mother and grandmother. As with Pascual and Miguel and the thousands of other Mexican immigrants in the 1920s, America greatly needed workers, and so my mother and grandmother were plucked as they crossed the line.

My mother wrote in her memoirs that "trucks were lined up waiting for us . . . we accepted the offer [to pick cotton], and the men led us to an open truck." She and her mother climbed aboard, along with "many other *reenganchados*" who had also crossed the international border that morning. They all drove off in the direction of Tucson. A monsoon preceded by flying dust caught them en route, and the hapless Mexicans riding in the open, including my mother and grandmother, were first blinded by the airborne sand particles and then soaked to the bone when the storm released its downpour. Even though the truck got stuck in the mud at one point, they were delivered in an area near Tucson with tents already set up. They also found food waiting as it was dinnertime. Although she was tired from the trip, Guadalupe remembered that she didn't sleep much that first night in the United States because the tents were located on an anthill teeming with "big ants," some which bit her. "It was awful for me!" she exclaimed but didn't dwell on it and neither did she mention any nurses or medical assistants who might have come to offer her liniments, salves, or ointments. She nursed her own wounds somehow. The following morning, after eating some regular American hotcakes (*jatqueques*) for the first time, they were put on a truck once again and driven to a place called Escatel, probably a farm, where they were assigned to yet another set of tents. Here, in the last days of summer, they would live and toil for about three months picking cotton under a scorching desert sun. Weather in their native Santa Rosa was never as harsh; nevertheless, they got used to it, slowly.

"We were not good at that kind of work," my mother remembered wistfully. Picking cotton or any other type of crop was not something that Carlota or Guadalupe had ever done. The reader will recall that while they worked very hard to get by and save a penny here and nickel there, in order to keep moving north on their long, slow journey, they concentrated their work experience on domestic chores already familiar to them. Picking cotton was not something they had experienced. Like the countless other Mexican immigrants who arrived in the United States in the 1920s, my ancestors were not necessarily experienced in doing harvest work on a large and intensive scale as they found once they crossed the US border.

Mother was right. They were very deficient cotton pickers. They hadn't done it before, and they didn't develop the knack for it. "Between the three of us (my mother, Juárez, and I)," my mother wrote, "We didn't pick more than one hundred pounds!" Each picking about thirty-three pounds per day was an abysmal amount! She acknowledged that others could pick more, and she was correct. A good "picker" in the American South could pick 350 pounds per day which might mean that an average picker might have harvested anywhere between 150 and 250.[45]

A Word about "Juárez"

The reader will notice a new name above. "Juárez" is inserted in the preceding quotation by my mother in the most casual manner, as if we had known about this person all along. The truth is that my siblings and I heard this name many times when we were growing up in San Fernando—it belonged to Grandmother Carlota's male partner at this time. Guadalupe mentions him quite offhandedly here, and this deserves a word of explanation.

His full name was Florencio Juárez, although he was known to most of my brothers and sisters only by his last name. This suggests that in addressing him or referring to him, Grandma commonly used his surname instead of his first name. My elder sister, Mary Valdez, addressed him as "Grandpa" when she evoked a memory of him in 2007 and said she believed that he and Carlota met in Mazatlán. Mary remembered him as man who was *moreno y chaparrito* (a dark-skinned, short-statured Mexican male); someone who was very kind and attentive to her when she was a child. She confirmed my mother's statement, made in one of her amazing moments of mental clarity at age 101, that Juárez had indeed befriended Carlota in the Mexican port city and joined her and her grown children when they embarked by train to the US border. This means that Juárez was already in their company as my grandmother's partner when they reached Nogales and later when they crossed the border into the United States. Curiously, my mother's memoirs do not mention him until after they cross the border, as we have seen, and Miguel does not mention him up to this point in his recorded interviews either. They may have seen his relationship with their mother, Carlota, as too recent and short-lived to give him more attention in their memory.

Early Courting Issues Involving Mother

Guadalupe remembered spending her first Christmas in the United States in the cotton fields near Tucson. "There was a lady who organized a celebration for that day," she wrote. Doubtless because they were not near a church and far from any known community, the woman who organized this seasonal observance in 1922 mostly likely included some prayers, perhaps the rosary, as a way to make up for the traditional midnight Christmas Mass which many Mexicans observe. Whatever kind of prayers were said, they were followed by a dance. Guadalupe continues, "Some friends of mine came by to ask my mother permission to take me along, as they had done before, but that night we stayed out until four o'clock in the morning! My mother got so mad! She didn't like to take me to these dances as other parents did with their girls—I would have liked that very much."

Here we see an early example of the difficult balancing act in which the mothers and daughters in our family engaged with regard to the eminently human practice of courting. Carlota's hawk eye on her daughter's social relations had already become quite evident—she monitored Guadalupe's activities very closely. Carlota may have ruled with an iron rod partly due to the fact that she and her daughter were constantly on the move, shifting from one set of neighbors to another—who could you trust in these circumstances? Not knowing the fellow migrant families well enough may have contributed to the strict supervision that Guadalupe lamented, but there were other issues too as we'll see. Despite their meager situation, Carlota was very stringent with her daughter and being poor and on the migrant trail didn't mean relaxing your mores.

Even with her mother's strictness, Guadalupe's teenage years would not be diminished, however. "A young man became interested in me—Luis Campos." This was one of the thoughts that flashed in her mind concerning these days near Tucson.

> My mother found out [about Luis Campos] and, as a result, had us moved to another cotton camp. A lady with a horse and buggy helped us move. But the next day, we learned the boy had followed us. In the morning, noticing that the young fellow had gone ahead of us to work in the fields, my mother acted as if we were going to work there too. Instead, she had the lady with the horse and buggy move us to another camp. We were almost there when the boy caught up with us (he was riding in a car), and he told my mother he wanted to marry me. She told him no because I was too young! And I didn't even have anything to do with him!

As a young lady, my mother seems to have attracted *pretendientes* at every turn (a male seeking a serious relationship with a female). To be sure, she made friends easily as we saw in Mazatlán, then later in Nogales with the family who took them in, and here in the cotton fields near Tucson with the young folk of other migrant families. We can't doubt she attracted young males in these early years because she recognized the fact in her memoirs and referred to it numerous times in her discussions about her early life with her children. While she wasn't a striking beauty by any means, she possessed a homespun loveliness when she was young nevertheless, and this worked in her favor.

Carlota, Guadalupe, and Juárez were not destined to stay long in the cotton fields in any case. Regardless of whether they were trying to keep a distance from any and all *pretendientes*, they surely had to continue their journey to catch up with Miguel and Pascual. "Thus," my mother writes, "We retook our path north," probably in early January 1923. She told Luis they were headed for Fresno.

They Finally Arrive in California

After walking along desert roadways for about a day and a half and sleeping out in the open, they arrived at a barren place called Mohawk. Here they found some men repairing a highway nearby, possibly old US 80. Guadalupe informs us that Juárez got a job there, but being the teenager that she was, she fails to give us any details about what his tasks might have been. She only notes that "we stayed there about a month," probably meaning that Juárez worked on this highway job, probably as a laborer, and they all presumably saved a few more dollars to continue their trip. We don't know where they lodged or how they managed otherwise.

When they had saved enough, they began walking again in the winter desert sun, prone to chilling spells, and headed to the "Santa Fe" railroad line that ran nearby although I believe Mom meant to say Southern Pacific. There they caught the first train going west on the same rail line that Pascual and Miguel had taken ahead of them—it still comes from Tucson, past Picacho Peak, and then heads due west through the parched Gila Bend Desert before veering southwest into scorching Yuma. Crossing over the Colorado River, it skirts the underside of the Salton Sea and then heads northwest toward San Bernardino. "We took it all the way to Ontario, California," she remembered. She couldn't detect the presence of any Spanish speakers here, so they had a hard time getting even the most basic services, like finding a bathroom. Still, she goes on, "We rented a hotel room before our money ran out."

"I also remember that my mother didn't want to sleep on the bed because it looked so pretty. She said she would rather sleep on the rug in the room," Guadalupe recalls. This is a reminder that Carlota and Guadalupe slept on *petates* most of their lives in Mexico and were not yet used to seeing a bed fully dressed with a bedspread folded over enclosing the pillows. A *petate* is a thin Aztec-origin mat made from woven palm leaves used by the Mexican peasantry as a bedroll. As a child, Mary learned a slightly different version of this story which itself became an item of our family lore. Mary's memory placed this episode in the American Nogales right after Carlota and Guadalupe crossed the border. In this version, Carlota and Juárez were so dirty from their traveling up to the border that they refused to sleep on the bed, so they designated Guadalupe to take her forty winks on it while they slept on the floor. Here again is a reaffirmation of the backcountry origin of our immigrant ancestors as it also suggests a tough and gritty trip to the border from inside Mexico, all fitting dimensions to the immigrant story.

Guadalupe remembered that even though Ontario lay on the eastern edges of the prosperous Los Angeles basin, far from the bare bone communities of the Arizona desert, Juárez said he was worried about what they were going to do next.

Going out into the streets of Ontario the next morning, our trekkers noticed an older Mexican gentleman walking down the street with a girl about Guadalupe's age, so they stopped to talk to them. The girl was the man's daughter. They also learned that they lived nearby, and so after some more mutual and friendly probing, "we asked for posada," Guadalupe put it simply, meaning getting a place to sleep. She and her mother asked the man and his daughter to let them stay with them for a few days given their special situation, and much to their delight, the request was granted. Guadalupe noted that "the man responded to our plea with kindness. He said 'come with us.' They treated us very well . . . so we stayed there a few weeks." The man, named Pedro, lived with his wife and daughter, Paulita. The daughter became a close friend of Guadalupe, and they corresponded for many years afterward, a pen pal relationship that reflected more on my mother's enjoyment in putting her thoughts down in writing. When Paulita married, she sent Guadalupe a photograph as a token of their friendship which was still in my mother's possession more than fifty years later.

During that interim in Ontario, Guadalupe wrote to Pascual informing him of their northward progress. He finally replied and sent forty-five dollars so that they could continue on their course. While Guadalupe does not offer details, she recounts that they again boarded the same railroad line that had taken Pascual and Miguel north and that it brought them to Los Angeles for the first time. Little did they know that in later years they would visit the city often. In fact, Carlota would die in one of the big hospitals nearby about thirty years later.

The fact is that they didn't know what to do once the train arrived at the Los Angeles Union Station. We need to keep in mind that when Pascual and Miguel arrived at a train station in the United States, they were both under supervision, along with the other *enganchado* workers, by a company agent who told them what to do and where to go. The most important thing for the *enganchados*, as we've seen already, was to make sure they wouldn't get off the train. They didn't even have to worry about food because the agents brought it to them. Carlota, Guadalupe, and Juárez, on the other hand, were traveling on their own without someone looking after them. So when they arrived in Los Angeles, they knew they had to change trains, but didn't know where or how.

> We moved from one car to another letting the people get off and then, finally, the conductor came along. I remember he said to us, "*camón*," but not knowing what he meant, we didn't know what to do. He had to gesture to us to get us off the train and then told us where to get the other one. This is how we finally arrived in Fresno on a morning of February 1923.

This is how Carlota achieved her goal in the middle of a California winter, in the middle of an entirely different culture, and more than a thousand miles away from Santa Rosa. She had cried and fretted that her son Pascual, and later Miguel, were not near. Now her worries, or these particular ones at least, were at an end. But she had paid a price. Guadalupe and Miguel described her as falling into depression many times while they made their way slowly to the United States—she had gotten sick on numerous occasions. Now they were back together again. They had come together and thus accomplished what they had set out to do five years earlier when they were still resident peons on the Hacienda Santa Rosa. The reader will recall that the hacienda owner scoffed at their reaching the United States, asking them, tongue in cheek, to whistle at him when they got to Mazatlán. Now they could whistle at Don Manuel Merino and feel proud of their determination. Indeed!

Pascual at age 23

Carlota at age 43

Chapter 5

The First Years in the United States
(1919–1923)

Pascual and My Father Team Up • Mother Nearly Marries Someone Else • Our Father Meets Our Mother and They Marry • The Family Moves to Southern California

ONCE IN AMERICA, beyond worrying about keeping food on the table and a roof over their heads, did my relatives make a choice one day that they were not returning to their community of origin? On a Sunday afternoon, gathered around a meal, did they reminisce about life as they knew it in Santa Rosa or discuss settling down somewhere else in California or the United States? Did they ever discuss America in contrast to Mexico and what it might offer them in the long run?

We don't know the answers to these questions because decades later when I asked my mother and my uncles to tell me their stories, they dwelled only on their efforts to find each other in this new land. They relived how they had come to terms with the new culture insofar as getting a job was concerned and finding a place for themselves in America, staying busy and hanging on to one another. They may have held elevated thoughts beyond their need to keep marching forward to earn their daily bread, but I was unable to stir them up. Their recorded memories only confirmed their attempts to move forward without losing a sense of themselves, but do so with a touch of dignity.

Their outlook was a positive one, at least for the younger ones. Unknown to them, as informants that they were at the time I interviewed them, and to me as their interviewer, the stories they shared with me revealed a certain zest. Pascual, Mom, and Miguel were young adults at this time, like the great majority of Latino immigrants crossing the US border in our time, and their appetite for life matched the hope which they raised against the hardships that would stagger any average middle-class American. They didn't mind sleeping on the ground or working to the point of exhaustion. Moreover, the three younger ones were single too and that mattered too.

When I came to this point in my story, about their lives as young adults arriving in the United States not yet married nor burdened with a family, I also came face-to-face with something I didn't expect. I came to realize that they were still in the process of becoming full adults; they were ensnared in their own evolving maturity which pulled them all manner of ways. I wasn't quite ready for this. Their hormones were raging, so to speak, and they were looking at the world with a singular expectation and a dab of the happy-go-lucky too. I began to understand that they were willing to fail and to move on because the whole world was waiting for them. In this sense, they were touched by the arrogance of youth and this carried them forward.

Pascual and My Father Team Up

As we've noted already, my father, Bernabé Gil, and Pascual became fast friends as early as 1919. Age-wise, they were close: Bernabé was twenty and Pascual nineteen. While we may not know the circumstances that first brought them together in Fresno, we do know they became very chummy and lived and worked together several years before Bernabé met my mother.

Two unmarried young men would naturally feel attracted to young women, and this contributed to Pascual's earliest memories of my father. Pascual remembered that they worked for a winemaker in Fresno and were busily engaged in crushing grapes old-world style when the winemaker, named Francisco, concluded that Bernabé was flirting too much with his wife. "Your father was a Don Juan!" "*Era muy enamorado!*" Pascual chuckled and looked impishly at me when he pronounced these words. "The man ran us off, and we didn't even get a chance to taste the wine!" "*Nos corrió y no probamos el vinacho*!"

Together the two friends bought an old Ford automobile, Pascual recalled—the first car they had ever owned. They bought it used for $120, and Dad did all of the driving at first because, as my uncle explained, "I didn't know how to drive, but he did." And he didn't know where Dad had learned.

One day, when both were out of a job, Pascual decided he wanted to go out and look for work, so he asked "Berna," as he called my father, to accompany him, but Dad declined. Pascual said that in those days Dad was living with a woman named María who had children and was happy to have him even if he was unemployed. Pascual said to him, "*Cuña,*[46] if you don't want to leave the house, then lend me the car. I'll drive." My father gave him the keys without asking any questions. Pascual ended this anecdote this way:

> He loaned me the car, and what did I know about driving! I went and crashed it into a telephone post, bending the front axle so much that the two front wheels came close together! The radiator exploded and water burst everywhere!

My uncle's remembrances stunned me a bit. Hearing from him that my father lived with a woman who was not my mother jarred me. That Dad flirted with a winemaker's wife and that he cozied up with María who had children jolted me. Should I exclude these images? I didn't know how to proceed, but, as I wrote further, I began to get a hold of my reactions. Cast against the larger context described in this chapter and the fact that he was a young, single, working-class guy who was busily engaged in trying out what the world had to offer, I began feeling relieved. I came to realize that my uncle's testimony had kicked out a leg holding up my puerile views of my father. Didn't I do something similar when I became an adult? Didn't most everyone? It all began to make sense as I kept on composing my thoughts; I calmed down and kept on writing.

In any case, Pascual and my father continued to spend a lot of time hunting for jobs together. Around 1921, they found employment in an area my uncle called Sugar Pine, up in the California sierras. This is where they worked as *muleros* opening mountain trails.[47] They drove mule teams yoked to plows that pulled the brush out of the ground. Once they cleared an area, they would substitute the plows with iron scrapers, also pulled by mules, and level the freshly dug earth. The trails might have served to control forest fires.

Pascual affirmed that they did similar work as far south as Fillmore, where they laid open pasture lands, again using mule teams as power engines. The two young bucks ran into some trouble here, however.[48] The boss didn't like the way Dad was handling the animals, "that he beat them too much," Pascual remembered. So he yelled at my father who apparently replied that the mule in question was too lazy and asked, just how did he suggest he deal with the animal? My uncle recalled that the gringo boss immediately got mad and threw a jab at my father. "He didn't like the way Bernabé spoke back to him," Pascual explained, visualizing the moment after many years. Taking umbrage at the way he was being addressed, my father apparently shouted, "You can take your job and shove it!" He then yelled at Pascual, "This son of a bitch wants to hit me just as if I was a kid!" Pascual described Dad, standing as tall and as strong as the gringo, and so he took the mule harness and threw it at the boss's head, nearly striking him. Ready with an iron brake lever in hand to use if necessary, Pascual yelled out to the boss, "Stop fighting because you're going to have to deal with the two of us!" He probably shouted all of this quickly in Spanish, but his tone and his readiness to strike put a stop to the situation. It was obvious their job had come to an end. Pascual groaned out loud, "I'm quitting," and both he and my father walked off the job. They were buddies and therefore stuck together.

Mother Nearly Marries Someone Else

While Pascual and Bernabé roamed in and out of Fresno in search of jobs and excitement, Mother seems to have been continuously enwrapped in romantic notions. After all, as a teenager she was driven by her youthfulness to relate to young men her age and probably, without being conscious about it, ultimately becoming an adult and having a family. Her behavior surely must have troubled Carlota, who knew all too well how slippery men could be in their relations with women, but we unfortunately do not have access to Grandma's thoughts and words on this account.

Mother remembered that she and her mother and younger brother stayed with Pascual for about three months after their arrival in Fresno. In his interview, Miguel noted that they took a house in the Mexican section of town while Mom was more specific. They lived on Inyo Street and later moved to a house on F Street.

This is about the time when Mother received notice about her old beau from Mazatlán, Pedro, whose family—the Santiagos—owned the inn in Mazatlán where she worked. He had been writing to Miguel all along, and the fact that Pedro did not write to her annoyed her quite a bit, apparently. She wrote in her memoirs, "I found it strange that Pedro didn't write to me because he had been my boyfriend. When I found this out, I decided to begin going out with Jesús López," a new admirer in Fresno who suddenly turned up in her narrative.[49]

Even as she was going out with Jesús, news also arrived about yet another old admirer—the one from the cotton fields of Arizona, Luis Campos. It seems that one day a priest at the Catholic Church they attended in Fresno's Mexican barrio announced that a train had collided with a workers' rail cart nearby and several men had gotten hurt as a result. He read the names of the injured to his parishioners one Sunday morning, and lo and behold, Mother heard the name of Luis Campos! He was the young fellow who had raced after her in the cotton fields of Arizona, yelling that he wanted to marry her as she and her mother rode away in a horse-drawn cart in order to get away from him.

> It was the young man from Litchfield [Arizona], Luis Campos, the fellow who had said he wanted to marry me and whom I had not forgotten. He was in a Fresno hospital, and my mother decided to go see him because she had come to know his parents. When we reached the hospital, we learned he had just been released, so we didn't see him. So I continued going out with Jesús.[50]

Who was this Jesús López? Where did he work? What did he look like? Where did he meet my mother, and how serious was their relationship? We don't have much information about him, and the little that we eventually learn fails to endear us to him. We also found that Mother dropped him cold soon enough.

As it turns out, Jesús decided it was time for them to get married. He gave Mother a trunk for her clothes which she viewed as a demonstration of his commitment. He also had to submit to the expected formalities, which included meeting Mom's family and making his marriage plans known to them. He had to dress in his Sunday best, to be sure, and visit Mother's home in order to ask Carlota in a formal way for her daughter's hand in marriage. This was no trivial affair, and there was little expectation of a quick reply. When I asked for the hand in marriage of my first wife, I underwent a similar experience, and it was not a lightweight experience. Unfortunately, we do not have a description of Jesús's oral petition to marry my mother. Mother wrote nevertheless that her mother's response was to slow things down, to wait a month. She wanted to mull things over and discuss the matter in a family conclave, which meant she wanted to talk the proposal over with her sons and neither were home at the moment—Miguel was working in a vineyard in nearby Le Grand and Pascual was up on the sierra. Mom recalled, "On the day that Miguel came back from Le Grand, Jesús gave me sixty dollars so that I could begin buying kitchen things, and he also said he was going to apply for the marriage license." He was clearly upping the ante.

In light of Jesús's obvious intention to marry my mother, the entire family finally got together. Pascual arrived with his lady friend named Cleofas. More importantly, new information came to light in this meeting. These are mother's words:

> They [Pascual and Miguel] both advised me to back out of my relationship with Jesús. They told me that he had another woman and even a child by her, and that he also lived with them. They helped me change my mind.

When Jesús arrived with a marital license in hand, proclaiming that it was time for them to present themselves at church for marriage,[51] Mother made her decision. "I had gone out to meet him and didn't let him enter our house. This is when I said no," she remembered quite clearly. She also recollects that Jesús's face "changed colors—the red on his face came and went" as if with anger and embarrassment. Cross words may have been exchanged out on the front door in old Fresno, but all Mom tells us about this difficult moment is that, "I gave him everything back." With the family behind her, there was little Jesús could say or do, and so it appears that he stepped away and disappeared from my mother's life.

These events must have shaken up young Guadalupe a great deal considering how romantic she appeared to be by her own admission. Her memory betrays a starry-eyed young woman eagerly looking for a man. While she doesn't describe her feelings for the boyfriends she knew before Jesús, perhaps in deference to our Dad, she does admit feeling great pain in her heart when she rejected him, feelings of betrayal no doubt. She doesn't mention anything else about Pascual and Cleofas's testimony regarding his alleged double-dealing, but she does say she came across Jesús's wife some time later. Mentioning this incident may have confirmed his deceit in her mind, serving as a way to feel better about her decision. In describing this entire episode in her memorials, Guadalupe keeps her feelings securely under wraps.

The only thought she adds to these events is Miguel's suggestion that she accompany him to Le Grand where he worked so she could get over the unhappy affair with Jesús. Miguel said to her, "There is a woman there by the name of Sofía who prepares my meals and you can stay with her." Sofía offered room and board to local Mexican workers. Guadalupe accepted Miguel's invitation, and her mother gave her permission to travel the fifty miles north. They undoubtedly took the train.

Our Father Meets Our Mother and They Marry

"This is where I met your father,"[52] she writes. He was living with Miguel in Le Grand, boarding with Doña Sofía. Pascual's more steady involvement with his girlfriend probably limited the time he could spend with my father, so it's possible that Miguel began filling in. "I stayed a month there, and this is when I began to get to know Bernabé," Mom wrote. She explained that although at the end of those thirty days she returned to Fresno, their romantic relationship waxed hot, so they wrote many letters to each other—letters that were lost with time.

Not long after, both Miguel and my father ran out of work in Le Grand, so they moved to Fresno to huddle near the rest of our family. Dad, who did not have one, gladly attached himself. "By this time," Guadalupe remembered, "we were already going together."

About three months later, they decided to run away and get married. We don't have my father's memory to shed his light on this important decision to flee and wed, but it does sound more like my mother's idea. It reflects both on her hormone-driven need to marry and an apparent desire to become independent of her mother. "I decided I didn't want to tell anyone because they were always saying no to me. They would not let me marry," she recalled. Thus, Mother short-circuited the advice and consent that her mother and two brothers might have offered and decided to escape with twenty-four year-old Bernabé. In doing so, my mother dealt a harsh blow to her relationship with her own mother, Carlota, and it is difficult to know whether my father jeopardized his relationship with Miguel and Pascual by courting their only sister. They seemed to have been such buddies—all three of them. In the end, it appears that things turned out all right—we really don't know the details. What is clear is that Mother and Dad eloped on August 13, 1923, a date Mother committed to memory. It was a Thursday—they didn't even wait for the weekend.

The two lovers fled back to the wood-framed boarding house they had left back in Le Grand to indulge in their happiness and to share the good news with Doña Sofía Lara who had become Mother's friend and advisor. They couldn't share their feelings more widely because they had run away, and this must have bothered the bride-to-be. Mom wrote that she and Dad stayed in Le Grand long enough to get married by the local justice of the peace, and Sofía and her husband, Dionisio, agreed to stand as witnesses.[53]

Soon after their marriage ceremony, they took refuge in the vineyard farm where Dad had been working earlier with Miguel. They might have run out of work months before due to the cyclical nature of raising grapes, but now in the middle of the harvest season, the grape farmer and his wife—the Stalders, neither of whom spoke any Spanish—ushered the newlyweds into a small wood-framed house where they could live. It would serve as their love nest and certainly remember it later many times.

This was their first abode together, and this was also the moment when Mother became pressed to experiment with English and to try to bridge the cultural divide that always surrounded her. Thus, my mother began her lifelong struggles with English and the exposure to Americans and their strange ways. Of these initial steps, Mom wrote, "The owner's wife would talk to me, but I didn't know anything at this time, not even an iota of English. We tried every possible way to understand each other because there were no neighbors nearby." The rural isolation pressed both of them to reach out. She added wistfully, "The *patrones* liked us a lot," referring to the farmers, the property bosses.

On the day they took out their wedding license, Guadalupe returned to Fresno with my father in tow to make up with her mother. Given the fact that she had enjoyed very close relations with her, strict and demanding as she might have been, Guadalupe simply could not stay away. "I asked her forgiveness," she wrote. This happened on Mexican Independence Day, September 16. She does not say how Carlota reacted. Considering how strict Carlota had been about these matters and how interwoven their lives had been during the four years they were moving north, it must have been shocking for her to discover the elopement. To have her daughter disappear without notice—and deciding to marry on her own! I think Grandma Carlota must have verbally lacerated Mom, feeling betrayed by it all. Her own life with men had been such a hard one and now her daughter, only eighteen, was behaving in ways that put her at risk socially and otherwise. Guadalupe's elopement must have been very difficult for Grandma to take indeed. After apologizing, the two lovebirds flew back to Le Grand, chastened by the experience, no doubt.

The Family Moves to Southern California

While Mom and Dad blissfully experimented with married life in Le Grand, Carlota and Miguel were lured to the south by Mother's former boyfriend from Mazatlán, Pedro Santiago. He had remained Miguel's friend, and they corresponded with each other. Pedro informed Miguel that he had found a comfortable niche in the Sunland-Tujunga district of Los Angeles, in the city's northeastern foothills where, according to my uncle Pascual, local builders were laying out new residential neighborhoods. So Pedro asked Miguel and his family to join him. Since Miguel had been having a hard time finding steady work in the Fresno area, he accepted Pedro's invitation, traveled to the southland, and Carlota and Juárez went with him. This relationship between friends thus led my ancestors away from the Fresno area and brought them to Southern California, where they would spend most of their lives and find a final resting place.

In the meantime, back in Fresno, my parents proceeded to do the proper thing. When the grape harvesting was completed in October, my parents once again enlisted Doña Sofia and her husband to act as their witnesses in order to get married properly or *como Dios manda* (as God commands)—in a Catholic church, in Fresno. They could not have overlooked taking this second step in legitimizing their relationship because it would simply have been unpardonable. Mother had already tarred her image with her mother by eloping, and so not getting a priest to bless their union would have made her a black sheep for the rest of her life.

When this ceremony was over—it was modest to be sure and without anyone from the rest of their family attending—Bernabé continued working in the vineyards. Grapevines always require a lot of labor, even when they're not being harvested—they need cleaning, pruning, and watering, at the very least, and he was the one to do it. This was my father's work right after he got married.

Dad took a moment to have his picture taken with a second man sometime during this happy interlude in Le Grand. The photograph in our family holdings shows my father standing next to someone who appears to be a male friend who is holding a dark-coated puppy with a large whitish spot (the puppy's mother sits in the darkened left foreground of the picture, barely visible). The puppy may have been a gift to the newlyweds. Dad rests his left arm lightly on his friend's shoulders and looks at the camera a bit sideways, expressing mild curiosity. Both men are dressed in work clothes; my father wearing a thick Irish-styled cap and a heavy dark open sweater over a pair of Levis-styled bib overalls with rolled up trouser legs. Work boots of the kind he would wear nearly all his life complete his attire. This photo is dated 1923, and it shows the two men standing in front of a tall, rugged-looking tree as a big iron-wheeled tractor sits behind them, all this suggesting the photo was probably taken on the Stalder farm. The photo also reveals some low wooden buildings, one of which might have been my parents' first home, their love bubble. Many years after my siblings and I were born, we all did farm work in order to make ends meet, as we'll see in a later chapter, and some of it included harvesting grapes, a type of work my parents learned in Le Grand. Afterward the Stalders later moved to another farm, in Stockton, California, and, according to my mother, they invited them to join them, but my folks declined because they had decided to move to Southern California instead.

"I became so sad because they [my family] had gone away from Fresno—I was no longer happy. I wanted to be by mother's side," my mother wrote. After about a year, she prevailed on her young husband who obviously would do anything to keep his new bride as happy as possible, and as he had no relatives to pin him down, they packed their bags and moved to Southern California as well.

Living in Le Grand may have been their happiest time together. They were young and probably earned enough money to put food on the table at least and otherwise still live with a touch of hopeful dignity. Their eight children and the hardships of raising them still awaited them.

Three additional photographs visually inform us about Mom and Dad in these first years of their marriage, their happiest. One of them, exhibiting Dad and Mom, hung in my mother's dining room for at least thirty years of my lifetime. It shows a happy, young, nattily dressed couple strolling in a garden side by side (p.101). My mother and father are dressed in their Sunday best—wearing a fine top hat he is garbed in a dark suit and vest and Mom shows off a light-colored knit sweater while she holds a fashionable flowered cloche-type hat in her hand. The puppy held in the arms of the man who must have been Dad's friend in the photo previously described is shown here calmly resting near their feet. It was probably a wedding gift. A second photograph in our collection looks like their official wedding photograph (p. 99). My mother and father pose in the formal fashion of the day. He sits in a chair with his legs crossed and is sporting a trim dark mustache. He is dressed in a three-piece dark suit and a white shirt with a rounded collar pinning a light-colored tie, and she stands beside him wearing a charcoal-colored, loose-fitting formal dress with an open white-lace neck accented by a pearl-like necklace. She wears black leather shoes with a modest heel, and he wears his favorite work boots. In the third photograph, marked "1926" by mother's hand and not included here, my father looking so young and handsome in a whitish long sleeved shirt and tannish pants, leans back against what looks like a 1926 Pilot Motor car with a black collapsible top. The photographer caught him holding a blonde colored twelve string guitar and he seems to be enjoying playing and singing at the same time. He was a crooner and mother often remembered that. These were their finest moments, no doubt.

Bernabé on right, at age 24, with friend holding dog, in Le Grand

Bernabé and Guadalupe, wedding photo (1923)

Bernabé and Guadalupe with dog (ca. 1923)

Chapter 6

Shuttling between Sunland and the Logging Camp
(1924–1927)

MOM AND DAD, as the newlyweds, caught up with Grandma Carlota, Juárez, and Uncle Miguel in Sunland, California, toward the end of 1924. Miguel probably received his sister with a great sense of happiness, and Juárez must have felt elated to see her as well. Carlota most likely welcomed Guadalupe and her new husband with veiled joy and slowly relented in her grouchiness as the days wore on; after all, mother and daughter had always been close, especially while en route to the United States. Having been Miguel's friend for several years, Bernabé probably felt he could easily become part of this extended family, so, when his old buddy, Pascual, arrived, Dad must have felt even more confident. Guadalupe writes that her elder brother Pascual arrived in Sunland in these days because he was unable to find a steady job in the Fresno area, but he told me differently. He claimed he could have gotten a job in the logging camps whenever he wanted to, so we can presume he merely wanted a change of scenery. In any case, his lady friend, Cleofas, joined them in Southern California.

Sunland sits in the northeastern foothills of the broad Los Angeles basin. At the time of this writing, Interstate 210—which funnels speeding automobiles between San Bernardino and the San Fernando Valley—runs nearby, allowing automobile drivers a glimpse of the brush-covered mountains that surround the community as they race along the concrete causeway. In 1924, however, Sunland was a hidden corner of Los Angeles reached only by narrow, winding, backcountry roads. It embraced several neighborhoods built of simple wood-framed dwellings shaded by towering California oaks which once covered much of this land. To this day, visitors can stroll through a sandy dirt park that sits in the middle of these houses, giving the area a sense of rustic, out-of-the-way tranquility.

Thanks to Guadalupe's old boyfriend, Pedro Santiago, the men in our family were able to find a job right away. He led the way and found them a job where he already worked with a local company that distributed natural gas, so he got them in. Pooling their money together, my mother wrote that they "were able to rent a good-sized house with a second floor near the park." As she had several children, one of Cleofas's family members, Celestina, also arrived in Sunland to join the family. When I was growing up, we visited the park often and invariably dropped in on old friends, including Celestina, who became a lifelong friend with our elders, but little did I know my parents were also reaching back to happier times this way. I simply considered Sunland a favorite place of rest and recreation for my parents, but Mary and Manuel made the connection, the rest of us kids just scampering about unknowingly. "We all lived together there and spent New Year's Eve of 1925 there," my mother recalled. It must have been a happy year end get-together.

After a few months, however, the big, happy family was unable to stay together. It began to break apart mainly for economic reasons. The jobs at the gas company soon disappeared, forcing the young men in our family to have to search for work elsewhere. The city of Los Angeles, with barely a million inhabitants in 1925, and probably offering more jobs than Sunland, lay only ten miles to the south, but our immigrant relatives didn't know anyone there, apparently. The consultation of any want ads in the newspapers didn't seem to play a role in their job searches most probably because nearly all of the newspapers were printed in English and our pioneers were as yet uninformed about printed job ads in any case. Obtaining information via newspapers was still an unfamiliar method for our pioneers. Except for Mother who could read in Spanish, they were not that literate either. Word of mouth is what drove our young workers, and this took them back to Central California once again, about two hundred miles away. True to his word, Pascual returned to the logging camps up in the sierra where he enjoyed plenty of contacts while the others fanned out in different directions. Bernabé and Miguel, for example, returned to Bakersfield, where they found a job delivering ice to railcars that transported perishable goods, before the arrival of Freon and other types of non-ice refrigerants. A family photograph marked with the words "Bakersfield 1926" shows young Miguel standing beside thirty-eight other rough-hewn workers like himself, wielding heavy-looking tongs ready to carry large blocks of ice.

After a while, my father, Bernabé, wrote his new bride to join him in Bakersfield, and Mom didn't think twice—she packed her bags right away. "I didn't even tell him when I was coming," she wrote in her memorial notes. She said good-bye to her mother and boarded the train. She remembered arriving at the Bakersfield train station, telephoning him at work and his picking her up and happy at seeing her again. They resumed their life as a newly married couple in a small duplex where they enjoyed some Spanish-speaking neighbors. Mother remembered their names very clearly: Ciriaco, Amanda, and their children. They all became friends right away.

Life for Bernabé and Guadalupe in the Bakersfield duplex, short as it was, unfolded in the middle of the so-called era of Prohibition, when federal law declared the manufacture and consumption of liquor in any form a punishable offense.[54] This prohibition of an age-old behavior lasted thirty-four years and naturally inspired many individuals to make their own spirits. Hollywood movies and television serials capitalized on this odd period in American history with such figures as the straight-arrow Elliott Ness, a federal agent, ever searching for liquor smugglers like the gun-toting Al Capone. In any case, the next-door neighbor in the duplex, Ciriaco, turned out to be a bootlegger too, a maker of the illegal spirits, one of thousands across the country. In the Mexican communities, people like him were called *bulégues* or *buleguеros* (based on "bootlegger"), and, like so many others, he made raisin-based liquor with the aide of a still. This was, in any case, the kind of liquor that Mother (who easily could have been an ax-wielding anti-moonshiner herself) identified with her old neighbor. He sold it on the sly, and sometimes Bernabé helped his neighbor manufacture the booze. "They would work at night," Guadalupe wrote many years after Bernabé's death, "in order to avoid people smelling the aroma." This might help explain why I have a vague recollection of an unmarked wine jug sitting under the kitchen sink when I was about six years old, perhaps a hidden nod to Bacchus which I would come to appreciate as an adult. In any case, my parents moved away, closer to downtown, leaving Ciriaco and his family behind—Mom must have felt good about their finding a new address not relishing living next door to illegal winemakers.

In 1926, my parents were already reporting mounting economic stress not only for themselves but for those around them as well. In her notes, Guadalupe mentioned families who lived nearby with hungry children and, of course, the great difficulty in finding jobs three full years before the panic of 1929. This is the year when the Great Depression is said to have started, eventually causing millions of jobs to disappear. What might explain my mother's claim that jobs were noticeably disappearing in California in 1926 was the fact that agriculture did not profit from the "good times" usually attributed to the 1920s, when waves of ever-mounting speculation on the stock markets reached a pinnacle and then came crashing down three years later.

The Depression might have gotten an early start in agricultural areas. Newspapers reported "labor surpluses" in different parts of California, but it seems they had a keener focus on industrial workers rather than agricultural ones.[55] A distinguished investigator of Mexican Americans in the 1930s confirms that "agriculture was one of the earliest casualties of the economic crisis" and that "the San Joaquin Valley and Imperial Valley declined even before the stock market crash."[56] Guadalupe did not refer to the unnerving markets that were all too familiar to men who could invest their surplus money, but she noticed widening poverty among folks like herself, and this might have been one of the reasons why people like Ciriaco engaged in selling liquor under the table, and why my father chose to help him out. Of course, having access to liquor under your own table when you couldn't buy it in the store probably helped a lot too!

In reference to those days in Bakersfield, Guadalupe wrote that "the Depression had arrived," like saying its front end was visible. It was three full years ahead of the crash of 1929, but she clearly remembered that Bernabé searched high and low for work and couldn't find a job. At one point, he found a job in another ice-making factory in Bakersfield—a job similar to Miguel's—but it didn't last very long.

While looking for employment in the midst of a worsening job market, my father seems to have been talked into a deal he couldn't resist. Guadalupe explains:

> At times he would help a nearby cobbler repair shoes. To make matters worse, he agreed to buy a small but brand-new house, plus six home lots in a place called Tijuanita! We even moved into the house! What I mean is that it should have been one, or two! But six! This is explained by the fact that everything was so cheap in those days. But Bernabé didn't have a job! So in order to make the payments, he even began shining shoes! He also resorted to selling sno-cones. One day he said, "Let's go pick cotton." But we didn't earn more than a dollar [a day]. They paid it at one and a half cents a pound. Sometimes we didn't even have a dime to buy bread! He would earn a quarter and

bring it to me so that I'd buy what we needed!

It seems my father was talked into a hasty decision, one hastened, no doubt, by the pressure of the worsening economic situation hitting closer to home. Slick salesmen preying on vulnerable buyers contributed to this unbelievable situation as well. Whether Mexican American workers who were only beginning to learn the ropes of how a market-driven economy functions were targeted, as my dad was, is not possible to know at this time. In any case, my mother avoids taking him to task in her memoirs and simply explains, "We abandoned the godforsaken lots with the little house because there was nothing to pay them with!" *"Dejamos los dichosos lotes con casita porque no había con que pagarlos!"*

Pascual's rangy pluckiness got them out of their economic bind apparently. He wrote Bernabé at this time, urging him to join him high up in the California sierra, east of Fresno, where he was working for a logging and lumber company. He claimed to be working as a foreman at an enterprise later described as ambitious, farsighted, but badly managed. This was the Sugar Pine Lumber Company (SPL) launched in the early 1920s by millionaire developers and lumbermen who invested more money into the venture than was needed, an over investment that reportedly led the way to its early demise.[57] In the meantime, the SPL built a modern milling center in Pinedale, immediately north of Fresno, to which logs from the nearby sierras were brought and cut into lumber. The logs were loaded onto special railroad cars that rode down the mountains on tracks owned by a separate SPL division called the Minarets and Western Railway Company. My uncle Pascual apparently worked for the latter division, and this is why he referred to the business that employed him as "Minarets."[58] He seems to have been unaware of the larger financial and organizational nature of the company for which he worked.

Pascual told me he was in charge of teams of men who transported timber that had been cut high in the mountains and brought down into the valley for milling in Pinedale, apparently. The work required binding hulking logs—each about thirty feet long—with steel cable onto flat railroad cars, six or seven at a time, and making sure that their weight and arrangement was properly balanced before riding them down the curving rails. If the cars were not loaded properly, the logs would fly off and cause the wreckage of both cars and rails—and men too, sometimes. My uncle mailed a post card photograph of a rail car loaded with the giant logs to Carlota, his mother, in these days, in which he scribbled a note in his untutored Spanish, "Mom, this is a logging car and I'm in this group of people." *("Mama, heste he un tren logero ý hen hese grupo de jente me ýencuentro llo.")*

Hank Johnston, who penned the history of the Sugar Pine Lumber Company, writes that Bob Haag, "perhaps the only survivor among the company's former railroad employees," whom he was able to interview made the very same observations as my uncle. He told Johnston that "derailments and wrecks occurred all the time on the logging lines . . . Since most of the routes were temporary, track laying and grading were rudimentary, to say the least, and this improper rail line work helped cause derailments."[59] So my *tío* Pascual wasn't exaggerating when he described log laden cars flying off on a curve, and Haag wasn't "the only survivor" either—my uncle was a survivor too. Moreover, Johnston's book often mentions lumberjacks and rail workers but never consents to the fact that many, if not most, were Mexican workers, just like *tío* Pascual.

Sometime in April 1927, while there was still snow on the ground, my parents drove their Ford automobile about ninety miles into the mountains east of Fresno and arrived at Camp 9 in a large network of SPL logging camps. This is where Dad took a job repairing the rail line that was frequently torn from the many wrecks that took place. Pascual worked in Camp 11, farther up the sierra.[60]

In these small communities, five thousand feet above sea level amidst pine forests, my mother, Guadalupe, joined forces with Pascual's lady friend, Cleofas, by making tortillas and feeding Mexican-style meals to many Camp 9 workers—for a fee, no doubt. This suggests that many Mexican workers chose not to eat at the "cookhouse" where all workers obtained their meals, American-styled food no doubt. They preferred their *guisados* (meat dishes cooked in pepper and tomato sauces) served with beans, rice, and tortillas, and possibly even enchiladas and tamales on the weekends. She discovered she could work under intense pressure while keeping her head about her because one day she was forced to do the work entirely on her own. The provisions or groceries to make the meals and lunches (the raw meat and vegetables, flour for making tortillas, etc.) were usually shipped up to the camp by train from Wishon, the nearest commercial center, but this time the shipment failed.[61] It thus became necessary for Cleofas to make the run herself. Guadalupe remembered, "She had to go to Fresno on an emergency and said to me, 'You stay and give the men their meals.'" Cleofas took the train to Wishon and Guadalupe held the fort. "Well, I don't know how I did it, but I did it!" Guadalupe recalled. She prepared the meals and served the men all by herself, and this sense of personal accomplishment came to mind in her old age when she wrote her life story for me. The experience would also help her decide whether she could handle a restaurant of her own, as we'll see.

Bernabé ran into trouble again while working in the California sierras. A cousin named Francisco,[62] working in Wishon, invited him down one day, and Bernabé, happy to make the connection, went to visit him. "This was the cousin who often suggested he [Bernabé] return home [to Mexico]," my mother noted. Being the young, hardworking men that they were and not having seen each other for a long time, they punctuated their reunion with some bootlegged whiskey "which the Indians came down to sell"—despite Prohibition laws, my mother recalled. In his study of these logging communities, Johnston omits mentioning this sort of extramural activity. They undoubtedly had a grand time reminiscing about their hometown and the old folks left behind, especially after they began to get sozzled. "*Se fueron de parranda,*" she termed it, which means they had a great boozing time. Mom noted in her handwritten notes that they sang their lungs out on their way home, "*hicieron una guasanga,*" and created the rumpus that heavy imbibing can encourage between friends—in this case, relatives. As they returned to the camp, walking along the train tracks, some guards stopped them just long enough to quiet them down and ask who they were and where they worked. Having answered the questions, they were let free to waddle along in a quieter mode. When they arrived home, the cousin didn't stay and managed to get back to Wishon somehow. The next morning, though, despite the achy and dreadful hangover that my father must have felt, some guards arrived at the door and asked him to accompany them. They seized him and turned him over to the police department in the town of Madera down below. He was charged with violating Prohibition laws because he was carrying a bottle of liquor when the guards stopped him. His cousin got away scot-free.

My mother makes no further comments about this incident other than the fact that the next day Bernabé's supervisor offered her a car and driver and encouraged her to bail him out, which she did. "It took us over four hours just to get to Madera," she noted dryly.

Bernabé and Guadalupe lived and worked in this region approximately seven months. She remembered that at the end of the season, marked by approaching snow, they became desperate to leave the mountain camps even though she had come to recognize the area itself was "quite beautiful," no doubt referring to the majesty of its evergreen covered mountains. She doesn't exactly say why they were anxious to leave, but it isn't too difficult to guess that Guadalupe longed to join her mother once again and return to warmer climes.

Returning to Southern California didn't take very long. As the cooler weather gained strength, Guadalupe learned that Carlota and Juárez had moved from Sunland, where they had lived in a big roomy house, to a nearby community known as San Fernando, about fifteen or so miles north. At their first opportunity, the newlyweds said good-bye to Pascual and Cleofas, who weren't ready to leave the sierras yet, and drove down the mountains in their Ford automobile, heading south about two hundred miles to the city of San Fernando.

SLP log rail car (ca. 1925)

Pascual at age 29

. . . Viejo barrio, Barrio Viejo,
Que en mi infancia te gozé.
Y con todos mis amigos,
Iba descalzo y a pié.

. . . Dicen que eramos pobres,
Pues yo nunca lo noté.
Yo era feliz en mi mundo,
De aquel barrio que adoré.[63]

("Barrio Viejo" written and sung by Lalo Guerrero in Ry Cooter, *Chavez Ravine,* Nonesuch 7559798772)

Part II

Putting Down Roots

Chapter 7

Settling in San Fernando
(1874–1927)

How San Fernando Grew Up • Why They Might Have Chosen San Fernando • San Fernando and Our Barrio in 1927 • *La vecindad* • Work in San Fernando

IN THE PRECEDING chapter, Guadalupe, my recently married mother, unexpectedly left her own mother, stepfather, and brother in Sunland to join my dad in Fresno at the beginning of 1927, if only for a short while. The reason was that the newlyweds couldn't live apart. Grandma was probably unhappy with the way that her daughter was behaving, having eloped in the first place, and now darting away once more with seemingly little forethought. She must have said to herself many times, "These youngsters just don't seem to learn from the mistakes of their elders!"

What is certain in any case is that Grandmother and Juárez, with Miguel tagging along, made the important move that would provide us with a hometown. They relocated to San Fernando, where Mom and Dad joined them a few months later, insuring that this would be where my siblings and I would be born and raised and where my ancestors would ultimately live to their last days.

Why did they settle in San Fernando? Settling there seems to have represented a chance at economic stability and finding our place in the sun, so to speak. Mother explained that the three of them—her mother, brother, and Juárez— moved because they couldn't afford to continue renting the big Sunland house which they had so happily contracted when they all came together a few months earlier. The biggest reason for the move, however, seems to have hinged on the fact that Miguel and Juárez couldn't find a steady job in Sunland and they both concluded somehow that San Fernando offered this opportunity. Unfortunately none of them stated exactly why they chose San Fernando leaving it up to us to speculate about it.

In contrast to the asphalted and cemented suburban jungle of today, San Fernando stood as a small community basking in the sunny desert of the north valley. When our pioneers moved there from Sunland, wheat was still grown and harvested in the ever expanding land patches ripped from the desert floor although much of the "developed" land was already giving way to lemons, oranges, and grapefruit—and more workers were needed. The sunny dryness of the San Fernando Valley contributed largely to the rise of the citrus-growing industry there and, as we'll see, became world famous. This business of growing oranges and lemons affected our lives without a doubt.

Let us briefly review how this northern part of the San Fernando Valley developed into an essential citrus bowl that presented job possibilities for the men in my family.

How San Fernando Grew Up

Despite the fact that our hometown was given the very fitting moniker of "The Mission City," San Fernando, as it turns out, can only claim a more prosaic beginning. It started as a railroad town like many other communities across the United States.

The nearby San Fernando Mission obviously provided the town fathers many decades later with the opportunity to link the city with the venerable historical monument built nearby when California belonged first to Spain and then later to Mexico. Its adobe-filled walls stood as the highest edifice in the northern rim of the San Fernando Valley for more than a generation, bravely resisting all of what Mother Nature could throw at them, but its massive ramparts eventually surrendered to the hot desert winds of summer and the eroding rain of winter, and to man's neglect, above all. The point is that the mission came first while the city followed much later.[64]

In 1797, the mission had been positioned by its Spanish builders at the northern end of a "very pleasant and spacious valley."[65] These are the words attributed to Gaspar de Portolá, probably the earliest European to set foot in the San Fernando Valley as he explored the possibilities of erecting missions in California to keep the English and the Russians away. Seventy-seven years later, after Spain lost control of Mexico and California, the foundations of the city of San Fernando[66] were excavated on some of the agricultural land that had once belonged to the now crumbling mission. It is in this sense that our hometown boasts the right to be called a mission city. The city was raised on mission lands.

Clifford M. Zierer, a geography professor from nearby UCLA who studied and wrote about San Fernando in 1934, affirms that "When it was assured, in 1874, that the main valley line of the Southern Pacific Railroad was to be completed between Bakersfield and Los Angeles through Fremont Pass, a group of capitalists purchased the north half of the San Fernando Valley from its Mexican owners and promptly started a town along the railroad near the early mission settlement."[67] San Fernando was thus induced by a rail line. That same year, the rail line snaked north out of Los Angeles and through the Glendale Gap[68] near present-day Burbank, ending up at the spot where San Fernando arose because the mountains immediately north blocked its northward access. Newhall and Saugus sitting atop of a wall of mountains were no more than dusty mountain crossroads connected by dirt trails in those days. A real estate flyer from these early years confirmed as much:

> A section of the Southern Pacific Railroad of California, connecting Los Angeles with San Fernando, and making the latter its northern terminus, was thrown open to general business on the May 1, 1874; and this is the stimulus that has made it necessary to lay out a town . . .

The phrase "a town" referred to San Fernando combined with land from an adjacent property known as San Fernando Ranch or Rancho Maclay owned by Sen. Charles Maclay.[69] W. W. Robinson, a clerk enjoying access to land records, wrote in 1938 that Maclay was the founder of San Fernando because in that year he "paid a visit to the county recorder in Los Angeles on the afternoon of September 15, 1874. He carried with him for recording a subdivision map showing streets, blocks, and several thousand twenty-five-foot lots . . . labeled 'Map of San Fernando.'"[70]

What we have then is the fact that the new city served as a terminus for the Southern Pacific rail line between 1874 and 1876. This gave Senator Maclay the opportunity to host many Anglo-American visitors from Los Angeles who arrived by train to view the open lots he offered for sale. His marketing campaign thus contributed to the construction of the first homes built mainly as a result of the senator's development work. He subdivided his Rancho Maclay north of the railroad tracks into town lots and a city was born, mainly of Anglos.[71] The eastern border of these lots extended to Pacoima Creek, which washes gravel and boulders down from the nearby San Gabriel Mountains to this day, and for this reason Maclay's house lots went no further east.[72] The desert community of Pacoima was later organized east of the creek or wash.

The new settlement soon included a Hispano family: Gerónimo and Catalina López, descendants of the majordomo of the old San Fernando Mission. They built a ten-room two-story Spanish colonial mansion near the center of the embryonic town, now a historic site known as the Lopez Adobe.[73] Other notable early homes were also constructed like the Henry C. Hubbard house, for example, built near Fourth Street and Brand Boulevard.[74] Hubbard, whose name graces an important roadway in the city today, became one of the earliest Anglos to begin farming former mission land alongside an Iowan named Francis Marion ("Bud") Wright and together they opened up Paxton Ranch near Pacoima and the Hawk Ranch near what is now Northridge.[75] City buildings like the First Methodist Church, the San Fernando Hotel, and a handful of saloons provided deeper roots for the new English-speaking settlers who agreed to purchase formerly mission desert land in the new community. This is how they made a concerted effort to recreate in San Fernando the same atmosphere of the towns they left behind in Illinois, Iowa, and other such places.

A tunnel that would permit the rail line to push north, connecting San Fernando with middle and Northern California didn't wait long; it was opened up in 1876. The extended rail line thus set off travel to Bakersfield via San Fernando and Tehachapi, allowing businessmen, ranchers, and tourists passage all the way from Los Angeles. This spurred the city's growth and its incorporation in 1911.[76]

When my mother and father arrived to join Grandma and Juárez in 1927, San Fernando, embracing about seven thousand inhabitants at the time, had been operating as a rural settlement for about fifty-three years and sixteen as an incorporated city.[77] Physically separated from the larger and older city of Los Angeles, it grew up as one of the first urban communities in the San Fernando Valley, followed closely by Burbank and Glendale. Except for some farms and orchards, the valley still lay garbed in the dark green chaparral that reveled along the creeks and gullies that drew moisture from the winter rains. My dad seems to have owned a 1922 Chevrolet sedan ('the world's lowest priced four-door sedan') in 1927, and it looks like he could drive south on US 99 with practically no stops all the way to the Glendale Gap and head from there to the *plazita* marking the heart of the city of the angels. There were few if any settlements to slow him down.

Why They Might Have Chosen San Fernando

Everything indicates that our *viejos* chose this relatively new urban settlement because of the citrus jobs it was already offering, as we'll see below. My ancestors could have gone elsewhere in Southern California but they didn't. Could there have been another reason for their choosing what turned out to be our home town, beyond the employment opportunities?

San Fernando counted two groups of Spanish speakers or Hispanos in 1927 who might have given my ancestors a sense of welcome.[78] One was the Spanish-speaking Californios[79] like the aforementioned López family. These were folks of Spanish-Mexican origin who settled in the valley many years before 1848 and eked out a living in grand isolation on their giant properties that were mostly undeveloped. It could be said that they held Alta California[80] until the Mexican American war when the American armies arrived to assert US control against Mexican authority. The general view is that these families lost all or most of their land eventually but stayed on and, as in many communities in the new southwest like San Fernando, they held on as best they could, some doing better than others. This explains why the Lopezes, the Rinaldis and the Picos are mentioned when discussing this early period in the valley.[81] It seems that some of them became part of the leading families in the region. Andrés Pico, for example, is said to have owned the entire valley after the war. A local historian claims that he lived in the main mission building often enough to entertain lavishly in its large, adobe-lined rooms; in 1858, after the hostilities, he became a brigadier general in the California Militia and also served as a state senator a few years later.[82]

When my parents arrived, some of these Californios still held remnants of the more extensive ranching properties they commanded seventy-some years earlier. Eager to nod to this legacy, the San Fernando Valley Chapter of the Daughters of the American Revolution commissioned a photograph of thirty-four members of these families for inclusion in a 1924 book paid for by a member of the Porter family, cofounders of San Fernando, along with Senator Maclay.[83] For this photograph, they rounded up about three generations of the local Californios; they all crowded into the eye of the lens, looking at the photographer as a proud assembly of seemingly well-heeled folks of the era.

So the question is, might my ancestors have chosen San Fernando because they learned about the survival and presence of these earlier Hispanos and figured they might gain an advantage somehow, treated better, perhaps?

The answer is, probably not.

A gulf seems to have separated the Spanish speakers, old and new. Many Californios seem to have stepped away from the newly arrived Mexican workers like my folks whom they began calling *cholos*, considered a contemptuous term. The perceptive journalist-turned-historian Carey McWilliams informs us that the word *cholo* was used by the Californio elite long before the arrival of workers like my family, and the term was used pejoratively to mean simple workers and herders.[84] In other words, it was a derisive term implying uncouth and low-class, so we are pressed to believe that they simply reapplied the label after the Mexican American war to the workers who began arriving from Mexico. It seems safe to say that many old Spanish speakers probably did not welcome anyone like my ancestors perhaps because they considered themselves more Spanish than Mexican, and this meant better, somehow, despite the fact that most of them had lost most of their land to the Anglos whom they seemed to have admired nevertheless. Regardless, the relation between these two Hispano communities at this time is not well charted. So it would be interesting to define with more precision what receptivity the Mexicans of 1927, like my ancestors, might have received from their fellow Spanish speakers who survived the American conquest seventy-five years after the war.

The other reason that may have attracted my ancestors in 1927, perhaps more so than the first, is that many Mexican immigrants like my own folks had already arrived in San Fernando by this time. They had formed a *colonia*, a part of town all their own, so to speak. Like my family, they had arrived in search of jobs and family stability. What Zierer wrote about them in 1934 holds true to this day, namely that they represented "workers . . . willing to do all kinds of jobs as the needs arise."[85] Indeed, in 1927, they stood ready to work as directed by the early English-speaking residents of San Fernando and, in this way, helped them build up San Fernando and the rest of California, as they continue to do at the time of this writing.

San Fernando and Our Barrio in 1927

In 1927, San Fernando with about seven thousand inhabitants already displayed the broad urban outlines that I came to know as a child later, in the 1940s.[86] For example, the township was already divided into two halves by the Southern Pacific rail line and US 99, both of which ran side by side at this point in their trajectory, in a northwest to southwest slant that continues to tilt the entire urban grid. The northeastern side of the town, closer to the rugged San Gabriel Mountains, held the *americanos* living on the first lots initially opened by Senator Maclay.

The avenue bearing the senator's name now intersects US 99 at right angles and stretches northeasterly from the highway toward the rugged, chaparral-covered foothills. In 1927, Maclay Boulevard acted as a commercial backbone for the English-speaking community much as it did when I was a boy. As early as 1918, the boulevard was already embellished by commercial enterprises, including a bank, a drugstore, grocery stores, meat shops, furniture stores, and churches built of quarried stone like the First Presbyterian Church at the corner of Second Street, and the M[ethodist] E[piscopal] Church on Third Street; the Morningside Public School could also be found at the corner of Fifth Street and Maclay. Attractive cottages and homes, shaded by leafy trees reminiscent of the Midwest, stood within a block on either side of the boulevard.[87]

The *mexicanos* lived on the southwestern side, literally "on the other side of the tracks." This is where our barrio was located although the word *colonia* was also used widely at the time. In 1948, McWilliams noticed that Mexican Americans tended to live "inadvertently 'on the other side' of something: a railroad track, a bridge, a river, or a highway."[88] Our barrio was circumscribed by the railroad tracks and San Fernando Road on the northeast side, by Mission Boulevard which extended southeast toward the old mission from US 99, lined with some of the city's finest homes, Huntington Street providing the northwest boundary which stretched down to some open pastures and orchards beginning where La Rinda Plaza is located now, and Amboy Street which acted as the south or southwestern edge of the city. Its high poplar trees marked the end of the barrio; you could see them from San Fernando Road looking down Kalisher Street. These trees seemed to act as windbreakers for the countless orchards that spread southwest from town in the direction of the old *misión* and what is now Granada Hills and Northridge. Today Interstates 5 and 405 funnel millions of vehicles speeding to the north or south where these orange trees used to stand. In any case, my parents and other Mexican immigrant families found housing more easily in this Spanish-speaking rectangle on the southwest side of town.

About five years after Grandma and the others in my family arrived, Zierer found the barrio to include "the most crowded and the least attractive residential district in which nearly all the Mexican population [was] found."[89] Here were the smallest of the residential homes in the city, most of them built on lots with twenty-five-foot fronts. Few, if any, streets were paved and almost none had sidewalks like what you could find on the other side of the tracks, the Anglo side. Luxuriant shading trees that harked back to the Midwest were absent here. According to Zierer, a geographer, 40 percent of the city's population was crowded into 10 percent of the city's municipal jurisdiction.[90] The city fathers clearly favored *their* part of town on *their* side of the tracks with the plentiful greenery and the municipal infrastructure that made life easier. A student of the first Mexican communities in California, like San Fernando, concludes that many of these Mexican "villages," as he calls them, were built by citrus fruit companies in order to attract and hold on to workers. My sources do not yet confirm the development of company villages in our hometown, though the citrus industry played a central role locally as we'll see below.[91]

Our side of town sheltered more people per square mile and encircled shabbier housing than the Anglo side but it also boasted a touch of diversity which seemed absent on *their* side. While Blacks were rare to behold, our barrio harbored Japanese residents, for example. Our family lore is quite clear about this and it favors the residents as being Japanese, not Chinese, although the 1930 census unveiled the presence of a number of Chinese and Filipino immigrants. In any case, our lore includes numerous references to *el Jadi*,[92] the supposed Japanese owner of a two-story wood building still standing at 1248 Griffith Street. My father rented business space from him in the late 1930s, as we'll see below, so our knowledge here is anchored on personal experience; other *chapos* or persons of Japanese origin were widely believed to have resided in that building. Another example of Asians living among us before World War II was the shopkeeper of a weather-beaten grocery store located on the northeast corner of Kalisher and Hewitt Streets. He was a gray-haired Asian man who attended to me several times when my mother sent me there on grocery errands. I remember approaching the open storefront door and seeing him sitting right in the middle of the doorway looking out on the street, presumably ready to greet his customers but he could've been musing about his life in America or back home. Many years later, I came to realize that this Asian man was replaced by one of the older men in the Barragán family after World War II so I never saw him again—the Barraganes, a large family with a bunch of boys who corresponded age-wise to me and my brothers, were well-known members at Santa Rosa Catholic Church. Several of us in the family also remember a large agricultural field tended by Asian workers from time to time; it stood on the city lot now occupied by the Santa Rosa Catholic School. We used to walk across the field when the earth there was fallow. Perhaps the church obtained this lot from Japanese owners.

These remembrances of Asians living quietly within our barrio were reaffirmed by a remarkable set of archival materials. Here I refer to the field notes compiled by fire insurance representatives who scrutinized every building in the city of San Fernando from 1922 to 1923, presumably for fire hazards. Their investigation produced a large book filled with, what I call, pictographs of the edifices standing in San Fernando in those years, each building symbolized on the large book sheets by a hand-drawn square marked with the street address, the composition of the building materials, and the type of business or activity conducted therein. For example, the fire insurance agents uncovered the presence of a "Japanese school" at 1335 Woodworth Street.[93] The elder members in my family didn't know about this school, not even my sister Mary who stored scores of anecdotes in her head about people and families living in our barrio during her growing up years.

The pictographs provide other details worthy of note at the same time that they confirm our reminiscences. They're instructive about the businesses in our barrio. These were found primarily on two streets: Kalisher Street and Mission Boulevard, an unchanged pattern twenty-five years later when I was a boy walking these same streets. Most of the shops and cafés that served our Spanish-speaking community, however, were found on Kalisher Street; here was the retail service backbone of the barrio. Unfortunately, Mexican American studies have yet to analyze businesses that operated within the hundreds of barrios spread throughout the American Southwest, so there is little printed material allowing a comparative perspective on our barrio business strip. In any case, Kalisher Street, which remains a one-mile ribbon of asphalt stretching southwest from San Fernando Road, held most of the Mexican American *comercios*.

Somewhat like Maclay Boulevard on the Anglo side of town, on Kalisher Street a visitor could find a variety of small businesses and places of worship with greater texture and color to be sure. Santa Rosa Catholic Church, providing services in Spanish to the burgeoning barrio, was raised on Kalisher and Hewitt and inaugurated only two years prior to the arrival of my ancestors.[94] Kalisher Street would also come to provide the southeastern perimeter of the Catholic school that the good fathers at Santa Rosa would decide to erect on what used to be an open agricultural field, as I've already mentioned; it would rise at the intersection of Kalisher and Mott. Stores and cafés for Spanish speakers were also strung along this street in addition to the inevitable drinking taverns and saloons and our own tortilla making shop. The church, the school, and these businesses are discussed in greater detail in Chapter 12.

La vecindad

After they left their Sunland residence in 1927, Grandma, Juárez, and my uncle Miguel, found lodging in *la vecindad,*[95]a peculiar Mexican immigrant microcosm located a half a block from Kalisher Street, right in the heart of the barrio. The reader may remember that Mom and Dad arrived from Fresno soon thereafter and they moved into a *vecindad* apartment next door to Grandma's and Juarez's, satisfying Mother's perennial desire to live near her mother. Other immigrant workers like my folks also resided here as we'll see.

La vecindad looms large in our family lore. On the material side of things, it refers to a street-level apartment complex located in the middle of the block formed by Kewen, Hewitt, Kalisher, and Mission Streets. The main feature we remembered took the form of an eighty-foot-long, wood-framed building partitioned into about ten two-room "apartments," each of these rooms measuring approximately 10 sq. ft.[96] My brother Manuel, who lived in the *vecindad* as a child, insists that (ca. 1940) the main building was one of three long multiunit apartment buildings. "*Eran tres viviendas* [of the long kind]," he claimed. In any case, the main one-floor main building was still standing at 1224 Hewitt Street at the time of this writing, though noticeably remodeled. Each apartment in this building opened into a common porch that faced a large open dirt yard in 1927. This covered deck, fashioned from rough, simple wooden boards, provided the residents with a comforting veranda, allowing them to look over the open enclosure and still be protected from the biting sun in summer and the drizzly rain in the winter. My sister Mary reserved some special memories about this open enclosure as we'll see below. The residential complex also included a manager's house facing Kewen Street, a detail that would later bring special meaning to us. At the time of this writing, a person could still follow a pathway across the middle of the block from Hewitt to Kewen and pass alongside the tiny apartments that filled up this eighty-foot building, a place that contributed heavily to our past.

When keen-eyed McWilliams reconnoitered the southwest in preparation for his celebrated book about Mexican Americans, he noted this kind of overcrowded form of housing in Los Angeles and elsewhere in the southwest. He referred to this kind of shelter as "house courts." He found them to be "a sort of tenement made up of a number of one—and two-room dwellings built around a court with a common water supply and outdoor toilets."[97] It may be said that my ancestors along with the thousands of other Mexican Americans who lived in dwellings similar to those described by McWilliams came to form the Southern California version of the "huddled masses" so poignantly proclaimed by Emma Lazarus except that these spoke Spanish and lived in "house courts" or *vecindades*.[98] It's noteworthy too that the Sanborn Insurance employees mentioned earlier did not overlook our *vecindad* when they surveyed the city. They properly marked it as a "Mexican tenement." In fact, they also uncovered nine other "Mexican tenements" in our barrio.

My eldest sister, Mary, introduces us to the other element connected to our *vecindad*—the socio-cultural dimension. Mary was born in this small and friendly ghetto-within-a-ghetto of Mexican families in 1928, and my two eldest brothers were also born there, Manuel being one of them. Mary's earliest memories, perhaps her fondest, are tied to this place because my family lived there until she was about ten years old:

> *La vecindad* was a big house with ten or twelve apartments. My mother and father lived in apartment 1, and my grandfather and grandmother lived in 2 . . . Apartment 1 was the first unit coming in from Hewett Street—the bedroom and living room were located as you go in the front door, and the kitchen made up the second room. Sometimes you'd see a bed in the kitchen. Mike[99] was [also] born there. They [Mom and Dad] put a steel baby bed for him [in the kitchen]— I [also] remember that my mother had a very beautiful and clean bedroom which [also] served as the living room. She had a very beautiful satin bedspread.[100]

Mary also remembers the open lot that stood in front of the long veranda. Her memory informs us that it served multiple purposes, one of which was to provide a place to wash clothes. It included a *lavadero*: an open, ground-level concrete washbasin equipped with a water spigot and a drain. It was built low, forcing the *vecindad* women on wash day to kneel around the edge of the six-by-six-foot basin and hand scrub and rinse their laundry. The dirty water would drain into an underground pipe. These are Mary's words:

> It was like a [low level] sink made out of cement with faucets in the corners for water. People who wanted their clothes cleaner and whiter, something they used to be so proud of, would put their *tinas* [galvanized metal tubs] on a wood fireplace near the outdoor toilets, and they would boil their clothes until they were nice and white. They'd come out so soft and beautiful because they'd boil them in the *tinas* that were jet black from the soot! It was so funny [too see this contrast]!

When Carmen Imperial was a little girl—she fell [into one of the fires] and burnt herself badly. When we were children, we were always chasing around [the *tinas*]. *Y luego los tendederos* [And then the laundry lines] were right there too—the wires to hold up the clothes which were anchored on the outhouses. They'd fashion some [long and narrow] boards with a tooth sawed out at one end [the top end] to hold the wire to raise the clothesline [off the ground]—I remember running through the [bed] sheets [that were hanging] and the cool smell [that they gave off]!

Mary reminds us that in her childhood days, the open dirt lot fronting the long veranda also served as a common meeting ground and a place for youngsters to play.

> There were so many children. We'd always gather in the evening. I remember the men would make a bonfire[101] and sit around it and talk, and we would dart here and there [all around them]. Anita Cárdenas would get us together, "Come here and we'll tell some stories!" That was our television, to sit together every night and hear stories. And they would come: Remedios, Lupe Pérez, and Fernando Brigil—Aurora of the Cárdenas family, then Ruben and Anita who was the tallest. We had so many friends, yet we were so poor too! We would play games like *El Matarile, El Agua Té, La Cebollita*, and many others. We used to have a wonderful time, and the evening would go by quickly!

Years later, I would stroll through the *vecindad* pathway, mentioned earlier, on my daily walk to attend grammar school. This would take me from Hewitt Street to Kewen Street past the *lavadero*. Decades later, this communal washbasin would be ripped out and replaced by an apartment building eliminating the open dirt lot where my sister Mary played with her friends, leaving us once more with the feeling of inevitable change—"*todo cambia, nada sigue igual*," as Mother would often say ("everything changes, nothing stays the same").

Another human dimension of the tight physical space of the *vecindad* is that it provided my family with social ties that lasted half a century at least. Mary's remembrances suggest that women especially held on to the relationships more so than men—clearly, women and children formed an integral part of the Mexican immigrant presence in the 1920s. For example, Mary flashed back wistfully, "I remember Ermelinda Luján living there as well as Doña Petra Espinosa and her daughter, Lupe. Lydio Alvarado and his wife lived there too. Alberto Prado likewise lived there and the Cárdenas [family]."[102] She continued, "I must have been about five years old when my grandfather became very ill, and Doña Petrita Pacheco . . . would bring him some tasty biscuits to nourish him—they [the Pacheco family] had been candy makers in Mexico [and therefore knew all about baking]." My sister could have gone on offering more names from her rich memory; still, most of them are preserved, though horribly misspelled, in the 1930 census form filled out by a Frank Richardson on April 10, 1930, including the names of our family as it was that year, and most of the persons named above.[103]

All of these names became familiar to me as well when I was growing up. The Espinosa women, who moved out of the *vecindad* years later, as we did, were steady churchgoers and helped Grandma Carlota make *cascarones* (confetti-filled egg shells) for the church bazaars. Ermelinda Luján and her husband, a musician, bought a house on the edge of town where I went to him for my first lessons in playing a string base. When I became a young man with my own automobile, I visited Lydio Alvarado, also a musician on the side, who moved from the *vecindad* to Oakland, where he and I played and sang in several cafés and bars of his choice—he strumming a mandolin and I a guitar. I knew many of the Pachecos, and my first teenage crush was, in fact, on one of the Pacheco girls. The point is that all of these relationships cultivated in the crowded "house courts" which we called *la vecindad* lasted a lifetime for the women in my family and also served me at one time in my life.

Work in San Fernando

Above and beyond the human relationships that my ancestors might have formed in the *vecindad*, the rent had to be paid and food and clothing had to be purchased. This meant someone had to work; luckily, San Fernando offered plenty of jobs in 1927, and, as I've already stated, this is probably the biggest reason why my ancestors made this town their own—and ultimately ours, too. Let us consider San Fernando's economic development for a moment.

In the days of the California dons (the Spanish and Mexican periods), the northern half of the San Fernando Valley was devoted to grazing mission cattle. Most, if not all, of the southwesterly sloping surface of the valley was covered in a "sparse growth of cactus, sage, and chaparral with some willows" shading the moist creeks flowing away from the eastern mountains.[104] As mentioned earlier, there were no towns until Senator Maclay created his urban lots.

After Anglo immigrants began arriving in large numbers with their hankering for bread and bisquits (ca. 1875), wheat fields began to spread over the pastures, thus creating the need for workers to bring in the harvests. This might have attracted the first Mexican laborers to San Fernando, although there is no record of this so far. In 1900, after spending the night in the old mission, one of the first American travelers to ride through here on horseback and write about it, noted that in the morning the valley "opened before me in league on league of grain, waving ready for harvest, a crop to be measured by the thousands of tons."[105] This wheat was shipped by rail to Los Angeles and beyond.

The golden oceans of waving grain were increasingly replaced with orange and lemon trees in the first decade of the twentieth century. This is how I remember our part of the valley—mile after mile of orange trees laden with their carrot-colored fruit.

Plenty of water had to be brought to the valley first in order to make it look the way I remember it. Fred Eaton and William Mulholland made all of this possible. Their infamous machinations ultimately brought water from about 240 miles on the other side of the San Gabriel Mountains to irrigate the citrus groves that attracted my ancestors and thousands of other Mexican workers in the 1920s. In 1913, their political brawn made it possible for the aqueous flow to spill in a showy cascade constructed just north of San Fernando for the entire world to see. The torrent coursed all the way from the Owens Valley, against the will of the local folks there.[106] Nevertheless, in November of that year, thousands of Angelenos flocked to San Fernando's northern entrance on US 99 to witness the splashy and wet display that boasted the power of a large and growing city over the needs of a small mountain community and, in doing so, reassured the expansion of the orchards. The sweet smell of orange blossoms, so prevalent in the spring, could now be guaranteed to spread across increasingly larger portions of the San Fernando Valley—and spread it did. This effort helped create lemon and orange picking jobs for Mexican workers like Juárez, Miguel, and my own father.

Once access to water was secured, the wheat fields that had adorned the San Fernando Valley were increasingly replaced with the *limones* and the *naranjos* (the lemon and orange trees). The larger picture is that the valley became part of a bigger network of citrus producing areas, leading to the creation of California's strongest industry in the 1930s. Writing at the time, Zierer noted in reference to the Los Angeles basin that "No other horticultural industry of equal importance in the United States is so compactly situated and no fruit district is more intensively cultivated or more productive of wealth."[107] Specializing on the subject sixty years later, sociologist Gilbert G. Gonzalez concurred, "By the 1930s, citrus was the state's principal agricultural product—" and key to the state's economy. He adds that "from 1890 to 1960, citrus produced more wealth than had gold in California history and ranked only second to the oil industry—"[108] Gonzalez's investigation also reveals, as Zierer had reported earlier, that the first and foremost citrus zones in California clustered around Pasadena, San Gabriel, Whittier, Pomona, Monrovia, Azusa, Corona, Glendora, Upland, Ontario, San Bernardino, Redlands, and Riverside.[109] Like San Fernando, these towns filled up with Mexican workers in the 1920s, and by the 1960s, they represented some of the premiere Mexican American communities in the southland, each with a history of orange and lemon pickers and a social community they could call their own despite the meager income the jobs provided over the years. There is no doubt that the citrus industry also became central to San Fernando, in addition to the towns named above, so it awaits young investigators to study its evolution there and ultimately place it on par with the other cities already named.

Did my ancestors know in 1927 about the citrus picking jobs also available in the Inland Empire that included the towns named above? Probably not. What is certain, though, is that they settled for San Fernando, where thousands of orange and lemon trees needed tending, and this is why we, the Gil children, grew up amidst citrus orchards and still conserve memories that connect our families to the work of the *piscadores*, the citrus fruit pickers.

This, then, is how our family found a place to settle in Southern California. After months of going hither and thither in search of a steady job, San Fernando appeared to offer the promise of longer work stretches given the fact that so many lemons and oranges had to be harvested. You could see them practically everywhere, the groves of low dark green trees loaded with fruit in late summer and early winter, stretching out over countless acres waiting for the hand of man. What's more, and as we've seen, San Fernando also provided a harbor for people like my ancestors, with its barrio populated with people who spoke their language and, in many cases, hailed from towns and villages already familiar to them in Mexico. By chance, the chock-full *vecindad* had room for them, and so our precursors settled there first and we children began to arrive.

Miguel with fellow iceworkers (ca. 1926)

Mary at age one in front of vecindad porch (1929)

Bernabé, Carlota holding image, Mary, and Juarez (ca. 1931)

Carlota, Guadalupe, Mary, and Juárez in front of Dad's auto (ca. 1931)

Chapter 8

Life Becomes Evermore Challenging
(1927–1938)

The Fear of Tuberculosis in the Orchards • The Depression and the Repatriation Program • Penny Capitalism Helps and So Does Self-Initiative • Juárez Dies and Carlota Presses On • Grandma's Tortilla Shop • Disaster Strikes but We Make the Best of It •

IN THE PRECEDING chapter we learned that Mother and Father settled into their little apartment in *la vecindad* in San Fernando in 1927. We now know that they arrived just as the American economy was beginning to shed jobs, having seen already that Guadalupe took notice of the growing number of agricultural workers in the Fresno area losing their jobs. Nevertheless, we, their children, began arriving, one after another. In fact, five of a total of eight Gil children came to this world during the years of the Great Depression. And birth control was simply an unthinkable option for my folks as well as for many Americans at this time.[110]

Hindsight tells us that their happiest time together was already drawing to a close, regrettably! Why? They would experience fewer moments of pure joy because our young couple would be walloped soon not only by the economic downturn that would begin unfolding, perhaps had already started when they arrived in San Fernando, and by us arriving on the scene, we, their newborn children. This would constitute a double whammy that would underscore the need for getting a job at any cost. Having employment would become more critical than ever, especially if you were hanging from the bottom rungs. Our parents would be tested individually, and their marriage would be put to the limit as well.

The Fear of Tuberculosis in the Orchards

As we've noted, jobs were available in San Fernando. Guadalupe didn't forget this contradiction when she remembered that while her husband Bernabé needed a job, he also didn't want to work in the citrus groves surrounding San Fernando and he told her so. These are her words:

> [Herbert] Hoover was elected and jobs became harder to find. This became our worst time ever because Bernabé didn't want to pick lemons even though these jobs didn't disappear [with the Depression]—the rumor was that you caught tuberculosis from them [and men avoided them]. But he had to do that work anyway—what choice did he have?

Mother and others in her circle insisted that tuberculosis was widespread. They said that the workers caught TB and got sick; that one or two workers survived from an entire family. Mother offered the example of the Gascas and the Ceballos. ("*La gente decía que se hacían tuberculosos y sí, mucha gente se enfermaba de eso. De familias enteras quedaban uno o dos [trabajadores] nomás. Allí estaba el ejemplo de los Gascas y los Ceballos.*") It's difficult to fully calibrate her statement. She may have been using "tuberculosis" as a catchall phrase referring to a resistant but crippling, and even fatal malady—not well-understood by the population, perhaps similar to the way Americans employed the word *cancer* in the late 1960s. The fact is that the fear of tuberculosis seems to have been widespread in any case, and this may explain my father's reluctance to work in the orange and lemon groves.

Everyone knew that chemicals were heavily used in those orchards. In fact, large quantities were sprayed on the trees, and workers like my father had to climb into them to pick the fruit. Interestingly, the citrus owners feared poisoning their customers but not the workers who did the harvesting. They were more concerned with creating "a new type of hazard for the consuming public" as a result of the chemicals penetrating the "subsurface" of the fruit than they were about the health of the orchard workers.[111] Indeed, scientists in the Department of Entomology at the University of California at Riverside ascertained that noxious insecticides sprayed on citrus trees could run from 1,000 to 2,500 gallons per acre.[112] They studied over fifty insecticides and acaricides[113] used in citrus orchards, including DDT and malathion, but found little or no danger to the consuming public. They concluded that the chemicals either remained on the surface of the fruit or did not penetrate deeply enough to affect it.

The impact on the workers was not a concern. To this day, we don't know if the fear that lived in the minds of my parents and their neighbors was unfounded. What is certain is that they weren't the only ones in the barrio to harbor it. Were orchard workers like my father more prone to contracting tuberculosis than non-orchard workers? We don't know the answer to this query. Recent scholarship studying Mexican American citrus workers in California seems to overlook this concern.[114] In any case, Dad did not die of tuberculosis in the end.

Parenthetically, a new tuberculosis "sanatorium" was installed in those days on the periphery of the citrus orchards in which my father worked. It appears to have been part of a larger effort at containing "consumption" (a.k.a. tuberculosis), the "single most common cause of death" at the turn of the twentieth century.[115] Seeking to relieve the Los Angeles General County Hospital from some of its tuberculosis patients, Olive View Sanatorium quickly filled up with tubercular patients, many of them "Mexicans."[116] Whether these Spanish-speaking patients contracted tuberculosis from working in the orchards is unknown to me at this time. Curiously, the Sanborn fire insurance analysts mentioned in the previous chapter sketched out a comprehensive layout of the sanatorium complex in 1927.[117]

When my parents arrived in San Fernando, many government officials were in fact concerned about tuberculosis among the Mexican people. Their anxiety triggered one of the earliest studies ever published about "the Mexicans of California," one that was issued by the state governor's office. Unfortunately, its sole purpose was to identify the worst aspects of people like us in San Fernando and other California communities harboring Mexican workers. The report called attention to a string of negative conditions: "the prevalence of tuberculosis among the Mexican population of California," the tendency "to live in colonies retaining [Mexican] traditions [which were] . . . not always satisfactory to his American neighbor," the "rapid increase in the number of Mexican births," high infant mortality rates, and so on.[118] The governor's report was properly condemned decades later as a shameless attempt to control unwanted immigration by emphasizing the negative aspects of the Spanish-speaking population. It seemed that on the one hand, Mexican workers were expected to work in the orchards and become exposed to a variety of chemicals which probably contributed to their frequent illnesses, but on the other, they were pilloried for being sick and weak.

Nevertheless, workers like my father had mouths to feed and bills to pay. Some people might have concluded that he was "lucky" to find work as a *piscador* (a picker) in the orchards at this time—after all, the citrus industry was the big attraction of San Fernando, and it offered jobs even in tough times—and these were certainly tough times and they would get worse. Looking back on these days, my mother sadly observed that Dad had no choice.

Dad's life as a *piscador* became etched in the memory of his children, indeed. His work demanded a routine that became unforgettable for us. He would rise early enough to dress in heavy *mezclilla* or denim clothes, including a Levi jacket for protection from the sun and the thorny branches, eat his breakfast, and get a ride at about 6:00 a.m. The open truck, on which he climbed aboard to stand along with many other *compañeros* early in the morning, probably picked him up at the entrance to the *vecindad* because many citrus workers lived there, as we've seen. Climbing onto the back of the truck, with heavy gloves secured and hat firmly in place, he would balance himself with the aid of his sturdy work boots while the truck bounced along the road headed for a target orchard. He would already be wearing his rough canvas *bolsa*, the bag that would swing from his shoulders all day long. He would also make sure he carried a pair of hand clippers in his pocket and a set of metal rings to measure the diameter of the fruit and thus help him cut the properly sized lemon or orange from the branches before dropping it into the *bolsa*. While riding on the truck, he would protect a black metal lunch box Mom filled with three or four soft tacos (now called burritos) packed alongside a thermos bottle filled with sweet, creamy coffee.

Arriving at the intended orchard about an hour later, sometimes less, his job was well-defined. It consisted of obtaining a heavy wooden ladder in order to begin climbing into the fruit trees with it and picking the proper-sized fruit. His *bolsa*, big enough to hold about fifty pounds,[119] was designed like a large tube that opened and closed with spring-loaded latches at the bottom. After filling it, he would carefully step down and get off the ladder in order to unload the bag into special wooden crates by unlatching the fasteners. The spherical fruit would tumble out with a soft thudding sound. Like his fellow pickers, he would start out working vigorously in order to warm up against the early morning chill. Then, with the heat of the day rising slowly, his heavy work shirt would darken with perspiration leaving behind lacey patterns of salty sweat. Often, the half-hour lunch sitting in the shade of a tree didn't come fast enough. In the end, the daily test was to resist the growing weight of the fruit inside the bag before climbing down to the ground to unload, making sure all the while that you didn't lose your footing on the ladder because falling with a loaded bag was very risky indeed. A sense of relief would usually come around three thirty or four when the majordomo would yell out for all to hear, "*Vamonos a la casa!*" ("Let's go home!")

Like workers everywhere, Dad and his buddies always seemed to find ways to lighten their labor, no matter how hard the job was. They chatted with each other across the trees, telling jokes and engaging in gossip, or just singing to pass the time as they clicked their special scissors to remove the fruit from the trees.

Many years later, when I was little boy, I occasionally accompanied my father to the orchards, and I was thus able to catch a glimpse of his work life and never forget it. He would sit me under a tree, and I would keep an eye on him, always afraid that he would wander too far from me. I would feel a sense of comfort hearing him talk with his fellow *piscadores* or singing his favorite songs. The one we often remember him by was "Cuatro Llantas," a parody of a popular Mexican song entitled "Cuatro Milpas."

Cuatro llantas	(Four tires)
Tan solo han quedado	(Is all that's left)
Del Foringo	(Of the ol' Ford car)
Que era mío	(I used to have)
Ay, ay, ayaai . . . [120]	(Ay, ay, ayaay) . . .

The laborer's truck would wend its way back to San Fernando and drop him off near our house at the end of the day. He would walk home wearily toting his bag, often containing oranges for us. Joyous to see him, my siblings and I would jump on his arms and shoulders as soon as we could reach him. This always tested his physical stamina in trying to remain upright after a tough day in the orchards, but we wouldn't think of this, of course. We've not forgotten the excitement and delight to see him come home nor the smell of his sweaty shirt mixed with the scent of orange peelings, they live in our memory.

The Depression and the Repatriation Program

As noted earlier, the Great Depression found my parents in the *vecindad*. This is where they lived on "Black Thursday," October 24, 1929, when the market executed a frightening free fall that led to a series of additional downward spirals known collectively as "The Wall Street Crash of 1929." Money invested in stocks disappeared, and many fortunes simply evaporated. This collective panic on the part of American investors fueled a widening circle of fearful withdrawals not only from the stock market but also from banks, large and small, making it difficult for factories and offices to remain open and to thus hold on to their workers. Bosses of every type across the country began handing out evermore "pink slips," thereby swelling the ranks of unemployed men in numbers that began to shock the casual observer. Americans lost jobs steadily, and within five months after Black Thursday, more than three million workers had lost their jobs. Local government agencies began doling out food to a growing wave of hungry and needy people who had never known what the word meant. A year later, the estimated number of workers who were now deprived of an income jumped to almost eight million, and by March 1932, about twelve million were jobless.[121] "Hobos" and "tramps" began to roam the country, as my uncle Miguel remembered in an earlier chapter, often riding in open railroad cars like he did. These are terms used when I was growing up to refer to homeless people, mostly single men looking for work or feeling anxious to leave failure behind and always seeking a place to sleep, even under a bridge. Tent communities, which became known as Hoovervilles (named after President Herbert Hoover), began to appear on the edges of many big cities. When the residents in these mushroom villages lacked canvas to block out the cold night air from their shelters, card board and newspaper sufficed. The most fearful years unfolded from 1929 to about 1933.[122]

Mom and Dad, of course, didn't lose any money in the stock market because, like most workers, they owned no stocks or bonds. They may not have known what a company stock was but they could easily measure the effects of the stock market panic around them. As we saw earlier, Mother had already noticed the spreading wave of unemployment in Fresno even before moving south to San Fernando. Here again she noted gloomily that ". . . the Depression that started about 1926 now became barbarous . . . everyone was suffering," she noted. My ancestors had known hard times but now "it wasn't just us," Mom wrote in her memoirs. By 1934, a year after Franklin Delano Roosevelt entered the White House, the country lay prostrate.

Having a steady job picking lemons and oranges in Southern California looked good in this context. My father, Juárez, and Uncle Miguel clung to their picking jobs as long as possible. The bottom line is that Dad's citrus-harvesting work kept our family from the poorhouse. As noted already, many Americans were beginning to depend on public kitchens organized to prevent widespread hunger around the country, but we escaped this experience for the most part. As my mother noted in a following letter to me:

> Roosevelt launched programs called the WPA, and they opened offices so that people could go there to ask for assistance. They gave out food [and] clothing and a lot of

> people benefitted quite well [because] they would send checks to their homes . . . we didn't ask [for anything] because Berna had decided to work picking lemons a short time after Manuel was born.

With one exception, our family lore doesn't include the memory of our parents ever relying on public kitchens or any other kind of public welfare—not even in the Depression. But in another part of her notes, Mother offers a slightly different explanation of why Dad avoided public assistance: "Berna said 'I'm going to go ask for [help]' [but] to avoid asking he later said 'I'll make some cheese [to sell].' He bought milk at the dairy, and we made it [cheese], but it didn't sell well." The exception Mother cites applies to 1939 when Dad was trying to earn money by selling cheese. In any case, Mom writes that ". . . when Marta was born, they laid him off for a few days, then we did [in fact] go for about a month and they gave us a clothing order and a check for seventeen dollars." Otherwise, my parents were able to get by. They didn't feel the pressure of the repatriation program either.

The "repatriation program" refers to an effort by various governmental bodies in the United States at the beginning of the Great Depression to reduce public welfare expenses by getting rid of Mexican workers. Government officials concluded this could be achieved, theoretically, by driving Mexicans back to Mexico. Griswold del Castillo and De León explain, "After 1931—government agencies undertook well-planned deportation campaigns, feeling it more economical to deport people than have them drain relief sources indefinitely."[123] Rodolfo Acuña added that "Hoover scapegoated the undocumented workers for unemployment, and the utterances of Hoover and other politicos encouraged racist nativist programs."[124] The subject of "repatriation" in fact became a major lesson for young Mexican Americans and others enrolled in Chicano Studies programs organized for the first time in the early 1970s in many American universities. The topic was always featured as an important chapter in the historical experience of people like us. Acuña further wrote that "In nearby Pacoima and San Fernando, INS agents went door-to-door demanding that the residents produce proper identification," otherwise they would be deported to Mexico.[125] Scholars estimate that half a million persons were either pressured to return to Mexico during the Depression years or were deported for the lack of proper documentation.[126]

The situation was more complicated, however. Our family, for instance, was not pressured to leave San Fernando nor go anywhere for that matter.

None came knocking on our door in these days, and if "INS agents" or their equivalent in those days went around knocking on every door, demanding to inspect documents, my ancestors did not record this in their memory. *La vecindad* would have been a perfect target for government harassment of the kind Acuña describes because of its compact nature located right in the heart of the barrio, and it was chock-full with Mexicans.

Still, my mother, who would have kept it in her memory to be sure, recalled no such activity, nor did anyone else in my family. In a letter to me about this subject she wrote, "I never learned that the government required them to leave but word did go out that those who wanted to leave would only have to pay half the cost...I need to stress that it was a barbarous depression that began about 1926...and it got worse when President Hoover came in. That's the why countless people left. There were no jobs. They paid ten cents an hour for agricultural work. In 1932 when my mother began making tortillas, they sold for six cents a dozen, a [piece of] steak cost fifteen to twenty cents, milk was sold at a penny. That's when Roosevelt came in and then they began projects called the WPA and offices were opened where you could get assistance."[127] Still, the phenomenon of repatriation was happening all around her and, as we can see from her letter, she knew that people were leaving for Mexico in large numbers but not in the gestapo-like fashion that Acuña describes. Here she offers more words about it:

> In those days, Manuel[128] was born. On the day that Manuel was forty days old, Pascual came by on his way to Mexico. He was a *repatriado*,[129] and he left Cleofas behind. I don't know why he left. [But the fact is that] a lot of people went back to Mexico! They left because of the Depression. People said that Hoover was not a good president. It was very much like today when the *migra*[130] goes around picking people up. That kind of thing has never stopped. Others went to colonize Eréndira [Baja California], where the [Mexican] government was offering land.

It's noteworthy that Mother places the intensity of the repatriation effort on the same level of the immigration raids that occur with certain regularity in Mexican communities like San Fernando, as we've already stated. Everyone in our family remembered them as we were growing up, and, of course, the raids continue to this day. She also acknowledges that her brother Pascual took part in the process of repatriation but admitted puzzlement as to why he might have done so. He didn't have to, she implied. She also questioned why he left Cleofas behind, referring to his girlfriend—she didn't have to go either, and she was a Mexican. It's useful to recall as well that Guadalupe and Carlota obtained immigration documents when they entered the United States but Pascual did not and neither did Miguel, his brother; we don't know if Juárez was properly documented. In any case, in the Gil family only Pascual returned to Mexico at this time, and he seems to have done so not because he was forced out, as he explains below. Mother's reference to Eréndira above reminds us that President Cárdenas did indeed seek to attract Mexican workers in the United States back to Mexico at this time by offering them land in certain localities—Eréndira was one such "colony" for repatriates.[131]

Pascual, who had been living and working up in the lumber camps in the California sierras, told me that he became unhappy at this time with his situation and quit his job. In his position at the Sugar Pine Lumber Company, he was able to recommend people for jobs, as he had done with my father, but someone "betrayed" him by accusing him of "rabble-rousing." My uncle blamed Agustín Ortega, one of his hires. This apparently brought Pascual certain criticism from his superiors, thus contributing to a sense of disheartening that overcame him. He made the following admissions to me:

> They accused me of rabble-rousing. I remember it was 1926 because I received a letter from Mexico informing me that my father had died. In 1929, they threw me out due to the accusations of those boys. I also got sick. [So,] I went to Mexico.
>
> I took advantage of the trips that were offered, and I went from— [Fresno] to Guadalajara for only ten dollars. I got this chance [of traveling at low cost] because of the great needs that people experienced. Mr. Hoover had brought things down, and people lost their jobs—I think he wanted to lower salaries—So the train I boarded [to go to Mexico], paid by [President] Calles or [President] Obregón, went from San Francisco to Mexico. But the main reason was Mr. Hoover's restrictions on citizens. Jobs disappeared. Farmers fired people. Banks stopped lending and then they froze the money. For me, it was my great disappointment [stemming from the accusations at Minarets] that drove me out of the country.

I asked, "Did you see any pressure exerted on the Mexican people to push them out of the country in those days?" Pascual answered, "I can't say anything about that because I had a job. What hurt me was the calumny raised against me. But things were so bad I decided to leave on my own." I further asked, "How did the Mexican people on the train feel?" Following was his reply:

> The Mexicans aboard were returning to Mexico on their own. There were no complaints [nor any expressions of resentment]; there was nothing. This is 1931, and people were leaving Mexico voluntarily since there were no jobs, no money [in the US]. A popular *corrido*[132] in those days said it all:
>
> Good-bye, California, good-bye, Good-bye, land of illusions. I'm going back to my stompin' grounds, I leave you all your millions.[133]

Pascual made sure that Cleofas and her family remained in good shape. "I also left them my car and a house I had bought on Pluma Street in Fresno for $1,000." The repatriation train he boarded in or near San Francisco—chartered by the government of Mexico and bound to Mexico—must have stopped temporarily in Los Angeles, giving Pascual the opportunity to visit his family in San Fernando precisely forty days after my elder brother Manuel was born in *la vecindad*, as my mother recorded.

As it turns out, my ancestors did not feel the pressure to return to Mexico although thousands of families in Los Angeles did. Some felt the pressure and some did not. This is one of the discoveries that George J. Sánchez offers us in his study of East Los Angeles, where he finds that residents in that area reacted in a multiplicity of ways to the pressures for repatriation. This lies in contrast with the simplified understanding on which we've relied in the past.[134] He also informs us that Los Angeles County officials organized special trains to transport Mexican families to Mexico every two months between 1931 and 1933, approximately. Pascual must have traveled back to Mexico on one of the first scheduled departures.

My parents didn't sink further into despair and poverty with the growing intensity of the Depression either. Perhaps part of what kept them afloat, at least, is that my nimble-fingered father made himself useful to people around him. As we'll see below, he became a rent collector and handyman at the *vecindad* in addition to being able to work in the orchards and "bring home the bacon" to help pay basic living expenses. Juárez, living with Grandma Carlota next door, did the same. After many months of working as a *piscador*, my father became a *cargador* or box loader on the trucks gathering the orchard fruit. This was a choice field job because he no longer had to wrestle with placing heavy ladders on the spiky lemon or orange trees—now his job was to ride a truck and pick up the boxes he used to fill and stack them aboard with care. My sister Mary said that the pickers considered this a special assignment and looked up to him for this reason.[135]

Penny Capitalism Helps and So Does Self-Initiative

Penny capitalism was another reason why our family avoided the public kitchens. Penny capitalism is a phrase coined in 1953 to refer to a system of micro financing and small trading long employed by Mexican peasants. [136] My immigrant ancestors kept food on the table during this dreadful time because they employed their native intelligence to manage their money and stay alive. This made it possible for them to maintain economic stability, save a few coins to supplement their abysmal wages, and eventually acquire some real assets.

My grandmother Carlota, who initiated the move to San Fernando, set the example first. She did so by making and selling tortillas—much as she had done to stay alive on the immigrant trail but taking it up to a higher level. Guadalupe described the situation:

> Witnessing the calamity that surrounded us, my mother decided to make tortillas for sale. She bought a small amount of corn on June 11 [I remember] because it was Bernabé's birthday [and she made tortillas and] then made some enchiladas for him [out of the tortillas]. She sold the left over tortillas for four or six cents a dozen. And she kept right on doing it—making *nixtamal*,[137] which she then transported to La Perla Market where they charged her ten cents to grind fifty pounds. We would take it [the *nixtamal* and the dough] in an old *bogue*[138] in which we used to carry Mary [when she was a baby].

Guadalupe's shorthand description of Grandma Carlota's plucky determination to survive and prosper requires more explanation. It means that after buying a supply of *maiz* or dry corn kernels, Carlota had to soak them in a tubful of water laced with limestone powder and then cook them slowly over several hours in order to convert them into *nixtamal*.[139] At least one galvanized tub full of *nixtamal*, if not two or more, had to be available to make enough tortillas to sell. These tubs full of cooked corn illustrate penny capital investments. The reader will recall that the *vecindad* apartments consisted of two-room units including the kitchen. This means that the tubs filled with steaming corn had to be set outside in the yard and fueled with firewood in the absence of "bottled gas."[140] Once cooked into *nixtamal*, the corn had to be milled. If Carlota had not been able to rely on the nearby La Perla Market, she would have had to do the grinding of the *nixtamal* by hand on a metate[141]—the ancient way as she did in Puerto Vallarta and Mazatlán. In any case, she had to transport the forty or more pounds of wet *nixtamal* to the mill and return with the same amount of masa or dough for making tortillas. This is where Mary's baby stroller, the *bogue* (buggy), saved the day as the transport vehicle. Carlota couldn't tarry at this point either because the masa could sour, so she and Guadalupe had to quickly proceed to further refine the corn dough on a metate and then hand-clap small amounts into thin rounds and cook them into tortillas—no easy task. This uniquely skillful phase lasted about thirty seconds per tortilla-to-be after which the thin corn cakes, slapped to about ten inches in diameter each, were lobbed on to a hot *comal* or griddle and cooked into a tortilla—the traditional way. They, of course, had to billow up with steam for a few seconds while cooking in order to be considered a properly cooked tortilla.

All of this work took place outside the *vecindad* apartment, out in the open lot where the children played fronting the small apartments, as Mary described earlier. The tortillas had to be sold, so Carlota obtained the help of a neighbor's son named Johnny Hernández to hawk them on the street. He remained a close friend of the family all his life thereafter and also became a good friend of my first in-laws. This experience later led Carlota to compete with La Perla Market in a minor way by opening up her own *tortillería* (tortilla factory) as we'll see below. This is a prime example of Carlota's engagement in penny capitalism, making it possible to survive in tough times. As we'll discover, Mom and Dad also engaged in mini-capitalism or microbusiness some time later.

One day an unseen opportunity arose for my father as well, right in the *vecindad*. One of the faucets attached to the *lavadero* (the common washbasin described by Mary) needed to be fixed—"the faucet leaked and no one would repair it," Guadalupe remembered quite clearly. Being a handyman, Bernabé fixed the faucets. In these days, the *vecindad* was owned by the Pacific States Savings and Loan Company,[142] and according to her, the company had also acquired many houses in the barrio due to foreclosures triggered by the increasingly difficult economic times. She noticed that an *americano* from the company would come by periodically to collect rental payments in the *vecindad* from María Saldaña, a tenant and one of Mom's friends, whose job it was to gather the money ahead of time.

The next time the gringo rent collector came by, Guadalupe, who seldom hesitated to speak her mind, went up to him and explained in her broken English that her husband had repaired the faucet. This information apparently impressed the corporate representative, and because he needed someone who was self-reliant, possessing handyman skills and spoke some English, told Bernabé and Guadalupe that they could oversee the *vecindad* from then on. It seems he had the authority to make this off-the-cuff decision. He assigned them the job of watching over the properties and collecting rental payments not only from the *vecindad* but from other houses in the barrio that were owned by the company. "There were a lot of houses," Guadalupe remembered. And my parents did not have to pay rent as a result—a godsend for them to be sure. As property overseers, they were able to move into larger quarters to boot—the *vecindad*'s manager's house at 1227 Kewen Street on the southwestern side of the *vecindad* property where I was born.[143] Maria Saldaña understandably "resented" being replaced by Bernabé, Guadalupe recalled, "even though she was my friend." But Mother had clearly placed family interests ahead of any friendship, gaining thereby a degree of economic security but suffering the loss of a friend.

Buoyed by the fact that they did not have to pay rent, my parents were able to accomplish something few people could do at this time: they made an investment in real estate. They bought a house on Mott Street on the southwestern edge of the barrio. As Guadalupe recorded, "We struggled to scrape thirty-five dollars together to buy a house," adding with exasperation that "that was all the down payment we could give." It seems the representative of the Savings and Loan Company, who got to know my parents to some extent, prodded them to buy a house and lot given the fact that home prices had fallen with the Depression. Bernabé and Guadalupe resolved to bite the bullet and, following his advice, bought the house, she claims, for $190.[144]

Was it Bernabé's idea to risk and buy it, or was it Guadalupe's? Did they argue about it and suffer from the mental hurt that comes from marital negotiations of this type? None of us in the family know the answers to these questions, but they surely must have felt considerable anxiety about this home purchase because it was a first time for them, and it also meant taking on debt in such dire economic circumstances.

It is likewise worthwhile to consider that in purchasing real estate, they had to be subjected to the bewildering paperwork that always accompanies this kind of transaction. This means that in order to secure this purchase, my parents had to visit business offices away from the barrio and engage the legal and financial services of men who didn't speak Spanish and dealt with Mexicans minimally. It must have been daunting to have to interface with individuals of this sort on their turf—in offices and parts of the city that were totally unfamiliar to them—and be confronted with the incomprehensible procedures that required some knowledge of English to know what was going on.

Nevertheless, they signed some documents (my father could barely write his name), and this led to their receiving a deed from the Pacific States Savings and Loan Company on November 8, 1934, for a parcel of land on 1417 Mott Street in San Fernando, "excepting there from all underground streams and all subsurface waters." Thomas Gardner, assistant secretary of the Pacific States Savings and Loan Company, signed the deed along with C. F. Adams Jr., the vice president, with a practiced flourish after which the papers were duly notarized and logged at the Los Angeles County Recorder's Office.[145] Guadalupe wrote in her notes, "All of this happened in 1933 when Miguel [Mike] was born, our third son." Her memory was off by a year, and the purchase price was $185, payable in five years.

It appears that our family became one of the few who were able to actually claim new ownership of a house when most folks were losing their homes or finding themselves on the verge of doing so.[146] The purchase enabled Bernabé and Guadalupe and their three children, Mary, Manuel, and Mike in swaddling clothes, to move out of the *vecindad* manager's house on Kewen and into the smaller wood-framed house on Mott Street about three blocks away. Our best recollections of growing up would be attached to this house, as we'll see.

Juárez Dies and Carlota Presses On

Grandma Carlota faced some life challenges of her own after settling into the *vecindad*. She was forty-seven years old when she and Juárez moved to San Fernando, but she would soon become a widow and would not have any other male partners. The reader already knows that my siblings and I knew little about Juárez. Photos reveal him as a dark-skinned Mexican male who preferred felt-brimmed hats and long-sleeved white shirts. While we allowed him enough space in our family lore to link him with Grandma, he loomed particularly large in my sister Mary's memory.

She called him "Grandfather," something we never did. The fact that she was the only child in the family at this time probably gave Juárez an opportunity to indulge my big sister in a grandfatherly way, attention always welcomed by a child. She never forgot how he took her to a "Japanese-owned store" on the corner of Maclay and San Fernando, about a thirty-minute walk from home, where he would buy her ice cream. Even though she was perhaps no more than three years old, Mary fondly remembered that they would amble home each enjoying their cones. She worried about finishing off hers before reaching the house of a boisterous Spaniard named Arsenia Sierra who lived on Mission Boulevard because the woman would tell Mom about it and then she'd get into trouble. Mary said, "Mom would complain that [my] appetite for dinner would be spoiled [by the ice cream]." Juárez also bought Mary "a turquoise parasol." She may have reminded him of a child left behind in Mexico. Her unusually early memories may have been bolstered by confirming testimony from Grandma and Mother. On the day we placed my mother's body to rest in a gravesite near Grandma's last resting place, I noticed for the first time that her name was engraved on her headstone as "Carlota H. Juárez," a surprise for me. If it was her wish to have her headstone carved this way, then her relationship with this man was more meaningful than most of us children realized.

Juárez died about the time my brother Manuel was born, in 1931. It seems Juárez became ill after self-medicating himself with a purging home brew of some kind. There was no medical insurance for most Americans at this time and much less for a recent immigrant like Juárez. Additionally, it must be said, home remedies were commonly used to cope with sickness; he had probably used medicinal home brews many times before, consistent with traditional Mexican ways. This one, however, turned out to be *la purga del diablo,* as Mary called it, the devil's purge. He became wrenchingly sick after taking it and suffered considerable agony before he died. With the help of Mother's memory, Mary talked about his last days and how "Doña 'Petrita' Pacheco," one of the shawl-wrapped ladies of the *vecindad* already bowing to old age, brought him some chicken soup and some Jell-O in the manner of old-time neighbors to forestall a mortal ending. Mary had never seen the bright rubbery American "food" before, and so thereafter she associated Jell-O with Juárez's death. He was buried in Oakwood Cemetery in Chatsworth, California, before it became a memorial park for Hollywood celebrities like Fred Astaire and Gloria Graham.[147] Guadalupe, as an adult, also remembered these days with a dose of practical bitterness.

Those were the days when my stepfather died. But there was so much misery everywhere that we couldn't even scrape together the twenty-five dollars to put down on his burial. We just couldn't find a way until my mother appealed to Father Mauricio, the parish priest at Santa Rosa [Church], and he loaned us the money.

Carlota must have been aggrieved from losing Juárez, but we know nothing about it. Her daughter doesn't mention her mother's heart break directly, assuming she had it, but she does say that she complained afterward about feeling ill a lot. Her son Miguel's almost-lyrical memories of his experiences as a young immigrant in America came to an end when they moved from Fresno to San Fernando, and so his interview statements do not contain any references to his mother's loss. Her other son's memory stream, Pascual's, is immersed in labor-related politics. If he became aware of his mother's grief from losing her partner, he doesn't mention it either. Mary and Manuel, who as children lived with Grandma at times, were too young to notice these things and consequently remember nothing on this score either. Years later, Carlota's younger grandchildren viewed her as flinty and stubborn, perceptions that added to her legacy as an old lady devoid of any feelings. I was one of her favorite grandchildren, so my views of her were not as negative. We can only assume that she felt Juárez's loss and that she shed tears for him, but her hard demeanor and the tough times that accosted her, and everyone else, drew a veil on her personal feelings. Times were not easy.

If she missed anything, Carlota must have missed Juárez's economic support. Working as a *piscador* in the orchards, he no doubt contributed steadily as a wage earner to her household budget. When he passed away, the rest of her family, Guadalupe and Bernabé, and Miguel, probably pitched in to fill the hole left by his death as they seem to have helped each other easily enough when they were living side by side in the *vecindad*, and Pascual may have also contributed from his lumber mill earnings. If Carlota sagged after the death of her partner, she didn't stay down for long, and all indications are, as we'll see below, that she propped herself up and in fact preferred to be self-reliant.

Carlota soldiered on by continuing to make tortillas in the *vecindad* as we've already seen, but, more importantly, she also moved beyond. She soon moved out of the complex of tiny apartments and progressed on her own partly because she built up a community network of sorts. As we'll learn shortly, she attached herself to the new Catholic congregation that was enjoying a newly built church in the heart of the barrio and made many acquaintances there; later, she also took on a leadership role in the church's women's lay organizations.

Her network went beyond the church, too. It appears that an acquaintance and neighbor who lived two blocks away played an important role in her acquiring property. His name was Conrado López, whom we all called Don Conrado. He was a paunchy and jovial white-haired man who differed from most other men in the barrio because he spoke English and drove an up-to-date automobile. He seemed at ease in the Anglo world even though he lived right in the middle of the barrio. What brought Don Conrado and Grandma together is that he wanted to sell a piece of property he held nearby at 518 Kalisher Street. We don't know how he acquired this property or how the two met, but all indications are that once she felt ready to take on the responsibility, he tutored her in the process of buying real estate. Hindsight informs us that whenever she needed to engage the Anglo establishment for legal or tax purposes he would often be the one to make the connections for her. Her inability to write much beyond signing her name didn't stop her either. Don Conrado would steer her to the right person or office much like a cultural broker, and whenever she needed car transportation to get to someplace quickly, she would call on him and pay him as if he were a taxicab driver—there were no cabs at the time, and certainly not in the barrio. When I was about ten, old Don Conrado would load us into his shiny black Chevrolet and deliver us at a lawyer's office or a doctor's office where I would serve as the interpreter; Mary and Manuel having preceded me in delivering these services to Grandma.

The oral tradition in our family informs us that Carlota purchased the Kalisher Street lot for $1,500. It faced the southwestern side of the first Santa Rosa Church built in San Fernando. The house address, 518 Kalisher Street, rings loudly in our collective family memory as I've already indicated, and we'll see more information about our family life at this address in later pages. Guadalupe simply writes that Grandma "bought it from *el señor* Conrado."

A title insurance policy dated June 15, 1938, in fact, shores up our family knowledge about this purchase. On that date, Carlota obtained a "joint protection policy" from a Los Angeles-based Title Insurance and Trust Company for a maximum of $3,000 that guarded her from any possible losses stemming from land title irregularities connected to the Kalisher Street property. The policy clearly states that the land title is vested in her. Schedule B in this document also declares that Carlota borrowed $2,000 from Security First National Bank of Los Angeles to pay off her debt to Conrado López, the bank officer obviously having been convinced that she was a good bet. Don Contrado sold it to her, and she paid him with borrowed bank money. The land parcel included a single-level corner storefront (at Hewitt Street), a garage, an outhouse, and some lean-tos built on an open lot modestly embellished by a young palm tree—all facing Kalisher Street.

After completing the transactions mentioned above, she moved out of her tiny *vecindad* apartment. In hindsight, here was a major reason for Grandma's neighbors to admire her as this was no minor milestone. In a move that suggests a certain amount of native shrewdness shedding light on how she would secure her economic independence thereafter, not only did she obtain a mortgage loan from an established bank, she also maneuvered a way to insure success. She did this by moving into one of the lean-to's on the new property and rented out the corner storefront to a cobbler and his family. This enabled her to save on rental expenses and begin paying her bank loan at the same time while staying within her budget. My mother persuaded my handyman father to fix the lean-to by providing it with more structural strength and then remodeling the garage into a tortilla shop for Carlota.[148] Given inside the family, his labor was free and absolutely critical for Grandma. His handiness would benefit her many times.

Grandma's Tortilla Shop

The remodeled garage became the "Tortillería La Esperanza," San Fernando's second tortilla bakery located only a half block away from the *vecindad.* My father outfitted the garage by closing the vehicle entrance with a light weight, wood frame wall ventilated by high-screened windows and then installing a door on the right-hand side of that wall. He also hooked up the electrical and water connections and plumbed in an outhouse on the side of the garage-now-turned-*tortillería.* When I was a boy, I spent many a day in the *tortillería.*

In the late 1930s, a customer, most often a woman, could make several observations upon entering Grandma's *tortillería.* First of all, her nose would immediately detect the smell of boiled corn combined with the mealy aroma of cooked tortillas. If a loud motor whine resonated the air, she could look more closely along the left-hand side of the room and discover that the engine noise issued from an electric motor anchored on a low cement table which drove a belt connected to a corn mill mounted about five feet away also on the cement floor. Someone would be standing in front of the vibrating mill pouring *nixtamal* or cooked corn into the mill mouth and a closer look would reveal that a rotating belt was turning a stone wheel inside the waist-high mill chamber at a high speed instantly grinding the corn kernels into a whitish blur of soft cornmeal. This flying smear of masa would fly out from underneath the chamber into a galvanized tub sitting on the floor. This was the corn masa needed to make the tortillas, ground fine in this case for tortillas instead of a course grind for tamales. In requesting the purchase of, say, a dozen fresh-made tortillas, the woman customer would have to speak up in order to be heard over the loud engine whine combined with the drone of the stone wheel grinding the softened corn. Another glance would reveal two or three large galvanized tubs filled with simmering *nixtamal* sitting on the floor over low gas burners waiting to be ground.

Our customer would also observe a lot of activity along the right-hand side of the small building. Two or three women would be standing making tortillas here, each one working at a metate or grindstone resting on a thigh-high table. The burners of a chest-high natural gas stove standing in front of each lady would be covered with three or four *comales* (griddles) within arm's reach—one *comal* for each tortilla maker or *tortillera*. Engaged in a constant and friendly chatter, each *tortillera* would stoop slightly to fine-grind the corn dough already on her volcanic metate with a mano, a near-cylindrical stone roller the width of the grindstone. The customer would notice that the *tortillera* would bend down slightly and grab the tapered mano at the ends and grind the masa two or three times, rub, rub, rub, pushing the reground masa toward the bottom edge of the metate. The *tortillera* would then scoop just the right amount of dough off the end of the metate with a swipe of her fingers, and with both hands slap it midair into a thin cake. Clap, clap, clap—clap, clap, clap—the *tortillera* would whap the tortilla dough cake in midair one more time and then foist it expertly onto the hot griddle in front of her. The tortilla lady would wait about forty seconds to turn the baking tortilla only once until it ballooned briefly with steam blowing from the seams. The hot vapor announced that the new tortilla was fully cooked. Avoiding overcooking, the *tortillera* would deftly pick up the golden disk from the griddle and flip it atop a nearby stack of tortillas. Here were the freshly handmade tortillas, the legendary corn cakes prized by the Aztecs made in the old way, not manufactured by an automated machine as they are today.

Carlota would count the tortillas into piles of a dozen, wrap them in slick, pale paper, and sell them to our waiting and observant customer. Deliveries would also be made to nearby restaurants. Homemade *menudo* was on sale on weekends, requiring each patron to bring a pot in which to carry it home piping hot. Fresh-made tamales were made available on Saturdays and Sundays.

Things went well for Grandma despite the Depression. Even though the business demanded a considerable amount of time and energy, she devoted herself to it and made her payments to Security First National Bank eventually paying off the loan. *"Le fué bién,"* Guadalupe remembered. Grandma did well, penny capitalism for sure. She was exceptional among her peers.

Disaster Strikes but We Make the Best of It

The fear of tuberculosis hanging about the orchards led my father to look for other jobs and occupations whenever the opportunity arose, and one of them was doing "flood control" work. This was available in Los Angeles County in the late 1920s and early 1930s to unskilled men like our Dad. We were living in the manager's house in the *vecindad* at the time—but the manager's job wasn't enough to feed the family. Government officials worried that creeks and small rivers snaking across the desert floor of the San Fernando Valley and the Los Angeles basin would flood in winter and cause economic damage.[149] My father became one of the many hundreds of laborers hired by the county to ensure that the waterways ran unimpeded whenever it rained. The Los Angeles River, for example, gathered rain water from the mountains bordering the San Fernando Valley, channeled it along the lower southern end of the valley toward Burbank, and then fed it south through the Los Angeles basin before delivering it out to San Pedro Bay. Years later, practically all of the waterways were later encased in large cement conduits, rendering them practically invisible to the growing number of residents.

This is the job my father held when he lost his left arm—a tragic mishap that affected our family in multiple ways. As a flood control worker, his responsibility and that of the other men who worked with him was to ready the water channels for the winter runoff by cleaning the water beds: grubbing, pulling, and otherwise eradicating any vegetation and annual growth that might obstruct the water flow. They also firmed up the earthen sides of the watercourses to prevent damaging over spill.[150]

One day, he was feeding brush into a big chopping machine and his glove caught on one of the branches. He couldn't remove his gloved hand in time, so the machine hacked into his left arm, crushing it below the elbow. The blow must have knocked my father unconscious right away. My mother didn't forget that day:

> They came to tell me that they had taken Berna to the hospital because he lost his arm in an accident. A machine had destroyed his left arm.
>
> How do you think I felt at that moment?

> I immediately went to him and found him on a bed. They didn't let me in because they were amputating his arm at that moment.

The doctors cut his left arm off, below the elbow. My mother noted the following:

> It was a terrible thing for him—and for me too because we faced such an awful [economic] situation.

Six-year-old Manuel remembered that

> On the day he lost his arm somebody took us—me and my mother—to the hospital. *Lo vi por la ventanita. Estaba llorando* (I saw him through the small window. He was crying). He waved to me as he lay on a bed.

Recently married, and looking forward to a family life of the kind he had sorely missed as a boy, his world must have come crashing down on him after recovering his senses. He was thirty-eight years old and fully expecting to remain an active head of the family he had married into, and now this! Good God on earth he must have said in anguish! *Qué suerte la mía!* What would he do now?

Our family lore doesn't include details about the mental distress he must have suffered, strangely enough. It doesn't address the emotional challenges he faced in the days following the removal of his trampled arm at the hospital where I would be born shortly thereafter. Guadalupe records precious few details about my father coming to terms with this loss and what this might have meant to him. He had been an able-bodied young man and now had become a one-armed man still needing to prove he could support a wife and children. He surely must have felt betrayed by Lady Luck, not being prone to beseeching God or Christ about his plight, but alas, his testimony is missing. We can only guess at the mental turmoil he faced privately.

What could he do now to bring economic support to himself and his family? In the end, he did what he had to do: get on with life and do the best he could. This was his legacy to us. So after a period of convalescence attended to by Guadalupe, he decided he would report to work at his flood control job again, but his boss sent him home—there was no work for him there anymore. What thoughts might have exploded through his mind on his way back home? We'll never know, but he was now being rebuffed on account of his physical condition, something he couldn't change! He might have said, "This is worse than being refused a job for being Mexican!" But our family lore doesn't include this kind of refusal as I discuss elsewhere, although he surely must have felt he was now in double jeopardy. His new reality had to sink in, and it couldn't have been easy.

Mom told us many times that the county compensated Dad's loss with fifteen hundred dollars (although elsewhere she cites $2,500). She also informed us on many occasions that Bernabé invested this money into a grocery store. We don't know how much negotiating went on between the two of them about this important move, but we know for a fact that he did open a small market called "La Flor de Abril." It stood a block away from *la vecinidad* near the corner of Kewen and Kalisher Streets in the heart of the barrio, next to a well-known but foul-smelling saloon, El Central Café, about which we'll hear later.

This, his first grocery shop, also became an important bit in our family lore for the reasons the reader is about to learn. Guadalupe remembered that "he supplied it well" with an array of grocery items. For example, a meat vendor from Los Angeles who was probably of Chinese origin to whom Mother referred to as *el chino* would come by periodically to make sure Dad had all the fresh meat he needed including not only beef, pork, and chicken but also sliced cold cuts, wieners, and sausages. She couldn't forget a Greek vendor who supplied him on the dry goods side including no doubt sugar, salt, canned goods, lard, etc. Mary, who was ten years old, remembered the store, "It was a narrow little store packed with soda pop [especially] Nehi [Soda]. I think they were the cheapest available—they cost two cents each. Coke and RC Cola cost a little more. I was in charge of selling candy."

Things should have gone well with this intelligent use of the money, but it seems that my father's frame of mind was not whole. The loss of his arm most likely demoralized him for a while, but more certain is the fact that he began to drink heavily, more than ever before. My brother Manuel also brought to mind that in these days father received notice of the death of Manuela Gil, one of the aunts who reared him in Mexico. My brother, who among us kids remembered Dad the most, next to Mary, affirmed that "he loved her" or at least held a special place in his childhood memory, and so we conjecture that this might have compounded his melancholy and depression in these days.

In any case, a covey of friends who stuck to him at the store throughout the day brought him down, according to Mother. As a small business man in the late 1930s, he was surrounded by desirable goods which his buddies coveted, Mom concluded, and he let them run a tab. What is clear enough is that in a time of high unemployment and economic depression, basic foodstuffs were at a premium everywhere. "He didn't lack friends," she said to us with a bitter irony many times, but they were not the right kind. One of them named "Quiñones" started to bring in liquor, and they would sip it during the day while chatting about a variety of subjects.

We lived on Kewen Street at the time and Mother must have been stomping mad about the way Dad ran the store, but she doesn't acknowledge it in her memoirs. She lets him off the hook. Mary and Manuel looked back on these difficult days and could only remember how outrageously bossy and unforgiving my mother was of my father. Mary, who always favored him, was nevertheless willing to accept "unpleasant things [that happened] because my dad began drinking heavily." Manuel, younger than Mary, simply admitted that "they [Dad and Mom] never got along too well, you know what I mean? He tolerated her a lot."

In hindsight, my father's foibles caused major financial setbacks for the family in part because he conceded greater importance to establishing and maintaining relationships with his buddies in the traditional Mexican way instead of drawing a line for business's sakes. Although my mother may have been a traditional woman most of the time, she gave little credibility to his being loyal to his buddies and condemned it outright, as a matter of fact. It seems my siblings were unable to figure out these larger considerations, but there is little doubt my parents got into furious squabbles at this time.

As mentioned already, rather than castigating Bernabé in her written memories, Guadalupe indicted "Quiñones." She maintained that he would advise Dad to be firm and "to stand up to women," meaning my mother, of course. Manuel did in fact recall that my father would ask his *compadre*, Don Rodolfo O. (my godfather), from time to time to keep an eye on the store while he would go to the warehouse to replenish the shelves. Manuel added that unfortunately, Don Rodolfo would compensate himself with "boxes filled with eggs and bacon" to the extent that my father had to say to him at least once, "You're taking too much home, *compa*." Manuel observed that, "My dad wasn't too happy with that." Guadalupe would try keep an eye on things whenever Dad had to make a run to the warehouse, and this is how she learned how some of these so-called friends felt comfortable enough to serve themselves food portions. "One of the Garcías (the owners of the Central Café) would serve himself from the best meat we had," she moaned many times. Mary remembered as much because Guadalupe would ask her to watch so "that people didn't take merchandise." She would also instruct Mary to "bring in any [extra] money [Dad had] and watch to see who takes what." Poor Mary! She was only eleven years old! The situation simply got worse so that the resupplying of beans came to a stop, then the meat deliveries thinned down and the other merchandise also became scarce.

Bernabé relocated the store in an effort to reorganize himself apparently and he even got it mentioned in the news. *Vida del Valle de San Fernando*, the barrio newspaper, ran a brief article about it entitled "The Grocery Store 'La Flor de Mayo' Moves to a New Location" in which the reporter and publisher, Carlos de Silva, announced that our Dad was planning to move his store to new locale at the corner of Griffith and Kalisher Streets. This would happen "in the first days of this month" as the new establishment found itself in the process of being "renovated" and "furnished with everything it would need." The barrio weekly advised Dad's "customers and the Mexican residents in the valley to honor him with their visit."[151]

Dad's situation didn't change significantly at the larger wood-framed, two-story building owned by "El Jadi," a Japanese neighbor. Mary remembered far too well that, "People would come by and say, 'I'm taking this. Put it on my tab.'" Manuel brought to mind a woman who would shop at my father's store and flirt with him in order to take advantage of him. Mother must have fumed in desperation about this situation and probably scolded Dad with frenzy many times, but she kept mum about this in her memoirs.

This is about the time that Bernabé asked the *chino* to supply him on credit, something he asked the Greek vendor as well. But Mother's summation of this effort says it all: "He [merely] sank into debt more and more." She claimed to have advised him to get credit with only one of the vendors, perhaps as a way to get a hold of the situation. She added, "I even told the *chino* not to give him [any more] credit."

Ultimately, my father went broke. The practice of opening tabs for his friends and letting them take merchandise without paying led to Dad's loss of the store. Guadalupe summed up the situation with biting words: "He lost everything—he came up with nothing." The Greek vendor sued Dad—took him to court "for a miserable sixty dollars that we could not pay," Guadalupe recalled bitterly. She added that "the Greek vendor would not accept little payments of a dollar like the *chino* did." Mary remembered endless bickering. Mother wrote that they closed the store and then, "They put our house on auction," referring to the house we moved to, on Mott Street, the one they bought against all odds when they were still living in the *vecindad*. She added,

> "I prayed entire novenas [of the rosary] asking Our Lady of Help (*Nuestra Señora del Socorro)* to assist us in this mo-

> ment of difficulty—because they wanted to take our house away—the idea was to see who would give the most for it in order to get the money we owed. A lot of people gathered at our front door. You had already been born."

Mother is referring to me above, the author. Her words to Bernabé were repeated to us many times:

> "It is entirely unjust that we lose this house for a lousy sixty dollars!" So I told [Bernabé] I would go see Negrete who went around selling fabric in our neighborhood—later he opened a store and he would lend money [from there] too. I said to [Negrete], "Lend me sixty dollars," and [after some more discussion], his heart responded when he heard our story, and he lent us the money. Then I went [to the auction officials] and turned in the money.

"Negrete," a private moneylender, perhaps of Lebanese or Jewish origin, who began as a door-to-door cloth merchant in our barrio, helped save our house on Mott Street. While he falls into the off-putting category of a "loan shark," he nonetheless entered our family lore because he bet that my mother would pay back the money he loaned her in order to preserve our house when no one else would. Even the *chino* vendor who supplied my father's store said to Guadalupe, "You don't have to worry about paying what you owe me." While the Asian meat vendor probably declared the money owed him as a business loss we became indebted to him as well. I was unable to recover his name unfortunately. Mother often said that Divine Providence intervened in our favor. "I came to realize clearly," she said, "that Our Lady of Help rewarded us with a miracle because even Don Basilio Alvarez, a foreman at the Lemon Heights Association, offered Berna a job now that the store was closed and no one else would give him a job on account of him having only one arm." My own recommendation would have been to give credit to "Negrete," the *chino* vendor, and Don Basilio instead. Mom does not berate Dad in her memoirs about this near loss of our house on Mott Street either; she leaves him relatively unscathed.

With "Don Bacho's" aid (Basilio Alvarez's nickname), Dad obtained a job after closing the store. This is how he returned to the citrus orchards, Don Bacho allowing him to pick as much fruit as he could with one arm alone and thus continue to earn some money. Dad became known to his friends as *El Mocho* (the man with a severed arm), a sobriquet that might have made him uncomfortable and which we children didn't like to hear. Mary formed the belief that when he went back to the orchards, he had to wrestle with loss of face because he could no longer work as a *cargador*, a job he cherished when he could easily stack fruit-filled boxes with both his arms. Now he had to come to terms with his new condition and learn how to grapple the ladders and do the picking with only one good arm. "He felt much diminished," Mary affirmed.

Soledad, one of the younger ones in our family, learned many years later that when Dad went looking for a job, he would try to hide his half arm—he didn't wear the prosthesis the county gave him. In fact, we children shrank from the clumsy and heavy artificial arm and it's possible our childish complaints might have worn down his resolve in using it. To us he looked natural with his stubby arm, and so the prosthetic arm landed in the back of a closet, and we kids used it only to scare each other with it. Soledad concluded that he avoided people with a camera for the same reason. Mary came to the belief that his diabetes set in at this time. A hard life's toll was beginning to manifest itself on my father when he was only in his forties.

Our time living on Kewen Street was a difficult one for our parents and it didn't get much better when we moved to Mott Street. As we've seen, my Dad lost his arm in those years followed by a convalescence that encouraged him to seek support from male friends who shared his cultural values when he ran a store but unfortunately also gave them the opportunity to take advantage of him too. This set of circumstances would have been a heavy burden for any man, to be sure, and, to compound matters even more so, my father could now count on having to feed one more mouth—my own! Had I been able to ask him about life on Kewen Street, he surely would have said it hadn't been a good time.

Chapter 9

We Stumble Forward
(1938–1942)

Our Family Keeps Growing • Living on Mott Street • Going "Up North"

Our Family Keeps Growing

Despite the loss of my father's arm and the near loss of our family home, our household kept growing right through the Depression. As already mentioned, we children began to populate the three dwellings we lived in, one after the other, and each abode we occupied stamped itself uniquely on our memory. The reader will recall that the eldest of us kids were born into the cozy but impoverished *vecindad* apartment already described: María de Jesús (Mary), the firstborn, in 1928, Manuel in 1931, and Miguel (Mike) in 1934. Aided by devoted neighbor women, Grandma Carlota served as a midwife to help my older siblings come into this world.

When my turn came to enter this world, in 1937, I was the first in the family to see the light of day in a hospital, the modern way. Family lore has it that when mother's doctor, Dr. Peterson, withdrew me from her womb, he called out for all to hear, "Well, here's a Mexican for sure!" referring to my dark skin and shock of thick black hair, now nearly white and sparse. As Mom said to me many times, "Bernabé had not yet gone bankrupt, and we were able to pay the hospital bill for the costs of your birth." So my parents brought me home to the manager's house on Kewen Street, having moved there from our tiny *vecindad* apartment when my father started collecting rent payments for the Pacific States Savings and Loan Company.

News of my birth even got into the newspaper. The December 2, 1937, issue of *Vida del Valle de San Fernando,* declaring in its headlines that Europe was feeling threatened by Japan ("Europea Temerosa del Japón") also carried a small notice on the front page about my arrival. Carlos de Silva, the publisher, must have become one of Dad's friends and acquiesced to greet my appearance in this world with a brief mention titled, "A Home of Good Tidings" ("Hogar de Plácemes"): "The historical stork of time immemorial visited the Gil family home Friday of last week at their residence on 1227 Kewen Street gifting them with a robust little boy. The arrival of the new born brought joy to the household and both the mother and the boy find themselves in good health."[152]

Two of my siblings were born in our Mott Street home, after we moved out of the *vecindad* which included the Kewen house. My parents purchased the house on Mott Street in the middle of the Depression and nearly lost it subsequently as we'll learn. Marta (Martha) made her debut there in 1939 and Enrique (Rick) in 1942. After Rick was born we moved to Kalisher Street where Mr. Stork dropped Soledad (Sally) off there in 1944 and Emilia (Emily, later "Country") in 1946, she being the last. (The reader knows by now that the latter names in parentheses are the Anglicized names we children adopted for ourselves—our parents never used them.)

Living on Mott Street

We lived on Mott Street, between Workman and Rinaldi Streets, from about 1937 to 1942, the years following Dad's accident. This is the period my siblings and I attach our warmest childhood memories to because we lived like a regular family here in contrast to our next home which would be on Kalisher Street where business pressures impacted our daily life, as we'll learn below. Life was enjoyable for us children on Mott Street partly because we lived on the periphery of the barrio, half a block away from open pastures, offering us the touch of the rural to be sure. There's no doubt our parents worried continually about how they were going to pay the mortgage because Dad was picking oranges with only one arm by now but we children didn't know about such things. We just loved our years growing up there.

In an earlier chapter, we disclosed that Zierer discovered that in 1933–34 the smallest houses in San Fernando were built in our part of town. Well, our Mott Street house was a pretty good example of the undersized houses designed for Mexican working families. It seems that the Anglo architects and developers said to themselves, "Well, smaller pocketbooks mean smaller houses no matter the family size!" Our wood-framed home was built on a 25' × 75' lot, so everything inside was pocket-sized, built for Tom Thumb.

The door on our little porch opened into a diminutive living room where after a hard day's work my father would sit in his favorite chair in the evening listening to Mexican radio broadcasts on his fine wood-finished Zenith radio, probably the best piece of furniture we owned. As he listened intently, the announcer's voice would ebb and flow competing with the static in the night atmosphere. The rest of the living room space was taken up by another chair that sat by a small coffee table and that was it. Nothing else fit. We, Gil kids, had no idea our house was so dreadfully small until we revisited it as adults; I was shocked when I did so.

One could easily step from the left edge of the living room into the largest bedroom in the house where we children slept, Mary, Manuel, Mike, and I slept here. My sister slept on a single bed on one side of the room, and we boys shared a larger bed on the other side. The living room also opened straight back into our teensy kitchen where only a gas stove and an undersized table fit in front of the sink, calling it a dinner table would have been an exaggeration. I hold fond memories of us gathering around that simple table and sharing our simple meals in this miniature kitchen-dining room. A door way on the left from the kitchen led to Mom and Dad's undersized plain board bedroom and this gave access to our one and only bathroom enclosing a tub and toilet. Dad built an additional room behind the kitchen which served as a storage and all-purpose room that was never finished on the inside where we raised fuzzy golden chicks on more than one occasion. The back door opened out into a smallish open dirt area that doubled as a vegetable garden and animal feed lot.

Mercifully, there was an unfenced, equal-sized, empty lot with a fig tree right next door. Another house the size of ours should have gone into the lot, and so in the interim, it served us as an unpaved driveway and a side yard allowing us to romp and play on and around the old fig tree. In this vein, Mary's reminiscences about Mott Street also reflect the fond recollections we all had about living in this micro house half a block away from some extensive pasturelands, now entirely gone.

> On Mott Street, my mother always had a *gallinero lleno de pollitos* (a henhouse filled with chicks). She seemed to have it well-timed so that as soon as she was finished giving birth [to one of us], the chickens would be ready to be put into a pot to make a *caldo* to restore her strength.[153]

> My dad planted *maiz* or *elotes* (corn on the cob), [and] calabazas (squash)—*como un* Victory Garden[154] on the side of the house. He had a chicken coop, and he also had some

> very fine roosters! He also raised rabbits, chickens—[Gosh] we had everything!

I too remember the rabbit cage and the chicken coop that Mary mentions above, plus a cow, a goat, and even a big, fat pig that my father butchered one evening shocking me into an early bedtime sleep. Carey McWilliams, who discovered backyards like ours in Chavez Ravine on the edges of downtown Los Angeles in the 1920s, where Dodger Stadium was built, wrote, "Goats staked out on picket lines can be seen on the hillsides, and most of the homes have chicken pens and fences. The streets are unpaved . . . In this socially regressive dead end, goats bleat and roosters crow and children play in the dirt roads."[155] That was us, too, but we wouldn't have agreed about being "socially regressive" although I do concur that social science in those days was shot through with heavy biases. Indeed, our roosters crowed early in the morning, our goats bleated at noon, and our pigs went oink! oink! all day long. It remains a marvel to me how my father crammed all these animals into the back lot that probably measured no more than 25'×30'. Although we really didn't have "garden" as such, we children considered our outside space a wondrous play lot. I'll never forget when five year old Martha, dressed in a spanking new white dress, stepped into a small muddy pond reserved for chickens, all because I enticed her into it.

Keeping a growing family fed and in stitches was not easy for an unskilled man possessing only one good arm. Our livelihood hung in the balance not only because of Dad's physical handicap but also because he didn't speak English. Still, he had no choice but to make money somehow—thank goodness our childish minds stayed busy with puerile fantasies.

This is about the time I presented a valentine card to him which I had created in school with the help of my first-grade teacher. I wrote the English words *I love you* on it, with childish crudeness, no doubt. I'll always remember he teased me about it as I played with him in our Tom Thumb living room on Mott Street. He pretended that the words really said *"Ay lo vi yu"* (a distorted version of "I saw you") and bid me to explain why I had written it that way. He was not only pretending he couldn't pronounce the words correctly but was also reminding me that he spoke Spanish, and the sum total of these contradictions exasperated me as a child. My brother Manuel claimed Dad couldn't read at all.

The Depression haunted us even after it began to lift and so it became necessary to shore up our family income in the years we lived on Mott Street. My parents had to boost the household budget in more ways than one because my frisky siblings and I grew in number and size and never stopped requiring more food, shoes, and clothing. Indeed, the economic marginality of picking lemons for a living in Southern California in those days, even when you possessed two good arms, guaranteed only a lowly living standard. It still does. So other strategies for income were in order for the Gil family.

Going "Up North"

One of the solutions for shoring up the family budget was to put us children to work. We represented extra sets of hands and arms that could pick fruit and help bring in badly needed cash—and we could do this in the summers when schools closed and the agricultural harvests in California kicked into full swing. These circumstances took us "up north" several summers in a row where we worked in the fields and orchards.

This is how we became farm workers and joined the countless thousands of families in the United States that followed the crops in order to make a living. "By 1940, nearly four hundred thousand workers, two-thirds of who were Mexicans, were following 'the big swing' through the cotton growing regions . . ." Thus begins one of the earliest descriptions of this important economic phenomenon that boosted farmers and growers in the American West bringing food to our tables, yet remains largely hidden from the consciousness of most Americans. The labor of these workers, who were always paid with rock-bottom wages, guaranteed sufficient earnings to help farmers and growers pay off their debts and keep money to go on vacation, buy a new car, send their children to college, or do whatever else they wanted. It brought wealth and power to them. When Carey McWilliams[156] wrote the description of the "big swing," he had Texas in mind—but, in the end, he was also writing about us.

Like the Tejanos of McWilliams's concern,[157] our family became a part of a similar "big swing" in California that swept up folks like us who lived in or near big cities like Los Angeles and couldn't quite make ends meet. It carried us north into the rich farmlands of the San Joaquin Valley and beyond. According to one observer, about a quarter of a million workers tended the fields and labored in Californian orchards in the 1940s. For example, César Chávez's family made up part of that quarter of a million. Like us, and many thousands more, they lived in or near big cities, and when their local urban jobs didn't produce enough income, they would try to patch up their family budgets by joining the armies of agricultural workers who migrated around the state, willing to exchange their labor for meager pay,[158] Ernesto Galarza, a well-known agricultural economist, saying as much. The Chávez family's headquarters, or "pit stop" as they called it, was found in an impoverished settlement near Oxnard called Sal Si Puedes. They fanned out across the state from there looking for agricultural work—full-time, all year long.[159] There were many families like the Chávezes.

Unlike them, our family worked full-time in the fields but only in the summers. Our cousins, the Naranjos, who lived a few doors down from us on Mott Street, engaged in agricultural work during the summer for ten years in a row, as we'll see in chapter 13. Mary remembers numerous other barrio families who would go "up north" to work in the walnut and cherry orchards. At the beginning of a school year she quickly came to understand what her classmates and church friends meant when they answered the question, "What did you do for the summer?" their reply being, "We went up north."

Our "big swing" up north took us to the "the factories in the fields," exposed and analyzed by McWilliams.[160] Going up north is how we became acquainted on a personal basis with Delano, Salinas, Gilroy, San José, and González in the 1940s —names that became nationally recognized in the 1960s, twenty years later, due to the take-charge efforts of César Chávez, after he became the famous farm worker organizer. His celebrated effort to finally create a farm workers union was bolstered by Robert Kennedy as I'll mention again in later pages.[161] We picked fruit in these same communities when César Chávez was but five years old.

In the summer of 1942, our family traveled to Gilroy to pick prunes, Mary reminded me. In response to my quizzing her about the preparation we had to undergo in order to travel up north, she supposed it to be a simple thing for the family to do: "[You] just throw into the truck what you were going to take with you and 'let's go.'" She was merely fourteen at the time and remembered only certain things although technically speaking she was correct. Easier said than done, however, this endeavor (preparing a family to travel to work on farms far away) had to require numerous steps executed by our parents that our childish innocence kept us from noting, much less understanding. For example, my parents had to have talked about taking such a trip before making a decision about it. Father couldn't have simply dictated his decision to our mother. How long they talked and how easy a conversation it might have been, at least for the first time around, is something we will never know. One reason for believing that the decision had to be accompanied by a lot of grief and worry is that Mom was always reluctant to stray far from her own mother, not to mention money worries.

Once taken, the decision had to be carried out. Getting a family of six ready, including my brother Rick who was a baby at the time, to travel by car and live on the road for two or three months had to be daunting because my parents hadn't done anything like it before, not with children. Many questions arose. What to keep handy on the road, what to leave behind? How much money to have on hand, in the absence of personal bank accounts and ATMs which didn't exist, not even in a pipe dream? Staying at motels and eating in restaurants along the way was out of the question, of course, although in Texas we wouldn't have had the option because "Mexicans" like us were not allowed this type of lodging on the road. For us, in California, however, it was merely a matter of cost.[162] We didn't have motel money anyway.

Mary was the eldest, and despite her young age, she no doubt bore the brunt of helping prepare for our first trip. Manuel, who was next in line, was only eleven, Mike was eight, I was five, Martha was three, and Rick was an infant. Curiously, my mother barely mentions the trips "up north" to earn family income by harvesting crops. Where I expected her to conjure these trips in her mind's eye for inclusion in her hand-scrawled memoirs, she merely acknowledges that the family came and went. "When we returned from picking fruit in Delano," she wrote, "we opened up a restaurant." Her memory skips the preparations, the trips, and the hardships involved in going "up north"—her thoughts turn instead to their decision to open up small businesses, again to ensure our income as my father was no longer in top health. Not emphasizing these experiences might have been a practical thing to do: better leaving some memories alone.

Mary did remember that we packed two mattresses, a bath tub filled with dishes and other kitchen equipment, an oil stove, a gallon of kerosene, a supply of clothes and shoes, and a big tarp to cover everything. Had John Steinbeck's classic novel *The Grapes of Wrath* been available and had we been readers at the time, we might have followed their lead in preparing for our trip up north. Below are the few excerpts from the novel:

> Tom said, "Ma, what stuff we gonna take from here?"
>
> She looked quickly about the kitchen. "The bucket," she said. "All the stuff to eat with: plates an' the cups, the spoons an' knives an' forks. Put all them in that drawer, an' take the drawer. The big fry pan an' the big stew kettle, the coffee pot—Don't do no good to take little stuff—Take the bread pans, all of 'em. They fit down inside each other." She stood and looked about the kitchen.[163]

Manuel recalled that in preparation for our trip, my father traded a car he owned for a 1927 black LaSalle sedan with long sweeping fenders that had already been customized into a truck. This meant that the sedan top was cut with a chisel and saw, removed and replaced with a wooden platform bolted onto the sedan frame, thus converting the sedan into a truck. We children considered it absolutely first-rate! In Steinbeck's novel, Pa Joad prepared the family vehicle, a Hudson Super-Six sedan, in a similar manner. He cut the roof with a chisel right down the middle and removed it and installed a wooden truck bed with boarded sides which he fashioned himself. It must have looked just like our LaSalle truck!

After loading the back with our travel belongings and covering them with a tarpaulin, Manuel, Mike, and Mary climbed aboard, in the back, and snuggled into the nooks and crannies. Dad sat behind the wheel and Mom rode in the cab beside him with three-year-old Martha and baby Rick between them. Tearfully, I stayed behind because my mother had instructed me to keep my grandmother company. Mom was always worrying about her. I remember seeing them off.

My family motored north on US 99, the only northern exit from San Fernando at the time. Dad would get to test the power of the LaSalle engine on the infamous Grapevine, that lonely and mountainous stretch of highway that connects the San Fernando Valley with the San Joaquin Valley. The two-lane road climbed the southwestern end of the Tehachapi Mountains and meandered amid rugged and towering coffee-colored mounds, testing the ability of drivers and the efficiency of automotive water cooling systems. The highway reached the summit at Tejon Pass, 4,160 feet above sea level, and our LaSalle did well enough but "the radiator began to lose water" as our custom truck approached the pass, Mary remembered. So Dad had to stop and walk off somewhere. Mary didn't know where he'd gone, but soon returned with a bucket of water which he poured into the hot and thirsty radiator creating a burst of steam. Today, water-filled drums stand alongside Interstate 5 for gasping radiators as it runs parallel to the old highway that my family traversed in 1942. Our one-armed Dad piloted our LaSalle smoothly down to the southern edge of the San Joaquin Valley and guided it down the main highway for another spell. Manuel remembered that the family stayed with some friends in Delano who owned and operated a tortilla making shop.

The next day, Dad drove farther north on US 99, turning west onto US 152 at Los Baños. Dad powered the LaSalle up Pacheco Pass, another towering ridge that separated the cooler marine air from the hotter inland valleys, and finally brought our family down to the extensive agricultural gardens that surround Hollister and Gilroy. Today the fields remain covered with verdant, ground-hugging vegetable tops and low trees weighed down with fruit—a veritable Garden of Eden that always makes me draw a deep breath and must have impressed my folks similarly in 1942. According to Manuel, we stayed with the Cárdenas family, our *vecindad* neighbors who had already moved to Gilroy. Don Benjamín Cárdenas, a tall, paunchy, light-skinned man recommended we seek work at the DD Ranch.

"We found a sign that said 'DD Ranch,'" Mary recollected. Noting that it was filled with plum trees and having been informed that the proprietors wanted workers, my father drove the La Salle into the property, humming past two tall pillars that guarded the entrance. We approached a house visible at the end of a long dirt road where an older Mexican couple greeted us. They served as the overseers. After the preliminary greetings and reciprocal eyeballing, they informed us that we were welcomed to settle in because the harvesting of plums was about to begin. Mary must have asked, "Where could we stay?" She only remembers the old man pointing to some stacking trays used for boxing the prunes and him saying, "Help yourself to whatever you can find!"

Mary claims that without complaining or asking questions, my father didn't hesitate. With the handyman side of his personality surely triggered by a keen sense of survival and pragmatism about the options facing him, he sprang into action despite his physical handicap. Breaking the trays apart, he somehow built a shed, and Mary helped. The details of how this construction took shape are lost in memory; what he used for vertical or horizontal beams, we don't know. In any case, the ranch overseers allowed Dad to connect an electric cord to the main house in order to turn on a light bulb in the evening. My sister also called up the fact that while the slatted shed offered some protection to the family, the wind nevertheless whistled through the cracks at night when the outside temperature cooled. Manuel recalled a slightly different story where Dad in fact built a shelter out of stray lumber, but he also remembered that my parents slept in the rancher's big old wooden house while he and Mike slept on some cots in an old gray tent. The slatted shed might have served as our abode at first. There were other worker families who lived in some barrack-like buildings. The proprietors, of Italian ancestry, lived in a large new home not too far away.

Never having done agricultural work together as a family, it must have been frustrating at times for my father to corral the young ones to work once the picking got started. Manuel and Mike most probably confused working with playing as both of them were just boys after all. Mary, an early teenager, didn't hesitate to help because she shared a better understanding of the larger economic situation facing the family, and she always prized assisting Dad anyway.

The work was simple enough, and that's why the kids were able to help. The prune trees were harvested three times during the picking season, and each turn required picking the fallen fruit off the ground, a procedure that made it necessary to stoop or kneel. Mary brought to mind Dad purchasing some rubberized knee pads from a nearby hardware store that you could tie around your knees. "Wearing these pads made picking plums much easier," she said. The third picking of the season was done with special hooks that helped shake the branches and finally clear the tree of its fruit. The pickers filled buckets which were emptied into the slatted boxes. The fruit was then placed into an oven whose high temperatures shrank them into the dark, waxy, wrinkly prunes of the kind and shape that most consumers know. The impact of the DD Ranch experience on eleven-year-old Manuel's memory was that "you had to drag yourself on the ground . . . it was dreary work." But he remembered that the rancher family was friendly, including the teenage daughters, "*unas güeras, simpatícas,*" light-skinned and good looking. Picking prunes nonetheless produced very sore backs. Needless to say, these were lessons of what kind of work to avoid when we became adults.

Next to getting shelter, if we were going to do an adequate job and make the trip worth it, we needed to be clothed and fed, and this job fell to Guadalupe, my mother. For this reason, she didn't work in the fields—she worked at "home" in the shed or the garage, preparing food, washing clothes, and caring for three-year-old Martha and baby Rick. Outside of the fact that Mother had to cook with a kerosene stove, Mary didn't retain in her memory any particulars about Mom's domestic supportive activity under these extraordinary circumstances—nonetheless, it seems that no one went hungry, and everyone had something to wear. Three-year-old Martha was encouraged to sit in a plum slat box cushioned with pillows in order to keep her out of harm's way.

Baby Rick, however, required special care because we believed that his *mollera* "had fallen." This meant that he had a sunken fontanelle; he was also feverish and cried a lot. Mary felt that his rolling off the bedding several times in these chaotic days may have affected his cranial soft spot.[164] Still an infant, the bone plates on his head had not yet come together, and this probably produced the soft, sunken spot. The ranch overseer's wife, "a thin, little lady of short stature" named Doña Petra who apparently struck a relationship with Guadalupe, offered to help. In doing so, she held up Rick by his legs, which she tied with a diaper to hold him securely and, as she shook him, inserted one of her fingers in his mouth. This procedure lasted a minute or two. She then sat him on a table and, with some water in her mouth, proceeded to suck the soft spot to make it rise. Mary believes this helped Rick. We don't know how my mother reacted.

Mary contracted polio in this trip too. An infectious disease caused by contact with contaminated food or water; it struck Mary with increasing and paralyzing pain in one of her legs.[165] She was one of many young people who contracted polio in the United States in the 1930s. "The pain developed within a week, and I could hardly stand up," Mary remembered. "I could feel the bone hurt so badly," she swore. And so, over and above the chores that my mother was tasked to keep the family working in the orchards, she now had to take care of her eldest daughter who was becoming an invalid right in front of her very own eyes.

My mother resorted to bathing Mary's leg with hot water and covering it with steamy towels. How mother managed to do this given our living circumstances at this time is simply unfathomable. While this remedy seemed to help, it was not enough; Mary continued to fall whenever she walked out into the orchards, so mother and Dad took her to a doctor. After an examination, the doctor confirmed that she had picked up polio, and that the afflicted leg was in fact not only thinning down quickly but also becoming shorter. He did not think Mary could be cured—it was too late, he said, but he called a county nurse anyway.

A nurse appeared at the ranch the very next day, eager to examine Mary. This guardian angel paid by the county of San Jose confirmed that Mary could not feel the pinprick applied to her bad leg, apparently a common test. She thereupon ordered my father to immediately place Mary in the San Jose County Hospital. "You need to take this girl to the hospital now because there is a polio epidemic going on," Mary recalled grimly. My parents must have been stunned and alarmed, but, apparently, they didn't hesitate. Specialists would confirm decades later that poliomyelitis was indeed reaching epidemic proportions about the time my family was harvesting plums in Gilroy.[166]

Mary was admitted to the hospital and treated according to a new polio therapy program called the "Sister Kenny method." It turned out to be very similar to what my mother had done by instinct. "Sister Kenny applied moist hot packs to help loosen muscles, relieve pain, and enable limbs to be moved, stretched, and strengthened,"[167] thus reads a web site to a medical institute that bears her name today. At the hospital, the 100 percent wool blankets applied to Mary's legs had been boiled in hot water, squeezed dry, wrapped around her body, and sealed with plastic (this was the first time that Mary saw plastic). She received two treatments daily for about five weeks and was released thereafter.[168] My mother kept up the hot water treatments back at the ranch, somehow, and soon the family returned to San Fernando, where Mother could resume the treatments there. Mary recovered eventually, perhaps miraculously, but she remembered that she was struck with rheumatic fever[169] not long after their return to San Fernando. Mary recovered from that too.

Because the Depression didn't end for us, we went "up north" two more times during the war years, and our experience as agricultural peons remained similar to 1942, except that none of us had to be hospitalized like Mary. Even so, our living conditions didn't improve significantly because in Salinas, for example, Mary remembered we lived in the farm owner's garage—Dad again fixed it up to make it habitable. Manuel remembered living in a barn there and sleeping on mattresses on the floor; his memory was sharper about some young men he met on the farm, one of whom owned a Plymouth sedan also cut down into a truck. In Gonzalez, Dad and Mary converted a chicken coop (*un gallinero*, Mary termed it) into our home away from home—Manuel called it a "hut.'" With her younger brothers by her side, Mary called to mind observing trucks filled with workers and produce going back and forth to nearby Soledad. Here the family worked in the *escarda de lechuga* or the thinning of lettuce seedlings using a twelve-inch hoe as the main working tool. A worker had to bend down to do the thinning. "We had to leave a thread of seedlings, separating each one by the length of two-and-a-half-hoe-blade widths. We used a six-foot hoe to weed," Mary specified. Manuel remembered almost the same details about the backbreaking effort, although he added that the work was so demanding and the rows were so long that the day could end and you would still be on the row you began in the morning. The thought flashed through his mind that "The [rows] might have been a half a mile long!" "They'd give you a hoe and that's what you'd have to do!" he stammered. Our family also worked the potato fields in Gonzalez, where Mary remembered working on a machine-driven belt used for sorting potatoes by size. Her job was to pick the "baker" size potatoes and place them in bags which were sewed up on the spot and hauled off.

World War II ended during our work trip to Salinas, Mary recollected. She didn't forget the moment when faraway automobile drivers honked their horns endlessly, rang bells, and set whistles blowing. The long-awaited news that the United States and its Allies had obtained victory over Germany came as our family labored silently in the fields of the San Joaquin Valley. Known later as VE Day, the celebration meant, among other things, that American boys would be coming home after a tense and vicious war. Mary remembered hearing the noise and commotion as she worked in the fields and feeling strangely removed and isolated. The fact that Manuel and Mike were far too young to have served as soldiers in battles that demanded so much from Americans made the war experience somewhat detached from us. The fact is that the rest of the world seems so distant when you're working in the fields.

When we didn't go up north, we did shorter stints of agricultural harvesting locally from time to time. At the age of ten, I joined my family in pulling carrots out of the ground in the patches of farmland still free of suburban homes in the western side of the San Fernando Valley, near present-day University of California at Northridge. We also picked tomatoes north of San Fernando, an experience that comes to mind when I handle tomato vines and get a whiff of their unique pungency. We picked olives in Sylmar many times, once an important olive producing center in California. They fell to the ground from the gnarly gray trees that grew among the *toritos* or prickly thorns that littered the desert floor (the *toritos* of course stuck to our knees often). Suburban houses now stand in the place of the olive groves. At lunchtime, we would gather in a dry gulch to warm up our meal which consisted of simple *taquitos* or tortilla wraps filled with beans, rice, or scrambled eggs, and perhaps a bit of cooked meat. We heated our tacos in the ambers of a quick fire. For us children, it was a joy to sit on the ground in view of Mom and Dad, eating our food around the fire, but our parents most likely didn't share in our childish delight.

Fifty-some odd years later, the deprivations we underwent in the name of supplementing our family budget, especially by going "up north" in the 1940s, seem nothing less than staggering. We may as well have been living in Mexico or some other Third World country. Our experience shows that our American capitalist system, based on "the survival of the fittest,"[170] coerced farmers to build their livelihoods on workers like us who labored in near-serf conditions. The system treated us like commodities, like a wheelbarrow or a tractor that you use up and throw away when it no longer works. The degree of our dispossession on these trips paralleled the sufferings and sacrifices of the legions of other families who worked in the golden fields of California in those days, Mexican, Okie, Filipino, or otherwise.

We, Gil children, have all but forgotten our childhood toil as farm workers, and it's safe to say that we barely appreciated our parents' distress over it. Moreover, our own bourgeois children know next to nothing about it and are capable of imagining much less. Yet, it goes on. We've been replaced by the multitudes of families, most of them from Mexico like our own, who continue to toil in the fields today under similar conditions and keep on enduring deprivations and challenges quite like ours.

Chapter 10

Our Toughest Years
(1942–1972)

We Open Gil's Café • How We Came to Know Our Clients • We Close Gil's Café • Grandmother Dies • Dad Becomes Ill and Passes On • Life without Father • Mother Begins to Renew Herself • Looking After Soledad and Emily • An Earthquake Hastens Mother's "Retirement"

We Open Gil's Café

WHEN WE RETURNED from picking fruit in Delano, we opened up a restaurant. My mother recorded this fact laconically in her notes. She meant that around 1942 we opened Gil's Café at 518 Kalisher Street. This is when we returned from working up North and found Grandma's storefront at this address to be vacant, including the living quarters in the rear. We had rented our Mott Street house, while we were working up North in the fields, so upon our return instead of ousting our renters Mom negotiated our occupying the Kalisher Street property for a fee from Grandma. Undoubtedly our parents had previously decided that we would open a small eatery.

Mom and Dad must have concluded that supplementing the family budget with our field labor was simply not the right thing for us, so they looked for other options, apparently. It appears that they decided to open up a food establishment as a way of putting food on *our* table, keeping us together yet surviving economically thanks to our common effort. Mom and Dad would be able to attend to the whole family, and on top of this, Mother could live next door to Grandma.

Dad thus put on his carpenter's hat on once more by converting the corner storefront into a small eatery with enough space to accommodate, perhaps, fifteen people. Despite his physical handicap, he was, after all, an informal builder. He constructed a wooden counter to harbor about a dozen swivel seats, fashioned three or four tables with chairs, and converted an adjacent room into a kitchen separated by top-to-bottom swinging doors. After fitting in other embellishments, this allowed us to inaugurate Gil's Café after returning from our last trip up North.

You, the reader, might be encouraged to visualize Gil's Café as a Mexican restaurant like those found in California today, but this would be incorrect. What is widely known as a Mexican restaurant at the time of this writing didn't exist in the United States at the time. This grand assertion is buttressed by the fact that the average middle-class American palate had not yet expanded beyond the traditional diet of meatloaf sandwiches, home-style hamburgers, liver and onions, pot roast, and other meat and potato dishes, the Depression having battered many middle class eateries. What's for certain is that the food preferences of the average American had not yet expanded to include enchilada sauces and tacos, for example. Besides, the habit and the financial wherewithal of dining out hadn't yet grown to the level common today. So, if any mom-and-pop eateries catering to Mexicans living in the United States could be found in the many barrios dotting the Southwest at this time, Gil's Café would probably fall comfortably into this class of eating establishments. We're talking about a basic mom and pop eating place.

Whether our parents planned it or not, Gil's Café ultimately catered to a niche market, the Braceros and their associates. This is to say, we focused our restaurant services on the many single working men living in the barrio. The Bracero Program stimulated their arrival. We've already seen that Mexican workers took up residence in San Fernando as early as the 1920s, but by the late 1940s, they came in droves, thanks to the US-Mexico guest worker program launched in 1942. Braceros were officially approved Mexican farm workers who helped us bring in the nation's harvests while Americans who might have labored in the fields could now devote themselves to the war effort, namely the Second World War. In simpler terms, the program allowed Americans to work in the nation's war factories while Mexicans brought in their agricultural harvests. This arrangement ironically contributed to ever larger waves of Mexicans arriving in small towns like San Fernando.[171] If one male adult member of a Mexican family managed to sign up as a Bracero worker, another one simply traveled to the United States on his own to work outside of the program. These I call the associates of the Braceros. The border was still quite porous in those days, and the links of economic integration at the level of the small towns and villages in Mexico had already locked into place, connecting towns like Mascota to American communities like San Fernando. This brought customers to eating establishments like Gil's Café.

While the Braceros were supposed to be fed at their special camps, some of them looked for alternatives like our small restaurant from time to time. The others who didn't live in the Bracero camps avoided cooking at home and preferred getting their meals in the small eateries like ours on Kalisher Street.

Many of these customers became our food boarders. Mother's experience helping Cleofas feed workers at the Sugar Pine Lumber Company near Yosemite undoubtedly helped clinch the decision to open the restaurant and focus on getting some boarders or *abordados*. For a weekly or monthly sum, an *abordado* could count on all three Mexican-styled meals at Gil's Café, including a packed lunch.

Mary easily brought to mind the menu at Gil's Café. It included pork meat stew with green chilies or beef stew with red chilies, shredded beef in a special sauce, meat-ball soup, beef soup, oven-roasted lamb or beef heads, beef tongue in a sauce, *menudo* (a tripe and hominy soup prepared with tomatoes and red chilies). Her exact words were *[C]arne con chile verde ó chile colorado, picadillo, albóndigas, cocido de res, cabezas al horno de borrego ó de res, lengua, menudo, tamales*, and of course, the customary sides of *frijoles* and *arroz* [beans and rice], and *tortillas*, corn, or flour. We also served *tacos* filled with seasoned shredded beef and chopped salad ingredients in tortilla shells which we fried to toasty crispness, and *enchiladas* filled with salad ingredients enhanced with dried crumbly Mexican cheese, not the baked kind smothered with Jack Cheese.

Mary's memory placed my father in a more important kitchen role than Mother. She explained that "Dad was more the cook, and he always had a better taste. Mom was not a good cook at the time. [If] she did cook she'd say, 'However the dish comes out is the way it'll be' or *Sale como sale* (but) not Dad, [he was more careful]. We didn't serve liquor because the church stood right across the street."

We Came to Know Our Clients

This is how we, Gil children, came to know a fair number of Mexican immigrant workers in these years—they became our customers and also our friends. In the early years, many of them were only a few years older than Mary and Manuel, if that much. My older siblings enjoyed lots of things in common with these guys in part because our parents had insisted we speak Spanish at home and also because Mom kept us conversant about her hometown and about other things going on in Mexico, as we'll appreciate below. When the rest of us Gil children grew older and took our turn to serve the customers, we also conversed with them easily enough, depending on our maturity. This is why we personally remembered many into our old age.

They were an interesting mix of men folk. Many were of the rural kind. I remember one who appeared as if he had stepped away momentarily from his farm, his *ranchito,* wearing sandals and covering himself with a heavily-woven *poncho,* just like a campesino would in Mascota on a cold morning. Most of them, though, were just a bit more citified or at least small townsmen-like, not yet altogether comfortable wearing jeans and Levi jackets or walking at ease in leather shoes, as opposed to sandals. Don Ciriaco and his two nephews, Manuel and Miguel Gonzalez, come to mind. They crossed the border as a family unit with Don Ciriaco, acting more like a chaperon, doing supervisory duty over his two nephews. He was a tallish man with a small lump on his forehead, seasoned, in his early sixties. Manuel and Miguel were in their twenties, all of them *güeros* with fair skin, brown hair, and brownish green eyes. While they could have come from any small town in northern Spain, they hailed from somewhere in the Los Altos region of Jalisco, where many inhabitants retain these physical characteristics, Jalisco being one of the strongest immigrant-sending states in Mexico. Don Ciriaco and his nephews lived in rooms Grandma rented to men like this, and so for many years they also patronized our little restaurant somehow being able to avoid the immigration agents who conducted roundups every so often. I remember the three men as real gentlemen of the country bumpkin sort.

We also remember those who were not ploughmen or hat-wearing *rancheritos.* Mary dredged her memory up for the A. brothers, Ricardo and Antonio, who gave off an urban air about them. Ricardo was a pleasant young man of about eighteen years, his dark skin complementing his black curly hair and carefully trimmed moustache. We nicknamed him Shorty because he was not as tall as most of the fellows in the barrio. Mary summoned to mind the fact that he seldom rushed off to work in the morning, possessing a more leisurely approach to life. I remember that he was always relaxed and willing to stand outside our establishment on a sunny morning and casually smoke a cigarette, watching the world go by. Mary knew him better than I, and she maintains that he managed to work from time to time. His brother, Antonio, was the opposite. Perhaps a year older, he was the diligent one. He arrived at Gil's Café early for breakfast and rushed off with one of our hand-packed lunches in hand, just at the moment when Jerry Avalos would come by and honk for him—Jerry owned a large truck in which he collected chicken manure to take to the orchard growers who needed fertilizer. Jerry was *el estiercolero* (the manure guy), and Antonio was one of the *paleros*, the fellows who spread the manure with a shovel while standing on the open truck platform in the back. With a note of respect in his voice, my brother, Manuel, who would soon join the US Air Force, added that "Tony" joined the US Navy and, like Manuel himself, received an honorable discharge about ten years later.

Ricardo and "Tony," like nearly all of our customers, always acted respectfully toward our family, including young Mary. And they always paid their bill on time. Mother would have been the first to protest had they behaved otherwise, and they would have deferred to her without hesitation. Shorty had so much time on his hands one day that he offered to do a reasonably good pencil-sketch portrait of Mary, which my mother kept for many decades. In the end, the A. brothers went their own way. Antonio or "Tony," the conscientious brother married one of the girls in the barrio and settled into our community, while Shorty, who preferred a happy-go-lucky approach, was picked up by the *migra* or the immigration officials and returned to Mexico, and we never saw him again.

Luis was another unforgettable guy in those days. Mary recalls that he too was an urban kind of fellow who married one of the prettiest girls in our barrio, Esperanza. My sister also summoned to mind that a couple of friends from back home came to stay with him, and they also ate their meals at our café. She considered them upper-class fellows, who seemed unfamiliar with manual labor. She remembered that both wore safari-styled helmets when they boarded the trucks that took them to work in the orchards alongside Luis. They obviously wore them for protection, but nobody wore that kind of headgear made popular by Hollywood films. It made them stick out like a sore thumb, most citrus pickers wearing cloth hats or caps of a more conventional style in those days. Their stay in San Fernando didn't last very long, but Luis did. Mary described him as someone who worked hard, saved his money, married as properly as possible, and opened up a dry cleaning shop, a block away from our restaurant, next to La Mexicana grocery on Kalisher Street. He did well. As Mary said, "*Luis no era de rancho* (he was middle class)," a status that was not yet within our reach.

Mary also remembered Nacho. He was one of the first Braceros to arrive in San Fernando, according to my sister. He would arrive from the Bracero camp at Pico Court with a group of friends on weekends, all of them in their twenties and thirties, Pico Court being located near the San Fernando Mission. Like most of our customers, Nacho and his friends were single young men who seemed to enjoy their meal more when listening to music from back home. They did this by endlessly dropping coins into our colorful juke box, which allowed you to view the records being changed through a small front window. They gained pleasure from the latest Mexican *bolero* (slow tempo danceable romantic tunes) or *canción ranchera* (Mexican country-western songs usually accompanied by a mariachi) supplied by our Jewish music vendor, a tall husky fellow, who knew what was hot in Mexican music.[172] Mary recalled that although Nacho was married to a woman who awaited him back home, he developed a relationship with one of the local girls and went to the extent of telling Mary's friends that he was going to marry her. Someone, it seems, warned his wife and even supplied her with a false birth certificate to get her across the border, so she showed up in time to foil whatever spurious wedding plans Nacho might have put together. The reunited couple ate at our café many times and maintained a relationship with our family long after Nacho became deceased.

In my own memory, Narciso stands out as a customer who really knew how to dress, at least, on weekends. It was about 1950, and I was getting ready to transfer from Grammar School to Junior High in those days. I must have begun paying attention to good dressers—subliminally at least. My siblings and I thought he was the best dressed male around, to be sure. Even though he lived in a nearby courtyard of single rooms—not unlike our own *vecindad* in our earlier days—and dressed in tan khakis and cement-crusted boots Monday through Friday, he always impressed me on Sundays when he would show up for breakfast or lunch, dressed up as if he were strolling down Broadway in his sharkskin suit and shiny black shoes. Mary remembered a "brown suit with red tinges," which impressed her well enough. He maintained a slim figure and his dark, reddish, naturally-waved hair complemented some gold fillings, which sparkled when he smiled. He also behaved respectfully and soon became a family friend. More than a half century later, he showed up as the best dressed man at my mother's funeral even though he moved with the sluggishness of an old man, but his hair remained curly, but now thin and gray. I noticed that the gold in his smile had also survived.

Then there was Isabel, who was quite a special case. He was a chubby, olive-skinned Mexican American who wore a shock of dark hair across his forehead and disarmed you with a dimply smile. He stood out because he was bilingual in English and Spanish and was one of the few Mexican Americans (born in the US, apparently) who frequented our establishment. When he came into our life, he was a veteran in his midthirties; Mary placed him as a former coast guardsman of the early 1950s, and he might have served in World War II. I remember him mostly because his mind was not right. He lived for several years in one of my grandmother's boarding rooms, less than a stone's throw from where I slept when I was twelve, and every so often he would run around our yard in his underclothes, howling with fear. He was hounded by hallucinations, surely. But on the days when his mind was free of demons, he was a very kind and charming fellow— just a bit spooky for us.

There were many others. Mary also remembered José who married one of her best friends. Another fellow by the name of Alfonso married the daughter of one of our neighbors, and then I can see in my own mind's eye the chaps whose real names we rarely ever used because they were known only by their nicknames like El Zapo (Frog), El Chino (a man with curly hair), and El Tos Qué,[173] a Mexico City *pachuco*[174]—all of them customers and friends who hung around our café frequently.

Unsociable customers at The Gil Café were rare, thank goodness. Most of our regulars might have originated in the most remote areas in Mexico and attended school minimally, but their behavior inside our establishment was nearly always gentlemanly. We were spared of any rough behavior although Emily, the youngest sibling in our family, remembered a time when one of our customers misbehaved in our little restaurant. She also recalled that the fellow was dealt with summarily.

> Dad was sitting at the counter one day and this man was [also] sitting at the counter, eating some soup. I was sitting there with Dad. The man got really nasty and belligerent and my dad told him to leave; [that] if he didn't like the food to leave. The man got very derogatory and took a swing at Dad and [suddenly] my dad lifted him up in the air and hit him once, knocking him into the two doors [forming the exit at the front of the restaurant] and he fell out the door . . . Dad just picked him up, threw him in the air, and he was just gone.

We Close Gil's Café

We closed Gil's Café in 1953 for several reasons. One was that the work team my parents had put together in the beginning had come apart by this time, as we'll see in more detail in the following chapter. Suffice it to say here that the elder Gil children were going their way and leaving the load of restaurant work to Mom, Dad, and their younger siblings.

Mom cites another reason for our closure: Government pressure against our most important customers. She cites this as the culminating motive for our closing Gil's Café. In fact, the shuttering of our little enterprise coincided with the days of Operation Wetback when the US Government began to hunt "wetbacks" more consistently (i.e., Mexicans living in the United States without proper documentation) in order to deport them. As we've seen within the context of our own business, the Bracero Program invited registered Mexican workers, but it also attracted their friends and relatives who often came from the same community. This is the type of immigrant who became our customer but also served as the target of Operation Wetback. The Eisenhower administration gave it a green light in 1954, thus bringing about the "mass roundup of 'wetbacks' . . . planned and conducted with all of the intricacy of a military operation," write historians Griswold del Castillo and De León.[175] They claim that more than a million persons were gathered up throughout the country as a result.

Operation Wetback hit us hard in San Fernando. We saw more roundups than ever before, all of which caused grief, panic, and the disruption of local economic life. There were many instances in which tall Anglo men wearing crow-colored felt fedoras and knee-length gray coats over dark suits appeared suddenly on Kalisher Street around breakfast time. Someone would catch sight of these men dressed in the G-men style of the Eisenhower years and yell out "*la migra*!" and within seconds, our café would clear out. Customers without "papers" at our counter would dash into our kitchen and disappear out the back door, some escaping and others not, the immigration officials barging into the restaurant at will. I remember *migra* agents stopping me on one of these occasions and questioning me but letting me go soon thereafter. In any case, the foregoing explains why my mother wrote the following words: "I stopped offering board and shut down the café because the *imigración* would periodically take all of the *ilegales*." She added, "I was better off working at the sewing factory." This is about the time that Mom took a factory job to help make ends meet in 1953, the beginning of her dark years.

Grandmother Dies

Our Grandma's final illness also helped close the doors of Gil's Café in part because Mom felt it was her duty to care for her. Grandma Carlota had lived next door to us over the years, tending to her tortilla business and feeding and otherwise caring for her dozens of canaries housed in various cages, but now, in her final months, she was forced to move in with us. So, having shuttered the café in one of his last jobs as a handyman, Dad reconverted the space we had devoted to the restaurant into two rooms, the larger of which became Grandma's final sleeping quarters. His carpenter's skills enabled us to bring her in into our living quarters where we installed her bed so that Mother and the rest of us could more readily attend to her. I remember catching sight of her resting in her bed, robed in a long, loose, egg-white nightgown as her big eyes kept track of the comings and goings of the family. She had always worn her hair in long braids and now it was silvery but still thick. Even though she became an unforgiving hag for some of us children, as her old scolding ways didn't entirely fade, we dutifully attended to her nevertheless, my sisters often combing and braiding her long tresses, the memories of her harshness weighing more on some of us than others. Seven-year-old Emily, the youngest in the family who confessed being free of grudges against her grandmother, served as her aide in her last days and thus witnessed the impact of Grandma's death on her daughter, our mother.

Mom was devastated by her mother's death when it came, needless to say. According to Emily, "Her world had crashed [as a result]" and after the funeral rites, she shut herself in her bedroom and spent long days grieving and crying. Guarding her feelings, Mom wrote in her memoirs, "She died on July 20, 1954, and I felt like an orphan."

Emily remembered being in the way. "We were a bother to her grief," she said, referring to herself, Martha, and Soledad, the youngest children still at home and heavily dependent on Mother. In fact, Martha had been stricken with rheumatic fever at this time and required almost complete bed rest. "She would get feverish if she did too much." Emily remembered of Marty. Nevertheless, "Mother wanted to spend all her time crying," Emily told me in a dispassionate tone, adding, "My existence interfered with her grieving . . . Mom had no patience for my size. I was a bother; [I was] in the way." I concluded that it must have taken my kid sister many years to be able to make these statements without expressing any emotion because she must have sorely missed the nurturing that a normal seven-year-old girl required. What remains clear is that in the days leading up to Grandma's passing away, in addition to a stack of other concerns, Mom had to worry about three family members who were ill in her house: Grandma, Dad, and Martha. My little sister Emily's childhood had indeed unfolded during Mom's worst years and she suffered from it consequently.

Having been close to Grandma, Emily now sought Dad's reassurance with greater insis-tence. "My refuge was to hide with Dad, [to] take care of him." Emily insisted she stayed "as far away" from Mom as possible, and if she asked her to do a chore, she would do it as quickly and efficiently as she could in order to fend off any negativity; "[doing the chore] would get me out of the way," Emily clarified—and she might have added as close to Dad as possible.

The family budget demanded income no matter who was sick or dying. As we've already stated, Mom filled the gap by setting aside the micro business and joining the labor force. She did this by working in the small to medium-sized factories that developed just north of downtown San Fernando in the 1950s; this is where she tried her hand at several jobs. These included working in a sewing factory, a commercial laundry, and, worst of all, a turkey-plucking plant. At age fifty, she discovered that her eyesight wasn't good enough for sewing, and her hands weren't strong enough for lifting wet clothes to push into the squeezer rollers at the laundry or for plucking dead, smelly fowl at the turkey plant—and she simply didn't care for these jobs, in any case. They were very hard on her. She complained about it, but we children, thick-skinned with our own little world, didn't appreciate her plight very much.

Dad Becomes Ill and Passes On

Dad didn't tarry either. Despite his growing frailty he refused to sit at home turning to what he knew best: micro businesses and doing field work. Always honing in on her father, Emily remembered fifty years later that he worked in some of the onion fields near Saugus at this time, more likely during the summer. She remembered that he often took her along with my younger brother, Rick, thirteen at this time, and Soledad, eleven, and they both helped Dad unearth the odiferous bulbs vital to cooks and chefs. Rick probably helped more than Emily. This was hard work, of course, and bad for the human back. Any assistance must have been appreciated by our one-armed Dad, who was about fifty-five years old at that time and not feeling well. The work took a toll on him. Emily put it in her own words as follows:

> . . . [I]t got very destructive for Dad. [His body] would swell up in the fields, and we would find him unconscious. [When we stirred him] he would say, "No, no, no, [don't wake me up]. Let me sleep a little bit more and tell me when you've gotten to the end of the row." (*"No, no, no. déjame dormir un ratito y me despiertas cuando ya lleguen a la orilla del surco."*) [Sometimes] there was no way of waking him up.

She also remembered that the field supervisor would come around to check on things and overlook my dad's prolonged napping as long as the children were packing the boxes with freshly pulled onions. In the end, the little money that my dad and the kids earned in the Saugus onion fields probably helped the family budget in important ways but, as stated already, we children remained largely unaware of the financial stresses our parents suffered at this time.

Mom's factory work and Dad's desultory picking jobs didn't pay off, in the end. Funding the needs and wants of five children including me, even though I was already working part-time after school, was not easy to do and so my parents found it hard to survive economically. So they reengaged micro businesses in the hope that this would make ends meet as before. This led to Mother reopening Grandma's *tortillería* (tortilla factory) and Dad starting up a grocery store—his last.

The strongest memories I have of my father coincide with these fretful years. They find him sitting patiently behind his grocery-store counter at Kalisher and Hewitt Streets—across the street from where we had operated Gil's Café. We used to refer to this store front as the "Landín's store" because Eusebio Landín, the publisher of *Vida del Valle de San Fernando*, the barrio's first newspaper, operated a store on this site. Here Dad would wait head down for customers as if he were meditating, often napping, wrapped in a soiled butcher's apron. I remember him wearing his customary light-colored, long-sleeve shirt with the empty left sleeve rolled up as usual, his durable gray cotton twill-work trousers, and his scuffed but sturdy half-length brown work boots—I don't recall him ever wearing "dress" shoes. He often wore a sweater because he complained about being cold, especially in his last years. His thinning *chino* hair (i.e., curly) was more pepper than salt by this time but still long enough to allow us to comb it.

He would shake off his doziness when a customer approached and engage in friendly banter during the sale. Despite extremely poor eyesight in his last days, he never wore eyeglasses and when measuring out meat or cheese he would have to crane his neck forward and squint at the grocery scale to make sure he was serving the correct amount, his diabetes-induced blindness being on the increase. After the customer walked out, he would regress to his meditational doze. These were the days when his legs swelled up from advanced diabetes, when I joined in to give him his insulin shots on a regular basis. This was about the time he tearfully confessed to Mother, "I can't work anymore!" With an ache in her heart, Mother reminded us of this confession several times after we became young adults.

My younger sister, Emily, preserved a more cheerful recollection, however.

> He used to love to talk to people about really serious stuff; I would stand with him on the corner when he would talk to people. He was like a counselor to people. People would stop by and tell him their stories. He would stand at the corner and talk to them, *"no, no compadre, eso no."* He was always talking to people [although] he couldn't see them anymore . . . [All he could see] were *bultos* [fuzzy objects]. He couldn't recognize people anymore but he recognized their step. [D]riving [in a car] with him was very dangerous. I had to tell him when to stop, when to turn, where's the curb . . . That was a "trip," being my dad's eyes while he was driving!

In the 1950s, my father also organized and operated another grocery store in what we called Orcasitas, a Mexican barrio of sorts in North Hollywood. After Mother's death, we gathered the various and sundry papers she had preserved in an old foot locker, including a tax record associated with Dad's store at this location in this central-eastern part of the San Fernando Valley. It showed a payment in 1954 of $12.53 for unsecured personal property taxes my father had declared in 1950 in connection with his store on 7834 Beck Avenue, North Hollywood. H. L. Byram, tax collector for the county of Los Angeles, threatened "seizure and sale" of this property if the taxes were not paid "at once." It seems father operated this store even while we were running Gil's Café. I would help my dad at this store on occasion when I was about fifteen and remember him driving there in an old 1934 Ford sedan that usually boiled over somewhere on Lankershim Boulevard. Dad would have to stop and let the radiator cool down before refilling it.

Dad died at the end of 1955. He was forced to abandon all efforts at managing a grocery store a year or so before due, in part, to his increasing blindness[176] which naturally restricted his mobility, as Emily mentions above. Mom confirmed Emily's observations when she wrote that on the few occasions she and Dad drove eighteen miles to Glendale to see a doctor, she had to guide him and tell him when to bring the car to a halt at a traffic light. I remember driving Mom and Dad to Glendale, perhaps more than once during these awful days. Mary recalled that "Dad was very sick . . . he would lie down close to the stove *porque tenia mucho frio* (because he felt very cold)." We didn't have central heating. Soledad (Sally), eleven years old at the time, also remembered Dad being very ill and saying one day that he didn't want to go to the hospital.

> I remember his looking at us . . . Emily and me . . . and saying . . . with tears in his eyes . . . I don't want to go to the hospital because I know I won't return. That was the last I [remember] of my dad alive.

Like other poor people across the face of America at this time, Dad didn't enjoy preventive medical care; he couldn't afford to see a doctor very often and so he died relatively young, at age fifty-six, as a consequence. These were Republican years. The social programs that would bring relief to America's poor and elderly would come later, thanks to the Democrats. Medicaid, a federal program providing health care for low-income families and individuals, might have helped us, but along with Medicare it was created ten years later, when President Lyndon Johnson launched his Great Society program.[177] In the absence of any reliable medical assistance, Mom would be overtaken by desperation over Dad's condition, and they would sometimes travel as far away as Tijuana on the US-Mexico border in search of medical care—where they could pay less for needed drugs and, at least, relate their needs to a medical doctor in a common language. "It was so difficult to go there," Mother admitted, "because we couldn't even afford to rent a room there, so we would sleep in the car."

Mom evoked the final days as follows:

> One day he [Bernabé] needed a blood transfusion and the nurse [we went to see] instructed us to take him to the county hospital [right away]. It didn't take longer than fourteen days and that's when I lost him. I felt so desolate . . . I didn't know what to do.

Mary, who was living with us at the time, accompanied Mother to the hospital, and she remembered more details:

> Dad was taken to [the Los Angeles County] General Hospital and I just remember he went into a coma. They didn't have dialysis yet [in those days] and [so] they were trying to flush his kidneys with the IV [so] when the IV water reached his heart, that's when he died. He began to fill up with water from his feet to his chest. [178] He was just like a balloon . . . We had to suction his chest because the phlegm would build up. That was our job—to be taking it out of his chest because he would choke on it. The doctors would only come when something bad would happen.

Manuel claims we all stood around Dad's hospital bed in his last moments. He also stated that Dad looked for me and didn't find me as he gazed around his bed; Manuel believes I arrived late at Dad's bedside. Then Dad closed his eyes, never to open them again (I was also hospitalized in these days and this may have prevented me from being at my father's bedside). Manuel summoned Dad's last moments to mind and gave them a comforting interpretation at the same time, as follows:

> He closed his eyes, and then he woke up again and looked around. To him it was a job well done. Yeah [, we were what he had worked so hard to keep together]. That was my father's life: *su vieja y sus hijos* [his old lady and his children]. Mission completed. [Then] he closed his eyes forever . . . It was a big shock; [it] tore me up.

My memory of my father's death revolves around my arranging his funeral. I had just turned eighteen at the time and while I must have been beaming at finding myself as the first in the family to finish high school (I had graduated six months earlier), my self-pride surely had to be toned down by my father's approaching end. I don't remember things clearly, but I do recall we were so broke that we didn't know how we were going to give my dad a deserving burial after he was pronounced dead. Mother was naturally engulfed by her grief, and my older siblings were wrapped up tightly in their own evolving lives, so I stepped into the breach and took it upon myself to make the final arrangements. I had worked part-time during my high school years for a Russian–American family that owned a trailer park at the southern end of the town and so I went to my boss, Rick Adams, the head of the family, and asked him for a loan big enough to pay for Dad's funeral expenses. Rick didn't hesitate one bit and, as a consequence, I was able to arrange and pay for my father's funeral and burial. I also remember assisting the undertaker to make sure my dad looked proper. I made sure he was interred with the one and only sports coat he owned, a gray gabardine jacket, and his gray twill-work pants plus a white shirt and a tie which he rarely ever donned. I remember summarily approving the cosmetic coloring on his face because he had lost his natural blush by this time. He thus appeared presentable for the viewing and the rosary service that followed soon thereafter.

My dad, the orphan, died on December 23, 1955, surrounded by his family, so we had no Christmas that year. His remains were interred at the San Fernando Mission Cemetery, just a few feet from my Grandmother Carlota's headstone. So even in death he could not get too far away from his mother-in-law.

Life without Father

Our family life thus commenced without Dad at the beginning of 1956, the year I entered junior college. We all missed him, of course, because he was always there for us despite our most difficult and penurious times. He stood by us during the many difficult moments he and Mom experienced and the wrenching relations we children had with Mom as we took our first steps toward independence. We came to miss his moderate responses to our sometimes calamitous life on Kalisher Street in contrast to Mother's stringent reactions.

Looking back, I can also affirm that his reaction to the world outside our home was generally moderated too. I am reminded of his cheerful whistling to pass away the time while he picked oranges and lemons while I awaited him anxiously under a nearby tree when I was a child. The point is that he whistled a happy tune despite his having to pick lemons with one arm in order to support a large family as he perched precariously on a ladder five feet off the ground.

Mary and Manuel, our eldest siblings who were fortunate enough to come to know Dad as young adults, acknowledged the gaping hole he left in our family. Mary, who always viewed him in a positive light, admitted that "it was a great loss, but at the same time I wanted him to rest too. He had a hard life with my mother." Manuel confessed to being stunned by it all: "[His passing away] was a big shock [to me, it] tore me up . . . I still feel a loss," he admitted at an age far older than my dad when he died. My brother Mike, had I asked him before his passing away, surely must have experienced a similar loss and I did too, of course, but my recall fails me for these days. My younger siblings, Martha, Rick, and Emily, might have felt like Soledad, one of the younger ones, who remarked that "it was all a blur; we were all traumatized by his death." She remembered the *novenas* (a novena is a series of nine prayer sessions conducted in the memory of some one who has died) said in his name, but for her, they also faded into a memory haze.

For our mother, it was not a blur. Having lost her own mother two years earlier and now losing her husband too; it had to be a heavy cross to bear. It was a daunting test for her—certainly her biggest up to this point. None of us children could remember anything about the days and weeks following my dad's internment at the cemetery, as it seems, we put those dark days out of our minds and fast-marched into our unfolding lives. Mom remembered, though. She made it clear in her memorial that she was devastated by Dad's death; "desolate" is the word she chose, and then she added, "I didn't know what to do [or how to carry on]. Even María de Jesus [my sister Mary], who had assisted me in these days had gone off with another man. I felt so alone."

Life had to go on, of course. Mary and Manuel had to go off on their own, as Mom complains about Mary above, because they were the eldest. They had to search for their own horizons—college was not an option for them so they had to prepare for a marital life in some form and a livelihood to support it. At home, my siblings and I had to continue to go to public school, ideally with clean and proper clothing, breakfast in our bellies and lunches packed, and of course, the bills had to be paid to safeguard a roof over our heads.

Mother felt annihilated in the face of all this. Soledad remembered that we lived *en estado de luto* (in the state of mourning). She reminded me about the Mexican custom requiring a woman to wear black clothing for a period of two years when losing a family member. Mother had been wearing black from the time Grandma died two years earlier, and now with Dad's passing away, she was expected to continue to wear black for another year at least, if not more—a cultural requirement that probably punished Mom psychologically. It was also bad form for us, the children, to listen to recorded music or the radio. Soledad claims I brought some relief to our culturally dictated gloom at home because I was learning to sing and play on the guitar at the time, and apparently, Mom chose not to stifle my efforts as I was the only one in the family who played an instrument. Soledad claims that the feeble plucking of my lute and my untutored singing relieved her melancholy, and it may have soothed Mom's heart as well. "You were the one who brought music to the house in these gloomy days," Soledad said to me.

Curiously, ten-year-old Emily remembered other dimensions of Mom's grief that no one else noticed:

> . . . [S]he just isolated herself and had nobody to talk with, closed herself up in the bedroom . . . she would go to work [at a factory] with a broken heart; she felt abandoned by her mother and my dad . . . When her [own] mother died, Mom became very mean with Dad and so when he died, she was blown away; she didn't expect that. She expected him to continue [living but] he was already too far gone. Mom felt the grief of not having taken care of Dad right . . . she would cry, "I didn't know he was so ill!"

Mother Begins to Renew Herself

Mom repaired herself slowly. She did this by trudging forward with the requirements of life: going to work and watching over her children. She even applied for U.S. citizenship and received approval of her request for naturalization on March 28, 1958.[179] She then opened her own *molino* (mill) for tortillas. As she explains below, she reopened Grandma's old *tortilleria* on the corner property, where we had operated Gil's Café and where Grandma and Dad spent their last days. Other tortilla shops had opened in the barrio by this time, but we could still claim enough customers to be able to pay our bills and live as normally as possible. A new corn-milling machine was installed, far more compact and more powerful than the long-banded one Grandma had operated as described in chapter 8, but in my father's absence someone else installed it. Stoves and all of the other equipment necessary for a small *tortillería* were also put into place. Mother estimates that her tortilla shop lasted about fifteen years or up to about 1970. She wrote as follows:

> I restarted the [*tortillería*] even though I worked [full-time] elsewhere. I worked Saturdays and Sundays in [the tortillería]. It was worse this way because I couldn't rest very much. Every weekend, I had to go fetch the three or four women who helped me make tortillas. Monday through Friday, I would get up at six in the morning, mill the [necessary amount of] corn, the women [who made tortillas for me] would arrive and [make the tortillas], wrap them, sell them, and leave me a note [about it] . . . Then my daughters would come home from school, Marta, Soledad, and Emily [and they would follow up].

Mother regained her moral and physical strength by working very hard. At age fifty-one, she took a sweatshop sewing job in Panorama City about eight miles away at the same time that she embraced her own business and pressed it forward. The factory earnings would allow her to keep the tortilla shop going and help pay the bills. Emily remembered the tortilla shop helped Mom begin to shake off her blues. I owned my first automobile, a 1937 Chevrolet two-door sedan, which my grandmother bought for me before she passed away, so I would do some of the *entregas* or deliveries of fresh-made, hot tortillas to various restaurants located around the San Fernando Valley. Soledad also remembered she delivered tortillas to La India Market a few blocks away from our place on Kalisher Street. But Mom wasn't out of the woods yet; she still had to finish raising Martha,

Rick, Soledad and Emily, the last of the eight children.

Mom began to leave her gloom behind in the 1960s. She continued working long hours in the sweatshops but saved her best effort on her tortilla shop on Kalisher Street. Setting her black dresses aside once and for all was probably the most important measure she took in those days. Soledad, who remained close, concluded that "someone advised her not to wear black anymore because black was making her sick," and these words to the wise might have contributed materially to a change in Mother. She switched not only the color of her clothing but also her spirit—both began to lighten up. Soledad vouched that as time went on, she began wearing garments shaded in light pastels or white trimmed with bright colors, especially green and red.

Soledad chuckled as she harked back on those days because she believes Mom took a sharp and surprising turn in her recovery. She made friends with Virginia, a kind of woman who struck my sister as a friend unlike any Mom could previously claim. Soledad flippantly referred to Virginia as a "loose woman" because she taught Mother how to enjoy herself a little bit: "She played cards [with Mother] in her bedroom behind closed doors! They would giggle and talk about all kinds of stuff," Soledad recalled, laughing with delight at the same time. It seems that my sister would come home from school and find Mother ensconced in her bedroom, playing cards—an activity that might appear as ordinary to some but not to us, the Gil children—and enjoying a private moment with her friend, Virginia. Card playing had been forbidden in our home (I rarely played cards, and I don't recall my brothers and sisters ever playing cards either). Mom squelched it as a morally loose pastime in our growing up years. I can thus appreciate Soledad's ironic use of the word "loose" in reference to Mom's friend because Mom would have labeled her this way back in her earlier years and now she was playing cards herself! It stands to reason that Virginia helped Mother release her tension and helped tow her out of a painful past. My sister affirms that they became lifelong friends.

When I graduated from Seattle University in 1960, I unknowingly helped nudge Mother away from the cheerless mourning practices she had been observing, my sisters informed me many years later. My graduation from college appears to have inaugurated Mother's willingness to turn a new leaf and welcome new vistas. In the company of Soledad, who was sweet sixteen, Mom took the train from San Fernando to Seattle in June of that year to present herself at my graduation. I was living at the St. Edward's Catholic Seminary in the north end, where I had worked for three years and boarded at the same time in order to pay for my schooling. My mother and sister were able to stay at the forest-shrouded seminary on Big Finn Hill during their week-long visit, thanks to the generosity of my boss, Rev. Justin E. Knuff, Treasurer. He instructed the French Canadian nuns, who cooked and washed for the Sulpician faculty and the young seminarians, to ready a room for my mother and sister and prepare them meals as well. The nuns treated my relatives with such favor that they never forgot.

Mom and Soledad attended my college graduation exercises. These included a High Mass held in honor of the graduating seniors at St. James Cathedral in the First Hill neighborhood of Seattle. Given her pious upbringing, Mom must have been overwhelmed by the graduation ceremonies intermixed with the pomp and circumstance of a cathedral mass presided by an ornately vested bishop topped by a golden miter and a slew of acolytes. Added to this, the fact that I, her son, was one of the graduating seniors, all this must have taken my mother's breath away. "She was as proud as can be," my sister assured me, admitting at the same time that the entire Seattle experience was like nothing she had ever known before. "I was like Alice in Wonderland," Soledad recalled decades later, probably referring not only to the college rituals at the cathedral but also to the forested seclusion of the seminary during the superb spring weather that spread over emerald Seattle.

Following up on Mom's greater sense of freedom after my graduation in Seattle and holding a newly acquired American passport, she flew to South America all by herself six years later. She visited me and my growing family in southern Chile where I had gotten a job. Emily believes this excursion helped Mother's attitude in a large way. "You brightened up her life by telling her to come to Chile," my sister told me in an interview. "[The trip] made my mom recognize that she was not dead, that she had a future—remember that she began to teach herself how to drive [an automobile] after she came back," she added. I worked in Chile as a young Foreign Service officer at the time, so we spent several weeks touring that lovely country and meeting many gracious and generous individuals. On numerous occasions, my friends and associates went out of their way to treat Mother with the utmost generosity and respect, a pleasantry that often prompted her to let them know that she didn't deserve so much attention as she was nothing more than the daughter of backcountry peasants. This affirmation usually caused her listeners to nod their heads, stifle expressions of puzzlement, and smile sympathetically at the same time. Ever conscious of her origins, Mom was sixty years old when she visited me in South America.

Emily's view that Mother's outlook on life brightened up after her visit to Chile is supported by the fact that afterward Mom launched other trips away from home like never before. Her visits to Mascota to revive old relationships, for example, became more frequent. Before my father's death, she had returned to her hometown only once or twice, but after 1960, she began visiting the old folks more frequently, even if getting there was not easy.

Prior to the 1980s, traveling from Guadalajara—where one could make major travel connections—to Mascota could easily turn into a physical endurance test. When not willing to expose your own vehicle to a serious road test, the only way to travel to and from was via second-class busses that ran with certain regularity over dirt and gravel roads, but passengers had to share space with chickens and roosters. Not infrequently, travelers had to sustain a degree of risk and excitement because traversing high mountain passes on dirt roads was normal and fording rivers occurred often enough. This is why the degree of exhilaration for the passengers of the Guadalajara-Mascota line usually went up during the rainy season although now, sadly, getting to and fro is easier and safer.

Once in Mascota, Mom wouldn't hesitate to hire a ranch truck or a jeep to traverse more challenging dirt roads in order to revisit her old haunts in what was left of the old Hacienda Santa Rosa where she grew up. By this time, the hacienda had long been divided up by government fiat and doled out to local farmers thus making Santa Rosa an ex-hacienda. On one of these trips, the locals never forgot that Mom hired a river gravel hauler and his mule-driven cart in order to reach another former hacienda in the Mascota backlands, the ex-hacienda de Galope, where our relatives farmed their small *ejido* plots. She had walked much of this terrain as a child, so there was no reason for mere rough roads to stop her from getting to her objective. Our relatives in Galope let me know several times how astonished they were to see Mother arriving aboard a gravel cart, standing next to the driver who was having trouble staying on his feet and wielding the reins at the same time; he made sure Mother, who gripped the wooden rails with her white knuckles, didn't get spilled over the side. On another occasion, before the main road was paved below Puerto Vallarta, Mom wanted to visit her cousin, María Ramos, in Tomatlán, but the monsoon rains had literally mucked up the dirt highway. Most of the automobile traffic had been halted as a result, so Mother, who wouldn't be deterred, persuaded the driver of a Coca-Cola truck who made rain-or-shine deliveries to let her ride with him since he was headed that way anyway. Her arrival in a Coca-Cola truck flabbergasted her relatives as she stepped off the truck totting her valise at the same time. The pluckiness that drove

Mother from the start impelled her to rise from the ashes, and she did so with certain gusto.

Looking After Soledad and Emily

"My daughters, Soledad, Emily, and Martha, helped me very much," Mother remembered with singular clarity in her memoirs. My two younger sisters spent considerable time helping Mom in the last years of operating her business. (I left home to attend college in Seattle and lived away for many years thereafter.) Soledad and Emily went to school during the day and hurried home in the afternoon to work in the tortilla shop. They counted the tortillas, wrapped them, delivered them, and cleaned the shop to begin fresh the next day. In sum, they helped keep the tortilla money coming to supplement Mom's meager factory wages and thus pay the bills that kept the collection agents at bay.

Much to their credit, my sisters fared reasonably well under the pressure. Despite their solidly packed days, Soledad remarked straightforwardly that she still found time to do her homework. "We were able to do whatever it was we needed to do. It wasn't a big problem," she insisted after I asked her if her school work suffered because of this hectic schedule. My sister reminded me that I had left an encyclopedia behind before moving to Seattle, and she claimed that it made it easier for her to do her homework.

My sister Emily's memory of these years was a bit different, however. Her most important remembrance is that she enjoyed helping Mom operate the *tortilleria*. It brought a measure of comfort and reflection to our youngest sibling, who was treading on her early teens but not enjoying her school days. Rather than complaining about the work that the tortilla business demanded, she confessed she actually liked it.

> That's when I began to learn how to make tortillas, get out from [always] being in the back [of the house]. [I]f I made tortillas, then I could stay in the front and hear all the stories [that the *tortilleras* told]. It was more interesting than all of the bickering that went on in the back with my brothers and sisters and with Mom . . . It was my escape. Being with the women and hearing them talk [about] all these stories and all these fascinating things about their life, how they grew up . . .; by listening to their stories it made mine [i.e., my own problems] nothing. What I was going through with Mom was nothing compared to these women who had gone through tragedies galore! Martha

and Sally didn't want any part of the *tortilleria*. I did.

In pouring her mind on paper about these days, Mother expressed her gratitude to my sister Martha particularly—"*Marta que venía de Los Angeles* (Martha who would come all the way from Los Angeles)." She had borne the brunt of Mom's ire and frustration during the dark days I've described, but she always stayed close. She would travel the twenty miles from her home in central Los Angeles to help with the tortilla chores—more likely on weekends as she was working for the county by this time. "*Me ayudaban tanto* (they helped me so much)," Mother wrote in reference to all three sisters.

So the time arrived in which my younger sisters also began to go their separate ways, beginning with Soledad, the elder of the last two children still at home. The reader will recall that during her high school years, along with her sister Emily, she stayed close to Mother, lending a helping hand in the tortilla shop. She graduated from high school in 1962, apparently following the path I laid out when I was the first to graduate from high school in our family. Martha followed me in graduating, then Soledad, and then Emily, who graduated in 1964.

In any case, Soledad met Javier Cruz, a youngish Mexican soccer playing immigrant who belonged to her church circles at Santa Rosa, and soon he became an avid buyer of tortillas after discovering that Soledad worked in Mom's *tortillería*. Three months after high school graduation, at age eighteen, Soledad married Javier.

He did things properly. When the local priest came to our house at Javier's behest to ask for Soledad's hand in marriage, Javier took a first successful step in captivating Mother's favor and ultimately gaining her permission to allow him to wed my sister. He did this by employing Father López, the pastor of Santa Rosa Church, as the petitioner to allow Soledad to tie the knot with Javier in the absence of his parents who resided in Mexico. Had they lived locally, my mother would have expected them to present themselves before her in order to ask for my sister's hand. In this way, my brother-in-law followed Mexican rules and so Mom couldn't easily oppose Soledad's commitment and betrothal with Javier. "Yes, he did it the right way—in the traditional style that Mother was used to." Soledad recalled more than forty years later, adding that she had not been allowed to date boys "in the regular fashion" outside of church circles.

The *petición de mano* (asking for a young woman's hand in marriage) is, in fact, an age-old custom, deeply rooted in the Mexican psyche. Embedded in Mom's consciousness in this way, it represented the time-sanctioned manner in which the parents of a young man requested the father and mother of a young woman for her hand in marriage. This custom obviously survived in the Mascotan highlands in a way that impelled Mother to put it into practice in San Fernando when it came time for us children to consider marriage—whether we knew what we were getting into or not.[180] This explains why each of us in our own time didn't hesitate to involve Mom and Dad when we reached this point in our young lives. My eldest sister Mary's new husband, John Valdez, had personally petitioned Mother for Mary's hand in marriage in the absence of his parents, and my eldest brother, Manuel, asked Mom and Dad to walk about five blocks down Kalisher Street to request the hand of his sweetheart, Cristina Méndez. Her parents complied, thus giving my brother permission to officially woo their young daughter. When my brother Mike thought he wanted to marry Esperanza Guerrero, my parents travelled to a small farm in Baja, California, to petition her hand in marriage, but her parents balked. However; when he later decided to marry Pat Wallace, a red-haired girl of Irish descent, our mother seems to have waived the *petición the mano* at the same time that she allowed Dad to help them wed in Las Vegas on account of their young age. When I decided I wanted to marry my childhood sweetheart, Rosemary Ruiz, who was a mere seventeen-year-old, I stood beside my mother as she rose on her feet in my then girlfriend's living room and asked her somewhat-miffed parents for her hand in marriage—we were asked to wait a year or two because we were too young.

Back to Soledad's wedding, Mom called a family meeting after Father López's visit to discuss Javier's request to marry my sister. She asked my elder brothers if they knew anything negative about Javier. I lived in Washington DC at the time, so I didn't participate, but Soledad, who listened intently, described the family gathering as follows:

> We had a family meeting and everybody questioned Javier to death, especially Manuel and Mike, who knew more about him. Mike said, "What are you doing with my sister! You're an older guy! Haven't I seen you around?" Don't forget he was nine years older than me.

Age differences aside, Javier and Soledad's nuptials became the first white wedding in our family. It effectively ended Soledad's direct reliance on Mother and placed her one step closer to retiring as she would now only have one more dependent on her hands. Soledad had been waiting to be released from Mother's shackles even though she played a big role in the *tortillería*. "I had other plans," Soledad admitted decades later and then clarified, "I just knew that the only way out of the house and out of my mother's control was to get married!" Emily was next.

If Soledad had been secretly waiting for the opportunity to escape my mother's domination, the same thing could be said regarding Emily but multiplied several times over. Most teenagers tend to be a handful, but Emily's case might be described as out-of-the-ordinary. We've seen already that her needs as a child were largely clouded over by Mother's dark days and so, as Emily got older, her relationship with Mother became quite complicated, to say the least. Emily already revealed to us that when she was a child, she trailed Grandma because she found her more nurturing than Mom and that when Grandma died, my kid sister sought out Dad's presence and protection. After his passing, Emily no longer enjoyed a shield and so her relationship with Mother entered into a fragile state of affairs that tended to hover somewhere between passive aggression and overt abrasion.

Looking back on her teenage years, Emily saw herself as not having any major problems with Mother as long as she stayed busy. "[As] long as I was a good worker—[and] I *was* her top worker—of course, there was no problem [between me and Mom]," my sister said referring to the work of making tortillas. As she stated earlier, "It was my escape . . . What I was going through with Mom was nothing compared to these women who had gone through tragedies galore."

However, after Soledad's departure via the altar, the relationship became more aggravated, according to Emily. "That's when the shit hit the fan," my sister remarked acidly. She concluded that "Mom felt abandoned by Sally [i.e., Soledad]" and, as a consequence, Mother began to "take it out" on her.

> Mom always said to me, "Why didn't you get married?" "Why aren't you like Sally?" "Why don't you talk like her, why don't you behave like her?" "What's wrong with you?" It got to be a broken record of how you're not good enough.

It seems that Mom mishandled Emily the way she had mishandled Martha. In the years that Grandma died followed by Dad's death three years later, Mom heaped considerable abuse on Martha by all accounts, flaying her over teenage foibles. It got so bad that she had to be given special medical attention and eventually persuaded to move away. Something similar was occurring with Emily after Soledad moved away.

One of the most regretful moments came during Emily's tenth grade year when "Mom became really cruel—[things got bad] between her and me," Emily explained. With Soledad gone and Mom having to continue working full-time at one of the factories in the valley, Emily bore the brunt of getting the tortilla shop ready each day, before leaving for school. Before Soledad got married, both of them had collaborated in this preparation as a way of helping Mom out, but now Emily had to do it alone. She had to get up very early by herself and grind the already cooked corn into *masa* so that the tortilla-making ladies wouldn't tarry when they arrived for work.

> So I never had time to fix myself a lunch. That day I asked Mom to give me a dollar so I could buy lunch and in front of the girls [i.e., her friends] my mom looked at me in total anger and hit me as hard as she could, tossing me against the wall, and then threw a five-dollar bill at me [saying sarcastically] *A ver si te ayuda!* [See if that helps you!]

This was the last straw for my sister, although she didn't know it right then. She collected herself in front of her astonished friends, who customarily came by to walk her to class, picked the money off the floor, and went off to school with them. Not surprisingly, her anger and resentment welled so high that she couldn't think straight, so she not only decided to interrupt her schooling that day but also decided to quit school completely and do something to alleviate her frustration. She left school and walked to the house of some notoriously delinquent girlfriends where she took her first taste of liquor. Thereafter, she proceeded to get drunk enough to lose her sense of time and place. Mom learned of her whereabouts somehow and soon retrieved her, and after some vile and acrimonious exchanges between the two of them, beat Emily so hard that when my elder brother, Mike, was called in to bear witness, "he just began to cry," according to Emily. It must have been a pathetic scene. Emily remembers that he scolded Mother and immediately sensed that there was no better idea at the moment but to remove her from Mother's clutch. He offered her a place to live with him and his family, but my kid sister opted instead for living with her eldest brother, Manuel, who lived with his growing family in Anaheim, about fifty miles south. This dismal episode thus served as a loosening of the taut bonds that Mother held over her last child.

This is how Emily came to live with her brother, Manuel, and his family for about six months. This half-year allowed a cooling off between daughter and mother, and it permitted Emily to return to her high school studies near her brother's home and do some reflecting and repairing as well. With time, Mother cooled off and asked Emily to return home and so when Manuel's son, Mario, was born prematurely and the doctors finally allowed him to go home, Emily understood it was time to accept Mom's invitation to return home despite grave reservations. Manuel encouraged the reunion.

We can't doubt one bit that the relations between Mother and her last child at home remained edgy and uptight. After all, Emily was now straining to become an independent-minded adult who had to fight off a micro-managing mother insisting on rigid behavioral norms from her daughter. Thank goodness my sister returned back home intending to resume her high school studies at San Fernando High School and, much to her credit, found a sane way to stay away from Mom whenever possible. She took solace among the books of the local library. "I began to hide in the libraries," Emily confessed. She had done this while living with Manuel and continued the practice in San Fernando. The library became a quiet place for reading and thinking. "I read and I read and I read; I lived in the library," she remembered, and this is how she discovered Sherlock Holmes, spending many hours enjoying his sleuthing yarns.

Mother employed an interesting tactic to open communication with her wounded seventeen-year-old daughter. She took her to Mascota. Toting a complete collection of Sherlock Holmes in her luggage, Emily traveled with Mom to beautiful Guadalajara and then rode a tired old bus for about fifty miles on unpaved and bridgeless back roads before finally arriving in Mom's hometown. Emily recalled that they traveled in silence most of the way while she absorbed details about London's favorite detective while Mom looked out the window enwrapped in her own thoughts.

Once arriving, my sister began to forget about being upset with her mother because she was distracted by world entirely different from her own. Here she encountered archaic buildings, cobble stone streets, homes with dirt floors, outhouses with pit toilets, and rudimentary home fixtures. She came across odd novelties such as open air kitchens built around earthen hearths fueled by firewood or dried-up corn cobs, people riding on mules or horses as there were few cars to be had, no easy access to a telephone or radio, and so on. She found herself immersed in an archaic world that was poles apart from anything she had ever known. "I began to let go of my anger," she remembered.

"Seeing how other people led their lives made a difference in mine," she remarked, adding that "I got to see other people in a worse condition than me." She brought to mind that in one of our relatives' house, drinking water didn't come from a faucet, it was fetched from a small depression in the ground called an *ojo de agua,* where natural spring water collected. On clothes-washing day, she helped women relatives scrub their garments against rocks at a nearby river. Comfort and convenience were acquiring a new meaning.

There is yet one more example of how Emily benefitted from an unforgettable perspective. On a day that they traveled farther into the mountains to visit Mother's birth place, the Hacienda Santa Rosa, now in ruins, Mom became so excited that she sprinted ahead, leaving Emily behind to walk more casually with one of our relatives. This is when she came opposite a young woman possessing a deformed face. "Oh my god, she was hairy, and she didn't have a jawline!" she exclaimed forty-seven years later, still remembering the trepidation that turned into a panic. The hapless young woman walked alongside a young man later described as her brother who also revealed a massively deformed face, and this shocked my sister even further. She remembered becoming panic-stricken and had to be calmed down.

Looking back on the trip to Mascota, Emily immediately labeled it as an attempt by Mother to give her a different perspective on life. This is how she came to realize that her problems were not as bad as she had thought. "You look at it and you go, 'Damned, I'm looking good!' I'm not as ugly as they keep telling me I am! Me [*sic*] and my stuff looked like nothing!" Things, indeed, could always be worse.

She also saw Mother in a new light. She chuckled when she described her mom doing things she never could have imagined. "I got to see another side of Mother, riding side-saddle on horseback or with no saddle at all [at other times]!"

Emily's life actually changed more speedily than she may have wished after her trip to Mexico. She graduated from San Fernando High School in June 1964, and by the end of the year, she too got married. Like the rest of my sisters, she married a youngish immigrant from Mexico, Mexican Americans running a distant second for my sisters when considering eligible bachelors as Anglo-Americans were too far removed from their social circles. In any case, Emily moved away with her new husband right after their civil nuptials (there was no white church wedding for them) and within six months, she returned to the San Fernando barrio to live nearby. Ironically, she continued helping Mother in the tortilla shop as a young bride but more important is the fact that Emily no longer belonged to Mother's household. "Now I was alone (*Yo quedé sola*)," Mom wrote in her memoirs.

An Earthquake Hastens Mother's "Retirement"

Mother continued directing the tortilla shop on Kalisher Street up to about 1973 while working full time at a nearby factory. While both Soledad and Emily continued to help by pinch-hitting whenever one of Mother's tortilla makers didn't show up for work, their assistance now became occasional because each one of them had to attend to their own households: their husbands and, soon, their children. My sister Martha, who remained childless, also continued to travel from Los Angeles to lend a helping hand on occasion. Mom benefitted in a considerable way when a new daughter-in-law filled the void for a while. This was Victoria Escalante, who married my younger brother Rick in 1963 in Washington D.C. and then both came to live in San Fernando. In her handwritten chronicle, Mother singled her out along with Uncle Pascual's last woman companion who lived next door: "Victoria helped me out a lot [as did] Doña Ester," meaning that they rendered assistance whenever Mom saw herself in a tight squeeze. They were willing to help, in part, because both lived right next door. Mother Nature, however, intervened by shaking things up and speeding Mother into retirement as a result.

The so-called Sylmar Earthquake contributed significantly to her giving up work and closing down the tortilla-making business. This violent temblor occurred in the early morning of February 9, 1971, with Sand Canyon in Santa Clarita as its epicenter—only ten miles north of San Fernando. An aerial bombing of San Fernando could not have looked worse. I was living in the heart of the San Fernando Valley by this time, having already returned from my overseas work, and I clearly recall the shock I felt upon seeing major buildings in downtown San Fernando strewn on the street, littered with chunks of brick walls and glass everywhere. Minutes after the first big undulations, I sped across the valley in my old, blue Volkswagon Bug, avoiding dislocated roads, to check on my family; I remember coming upon men and women still dressed in their night clothes, walking in a daze down the middle of San Fernando Boulevard, some with bloody wounds still unattended. Fires roared from broken natural gas pipes at various places along the length of major streets in the city, including Kalisher Street near Mother's tortilla shop. Much to my relief, I discovered that my family was stunned, to say the least, but unharmed. Mom's house and tortilla shop were shaken so severely by the tremors measuring 6.6 on the Richter scale that everything was hurled to the floor. We began the cleanup, filled with dread and alarm, and then began to take notice of cracked walls and ceilings.

The shaking of the earth under the city of San Fernando changed the lives of many people and Mother was no exception. Her Kalisher Street building was damaged but not as much as the structure next door where my brother Rick lived with Victoria—where Grandma had opened her tortilla shop forty-some years earlier. It was declared uninhabitable until further repairs. Rick and Vicky were thus forced to move elsewhere and so this removed Victoria from being able to help Mother with the business. Mom's last chief supporter was now out of reach. She was thus left on her own once again.

Federal authorities arrived on the scene within a few days to organize relief operations and render assistance. Part of the services they offered included government-backed loans for victims of the earthquake, and this is how Mother eventually accepted a loan from a federal disaster agency aimed at repairing her property. The trauma of the actual earthquake combined with the enormous effort of having to clean up and get her home back in order and revive her business led her to seek a way out. We, the children, helped out, of course, but replacing broken dishes and fractured furniture and repairing faults in the walls seemed to have drained her enterprise. She must have said to herself, "What's the use? Do I have the strength to get back to where I was?" In the end, she resolved to make the last big move in her life. She dug deep into her savings and purchased a nearby home. She also rented the Kalisher Street building once it was repaired and triggered whatever the Social Security Administration would offer her, which she assessed as something that "wasn't very much."

This is how she moved to 603 South Huntington Street at the age of sixty-seven. She took out a mortgage on what would be her last home, about four blocks away, in a locale that used to mark the northwestern edge of our barrio when it separated our homes from grassland and pastures, these now covered over with streets and houses. Mother's new home stood about a block and a half away from our old Mott Street house. The fact is that all of the homes that saw us grow up and go our separate ways—the *vecindad*, the "big house" on Kewen Street, our little abode on Mott Street, and our restaurant on Kalisher Street—were located within a handful of blocks of each other. In this way you could say that the barrio functioned like a small, rural town for us where you couldn't move too far away. Mom wrote in her notes thus:

> It hurt me to move because the house I was leaving [on Kalisher Street] held so many memories. It was hard to accept the idea of leaving it behind.

Mom eased herself into a self-fashioned retirement on Huntington Street, where she resided for the next thirty-three years for the most part. By dint of her dedication to the family she had helped procreate, her simple two-bedroom home evolved into the heart of an extended family. We, her children, grandchildren, great-grandchildren, and great-great-grandchildren, all came to Huntington Street to render tribute to her, our steadfast matriarch, in one form or another.

This thirty-year period, then, enclosed our toughest years. It started out with everyone on board, together, eagerly pushing and pulling forward, and it ended with nearly everyone gone their way including Grandma and Dad, who passed on to meet their reward, up in the sky. Mother, who suffered the most because she lost both her mother and husband and then found herself having to support the younger ones in the family, ultimately became the lone survivor.

Cannery in San Fernando (ca. 1940)

The Gil family in front of the old Santa Rosa Church (ca. 1949)

The Gil's and friends in front of Gil's Cafe (ca. 1950)

Grandma Carlota with her daughter and grandchildren (ca. 1952)

Chapter 11

Looking Back at Our Toughest Years

My Siblings Had a Different View • Why the Restaurant Years Were the Hardest • Two Other Reasons that May Have Contributed to Our Unhappiness • Why Was Mother So Compulsive? • Mexican Rules of Behavior Had a Lot to Do with It • Could There Have Been Yet Another Reason? • Could It Have Been a Mother-In-Law Problem? • Mom Becomes Grandma

THE YEARS MOM and Dad owned and operated Gil's Café on Kalisher Street were the most arduous for all of us children, but we didn't comprehend it fully at the time. My siblings and I came to this realization only after I began asking them to reflect on these years. We eventually admitted—perhaps I should say, *I* eventually admitted, as we'll see below—that we faced many disagreeable moments in the back rooms where we resided, behind the swinging doors that separated us from the public eating area. Had I not interviewed my brothers and sisters and risked sharing my own views with them about these years, I could not have written chapters 10 and 11. One reason is that I was a bit too young during our early restaurant years to understand what was going on in our family, and another is that when I got older and enrolled in high school, I began to bury my nose in my books more often than not. It's surprising how you can bury your head in the "sand" of thoughts and ideas in order to avoid the unpleasant world around you. After high school, I spent even more time in libraries and so I didn't witness and experience the family as much as my siblings did—it could be said I avoided it all, I was always saying *ya'm voy*, "I'm leaving [to go to the library to go do my homework]."

After asking my siblings to look back from their own vantage point at our parents and our family life, I concluded that our years on Kalisher Street were the most daunting, that leading up to the closure of our restaurant in 1953 and the dozen or so years that followed were disheartening for us all. This discovery led me to weave this notion into the preceding chapters in order to have them read as they do now. I try to get at the roots in this chapter—why did we suffer as we did?.

My Siblings Had a Different View

At age seventy-seven, my brother Manuel caught me off guard when I first asked him to evaluate our growing-up years. Sitting in his trailer home, anchored on the Arizona desert floor overlooking the Colorado River, his immediate response jarred me. After pursing his lips and deeply furrowing his brow while he seemed to study the knots on the floor rug, he summed it all up with a quick comparison. "On Mott Street everything was just [like with anyone else, we were] going to school, [Dad went to work, and so on,] but on Kalisher, that's when the problems arose." He then let out a big sorrowful sigh and then looked at me like saying, don't you remember? This was a reaction I didn't expect. "What problems was he talking about?" I said to myself.

When I asked eighty-year-old Mary if she remembered any conflict between Mom and Dad, she informed me immediately that she preserved vivid memories of quarreling as early as the 1930s. She traced it back to *la casa grande*, the "big house," (the manager's house) on Kewen Street, long before we moved to Kalisher. Being older, both of them undoubtedly saw more in our family life than the rest of us who were younger, and they harbored more feelings about it too. I was learning more than I expected.

Manuel said to me as follows:

> I remember breaking up a lot of fights. There were a lot of fights between my mom and dad. One day he went out drinking and returning, he parked [the car] out in front. And there goes my mom to raise hell with him. So he takes out the crank [from the car] and [goes] chasing after her . . . and they go round and round . . . She had her own devils to work out. [She had] many more than my father.

Manuel also dredged up from his memory the time when he felt he could no longer tolerate things at home. This was on the eve of his enlisting in the US Air Force in 1949.

> They made me cry. Martha [age ten] would hide [to avoid hearing them]. Mary had already run away with Irineo [a

> restaurant customer]. When Mary returned, [mother] treated her like hell! [All this] made me cry. I [would] cut in to calm them down and this usually stopped it. I didn't want to hear it [anymore. One night as I slept] I even knocked a window out [in my frustration; I guess], I hit the window twice . . . It was the anger and ill-feelings [that hurt me]. [Such] anguish! The goddamned business [had a lot to do with it]! [But] I loved my mom!

In Manuel's memory the restaurant years were synonymous with the constant conflict that took place between my parents. Mike's recollections would have helped here too, but he passed away before I could interview him. Having missed this dimension of my family life, I had to think more deeply about my own thoughts.

Why the Restaurant Years Were the Hardest

After a certain amount of pondering, I concluded that Mom and Dad, indeed, confronted their deepest travails in these years. Let's consider why.

To be sure, there was the pressure of business. Keeping customers happy is not a simple thing—some of us children opened our own small enterprises when we became adults, and each of us discovered this in the flesh. My parents were ultimately responsible in keeping the customers satisfied and keeping the business on track, no easy task. Manuel's complaint summarized the matter. "The goddamned business [had a lot to do with the conflict in our family]!" The restaurant represented our economic lifeline, but only a unified team of managers and employees could safeguard it. In our case, the managers didn't always see eye to eye and past business experiences involving Dad had not been positive, as we've seen already. But we children didn't know this.

Keeping the restaurant on track was up to all of us, but that was easier said than done. The Gil Café worked as a family-operated establishment, and this meant that we the Gil children had to lend a hand. Our parents were the bosses; they commanded the kitchen and directed the larger operation at the same time. Manuel, who was a teenager in these the first years of the restaurant, brought to mind that "Mom did the cooking . . . [Yes,] my mother had the big tough job," he observed when I asked him who did what. Then he added that [Dad] assisted in the cooking [but] mostly worked as a waiter. The reader may recall that Mary allowed father a greater role on this point. Regarding his own role, Manuel explained, "I killed the chickens [then the rest of us would have to skin them but] Mary helped out as the waitress [too]."

Three years older than Manuel, Mary saw the tableau from a different angle. She remembered her morning routine very clearly. "We had to get up early, about five in the morning, *y hacer todo* (and do everything)! [We had to] Prepare the dough for making flour tortillas [in order to make the *tacos*] which we packed in the [carry out] lunches and [used] for the boarders' breakfasts [too]—and for the other customers who were not boarders. When school started, we had already done a lot of work." At other times, the rest of us who were younger, washed dishes, mopped floors, peeled potatoes, cut tripe for *menudo*, and so on.

The challenge was running a business and a family all at once. Mom and Dad had to work together as co-managers and supervise their own children as employees too. This was the rub, business pressures colliding with family needs! We, the employees, were finding it harder to wait on tables, do the dishwashing, and execute the food prepping and otherwise fulfill the role of proper and efficient staff members because we wanted to grow up just like the kids next door who didn't have all these heavy chores. Mother-in-law tribulations also flared up to upset my father's composure as we'll see below. And last but not least, both Dad and Grandma were not well in these years, their health beginning to decline.

A cherished black-and-white photograph permits a glimpse of the business pressures on our family and the wear and tear on Dad, probably taken on a warm Sunday afternoon in 1949. It puts us on view as a family that hurriedly gathered for the camera, no time for sprucing up except for Mom. She seems to be the only one who knew someone would take a picture, or she dressed up a bit to visit someone and then he or she showed up unexpectedly with a camera. In any case, she appears as a vigorous but friendly middle-aged woman with carefully combed black hair, wearing a black, long-sleeve sweater over a light-colored blouse. Dad, on the other hand, didn't dress up at all for the occasion. He was probably cajoled out of the kitchen, pressed to cross the street in order to pose under the sun in front of the peppermint tree that stood near the front corner of the old Santa Rosa Church on Kalisher Street on that afternoon. He wore a whitish long-sleeve shirt and a pair of dark work pants that didn't quite close around his middle; they were cinched shut by an old black leather belt that he wore year after year. He must have been about fifty years of age, but he appears older in the photo, tired, and worn. Mary is twenty-one, Manuel eighteen, Mike fifteen, and they stand tall and confident. The rest of us children who at this time still depended on Mom for all of our personal needs reveal an edge of neglect: I am wearing a scruffy plaid shirt and a pair of heavily worn pants that plainly need a vigorous washing,

Martha wears a rumpled sweater over a wrinkled dress, and Soledad and Emily stand in front of Mother unsure of what is transpiring, both dressed in very commonplace frocks that confirm considerable use. How to keep a family restaurant in the best shape possible and do the same for your family too! It wasn't easy. Whenever I view this photograph, my mind whispers to me, "Those were tough times indeed!"

Who managed the money and the bills? Who kept on eye on the pantry, making sure it was full at all times? Who set the week's menu? The business details escaped our young eyes because we were too young and distracted by the fantasies of our own evolving youthfulness. Expecting a thirteen-year-old to be vigilant about waiting on tables, do dishwashing, or food prepping was asking a lot. Yet we could not be released from these annoying and often heavy chores because my father was unable to earn a viable wage due to his physical handicap. We were thus tied to the restaurant, and our parents had to be all things at once: business owners, managers, spouses, and parents.

Two Other Reasons That May Have Contributed to Our Unhappiness

Listening intently to the reminiscences of my older siblings, I concluded that beyond the business pressures, two other forces probably contributed to the difficulties that tore up my elders, causing a lot of collateral harm to some of us children.

One was my mother's compulsion to exercise control over her children's behavior. Mary and Martha, the first girls in the family got the worst of it as I've noted already, it being noteworthy that Mom couldn't control her sons in the same way. Mary, who felt the most injured by Mom's impulse to watch over her, like an eagle, confessed decades later that even before she became a teenager, she already resented Mom's micro control. She remembered thus:

> All I would do is work. That's why I would go to my grandmother's [house] because she was never on my back. [She] would never whip me just because she felt like it. She might [have beaten me but it would have been] for a [good] reason. That's why I cared for my grandma. My Dad couldn't say anything because Mom would rake him over the coals. I'm still shaking just from saying all this.

Mary's frustration escalated in her teen years.

> She always wanted me right there . . . I was not allowed to have friends, never allowed to have boyfriends, never allowed to go to a party [and return at my own time]. She would let me go with Carmen O[.] for thirty minutes, Terry [Carmen's daughter was] having a party across [the way] from us on Mott Street. [And, to make matters worse,] Don Rodolfo [Terry's dad] and Juan Imperial [a neighbor] would patrol the street to make sure no boys would ever show up! [Then] when the thirty minutes were up, she would send Mike [my younger brother with instructions to] "Tell her she needs to come home." She was so possessive!

Mary's distress didn't fade over the years. As the reader can appreciate, Mom was strict about our behavior but especially the girls'.

Over and above business pressures, we lived with a disparity in child-rearing terms. Mom was always on us, Dad less so, acting more moderately, going with the flow more often than not. He was not quick to spank us whereas Mother swiftly meted out our dues. This is what Mary and Manuel remembered from the time they were teenagers, and Mike and Martha probably would have said the same—I had overlooked this. I concluded that this discrepancy caused frustration in my folks and my elder siblings because I discovered that memories of heart-rending anguish didn't entirely fade away with the years.

Mary and Manuel evoked memories about Martha, our younger sister, who seems to have gotten the brunt of Mom's ire, as already mentioned. Manuel reminded me that Martha had to be sedated and taken away in a straight jacket for a while because she had become delirious with Mother's treatment. Martha's torment took place sometime between 1952 and 1954 when she was in her early teen years—toward the end of our restaurant period. My brother's memory rang a bell in my own recollection, to tell the truth. Mother's treatment of Martha became so hurtful that it required outside professional intervention. She eventually moved away in order to regain her health.

And Martha wasn't Mom's only injured party in this fashion.

Why Was Mother So Compulsive?

As a result of Mary's and Manuel's recollections, which served to rekindle my own cooled-over memories, I felt forced to bring some perspective to these hurtful memories. I couldn't have included their observations and remembrances in this book otherwise. Doing my best to understand what my elder siblings were really saying led me to recognize what I've asserted many times already, namely that Mother's hardest years, on herself and on us children, especially my sisters, coincided with the years we operated Gil's Café.

My siblings could not fathom why Mother was so compulsive. I asked them to try to explain her coercion several times, but their answer was simply that Mom had just been Mom. Except for Emily, we couldn't accuse Mom of disregarding our upbringing nor could we claim she cared little for us. We could only blame her for being too hard on us. Interestingly, while she was alive, Mom didn't explain her wicked moods and she never felt the compulsion to rationalize or explain her style of raising us either. It's as if she had long concluded that she had done only what she could do and no more and no one had the grounds to censure her. Yet, my sister Mary, well into her "golden years," literally shuddered when my interviews encouraged her to flash back on earlier times; she could only repeat, "She always wanted me right there. She was like that with Martha too."

I believe that had we possessed the temerity to corner Mom and ask her to explain why she was so cross with us, her children, especially in the years indicated, she probably would have pointed to the larger situation that I'm describing in this chapter. This is another way of saying that I began to understand that we children were focusing on our own feelings primarily, not on what was happening to our parents. We were missing the broader picture in concentrating on ourselves.

One consideration to keep in mind is that by the mid-1950s, we children were more demanding than we had been before. Dad and Grandma's emergent feebleness in these years coincided with the growing complexity of the requirements that we children placed on Mom. She stood like the Rock of Gibraltar and consequently caught the storms we created in our growing up. Several of us reached teenage during this time, and our bubbling hormones and more frequent bouts of believing that we knew what was best for us stirred already high levels of frustration in our parents, especially in Mother. We stood between being youngsters and adults. You could say that we were beginning to have a say for ourselves for the better or worse of it.[181] This psychological twilight pressed us to resist Mother or, at least, to pull in a different way because we were forming a vision of ourselves, one that differed from hers.

American culture encouraged us to behave this way too as we'll see below, and this clashed with her expectations, of course. Mary started her teenage years in 1941 and ended them in 1948 when she turned twenty, Manuel did the same during 1944 and 1951, Mike during 1947 and 1954, and I during 1950 and 1957. These years were Mom's worst. This larger panorama about our maturing process was difficult for any of us to see even from hindsight.

We saw already that the 1950s were filled with grief for Mom. Grandma Carlota died in our home in 1953, and Dad who was sickly for several years, died at the end of 1956. Life was leaving Mom alone at the rudder, and the current was becoming swift and treacherous. To make matters worse, she had all her teeth extracted about this time to prepare the way for dentures; I remember her applying hot, wet compresses on her cheeks, almost daily, in the middle of a sweltering California summer as a way to control infection and lessen pain until her last tooth was finally pulled out. How would I have felt under the circumstances, and how understanding could I have been with my own children?

We saw that the restaurant closed in 1953, and Mom had to resort to working in the dreadful local factories willing to employ immigrants like her. Our restaurant income had already ended, and there was no one else to bring in the "bacon" now. I've suggested already that Mother undoubtedly saw the writing on the wall about living without her husband and her own mother. In trying to understand the larger picture, I think it fair to consider that living on the economic edge and belonging to a minority culture could only make matters worse because it meant being ill informed about any available resources at the time. President Lyndon Johnson's War on Poverty spurred the formation of many outreach community programs in San Fernando, and these helped spread the word about obtainable help for needy families but, alas, this came twenty years later.

Beyond the related economic and social dimensions, other considerations I believe entered the picture. Mother's predisposition to demand certain behaviors from her children resulted in early defections too. As we've seen already, Mary eloped with one of our restaurant customers, a bracero. Happily, this led to a short but rewarding relationship that included a quiet marriage ceremony and living away from Mother for about a year and a half. Martha got out too. At age fifteen or thereabouts, she found refuge as a governess with a well-heeled professional Anglo family, which also provided her with some greatly needed psychological assistance and in this way started an important shift in her life, a situation that allowed her to live away from Mom as well. Manuel signed up for the Air Force and went away to Texas and eventually to England. It must be said, nevertheless, that none of us ever stayed away for long, but we did manage some space for ourselves.

In other words, the integrity of the family became altered in the second half of the restaurant years. Mother lost her lifelong partners, and her oldest children began rebelling and stepping away—by 1957, four years after we closed the restaurant, both Grandma and Dad had passed away and Mary, Manuel, and Mike had flown the nest, Martha had entered her most vulnerable stage before moving away, and I was packing my bags as well. My siblings and I had overlooked this convergence as a way of taking a second look at Mother's frustration and crabbiness.

Mexican Rules of Behavior Had a Lot to do with It

There is yet more to consider. Would she have been less cranky had she not lost her mother and husband in these critical years? Probably not!

My assumption is that Mexican rules of behavior need to be taken into account, especially where girls are concerned. By this I mean that traditional practices about how children should behave and the values behind these practices drove my mother's compulsion to watch over her children like a hawk, apart from whether her mother or husband was well or not. The rules clashed with American behavioral practices or, at least, those present in Southern California, and it's fair to say that Mom reacted more acutely about this contradiction, Mexican vs. American, than did my Dad. She was far more alert about my sisters breaking these social rules than us boys and, at times, her conduct became frenzied and hurtful to some of us. It's safe to say that the relations between Anglo children and their parents, at least those she might have been able to observe on the edges of Los Angeles, failed to impress her in a positive way.

The tenets Mom guarded about how children should behave were rooted in the backcountry of her birth, where she grew up—the Mascotan highlands of Jalisco. They were written and engraved in the minds of the local people there, rich or poor, and it's fair to say that other simple folks elsewhere in the rugged Mexican landscape held similar views. The rules rested on the belief that everyone's behavior was tied to a code of honor—and respect, above all. Children needed to absorb these lessons so they could become valued members of the community otherwise they would be ostracized. To allow these lessons to fall by the wayside amounted to great negligence.

In the world in which Mother grew up, children were expected to honor and respect their parents. No one except God stood above them. If there was a single value or moral cornerstone upon which the structure of our family rested, this was it. We learned this lesson from our parents, especially Mom, and she learned it from her own mother. Everything else cascaded downwardly in priority. She verbalized this to us in a million ways.

Even in her late nineties, she underscored this ideal when she insisted that Soledad, for example, her third daughter already married and in her late fifties, perform eldercare for her—and Soledad saw no leeway. In fact, she seems to have embraced it with filial loyalty. In other words, Mom seemed to be drilling into us that respect and honor for one's parents included taking care of them in old age. Mom had taken care of Grandma Carlota to the very end, and now it was one of her daughter's turn to do the same. It was Mom's turn to be taken care of and, in this way, be honored according to the world she left behind in the Jalisco highlands.

If we, the children, showed disrespect in some form, we got hit quickly. Sometimes we didn't know why we got into trouble but hindsight indicates that *la falta de respeto* or the lack of respect could take surprising and unsuspecting forms. If you consider the fact that we were also learning new behaviors outside our home, since we were growing up in America, then the possibility of breaking the rules or showing disrespect could be multiplied many times. Honoring and respecting your parents could take many forms, and we learned slowly and painfully as we went. For example, when Mary or Martha asked to be allowed to nurture friendships with classmates, like spending the night with one or more of them, she was usually denied, presumably because Mom could not trust these friends to subscribe to the behavior requirements she expected from her daughters.

Sitting at Mother's dining room table, interviewing Mary one day, with Mom following the proceedings with keen interest, I asked Mary about her school days. My sister reminded me that she had only attended up to ninth grade. Asking her why she hadn't gone beyond ninth grade, Mary started to answer the question when Mother suddenly interjected. She understood the question I had posed my sister in English and helped answer the question by admitting she was so *desconfiada* (someone who is untrusting), but she didn't say more, and I unfortunately didn't ask her to clarify. Without any objections from Mom, Mary, however, filled in for her with the following words:

> The main reason that they [our parents] were strict was that they didn't want to give a girl a chance to talk to a boy. That was their concern. Most parents [in the community] used to feel the same way. It was more important to keep you at home under parental surveillance [than to let you go on to school. At home I was always busy]. I was always responsible—all my life—for my brothers and sisters, like being the second mother. [I was] always there!

As a new immigrant, Mother distrusted the world that surrounded her family and believed that her children could fall into harm, her daughters in particular. Physical harm, possibly, but moral harm, most probably. This meant that by the time Mary started grammar school, Mother still could not easily trust the teachers or the schools in San Fernando and so it was better to have her daughter close by and safe—this was about twenty years after immigrating to America. If Mary or Martha (later Soledad and Emily) insisted on doing things their way by simply sneaking off to be with their friends, for example, not only did they put themselves in harm's way from Mom's point of view, but they also incurred *falta de respeto*, by dishonoring Mom's advice. Disciplinary action was sure to follow.[182] Mom expressed her old fears outright that day at the dining room table, *"Yo era muy sin [confianza]! A'y que diga ella! Yo ni quería que fuera a trabajar!"* (I was very untrusting! She [Mary] can tell you! I didn't want her to get a job [when she stopped going to school at the end of ninth grade]). Mother softened her *desconfianza* in later years, allowing a longer tether for Martha, Soledad, and Emily, but Mary experienced the shortest one.

Mother naturally inherited a Mexican provincial outlook on life. It included rules about how people should interact with one another, how young women should express modesty in their dress, convey deference both in speech and in nonverbal communication, show respect toward elders, and so on. All this had the practical effect of laying out an array of non-written rules that were strictly observed in our home. Had we been raised in Mascota, it might have been easier for us to follow them, but alas, we lived in Southern California and by trial and error we proceeded to learn what we could get away with, the boys their way and the girls theirs. The bottom line is that problems would arise when we tried applying American standards of behavior at home, or at least, what we thought they were. Mom's rules tripped us children repeatedly. It is safe to assert that gringo-inspired behavior at home generally created a lot of commotion.[183] My sister Mary was hurt by the conflict in cultural mores, whether she deliberately violated the rules or not, because she was the first girl in the family. The leeway she enjoyed was the narrowest. She felt caught in between.

> I was not a modern girl. In my world I was a very old-fashioned person. I never dressed up like that. I was always way behind, never went with the fashions of the day. Dora and I [wore] braids, long dresses . . .

While our transgressions were not about smoking or drinking or taking drugs, Mom would be first to castigate us. She would often pressure Dad to confirm the penalty with his muscle, which he did often enough although we don't know how reluctant he was to do so. The "hit" could take the form of sternly or harshly pronounced words by Mom, or it could take the form of some "physically coercive tactic." By Mom's hand, this could take the form of pulling of an ear, a slap, a *coscorrón* (hitting someone's head with your knuckles), or a just a plain good beating. Inventive combination of all these physical and verbal acts worked very well too. Dad spanked us only when we were egregiously out of hand although he did a thorough job of it too. It seems none of us kept a grudge against him.

Our family was not unique as Mary observes below. Most families in San Fernando probably followed similar rules. "Harsh parenting" as practiced by Mexican fathers and mothers was discovered to be so prevalent in certain communities that it became the subject of clinical inquiry many years later. One group of investigators confirmed this to be true in northern Mexico, for example. The report stated that "a common disciplinary strategy used by Mexican parents is physical punishment." The group also concluded that perhaps more in the case of Mexicans than other Latin Americans, "corporal punishment" was "seen not only as a necessary disciplinary method but also as a positive practice to produce good citizens."[184] It was good for the children, in other words.

Many examples abounded nearby for us. My sister Mary remembered, in her words above, that on those lucky times when Mother allowed her to cross the street and spend a brief amount of time at Teresa O's party. Teresa's dad, Don Rodolfo and his neighbor, Juan Imperial, whose family organized the Christmas-time posadas that Mary enjoyed so much, "would patrol the street to make sure no boys would ever showed up." This means that they too subscribed to child-rearing rules that called for a close watch over youngsters, especially girls. Mary remembered clearly that her closest friend, Dora, experienced similar treatment by her own parents.

It appears to me that Mother's bad temper became more understandable from this perspective. In other words, she fretted about our breaking the rules that she believed ought to guide our young lives, and if we add the anxieties that began welling up about Dad's and Grandma's increasing illness and what this would mean financially and otherwise to her, then the frustration and strict behavior she displayed toward us became more comprehensible.

Could There Have Been Yet Another Reason?

Is it possible that Mom's distress came from her longing for a different kind of life? Could her stressed aggravation in the hard years I've identified come from occasional flashes of what her life might've been like in another circumstance? Some of us are stirred by the what-if's that dash across our minds every so often. What if she had stayed in Mazatlán? What if she had married another man? Is it an aberration for us children to think that she might have dared picture herself in another situation, especially when her day-to-day life became difficult to endure? Do we not engage in this practice ourselves? Is daydreaming reserved only for the young?

The reader will recall that both she and her brother Miguel caught a glimpse of what life might have been like for the two of them had they remained in Mazatlán. Let us not forget that Miguel, for example, saw himself as a *fogonero* or a *maquinista* working for the South Pacific Railroad, riding trains hither and thither. He even had a mentor who offered to help him along. No wonder he kept that thought alive for over fifty years! And, as many years later, Guadalupe likewise remembered her best friend's parting words, "If you didn't have your mother, you would stay and live with us." She repeated that phrase to us several times but never expanded on what all it meant to her, and we didn't ask.

Memories of this sort have the power to abide in our minds for many decades and become rekindled at unexpected moments. We ought not forget that Mother left a *pretendiente* or a brokenhearted admirer behind in Culiacán: Miguel, the telegraph operator. She nearly married a fellow named Jesús, and scattered other rejects by the wayside as well. Is it impossible, therefore, to imagine that when we children were beginning to storm her sense of propriety with our imagined self-importance and grown-up wisdom as teenagers, she might have nursed her disappointments by engaging in the what-if's of her life even though she apparently never disclosed any of them? Having to return to the reality of two or three ripe teenagers walking around in a pubescent haze ought to have contributed to her daily crankiness.

Could It Have Been a Mother-In-Law Problem?

Another factor that contributed to our family distress was Grandma Carlota. Her daughter always wanted her nearby, and this became a problem. Being the older and more battle-hardened of the two, it seems that Carlota believed she was entitled to a say about how we, the children, were raised and even about how her daughter might relate to her own husband. Her constant proximity to Mom and Dad encouraged this situation. Mary, about ten years old at the time, remembered that when Grandma was enjoying her own room in our Kewen Street house in the late 1930s, the situation could put a person on edge:

> Whenever my mom got pregnant, Grandma would pick a fight with her. My dad would try to show his affection to Mom, and Grandma would get upset. After showering, he would go to the mirror to comb his hair [and Grandma would criticize him] . . . She didn't like men who perked themselves up. "Look *el chino* [someone with wavy hair] is fussing with his hair!" One time . . . he passed by the window and looking in, he smiled at Mom [and] Grandma carped at her, "You should be ashamed! [You act like] you were sweethearts!" (*"No te da verguenza! Andan como si fueran novios!"*) They [Dad and Grandma] fought for the strangest reasons: because he was reading a newspaper, because he and Mom would go to the movies [and so forth. Such activities] were things of the devil. My Dad would get away by going to the corner to get a beer . . . In those days [Grandma] might have been going through menopause; that's what I figure.

Throwing her weight around, so to speak, had some positive sides at times. Mary remembered that when Manuel was born in *la vecindad*, Grandma took the situation over very quickly. Mom had apparently agreed that Carlota and Juárez would be the Godparents, not unusual under the circumstances, and Grandma soon organized a party for the entire family plus the neighbors. Musicians too attended, according to Mary. Grandma's cousins from Santa Rosa, the Peña brothers (Aurelio and Lupe), musicians, arrived and put on the entertainment, having been invited down from Oakland (they too abandoned the hacienda about the time that Carlota and her children walked away from it and ultimately ended up in the Bay area). The cousins always attracted fellow musicians wherever they went, so Manuel's baptism was livened with good food and much song.

Manuel also viewed Grandma as the source of considerable trouble between Mom and Dad, especially during the restaurant years. Grandma may have lived independently, but she did so next door! I was too young to understand this kind of conflict between my elders, and so I pay heed to Manuel's observations, which struck me as a bit over colored at first, but considering that they ran parallel to Mary's, I finally relented in his favor. He confirms that my father was caught in a Mexican version of the mother-in-law contest, and he just couldn't win. My brother remembered as follows:

> Grandma was tough as nails, especially when she was in her monthlies, you know? [This is when] she'd be yelling at Dad and the whole world could hear she was yelling at him! The bad part about it is that my mother never intervened. There was my Grandma in full fucking force [and] everybody was listening [to her] giving my father hell. *Tu eres esto, tu eres el otro y quién sabe que más!* (You are this, you are that, and I don't know what else!). I couldn't understand it . . . [That kind of behavior] made me fucking nervous. She was fucking with our lives [because her words collided with] the way we [felt] about ourselves. [Here stand our] Gods [who are] going to fucking pieces!

My brother obviously loved Dad and hated to see him attacked, no matter what the reason might have been—he was very conscious of Dad having to deal with so many problems. I would have felt the same, no doubt.

Both of my elder siblings felt Dad was getting a raw deal because they remembered the work that he had performed for Grandma over the years. For example, when Grandma Carlota first bought the corner lot on Kalisher Street, renting out the residential building on the corner and opening up a tortilla shop in the garage, Dad's carpentry work made this possible because he converted the garage into a one-room tortilla factory as related earlier. He also installed an outhouse with a flushable toilet on the lot and fixed up a shed for her to sleep in while he built a two-room dormitory for her, completing it about the time I was five years old. His services for her ran the gamut. Mary summoned to mind the time that Grandma had gotten sick enough to lose a considerable amount of weight and that the doctor prescribed a glass of wine for her with each meal. This is when liquor was illegal, so it was Dad who procured the ruby brew from an Italian bootlegger in Sylmar. Dad, of course, wouldn't have done all this for Grandma if it hadn't been for Mom asking him. All this constituted an investment of time and labor on his part, and he probably appreciated the larger reward of it all too—the family which he missed as a child. So he put up with the headaches. Manuel recalls that my uncle Miguel, who lived nearby, helped out from time to time, but his own family was growing so fast that he didn't dispose of that much time although Rose Marie, my uncle's eldest daughter remembered he fulfilled his quota well enough.

Guadalupe was very devoted to her mother, Carlota, and the reasons were abundant. To begin with, Mother never questioned having to show honor and respect to her. Both had learned this fundamental rule in the culturally conservative communities of central west Mexico, and Mother never thought twice about it. This may be the main reason why Manuel doesn't remember Mother ever defending Dad from Grandma's caustic disparagement. Another reason Mother was devoted to Grandma is that they had experienced so much together. They embarked on the immigrant trail together and shared many moments of joy and despair along the route.

This devotion and concern on Mother's part understandably increased as Grandma got older, considering she remained single after Juárez's death. This may explain why Mother arranged for Mary and Manuel to spend weeks with her at a time when they were youngsters, especially after Juarez died. I followed in their footsteps in the late 1940s when Grandma was in her late sixties, living with her for all practical purposes, and then Emily did the same in the early 1950s. Manuel believes that my father complained about my spending too much time with Grandma, even though we were separated by only a handful of city blocks and I went back and forth between our house and Grandma's all the time, "My father used to say, [presumably to Mother] 'he belongs with us! He's my son, he belongs in this family! He doesn't have to be over there!'" Mother would interject by saying, "No, no! She's all alone. My mother needs somebody to be with her." My sleeping away from the rest of my family "was my father's biggest bitch," according to Manuel.

Mom Becomes Grandma

However our trying times might be explained, our hardships receded. As Mom used to say, *No hay mal que dure cien años* which in more common parlance means that bad times don't last forever. Something always changes. This is how Mother gradually consented to her widowhood, slowly ascending from the dark days and long nights that accosted her as we saw in the last chapter. This is how she ultimately became Grandma Lupe, the octogenarian-and-then-some who could be sweet to her friends and great-grandchildren but steely with her offspring, if need be. No one will argue in the family that she maintained a certain clout over her children even when they could no longer hide their graying hair and budding doses of rheumatism.

In the end, to her credit, given her socioeconomic origins, she eased herself into a self-fashioned retirement, which might have been envied by some of her contemporaries. She outlasted Grandma Carlota, Juárez, my two uncles, Pascual and Miguel, and my father, Bernabé, and she probably outlived all the men and women who crossed her path on the immigrant trail from Santa Rosa to San Fernando. She was like the craggy bluffs that remain upright on a weather-sculpted plain.

Was our experience during these most difficult years unique onto ourselves? The answer to this question is that it probably was not, and this is one of the reasons I chose to write this book.

Chapter 12

Connecting and Celebrating

Our Mott Street Neighborhood • Kalisher Street • Santa Rosa Catholic Church • *La Misión* at Santa Rosa • The Local Schools • Community Cultural Events

A MORE COMPLETE VISION of our community and how we were able to relate to it is offered in this chapter. So far these pages present the reader only a glimpse of the world outside our humble abode, whether it was on Mott Street or Kalisher Street. Our ancestors arrived as immigrants, so how did they begin connecting to the immediate world around them? The purpose here is to explain how we linked up to this little universe that surrounded us and how these early connections affected us children growing up in America. Some of the preceding chapters provide part of the answer as they dwell on the jobs that the men in our family secured in order to keep us younger ones fed and clothed. Here we look beyond the jobs.

We can begin with our neighbors on Mott Street when we lived there in the early 1940s. Afterward we'll broaden our vision to include the Kalisher Street corridor, which held the barrio's commercial strip in those years, and then we'll focus on the institutions, especially the church and the schools, that served as our windows into the much larger world beyond. We'll finalize by examining other cultural activities and influences that impacted our barrio and our family in particular.

Our Mott Street Neighborhood

This one-block neighborhood constituted the first layer of the world outside our window, where we children conducted the earliest expeditions beyond the reach of our parents. For Mom and Dad especially, our neighborhood meant a handful of adults, all Spanish speakers of Mexican origin, who lived within a stone's throw of our front door and who required daily greetings at least, if not engaging into a conversation of one kind or another. For us children, it meant finding playmates for our games, and it also afforded us comparing adults with our own folks. Incorrectly or not, we viewed some of our neighboring families as being different from us because we thought some of them were better off than we were or, at least, not as country-bumpkinish.

For example, looking back in our minds we can see the Imperial family (that was their surname), who lived across the street and off to the right of our house, whose family members seemed to adapt more easily than we did to life in Southern California in part because their dad seemed more comfortable than ours in making a living. He transported chicken manure to the citrus groves, and so we thought that was a pretty smart thing to do. My memory etches him as a slightly paunchy, olive-skinned, curly haired fellow with a face and a black moustache suggesting something of the Arabic. He wore cowboy boots, and in my memory, he used a tooth pick to clean his gold-lined teeth. Mary believes he came from Arizona. Clearly, our dad was not at all like him. The fact that Mr. Imperial and his wife had two daughters only, as opposed to our larger and rambunctious family, certainly would have contributed to the feeling that they stepped to a different drummer, giving us the impression that they enjoyed themselves more than we did. The reader may remember that my sister Mary brought to memory that they organized the posadas, a traditional reenactment of Mary and Joseph's search for an inn, and this brought a lot of delight and harmony to our neighborhood and undoubtedly self-esteem for the Imperials.

Two other neighbors included Chuy or Jesús Landeros who lived next door to us on our left and spoke English like Mom never could. This suggests she too may have arrived in our neighborhood from somewhere along the border where Spanish and English were commonly spoken, instead of Mexico's interior like Mother's Jalisco, where no one spoke English. My brother Manuel remembered Chuy as a "middle-aged, skinny lady, with three children, married to a short, dark-skinned, hard-working man—*muy trabajador* (a hard worker)." Then there was the Puga family, two doors to our right, whose mom unashamedly let everyone know she was Protestant. Mrs. Puga, an older woman with sagging jowls wearing long, loose, silvery hair, would amiably stop at our front fence every so often and chat with Mom, mildly shocking her whenever she quoted a line from the Bible as part of the conversation. Mother wasn't used to this kind of tête-à-tête, having been raised a Mexican Catholic and naturally averse to anyone reading the "holy book." Catholics were expected to attend Mass and go to confession and leave the Bible-reading to the *padrecitos*, the priests. Little did either of them know that this avoidance of the Bible on Mother's part reflected decisions made by Catholic bishops hundreds of years earlier to discourage bible reading without priestly supervision as a way of stifling the formation of more Protestants.[185]

To complete the roll call of the families living in our Mott Street neighbor, there was old *el chato* (flat face), as everybody called him. Perennially inebriated and babbling as he stumbled, he presented yet another kind of head of household in our quarter, apparently childless. This man, who brought pangs of fear to my sister Martha and me whenever he staggered by, lived with his wife in the far corner of our block in a house almost entirely concealed by shrubs and vines. My uncle Miguel was another neighbor; he lived between *el chato* and Mrs. Puga on our right with his wife and twelve children, a family we considered to be more like us or so we thought. Also residing in our block was *Don* Rodolfo O., my *padrino*. He lived directly across from us, claiming a close relationship with Dad mostly because he also hailed from near Dad's hometown and both of their own fathers might have known each other. My Dad might have selected him as my baptismal godfather for this reason. According to my sister Mary, his wife, Doña Carmen (my *madrina*), grew up in Arizona, not Mexico. Their daughter befriended my sister, but their boys didn't chummy up to my elder brothers. They're the ones who introduced us to ice cubes, as Mary tells us elsewhere in this book, and I too was pretty impressed by that technological marvel. The Murillos need to be accounted for here because they lived next door to us, on our right. Inhabiting a small house like ours also filled with children, they stayed in our memory for at least two reasons. One is that they bought a player piano that tinkled on its own with the aid of a paper roller causing a sensation for everyone to witness, and the other reason is that a handful of decades later, my sister Martha married Johnny, one of the Murillo boys.

Kalisher Street

Kalisher Street, the next layer of the world outside our Mott Street home, stood three blocks away. It was then and continues to be today a one-mile-long asphalt avenue, introduced in chapter 7, trimmed with important businesses for our community all of which we, Gil children, came to know like the palm of our hands. The *comercios* on this street provided us with the things we needed if we didn't care to shop at the larger American shops located on San Fernando Road or even farther away on Maclay Avenue, giant box stores like WalMart not yet conceived. The businesses on Kalisher were attractive to people like us because all commercial transactions were conducted in Spanish there. If someone like Mom or Dad chose to do business in the American section of town, doing so required some knowledge of English. Besides, you had to walk a minimum of fifteen minutes to and fro, just to get there.

For these reasons our little *comercitos* on Kalisher were indeed quite handy, although now they're practically all gone. To illustrate, Mom relied on these shops on Kalisher Street for our everyday needs in our Mott Street kitchen. For example, we could purchase *carne para picadillo* or shredded beef, which Mom cooked in a light tomato-pepper sauce, at La India Market at the corner with Mott Street operated by the business-minded Sevilla family, or at La Mexicana Market run by the equally enterprising but gruff, smart-talking García brothers at the corner with Coronel Street. When we could afford and deserved a treat, we could always look for fresh out-of-the-oven, mouth-watering Mexican *pan dulce* (sweet bread) purchased from Doña Lupe at the Panadería Las Palmas at the corner with Pico Street. If we wanted the latest news, we could apply at Landin's tiny grocery store, at the corner with Hewitt for the latest copy of the local newspaper, *Vida del Valle de San Fernando,* which Mr. Landín himself wrote and published, a store site that would also be Dad's last store. Eusebio Landín's smoke-colored eye glasses gave me the vague impression, many years later, that he might have been a formally educated man from a big city in Mexico, so different from our folks.[186] Don José Audelo, whose kind and avuncular demeanor veiled a former life as a copper mine union organizer in Arizona, according to Mary, who established a lifelong friendship with their daughter Ernestine, operated a tidy tortilla-making shop with his wife, Doña Ester, near the corner of Hewitt Street. A shoe-repair shop run by another old *guero* merchant named Don Casimiro occupied the building we would inhabit on Kalisher and Hewitt, beginning in 1942 (this is the building that Grandma Carlota purchased and rented to him before we moved in). I still remember the sharp smell of leather and tannic acids that permeated his shop. Bolts of cloth and other mercery items needed for mending clothes could be obtained at *el judío's* solid brick building store at the corner with Kewen Street, which included a gasoline pump by the street curb, we Gil children honestly not knowing whether he was really Jewish, just knowing that *el judío* was Mom's sobriquet for him although his Spanish sounded different from everybody else's in the barrio. When I would go buy sewing thread for Mom his waning white hair and striking

European features always suggested to me that he was indeed different. Others in our barrio called him *el judío* as well.

As we've seen already, our barrio hosted many single Mexican males who worked in the agricultural fields of Southern California and lived on our side of the tracks or nearby and so, therefore, Kalisher Street also held space for their leisure-time activities, including their "watering holes." Some of the men requiring alcoholic beverages served by a bartender consumed their meals at Gil's Café and so we, Gil kids, knew pretty well what went on in those beer parlors. Luckily, I can say with great relief that the drinkers in my family, like Dad and my *tio* Pascual, tended to do their drinking at home and only occasionally at these swill holes.

In any case, the biggest saloons stood opposite each other right in the midsection of Kalisher Street between Hewitt and Griffith Streets. These were the Central Café and the Rialto Café plus Martínez Café, a block away on Mission Boulevard. It seems that these three drinking holes attracted the greatest number of boozers from the barrio, single men for the most part who developed the habit of drinking a beer or two or more at the end of a workday before going home to rejoin family or reenter their lonely bedroom, or on Fridays or Saturdays imbibing one too many beers and causing a ruckus. Sarabia's, a smaller, perhaps calmer tavern, located down in the *rana* (frog) part of Kalisher Street, below La Perla Market, also provided barrio men with a chance to drink and talk after work, especially on weekends. Some barrio pachucos may have sat at Sarabia's bar to wet their whistle more easily because they may have felt unwelcome by the mostly Mexican immigrant male clientele at Martinez's or the Rialto, the cultural differences simply being too great, according to my brothers. Federico Maldonado's pool hall located between Hewitt and Kewen Streets gave this part of Kalisher Street an added bohemian touch. His three tables, two for regular pool and one for carom billiards, attracted many players who could earn good money with their skillful handling of the cue stick while the everyday gawkers quietly sucked on their smoky cigarettes watching the balls roll and crash.

The presence of these establishments of questionable repute no more than a block or two away from our own Gil's Café provided a great source of concern for my parents, Mother especially. This was part of her ongoing concern over my sisters, above all, because a handful of drunks and worn-out prostitutes tended to cluster often at the doorways and spill out onto the sidewalks. This distinctly honky-tonk atmosphere invited trouble from time to time, especially on weekend nights. It was not uncommon to see police cars arrive with flashing red lights and black-uniformed officers jumping out to put a kibosh on a growing fracas often handcuffing someone and driving him away. This led city authorities, many years later, to rezone Kalisher Street and eventually close down the disputed enterprises, especially when narcotic drugs began infiltrating the barrio. This clamp down also had the effect of neutralizing what was once an untamed but colorful dimension of our *colonia*.

Santa Rosa Catholic Church

The most important place of worship in our part of town, and the spot where we would most connect with people in our community, was at the Santa Rosa Catholic Church, a stone's throw from the malodorous saloons and the smoky pool hall. This place of worship stood at the corner of Kalisher and Hewitt Streets across the street from our small restaurant after we opened it. Erected in 1925, Santa Rosa, named in honor of a Peruvian *mestiza* saint from the city of Lima, was the second Catholic Church built in the city. The city's first Catholic place of worship, St. Ferdinand's, stood near the dividing line between the English and the Spanish-speaking communities at the corner of Maclay and Celis. His Excellency, John J. Cantwell, bishop of the diocese of Los Angeles (elevated to an archdiocese a few years after Santa Rosa was opened), was persuaded that the growing Mexican population in San Fernando merited its own place of worship. This led to the inauguration of Santa Rosa in the year already cited consequently adding to the crazy quilt diversity of Kalisher Street.

The management of Santa Rosa Church was assigned to the Oblate Fathers of Mary Immaculate (OMI). These men represented a Catholic missionary order whose emissaries were allegedly described by Pope Pius XI as "specialists in difficult missions."[187] With stinky saloons only a block from its front door you'd think that these hardy priests may have been dispatched by the Vatican to shut them down, certainly a difficult undertaking to accomplish in our barrio. The truth is, however, that if these special missionaries were assigned to San Fernando, it wasn't because of the handful of drunks and prostitutes that graced the corner of Kalisher and Griffith Streets on weekends. Rather, it was us, the Mexicans and Mexican Americans of California. Places like San Fernando were viewed as a special mission or challenge by the American Catholic Church, culturally and linguistically. The church enjoyed a long track record of trying to spread the Christian Gospel in the poor neighborhoods of Boston, Baltimore, and Chicago, but the Spanish-speaking workers who were slowly filing into the newer towns of the American Southwest, like ours, in the early 1900s represented a unique challenge. They demanded a tailored solution, and this is where the French-inspired Oblates of Mary filled the void. Founded by a French nobleman turned cleric, Eugene de Mazenod, in 1826, by 1925 the Oblate Fathers possessed a solid track record of ministering to the working poor in Europe and Canada, and so they took advantage of their Spanish-speaking connections in Europe to carry out their assignment. The priestly organization turned to their Spanish-speaking Frenchmen and Spaniards, and this is how the *Oblatos de María* began trickling into my hometown.

Assigned by the American provincial director in San Antonio, these black-robed men who could speak in the tongue of Miguel de Cervantes began arriving in San Fernando in the late 1920s with the purpose of laboring in the sun-drenched fields of the lord in Southern California. Father Mauricio Jean, also known as *Padre Mauricio,* arrived first and by all accounts, including the churchgoing women in our family, set a positive example for the others who followed him. A Spanish-speaking Frenchman, apparently, he won the hearts of many parishioners including the women in my family in part because he spoke Spanish with a slight accent, albeit, and echoed an appreciation of Mexican culture at the same time that he strove to spread the Christian faith. Afterwards, Spaniards tended to be assigned to San Fernando in the early years and to this date my hometown remains Oblate territory. [188]

This background glimpse helps explain how the church across the street from our café became for us a significant bridge to other individuals and families in the barrio. Doña Petrita Pacheco, who resided firmly in my sister Mary's memory from the early days when we lived in *la vecindad,* as discussed in chapter 7, is a convenient stand-in for the many women like my own Grandmother, who found a haven in the religious exercises that the Spanish *padres* organized for the pious followers of Santa Rosa parish. The daily rituals typical of Mexican Catholic churches brought them together from wherever they had started in the Mexican backcountry. Wrapped in their traditional charcoal gray shawls or *rebozos de bolita* to fend off the morning chill, they would amble into church in the early morning to greet each other and hear Mass, or in the early evening to say the rosary, just as they or their mothers had done back home in the small towns of Jalisco or Michoacán. These were the commonly shared acts of devotion practiced by immigrants in a foreign land which helped accept the migratory moves and contributed to the formation of lifelong bonds.

It merits noting too that in reaching out, the older women in our family could easily rub elbows with some people but not with others. Grandma Carlota related effortlessly with Doña Petrita Pacheco and her daughter

Margarita, for example, and Doña Petra Espinosa, or even with Ermelinda Luján because they shared a socioeconomic background, so to speak, because they came from modest, not to say peasant families, very much like ours. However, the parish body of Santa Rosa Catholic Church, like the barrio itself, reflected certain diversity too. It also embraced families who hailed from higher economic strata than ours, and it's probably quite safe to assert that the trajectories of people like Lola Ortega, Juan Najar, the Zamoras, the Camperos, the Padillas, and others, differed markedly from ours because they were able to claim some degree of middle-class origin all the way from Mexico, perhaps Spain. They probably didn't emerge from hacienda peasantry as our family did and never knew what it was to see the world from the long vegetable rows awaiting harvesting under a hot California sun or the orange trees needing to be picked or pruned.

This socioeconomic dissimilarity was revealed every Sunday at Santa Rosa Church. Their dress, the vehicles that brought them there, the way they spoke and carried themselves in public and, of course, their *güero* or lighter complexion tended to identify these better heeled families more often than not. The women who headed this type of family didn't dress in the peasanty rebozos like Doña Lugarda Elías, for example, one of Grandma Carlota's comrades. They dressed in suit dresses and matching hats and wore shiny heels. Standing by the rectory door after Mass, they could look at the Spanish priests in the eye and speak nonchalantly with them as if they were enjoying tea with them on a Sunday afternoon, which is something they probably did. They could even laugh with them like long-time friends do, something the rebozo-clad women could never claim.

Even so, these veiled differences didn't hinder the moments of soulful distraction that the activities at Santa Rosa presented to most of us in the Gil family. Grandma Carlota, for example, was the first person in our family to become involved with organized religious pursuits at Santa Rosa. We Gil children knew her as a zealous Christian woman, but we didn't know whether she held this fervor all of her adult life perhaps reflective of the piousness of Mexican peasantry in the late 1800s or whether her attentiveness to religious worship grew as a counter force to her difficult relations with men. The earliest photographs we conserve of Grandma often show her holding a portrait in her hands of Jesus or Mary and wearing a scapular (a neck band holding a religious image) over her breast as a protective icon[189]. My sister Mary remembers her creating a home altar in the minuscule-sized, two-room apartment at *la vecindad,* where she would organize novena prayers for her neighbors in commemoration of one or another religious personage. We know that after settling in San Fernando she sought membership in some of the women's lay organizations like the Society of the Perpetual Light (*La Vela Perpétua*), The Daughters of Mary (*Las Hijas de María*), and the Followers of Our Lady of Guadalupe (*Las Guadalupanas*). These organizations were probably encouraged by the pastor as a way of channeling some of the spiritual fervor that drove women like Grandma; in fact, she may have even helped found one of these groups. She became president of at least one of these organizations in the late 1940s because on one occasion she had me jot down some notes for her in preparation for a meeting she was holding in one of the church offices, her own writing ability having been extremely limited due to the lack of schooling.

The benefits of belonging to religious groups of this kind must have been particularly important for women like our grandmother. Older women like her who emigrated from Mexico as adults probably yearned for some kind of society that could provide an outlet for the challenges and frustrations that life in Southern California might have brought them. Like our Grandma, many of these older *señoras* who trekked to seven o'clock Mass every morning surely must have found themselves bewildered from being wrenched out of their small home town back in Mexico and so must have welcomed joining *La Vela Perpétua* if for no other reason than to exchange their experiences in America with someone like themselves or perhaps obtain news from back home or simply vent about the latest bout with rheumatism with a friend.

All indications are that the decades of the 1920s and 1930s provided even greater reason for émigrés like our grandmother to gather at Santa Rosa Church. This is the time when the Mexican Catholic Church came under attack by the government as part of Mexico's revolutionary experience discussed in Chapter 1. One of the aims of the revolutionary leaders was to destroy the long-held economic and political power of the church, and so this historic struggle became red hot in the mid-1920s when President Plutarco Elías Calles finally put the screws on the church, triggering a rebellion known as the Cristero Revolt. Devout Mexicans mounted a defense, which included motley battalions of poor, illiterate peasants cut from the same cloth as our own grandmother and her siblings, all prompted by clerics and landowners to fight to save the church. The worst fighting took place in Jalisco, Grandma's home state, and in other nearby states many of whose families like ours had already immigrated to Southern California. Our grandmother seems to have been a good example of the puzzling reactions that this struggle engendered among the ordinary populace, particularly in rural areas. As we've seen, Grandma hailed from impoverished peasant families that had been subjected for generations by dominant landlords who themselves enjoyed the moral backing of the local priests and the Catholic Church in general. Despite this contradiction, our grandmother stood as a vociferous critic of government leaders like Calles who dared to strike against the church. I remember her saying several times that Juárez and Calles represented the anti-Christ.

Grandma Carlota and others of her circle supported activities on behalf of "the persecuted" Cristeros in ways that most of us grandchildren failed to understand or remotely appreciate. This included paying dues to maintain a political party known as *El Partido Sinarquista* and its publication called *Orden,* which was sold at the church door for many years after Sunday Mass at Santa Rosa by a wiry, peasant-looking old crone named *el Señor* Tomás Gasca. The *sinarquistas,* as they were called, struggled to bring about a government that would allow the church a vital role in Mexican society, and their political punch withered over the years. Even our own mother became involved with the local organizers and attended several meetings in the late 1940s, but her participation ebbed as well. Indications are that many local San Fernando families were affected by these happenings. A church-sponsored pictorial directory circulated in 1975 gingerly refers to this cross-border phenomenon with the following carefully chosen words:

> [In the late 1920s] Santa Rosa began to serve as the gathering place for its church members and also for those who fled religious persecution in Mexico . . . [190]

Whatever our family travails might have been, whether we were living on Mott or on Kalisher Street, the *padres* of Santa Rosa offered us many ways to connect with the larger barrio community, and we responded enthusiastically at times. For example, sometimes we would learn of a baptismal ceremony taking place, and this would impel my siblings and me and other barrio ragamuffin children to stand eagerly at the church doors, usually on a Saturday morning, ready to catch the coins the new godfather would toss into the air as an age-old gesture of good luck at the moment he and the proud new parents emerged from the baptismal ceremony, or of a wedding mass that would give my sisters the opportunity to gaze admiringly at a new white-veiled bride offering red roses to an image of the Virgin Mary at a side altar, or of a significant funeral that triggered more than a dozen automobiles of varying trademarks en route to the cemetery. In May, mothers would take their elementary-school-age daughters to "offer flowers" to the Virgin Mary during the daily rosary hour in the evening, and in June, the boys would do the same in honor of the Sacred Heart of

Jesus. We Gil children took part many times in these religious ceremonies that required large quantities of daisies, gladiolus, and ferns at the same time that it offered us kids the chance to greet our friends, if ever so briefly. Then there was the *misión*.

La Misión at Santa Rosa Church

A *misión* at Santa Rosa when we Gil children were growing up consisted of an annual month-long religious exercise. It took the form of a series of devotional activities whose main objective was to renew Catholic vows, a spiritual workout that surely tested the ability of the local pastor and his volunteers in reaching out to the parishioners. It meant shaking the bushes for sinners needing repentance—even the Kalisher Street drunks and prostitutes were known to pay attention. A *misión* competed with Christmas and Easter in terms of the numbers of people trying to gain entrance to the church on the appointed days, and when they couldn't wiggle all the way in, they conformed themselves by listening at the doorstep, whole globs of them.

Given the importance of a *misión,* the Oblates in San Antonio would send out a special missionary to conduct it, not leaving it in the hands of the local pastor. My sister Mary remembered that Father Andrés DeAnda, a fast-walking chubby-faced Spaniard with a disarming smile and receding black hair, performed the *misión* successfully for many years.

The launching of the spiritual exercises were announced at the Sunday homily by the local pastor several weeks in advance, and when the inaugural Sunday arrived, no punches were pulled. Father DeAnda would preside over a three-priest Mass accompanied with full organ and choir; all the stops were out. The sunlight would filter through the high windows and reflect on the sparkling vestments worn by the celebrants, while the heady scent of incense spiraling upward filled the front part of the church with a silvery haze. In these days, prior to Vatican II, the prayers were recited in Latin, rather than in the local language, and they would echo through the building crammed with wide-eyed Mexican faces eager to hear the fiery words of Father DeAnda, well-known for his sermons. The launching of the elegant three-priest Mass meant the *misión* was a go, and so the moment would arrive when Father DeAnda would stride up to the pulpit.

During the *misión* itself, his sermons were critical, of course. If the parishioners were going to renew their Catholic vows, they had to be reminded of how they had lapsed on them. And Father Andrés was ready to remind his rapt listeners. In his Spanish, resonating with a slightly lispy

Iberian timbre, his words would boom through the air regaling his listeners with simple stories of men and women who favored power, money, or fashion over the simple act of helping a neighbor. *Ayudar al prójimo,* he would say many times, help thy neighbor. Turn your back on the Devil and just practice the simple Christian virtues, he reminded us often. He favored unveiling the selfishness of rich men and overly dressed women who put on airs, but he also applied similar lessons at the level of the working men and women who seemed to heed his every word. Do good acts because you never know when you'll be knocking at the Pearly Gates. He also extolled the advantages of belonging to the "true church" and often urged us to beware of errant ministers whose line of authority reached back to Henry VIII, who broke away from Rome merely because the Pope refused him a divorce that would allow him to marry young and nubile Anne Bolyn. Father DeAnda enjoyed reciting that story for his listeners who likewise appeared spellbound by the seemingly common and familiar antics of kings and queens. Protestantism served as a whipping boy in our *misiones,* and these annual lessons from Father DeAnda no doubt fed Mother's occasional thrusts at "the little ministers" (*los ministrillos*) who presided over the Protestant churches to which some of our friends belonged.

Sermons filled with images of ordinary folks performing good acts were joined with spoken scenes from the Bible for an entire month, all aiming at spiritual renewal in weekly stages. The first week was reserved for the adult men of Santa Rosa, which included attending early morning Mass, Monday through Friday, for those who could fit it in, and confessions on Saturday afternoon. This is when Father Andrés and his assistant pastors would sit and patiently listen both to the *pecadotes* and the peccadilloes, all transgressions against moral purity committed by the contrite souls who formed long lines outside the confessionals, waiting for their absolution and thus be able to prepare for Holy Communion on Sunday.

This is when the key event would come for the men, at the sermon for the main Mass. This is when every man attending would stand up and be exhorted by Father Andrés to renew his vows at the top of his lungs, revival style:

> I renounce you, Satan, and all your profane deeds, and all your evil followers, and all your power, and all your evil traps and your army and your dominion and the rest of your deceit! I renounce you! I renounce you! I renounce you!

The second week was devoted to adult women, and it included a schedule of rituals similar to the men's. The third week was similarly aimed at the young men of the parish and the fourth was reserved for the young women in the same manner. The *misión* would culminate on the last Sunday when the church doorways would become simply impassable with people hoping to benefit from Father DeAnda's final blessing.

Almost everyone in our family felt lifted by the *misión* and its religious stimulation. In the days that we operated Gils Café across the street from the church, we had more customers, of course, as a result of the large crowds milling at church and this pressed us all the more so because we too were keen to witness the throngs and be part of the exaltation promoted by Father DeAnda. In the days when Grandma Carlota was alive and well, she, of course, prodded us all to attend and take part. With Mother's guidance, even Dad would relent and don his gray gabardine jacket over his khaki pants and walk over to the church, if he could edge himself in and, finding a place in the back, quietly listen and take part in the proceedings. Dad was never militant about church issues, so different from my uncle Pascual in this respect. Grandma would exhort Pascual to attend, and if he was in good mood, he would give in to her urging. Anti-clerical, as the day was long, he would enter inside the church and stand in the back, suppressing his disapproval of the entire performance. At the slightest remark about his going to church, he would voice his trenchant views about priests and the Catholic Church to anyone who would listen, "all they want is to take your money, don't be fooled," but we all pleaded deafness to avoid an uproar.

The Local Schools

Schools constituted our second most important connection to the world outside our home and our barrio. They would mark us, Gil children, in one way or another, some of us feeling the imprint more than others. Of a small handful of schools that served San Fernando, the one that most directly affected us all in the family was San Fernando Grammar School located a block from Kalisher Street at Mott and Mission Boulevard. This is where all of us Gil children formally began our American education, and our first encounters with *americanos* and their culture, although ironically, the majority of our classmates seemed to have been of Mexican-origin. Because there were eight of us, our collective experience at San Fernando Grammar was drawn out across the years creating in this way a lasting impression among all our long-term Anglo teachers who were prompted to us, "So you're another Gil!" or "So, you're Mary's little brother!" This left us to wonder what exactly lay behind declarations of that kind.

Mary's School Remembrances

Being the eldest, Mary had to smooth the way, and it wasn't easy for her. It seems that six years after settling in San Fernando and living in *la vecindad,* Mother wasn't ready to allow five-year-old Mary, her firstborn, out of her reach and protection just like that. By her own account, Mom loved her own school experience in Mascota, brief as it was, when she was about Mary's age, but that was different because the school was small as was the town. Besides, Mom's school was located only a few blocks from where she lived, and the teachers and the prevailing culture were all familiar. Not so in San Fernando. This may explain why she hesitated that day in 1933, reportedly the worse year of the Depression, to register Mary in school. It's entirely conceivable that walking into an unfamiliar school office where the officials spoke only English added to her quandary, and at age twenty-eight, ten years into her marriage, it might have been the first time she was expected to walk into an American office and conduct business. Apparently, the school officials took steps of their own to get Mary into class. Mary explained it this way:

> My mother didn't want me to go to school . . . *El Gordo* [the fat man] was the person . . . [who the school authorities] sent to get me, he was a bit daffy. They registered me [in the office], which was under construction, and *El Gordo* acted as my guide and took me to my first class [which happened to be] in a tent with a wooden floor [because some of the classrooms were also under construction].

El Gordo was a youngish pot-bellied man with bulging eyes who always wore a long-sleeved tan khaki shirt and khaki pants and walked as if he was always unhinged. Also known as Everardo Guzmán, he often stood on corners, offering to help people and run errands for many barrio residents. Mary called him "a boyish man approaching middle age" whose physical and mental handicaps robbed him of a normal life but not enough to prevent him from busying himself in the service of others. Apparently the registrar at San Fernando Elementary knew enough to draw upon his familiarity with the Mexican part of town to assist in Mary's registration into first grade, not a professional way of doing things, but this is what it was. So at the end of the day, Mother's first child was admitted at school despite her reluctance and suspicion.

In any case, Mary's entry into elementary school opened up the world for her. Judging from a sum total of her memories, perhaps her most important discovery was other adult women, besides her mother and grandmother. Meeting other children, particularly those who didn't know a word of Spanish was also a novelty. Teachers dominated her memory because they ruled her life at school, and she gave most of them a reasonably high mark. "I remember my first teacher being Mrs. Dunbar, and one day she told us she was going to go on long trip on a boat, sail a big ocean because she was getting married. She was my first grade teacher." A Mrs. Carpenter, possibly Dunbar's substitute, struck my sister as "very pretty," and then she recalled the others in succession without a note of disapproval: Mrs. Janey, then Mrs. Gallagher, later Mrs. Radditz. "All of them were very intelligent and soft-spoken," my sister affirmed. She even proclaimed Mrs. Radditz as "a beautiful person," recalling some of her activities as well:

> She made all her dramas about Indians. She'd make us study about American Indians; we'd make plays about them. Everybody wanted to be with her because she was sweet and lovable to everybody! She was chubby and endearing.

One of the exceptions was Mrs. Dill, who happened to live on the edge of the barrio on the corner of Coronel Street and Mission Boulevard. A cheerless woman in her fifties, always dressed in a suit, exuding a facial sharpness that matched her lean body, she always seemed to march instead of walk. Mary remembered this about her:

> Mrs. Dill was a very moody person. The first day in her classroom she'd sit us down and then she'd say, "In this room, I will not stand for any foolishness. Everybody put their hands out" and she would get the ruler and she'd go down the [row] and hit you with her ruler and you'd better not get your hands out of the way! This was to let you know she was the one who was directing things from then on. She'd give all these instructions like "Nobody is going to come running up the stairs! You wait for me in line!" It was all a lot of discipline.

In another teacher, Mary may have discovered the existence of prejudice for the first time, and it involved an instructor named Mrs. Rush.

> When I was in the fifth grade, with Mrs. Rush, you [the author] were born, and I was so happy [about it]. We were

> living on Kewen Street, and I went home during my lunch hour—all of us did that. So I got you out of bed, got you all dressed up, and I told my mom, "I'm taking Carlos to school so my teacher can see him!" I ran all the way from Kewen [back] to the school, and she [Mrs. Rush] was on the second floor, and I ran up the steps so hard I could hardly breathe! You must have weighed about 12 or 14 lbs; you were a big baby. I went to see her and said to her, "I want you to see my beautiful brother!" She said, "Aaah! Roly-poly *cholos*!"
>
> I was so sad, you know! [Mary's voice quavers]. I just hugged you and ran all the way home! I was able to make it all the way home and back before the tardy bell [rang]! This is when I really realized how prejudiced she was! When I got home, I told my dad, and he said, "That old woman, she's the daughter of the ugliest looking Indian around, of all San Fernando [referring to the López family]! Who does she think she is?" [Mary stiffles a sob] After that I didn't want to go to school anymore. I told my father, and he said, "Eh, that's all right [forget about it]. That's the way she feels! She can't change!" She considered herself so American because she married Dr. Rush. [Later] I got to meet some of her daughters—they were very beautiful people. They used to live on Brand and Mott Streets.

In spite of Mary's huge disappointment with her fifth grade teacher, she nevertheless recognized her teaching ability. These are her words:

> [S]he was very artistic, she'd teach us how to hand-screen our own kimonos for the Japanese plays we used to perform, there in her room. It was very beautiful! The whole front of the classroom was done in orange and cherry blossom. We used to have a little rickshaw that somebody would sit in, and we would make a little play . . . we made our wooden shoes. The only things that were store-bought were the sox you would wear in your wooden shoes. The kimonos, the sash—everything was beautifully done. Very few people go to that extent now. As far as being a teacher, I guess she was all right except for her prejudice against the Mexicans.

Mary stopped attending school in ninth grade.

Manuel's school remembrances, Mike's, Martha's, and My Own

Manuel, the second Gil child, began nursery school about 1936 and completed his elementary years by 1944; then he passed on to Junior High where he dropped out also from ninth grade in 1947. When he was seventy-nine years old, he set aside his favorite Buddhist texts and looked back at his San Fernando Elementary days appraising them as "all right" and proper. His hindsight view was that his school days were nothing more than his personal acculturation, becoming an American. In that sense, he added as follows:

> [I]t was the formation [given to us] for being in America . . . The impact on us was a culture thing, eating different food, [becoming familiar with the] history of US . . . That was good. It was OK. I was a functioning student.

He claimed having "no problem with English" but admitted that he just didn't like the grammar, "the mathematics of English," he called it. Then again, he added the following:

> School was OK . . . [It] didn't play a big part of my life. It wasn't what I wanted, although Mary liked it. I felt better working with my dad, he on the ladder and me down on the ground; he was my mentor, I liked being like him.

Had my brother Mike been able to share his views with me about his attending school, they wouldn't have been pleasant to read. Of all of us Gil kids, he was the most indomitable, like a mustang that wouldn't be broken. As explained in another chapter, he wasn't afraid of exerting himself physically or working harder than anybody else. But to concentrate on brainy or analytical matters that appeared only remotely connected with his daily activities was hard to do. His teachers must have strained and smarted over him, and Mother must have discovered his poor grades at one point or another, but when he got past his twelfth birthday, she could manage him less and less, he pulling in his own direction. His first wife, Pat, wrote to me saying, "He was like a horse wanting to escape a barn," in reference to school. She believes he quit when he was about sixteen years old, when we were busiest with the restaurant and just before Grandma and Dad started declining health wise. In school he learned enough to speak English perfectly and write it effectively enough to make his business pay off as we discuss later.

My own peek at the world through grammar school wasn't remarkable either. My elementary school experience began rather negatively in fact. I remember feeling alienated in my first days in school in 1942, but I don't recall why. I may have been homesick, and this could be the reason I clearly remember wanting to climb the chain-link fence in order to go home, which I knew was nearby. The all-English language environment in the classroom may have induced me to feel estranged, and while it's entirely possible that I knew a few words of English by the time I reached first grade, thanks to my elder siblings, this probably didn't make any difference. My memory, nevertheless, summons up crowds of children playing outdoors or otherwise milling about on the school ground, lining up outside the auditorium door to get a pinprick on your arm to ward off one sickness or another. Likewise, classrooms filled with youngsters sitting on the floor in front of the teacher—nothing of this excited me. The large marble-walled bathrooms in the building basements repelled me, and I recall being upset by the showers in these bathrooms where some of my male classmates were required to bathe, I myself being unable to remember whether that ever happened to me though I believe Mother would have raised a tempest had that occured. I also remember the cafeteria food smells making me queasy and so I avoided it and seldom ate there; I ate Mom's lunches prepared with tortillas and other homemade foods, and I also commit to memory having to hide at lunchtime to eat my lunch because eating *tacos* wasn't a popular thing to do. I had, at least, one favorite teacher, Mrs. Hershey, who made us feel comfortable around her, taking us to her home at least once, some of us riding in the open trunk of her tan Plymouth coupe automobile, as I remember, and I also admit having to endure Mrs. Dill for the reasons already presented above rendering her class unbearable for me. I can only presume I learned to read and write in a satisfactory manner, but any achievements that may have come my way did so only after elementary school came to an end.

Next in line was my sister Martha who entered San Fernando Elementary School about 1944. Her experience in that school is also unknown to us, but I surmise that her time in school, overall, may have been one of the few positive notes in her life. She reached junior high school about the time that the world was crashing down on Mom as presented in chapter 10 with Grandma dying and our father getting progressively ill and then passing away. These were the depressing events that marked the dreadful timeline that spanned Martha's junior and high school years, all of it contributing to Martha's extremely difficult relationship with Mother, oscillating between the adverse and the grievous. Martha contracted a severe case of psoriasis in these years, but she was always a trooper and in spite of it all, including her difficult relations with Mom, she nonetheless became the first girl in the family to complete high school. She deserved many encomiums for this alone.

My brother Enrique's earliest school experience also occurred during the nadir of our family life on Kalisher Street, and his memories too are gone for us. Rick began elementary school about 1947, and so the span of his grammar school years also coincided with Mom's worse years. It seemed to us, looking back on things, that Dad was unable to cast an imprint on him as a way of providing him the clear dose of self-confidence that Manuel, for example, drew from Dad and so my kid brother often landed in difficult situations, and he too quit school early.

School for the two youngest ones

Soledad and Emily, perched on the lowest rungs of the family ladder because they were born last, trod a different path because they were able to attend Catholic school. While they may have been the last ones in the family to begin school life at San Fernando Elementary, Soledad in 1949 and Emily in 1951 or thereabouts, their most significant school experiences, by their own account, took place not in public school but at Santa Rosa Catholic School nearby. Erected right in the heart of the barrio on Kalisher Street between Mott and Griffith Streets, about 1955, Emily was the first to attend there. Unfortunately, though, things never proceeded well for her to say the least.

Emily wasn't interested in attending Catholic school at all, but she ended up spending four years there anyway, her unhappiest school years. Looking back on this time, Emily grimly declared it to be terrifying. "School was a real, real, bad nightmare [because] they had some vicious nuns [there]."

One major predicament had to do with her being there in the first place. It seems that Mom was pressured into sending Emily to Catholic school. Emily's understanding is that once the school was opened for the first time, the parishioners of Santa Rosa were exhorted to send their children to it presumably to insure its success, the more the merrier. And, Mother, right in the middle of her gloomy interlude, didn't take command of Emily's registration. She was working at a factory during the day and supervising the tortilla shop in the evening and still grieving from having put her own mom in the grave two years earlier and seeing Dad's fatal health declining steadily. This seems to be why she required Emily to do the negotiating with the Franciscan nuns who operated the school. She instructed Emily to present herself to them and explain that she couldn't afford to send her daughters to Santa Rosa. Instead of listening to Emily, the brown-robed sisters decided they wouldn't take no for an answer. They insisted that she become part of the student body and that Mother could pay in kind with *tortillas, menudo, tamales,* and so on. Emily's religious education could be assured this way. Apparently, Emily felt disempowered to argue to the contrary, and decades later, she could only explain it all with exasperation, "By keeping me in school, my mom was forced to pay for my tuition [in kind]. They would order [what they wanted] ahead of time [and] you were forced to give it; they set you up in such a way that you didn't have a chance. [This is the way] they forced the issue on my mom." And Mom blamed Emily for this situation even though she herself felt unable to alter it. Emily claims that Mother complained to the local pastor but to no avail. "She was forced into that one," my youngest sister avowed, like seeing a child slip on ice. But that wasn't the worst part.

Another difficulty had to do with who would define the official school starting time. Mom or Emily's teacher? This question placed Emily in a constant quandary. "Mom had a thing that you didn't go to school until school started," Emily recounted. In other words, for Mother, school started when the pupils convened in the classroom in order to actually begin their school work. Emily's teacher, on the other hand, defined it differently. For her, school started when the students gathered on the school playground and then walked two blocks up Kalisher Street to Santa Rosa Church, past the smelly bars which were mercifully closed early in the morning or were being hosed out as part of a cleaning routine, to attend morning Mass, directly across the street from where we lived, the students sauntering back to their classroom after Mass. Following this routine, Emily would have to make sure any early morning chores on her list were completed, be dressed in her white and dark green school uniform, groom herself as best as can, and leave home, walk down two blocks on Kalisher Street past the closed bars, gather in the school yard, then walk back up the street in formation with her classmates in order to enter the church to hear Mass, across the street from where Mom could see her entering the church. This amounted to doing an early morning round trip, essentially speaking, before class.

Mom, who was undoubtedly dashing around herself early in the morning in order to leave for work at one of the local factories on First Street, considered this excessive hanging out for Emily and a waste of time to boot. Already having to swallow Emily's attending school under an unsatisfactory arrangement, which she felt unable to oppose because it involved contradicting religious authority figures, Mom seems to have placed the burden on her youngest daughter. Her response was to label the early starting time as nothing more than "ridiculous" and put the blame on Emily. "That's across the street, let them come this way [and then join them]!" In other words, she should be safe at home instead of walking up and down Kalisher Street more than necessary. Emily remembers Mom's rejoinder: "You do it only because that's what you want to do (*Nomás porque tú quieres!*)!" According to Emily, Mom would not see it any other way, "She refused [to allow me to go early]!" My sister remembers being physically punished in class for her lateness, "I got beatings so bad every day because of that, and Mom refused to acknowledge it." Mom's words still ring in her memory. "How do you expect me to believe that they're treating you like that?"

Emily's nightmarish memories went even further. Her teacher apparently decided to shame her into dressing properly.

> Sister Katherine decided that I was going to be made an example of. She began to undress me in front of the class to show my poor and shabby clothes. It became a nightmare to be in school because Sister Katherine had a real shit about it. [She undressed me] to show the shabby clothes I wore.

This episode may seem hard to believe. But it has a supportive explanation. Never known for natty or stylish dressing, much less in her teenage years when Mom was unable to watch closely how she dressed, my sister, no doubt, did what most unsupervised or semi supervised teenagers would do: dress helter-skelter for school. She would probably throw on whatever under garments she could find before donning her white blouse and dark green skirt and sweater in whatever condition these were in, and Sister Katherine, who was probably a childless spinster growing up as an only child in a middle-class family, decided she'd take matters into her own lily-white fine-fingered hands. She'd teach Emily a lesson about preparing for school properly. My sister's bitter cup was thus brewed, poured, and swallowed. "It was the most terrible time [for me] . . . between [the time I was] nine and thirteen [years of age]."

No one would believe Emily at home, not Mother or her sister closest in age, Soledad. "Sally never believed me until about six months ago," Emily complained fifty-three years later. In a chance meeting between Soledad and Laurie Elías, one of Emily's classmates at Santa Rosa Catholic

School, the former schoolmate inquired about Emily with a touch of concern. When asked to explain her apprehension, the answer was that she had always fretted about Emily. As Sally later told Emily, "She was very worried about you," adding that "she prayed and prayed for you because of what Sister Katherine did to you." Here was the confirmation! But no one would believe Emily all this time. And, as if this wasn't enough, Emily had to bear with Sister Katherine for several years.

> I never got a new teacher. She always went up with the class! Mom asked me, "Who turned you against the church?" They did! They did it, all by themselves! I hated going to school! I would rather go to work!

Soledad's experience at Santa Rosa Catholic School was entirely the opposite, like night and day. At the time that Emily was enduring the domineering nun, Soledad was attending San Fernando Elementary; after all, Mom simply couldn't afford to send both of them to private school—that would have meant even more tortillas and tamales! Walking to and fro, Sally would often walk past Emily's school and look through the chain-link fence into the school yard. She pined to attend Catholic school. "I remember standing at the chain-link fence on Kalisher Street, looking into the Catholic school [grounds], wishing that I was there [inside]," she recalled wistfully when we talked about it decades later. Soledad attended public schools reluctantly all the way to eighth grade. This is when Mother relented and sent her to Santa Rosa.

Soledad's happiest time in school was in eighth grade at Santa Rosa. Asked to explain this, she was crystal clear in her answer. One reason was the sense of belonging, a "sense of community," which she missed in public school. She relished the morning walk after roll call to attend Mass two blocks away at the church in front of our house. As we saw with Emily's experience, the entire class walked together, and this made Sally "feel special," like she "belonged to something beyond herself," she stated. Mom may not have complained about Sally's wasted time doing the round trip because she had already learned she couldn't change matters. Another of Sally's hindsight motivation was her conviction that the religious education imparted by the nuns at Santa Rosa was superior to "the old traditional way," in catechism classes and different from "the way Mother taught us," she added. "I remember admiring the nuns so much that I wanted to be a nun at one point," she confessed. It was a "whole new experience." And the third reason she considered Catholic school superior to its public equivalent is that "We all dressed the same, we were in uniform and somehow that was very important to me, I guess. Everybody dressed the same so nobody had anything better than [anyone else]." Mother was blind to dressing her daughters well. She recalled, "She made me go to church, wearing a frumpy little dress" and that simply wouldn't do; she chuckled when she thought back on it. Wearing a uniform meant that she didn't have to compete with classmates who might have dressed better than she and most did. Alas, at the end of eighth grade, she unhappily resigned herself to returning to public school because Mom couldn't afford more.

Summing up our primary school experience, you could say that it was patchy, indeed. Whether or not we had any learning disabilities, it didn't matter at the time. Still, it afforded us our first look at the larger world and provided us with basic tools at the same time. We all learned to read and write and gain at least a working knowledge and appreciation of what it meant to live in the United States as verified in the employment biographies that follow in chapter 14. Mary and Sally appear to have held the strongest attraction to institutionalized instruction and everything that goes with it, yet both underwent strikingly different experiences. It's entirely possible that Martha may have been positively attuned to it as well from the start; she did so well, but we'll never know. Things might have been satisfying for Emily but her rocky relationship with Mom and with her teacher-nun simply produced an awful muddle. Given Mom's life predicament including the fact that Dad was now too feeble to come to her aid and no one else could fill the void, she had to submit to unbelievably bad pedagogy with good grace. For the rest of us, the boys especially, primary instruction in these years at San Fernando Elementary, didn't arouse us particularly; although we obviously learned the basic lessons, even Mike and Rick, furnishing us with enough intellectual skills to grapple with the horns of life.

A word about organized sports fits here because it usually plays an important part in American school life. We Gil kids would have benefitted from organized sports or from taking part in youth organizations like the Boys Scouts or the Girls Scouts, but this was not to be; not for us of the second generation. To begin with, our parents didn't have any such experience, of course, and my father didn't work in a big American factory or a large mining enterprise where organized sports might have been encouraged as part of an extramural program, so he didn't promote it. Besides, Mother was perennially afraid of the contamination that we kids might acquire from the barrio in terms of bad friends, *malas companías,* as she so often advised. As far as she was concerned, we had to come straight home from school, right away, and while my sisters may have felt more obligated than us boys to tow the line, we brothers didn't feel pulled in by sports in any case. I was aware of a local CYO (Catholic Youth Organizations) sports program but, in the end, we didn't have that kind of mentoring. The valuable experiences that my grandchildren derive today from playing on this baseball team or that soccer league include discipline, an appreciation for team work, and a respect for your opponents but this kind of training simply did not fall within our reach. My son, Carlos, yearned for a more sports-oriented Dad when he was in grade school but he just didn't get one. My siblings and I learned about team work and respecting others, opponents or not, from life itself.

Community Cultural Events

Our family obviously connected to the larger world beyond Santa Rosa Catholic Church and San Fernando Elementary School. Hindsight, in fact, suggests that two parallel but invisible connections formed between us and the community outside our home. One served us, the children, more than anyone else, because it unveiled the ways of the other young people around us, mostly classmates or neighborhood kids, some more American than us, others less so. If they used English and adopted its popular phrases in their daily chatter, we did too; the same with language intonations and the pronunciation of certain words, in addition to copying what might have been regarded as American attitudes, or ideas, dress styles, even music. As we played in our backyard or out in the street, we probably sought the reaffirmation of things we learned at school. The barrio was unable to filter out the larger world, the external ideas and ways of doing things, and we didn't consciously keep track of this process either.

The other link came to the aid of our parents because it paid due respect to their old ways. This included their ties to the mother country which remained firm along with their life values, Mother being quite keen on this. Conserving the Spanish that Mother learned growing up in Jalisco was one such connection as was stigmatizing the use of "Spanglish." We learned the distinction between "good" Spanish and corrupted Spanish although we never called it that. We were taught to appreciate Mexican culture, keep in touch with our Mexican relatives, and be true to our Catholic faith. The sum total of these values led us to view the world through the eyes of our parents, and this set us apart from many kids who didn't do this.

These two connections always vied with each other. Sometimes they leaned more toward one cultural cradle and then inclined toward the other, sometimes creating stormy situations as we've already seen in chapter

11. Our minds sifted and stirred; our intricate world views formed slowly and inevitably.

If our parents endowed us with filtered elements of their culture and their way of life, the rest of the world nevertheless dribbled into our household, changing our lives and converting us children inescapably into Americans of Mexican descent. It's worth noting that the notion of being a Mexican American or a Chicano and identifying yourself as such did not arise until the late 1960s, long after most of us had grown up and grappled with our identity challenges in our own way. The truth is that we Gils thought we were Mexican in some way or another up until we became young adults although when the Chicano Movement came along, its cultural thrust encouraged us to refer to ourselves as Mexican Americans but only one or two of us paid close attention to this stimulus. I was the only member in the family who actually used the term *Chicano* as a self-referent.

The radio in our lives

In any event, from the 1930s through the 1950s, the years of our concern here, the local radio airwaves transmitted music and voices to us from both America and Mexico. Radio was the best means for this, and it brought us more American sounds than Mexican, as you would expect. Reliance on it may be hard to understand at the present time when our brains are pummeled furiously by images and information arriving from almost anywhere via television and the Internet. Still, in our time, radio served us best with regard to Mexican music and culture even though we could only enjoy it during "dead air time," as George J. Sanchez reminds us, when few Anglos were listening, as in the early morning hours, Sundays especially.[191]

Elena Salinas was one of the individuals who spoke to us over the air waves, and she did so in a way that made us think of her as a friend. When there was no other Spanish language radio program in San Fernando,[192] her friendly voice dominated our early mornings, making us feel she was there by our side as we got ready for the day. She was like a super-talented disembodied aunt who soothingly informed us about what was going on in the vast Los Angeles area; she linked us in San Fernando to other corners of the metropolis. I can remember standing in Grandma's yard on Kalisher, listening to Elena Salina's voice filtering through Don Secundino's window; our next door neighbor and tortilla-making competitor who tuned into her program daily loud enough so that the tortilla-making ladies could enjoy it as they slapped corn dough tortillas together, and I could too. She'd also play the latest *canciónes románticas* (romantic songs) or share a recipe for a Lenten meal like *capirotada* (bread pudding), perhaps, or endorse a product like *Sal de Uva Picot* for an upset stomach, plugging it in a disarming and personal way.

Elena Salinas stands as one of the unsung pioneers of Spanish-language radio in Southern California, and she knew how to curry favor with households like ours every morning from 4:00 a.m. to 7:00 a.m. on KWKW, "La Mexicana," reputed to be one of the oldest Spanish language radio stations in Los Angeles. When my sister Mary lived in the *vecindad* in the early 1930s, she remembered hearing about Rodolfo Hoyos, also a pioneering disc jockey in Mexican music, as well as the controversial Pedro J. González, who sang as part of singing group known as El Trio Los Madrugadores and broadcast other music along with pro-Mexican immigrant commentary from KELW (Burbank) which landed him in jail and then got him deported.[193]

There was another pioneer who transmitted Mexican music to radio listeners in the San Fernando Valley. He was an *americano* who featured the latest Mexican ballads on KMPC on Sunday mornings when most folks were singing gospel songs at church. I remember driving on Lankersheim Boulevard one day, around 1955, delivering a load of tortillas to a restaurant in North Hollywood, trying to mentally digest how an Anglo could affectionately present the latest musical sensations from Mexico City. The first time I ever heard "Historia de Un Amor," by El Trio Los Panchos, was on his program as well as Pedro Infante, the crooner par excellence singing "Amorcito Corazón," one of his many hit songs. Between him and Elena Salinas, we knew of no other radio stations that broadcast in Spanish at the time; a fact that compares so dramatically to the present day in which Latino radio stations abound everywhere in the Los Angeles area including San Fernando, and Latino music of varying caliber is found on the radio dial even when you're not looking for it.

American music, however, dominated the radio air waves, of course. We didn't have to wait for a special time of day or night to tune in; we could hear it anywhere at any time even on the lips of our siblings or best friends. It flooded our house when our parents weren't listening, we opening the flood gates, of course. Mom resisted most forms of American music, reminiscent of the way my siblings and I as adults detest certain forms of popular music today. Before the age of rock and roll, we often listened to Al Jarvis and his "Make Believe Ballroom" on KFWB or tuned into Dick Wittinghill on KMPC, "The Station of the Stars," as well.[194] These two disc jockeys led the list of other transmitters of the contemporary American music scene, helping us join the rest of our contemporaries by becoming fans of Bing Crosby, Frank Sinatra, Vic Damone, Vaughn Monroe, and so on. Most of us in the family committed to heart, as did American youngsters across the nation, the lyrics of "Doggie in the Window" popularized by Patti Page, "I Believe" by Frankie Lane, "Pretend" by Nat King Cole, "Till I Waltz Again" by Teresa Brewer, and "Your Cheatin' Heart" by Joni James, among legions of other songs in this category.[195]

After rock and roll bopped into the American music scene, most of us Gil kids readily accepted it but didn't join the craze for it. When Elvis rose to fame, we enjoyed his music and his gyrations but didn't go wild about him. Other radio art forms also penetrated our household, of course, like the work of the comedians Jack Benny and Red Skelton whose clownish routines triggered us to laugh many times as we narrowed our fingers to further fine-tune the radio dial and place our ear closer to the felt-covered speakers. Mary became a fan of The Shadow, in the 1930s, a mysterious crime fighter who could make himself "literally invisible," manipulating "the minds of his opponents so that they couldn't tell where he really stood physically."[196] I was keen on the Lone Ranger and his friend Tonto in the 1940s.

The Movies

Movies or commercial films played an important part in the parallel cultural connections mentioned earlier, one for us the children and another for our parents. As with the radio airwaves, we children benefitted from both and, happily, San Fernando offered plenty of celluloid in either connection. Two theatres offered American movies, and one specialized in Mexican films when we were growing up.

The Towne Theatre and Rennie's Theatre on Maclay Avenue on the Anglo side of the tracks presented American films from nearby Hollywood. This means that our earliest and most delightful movie-going experiences involved the classic Walt Disney movies like *Snow White and the Seven Dwarfs* and *Bambi*. And as we got older, just like everyone else in the United States, we cheered when Tom Mix held on to his big felt hat as he captured a bad *hombre*, and we marveled at Roy Rogers's silver-studded saddle and gaped at Trigger, his gorgeous golden palomino. We also laughed until our sides hurt with the antics of Laurel and Hardy and Bud Abbot and Lou Costello. We became fans of Hollywood's golden era movies stars' too like Humphrey Bogart, Judy Garland, Betty Davis, and John Wayne.

We differed from most other youngsters in Southern California however, because we also enjoyed Mexican cinema. We shared it with our parents at the San Fernando Theatre on Brand Boulevard located on our side of the tracks, and I suspect that film going here played an important psychological outlet for my parents and certainly an enjoyable cultural event for them as well. It needs to be said that sharing these movies with them brought us commonalities that lasted the rest of our lives. My own first movies in the company of Grandma Carlota took place at this theatre about 1942. Mexican movie studios produced their own golden era as well about the same time as Hollywood's, and so my siblings and I, often in the company of our parents, enjoyed just about every single film produced in Mexico during this era and thus became familiar with Mexico's legendary actors. These included the famous comedian, Mario Moreno Cantinflas, the beautiful but fiery María Félix, the shy heroine made like fine porcelain, Dolores del Rio, the handsome Mexican *macho*, Pedro Armendáriz, and of course, the darlings of that period, Jorge Negrete and Pedro Infante, already mentioned, both of whom acted and sang to the delight of millions, including all of us in our family.

Music In Our Lives

Despite our many moments of tension and unhappiness at home, music soothed our frayed edges and this included singing; we were music lovers. Our family lore tells us that when they were young and freshly in love, Dad liked to play the guitar and sing *"Me he de comer esa tuna,"*[197] among other songs, to my mother. Grandma Carlota might have been a dour-looking woman in our photo albums, but we cherished stories about her as a young woman singing to the accompaniment of her uncles, Sotero who strummed the guitar, and Sabino who played the violin, back home on the Hacienda Santa Rosa as described already in Chapter 1.

Our lore also informs us that her cousins, Lupe and Aurelio Peña, mentioned previously, didn't have to shrink in the shadows, musically speaking, the two of them having immigrated to California as well. One played the violin and the other the mandolin and they lived in San Fernando for a time when we Gil children were little, we calling them uncles too. After their regular day jobs (my *tío* Lupe, for example, worked in the local cannery), they often satisfied their love of music by getting invited to play at private parties as they did for Manuel's baptism. Their dark Indian complexion heavily pocked by smallpox was framed by their thick black hair, making it easy for us to identify them in the few photos we preserve. In one of these, my *tío* Aurelio stands behind his son, Lucas, a blondish one-year-old boy born of a European mother, according to my sister Mary, the youngster looking past the camera as he stands on a wooden chair.

We have a photo included in these pages of their performing in the San Fernando Valley as musicians in community orchestras commonly known as *orquestas típicas* (before *mariachis* became popular and long before the so-called *bandas* found acclaim among young Mexican Americans). These *orquestas* were not unusual in the Los Angeles area in the 1930s; they were, in fact, known widely in other cities including Mexico City and Buenos Aires, although in somewhat different forms. We children were introduced to these musical ensembles very early, and as we grew up, we merely tolerated them in part because their performances were usually sit-down events rather than danceables, and they weren't as hip as American music.

The *orquestas* típicas consisted of stringed instruments, mostly, and could include as many as fifteen to twenty musicians. In our photograph, hand-dated 1935 (p. 265), fourteen male musicians dressed in white shirts, bow ties, and black pants sit on an elevated stage back grounded by two large flags, one American and the other Mexican, the venue somewhere near San Fernando. The musicians flank the director. He stands in the middle of the ensemble all dressed in white, trimmed by a black bow tie, holding a baton while three young women attired in elegant, fair-colored dresses, lovely dark tresses, probably singers, sit in front of him revealing silvery nylons and stylish white shoes. My *tío* Lupe, one of three violinists, sitting first on the left, holds his fiddle on his lap, while my *tío* Aurelio, four persons to the right, grasps the only mandolin in the group at the same time that four other musicians clasp what appear as *bandolones* or stringed instruments the shape of a banjo mandolin. Six others clutch guitars.

Antedating the proliferation of *sones* and *canciones rancheras,* the repertoires favored by these urban-styled *orquestas típicas* consisted of love ballads like María Grever's perennial, "*Júrame,*"[198] invigorating polkas like "*Jesusita en Chihuahua,*"[199] dreamy waltzes like Enrique Mora's classic "*Alejandra,*" and sensuous *danzones* like "Juárez" and "*Donde estás Corazón.*" They also played high-stepping marches like Genaro Codina's "*Marcha Zacatecas,*" considered by many as the second Mexican national anthem. In any case, Lupe and Aurelio moved to Oakland, where they died, I having attended my *tío* Lupe's funeral in the company of my grandmother about 1942. They may have died early and sorrowfully because they found themselves culturally and socially isolated in Oakland, far from any family support.

One of the important musical events that caught our fancy, as a family, and consequently pulled us into the tangle of the community was our parish's annual spring social extravaganza, most likely an Easter Sunday event. Organized by our pastor and the more important families at Santa

Rosa Catholic Church, it took the form of a *barbacoa* (pit-roasted barbecued beef served with rice and beans, etc.) and a *tardeada* (an afternoon dance) hosted at a ranch-like locale called Saxonia Park in Newhall. It attracted a considerable number of parish families whose youngsters, like us, became all excited and easily heeded our parents' requirements to dress up nice, being able to meet up with friends too. I remember climbing aboard an open truck, like the one that transported my father to the lemon groves, standing up in the back along with other parishioners, holding on to the wooden sides, and getting a ride to the park about ten miles away, in the mountains north of San Fernando, my parents apparently arriving separately. Beyond gobbling up the delicious roasted offerings and climbing the hills surrounding the park, getting my white shirt dirty to my mother's consternation, the main attraction was none other than listening to a live band performing in a large dance hall where everyone could swing and sway, parents and children.

I remember admiring my brother Manuel and my sister Mary, both dressed elegantly and dancing expertly to rhythms of the *música tropical* of Caribbean and Veracruz-origin, cadences performed expertly by the dance orchestras hired for the occasion. The tempo included the more established *boleros* and *danzones*, which were competing in these days with the newer sounds of the *cha-cha-cha* and the *mambo* all of which my elder siblings demonstrated for us younger ones with affable expertise. I remember Mary dressed in elegant heels, a full-skirted colorful dress, while Manuel wore a "Bing Crosby styled" one-button role jacket with pants that cuffed narrowly over his shiny leather shoes. Dancing together, they moved with effortless ease around the dance floor as the music wrapped us all with its sensuous pulsations.

At home, I learned to play the guitar informally after my father died, and as Soledad reminded us a few pages back, sometimes we would all sing and quickly fall into harmony too. There were many occasions, when we all happened to gather in our Kalisher Street house, that Mary would nudge me into playing and singing some of our favorite songs like *"Una noche serena y oscura,"* and *"A la orilla de un palmar."* Then Mom would join in followed by Martha and sometimes even Mike and Manuel would be coaxed into relaxing their young buck bravado and pressed to sing along.

The Santa Rosa Boys Band

One of the most singular musical experiences that transpired in our community during my growing-up years was the formation of the Santa Rosa Boys Band, and to our credit, our family was part of this experience.

My younger brother Rick and I took part in the band as did our parents because they had to foot the bill along with many other barrio families. In any case, the Santa Rosa Boys Band stood out for a handful of years as an outstanding experiment in youth formation; we took part in it and swear that it flourished unpredictably.

Our family possesses a black-and-white photograph dated approximately 1950, included in these pages, that brings it all back (p. 265). It shows thirty-seven uniformed boys and one girl, ranging in age from about eight to thirteen years, all seated on bleachers on a sunny day, some eucalyptus trees offering a bit of shade in the background. A portly man wearing a dark, striped suit with a black Mexican bowtie sits on the bottom bench flanked by his whipper-snapper musicians, all posing for the photographer. This was Antonio Bañuelos, our *profesor*. In this photo the young beaming instrumentalists are showing off their uniforms highlighted by silver satin shirts, black pants, and dark garrison-styled caps, each holding or connected to a musical instrument. Those nearest to *el profe,* as we used to call him, are holding woodwinds: twelve clarinets, one flute (the girl!), and six saxophones. My brother Rick, age eight, gazes innocently at the photographer as he sits in the clarinet section in-between his two Naranjo cousins, Mike and Tony. The brass section occupies the middle benches, and it comprises nine eager-looking teenage boys holding trumpets, two lads gripping French horns, and two others clutching trombones including my friend, Danny Rosales, one of the leading trumpeters who later became a professional musician and played and sang at my mother's funeral. The band's percussionists occupy the upper benches including three boys who are strapped with snare drums around their shoulders holding drum sticks at the ready and one other young fellow who stands behind the big bass drum trimmed with the words: "Santa Rosa Band, San Fernando, Calif." I too sit in the upper benches with a sousaphone wrapped around my shoulders, I, being the oldest at fourteen and one of the biggest, was assigned the silvery bass tuba.

One day out of the blue, it seemed to me, Mr. Bañuelos arrived in our part of town eager to create a band out of us barrio boys. I remember he piloted a shiny new gray Buick with a chrome grill that made me think of huge overgrown teeth gleaming brightly. No one in our barrio owned anything like it, for sure. He introduced himself to our local pastor, Father Sebastián Mozos, about a year or so before the photo described above was taken, and persuaded him to convene the parents in the parish to hear his proposal: In an age when few "Mexican" boys like us aspired to be something, he would mould us into young musicians. He would do this in exchange for monthly fees, which some parents ultimately agreed to, including our Mom and Dad. This was no easy thing for my cash-strapped parents, of course, but they must have been impressed with this well dressed Mexican music teacher who brimmed with self-confidence. They consented along with at least thirty or so other families because they wanted their boys to grow up to be something, if nothing else, at least, a well-trained musician. Let's remember that this was before the age of Upward Bound and ahead of other federal programs aimed at "disadvantaged" youth in America's "blighted" cities.[200] In any case, *don* Antonio pledged to make us musicians. The truth is that he could have been a smooth talking con man, dressed up fine, but he kept his word. He made musicians out of us; this is exactly what he did.

El profesor literally whipped us barrio kids into young, proud instrumentalists, and he did this by employing old-fashioned music study methods. He taught us to read music by singing the notes from special music scores, apparently, making use of a technique he learned in his home state of Zacatecas decades earlier. I discovered later that this technique, known even to this day as *solfeo,* and *solfeo de Do fijo,* was employed widely throughout the Hispanic world. Incidentally, our instruction took place entirely in Spanish; rarely did *Profesor* Bañuelos speak to us English.[201]

Thus, for many months before our instruments arrived, we met on a weekly basis and read the music and sang it in choral fashion, all together. Instead of singing words of any kind, we chanted Do, Re, Me, Fa, Sol, La, Si, Do, according to the notes written into the score we held in our hands. Guided by our teacher, who often resorted to shouts and grimaces causing his longish hair to air flop on his face, we intoned for hours and hours until we began to catch on to the printed music. Together we learned to croon a Do on the proper pitch and take it up a scale, to recognize whole notes, quarter ones, three quarters, eights; recognize half-time cadences vs. three quarters, glissandos, treble clefs vs. bass clefs, and so on. The mysterious dots with legs spread over endless sets of lines slowly became meaningful to us. It's fair to say that we kids stumbled and grumbled, and sometimes we cried, but *el profesor* led us forward, conducting us firmly and allowing for just a little bit of horsing around in order to let off the pressure.

The day finally arrived when our instruments were delivered! They all came at once, transferred to our church hall classroom where we used to gather. I remember some of us were delirious because this meant we no longer had to sing our music, now we could actually play it outright! But, of course, this didn't happen right away. The sounds we produced during our first few sessions after the instruments arrived were atrocious and frustrating because we wanted to play as expertly as we had learned to sing, using the *solfeo* method, and there was no way. With *Profesor* Banuelo's grim determination, however, we gradually improved. The pitiful sounds of air blowing through metallic tubes began to merge with occasional musical tones, then more tuneful echoes prevailed over ear-piercing dissonances. We had to practice at home, of course, and this meant that if you walked the length of the barrio on certain days, you could hear the mournful tones of a trumpet on one street and a reedy clarinet in a back alley, and in my case, the deeper breathy sounds of a tuba on Kalisher Street.

We improved gradually. In due time, we could play simple ditties, all in unison: brass, winds, and percussion, playing the same notes. Weeks later, our director introduced us to separate musical parts, and eventually, perhaps twelve months later, we started sounding like a youth band. Soon we improved to the point of being able to impress many a bystander with *La Marcha Zacatecas*,[202] which became our signature march.

This means we had to learn to march too! So, as a prelude to those of us who attended boot camp years later, we began marching practice, first without instruments and then with instruments. One day, as part of our marching-with-instruments practice, the *profesor* decided to strut us out of the church hall and into the street. He paced us out on to Kalisher Street and did a forward-left toward the church, and as we proceeded to where the already described stinky saloons stood, the *profesor* ordered us to begin playing *Zacatecas* and so we did.

The march begins with two strong musical jolts, so when we executed these, the puzzled patrons all came out to see what the racket was. We trod past them with drums pounding and reeds and horns a-blowing. At first, they gasped at the musical demonstration unfolding before their eyes, and then they cheered and applauded, some of the bystanders recognizing me and yelling out, "Hey, that's Charlie with the big horn! *Ese charli*!" Huffing and blowing on our instruments, we tramped beyond the little cafés and mom-and-pop stores, including our own Gil's Café, and then finally marched back on a side street and thus returned to the church hall. I was so embarrassed at being recognized like that!

The bottom line is that being able to march and play zesty marches drove us to show off not only our barrio-created musical talents but also our inspiration in Mexican composers. Soon enough, we even acquired rust-colored *charro* uniforms in the style of *mariachi* musicians, including the traditional wide-brimmed hats. We didn't wear them the day we marched on Kalisher Street.

Danny Rosales, one of the band members, recalled our first real public performance. He reminded me that our music director decided to do our debut, or "coming out," on September 16 in San Fernando for the upcoming Mexican Independence celebration, appropriate, indeed. And, we had no choice but to get ready for it.

And, by gosh, we got ready! This may have been when we showed off our *charro* outfits for the first time, proudly so, astonishing our listeners and making our parents very proud. Here we were, a collection of barrio youngsters flaunting our well-honed discipline and mastery of reading musical scores and playing some pretty respectable marching band music on this, our maiden performance. And to top it off, we again featured the *Marcha Zacatecas*. You couldn't get more ethnic-prouder than that! The main thing was that we were beginning to make the "Mexican" side of San Fernando look good in front of gringo eyes, a thought that brought pride to many of us and to our parents as well, not to mention what *el Profesor* Bañuelos might have felt. We had a great teacher; we *banda* kids were good, and we would become even better!

It wasn't very long before we started taking part in local and regional musical tournaments. Danny remembered that our first big performance, in front of the whole world to see, was in the annual San Fernando parade, but he also brought to mind that the Anglo organizers didn't give us a warm welcome. In fact, *Profesor* Bañuelos felt rebuffed, and he seems to have passed this frustration on to Danny.

The local organizers may have been ill prepared to accept a "Mexican" band like ours. After all, these were the days in Southern California communities when civic parades and other founding festivities ("pioneer days") dutifully included representatives of "old Spanish" California. Leo Carrillo, an aging Hollywood actor, who claimed lineage to the "old" prewar Californio families became a fixture in commemorative parades in the southland in these years always mounted on his white stallion greeting bystanders left and right. Anglo civic leaders often dressed up to impersonate Spanish "dons," and *mantilla*-draped *señoritas* strutted about clicking their castanets. The Santa Barbara Rotary Women, all Anglo females riding silver-bedecked palominos, were often exemplified as the leading examples of this cultural fakery that prevailed in the southland for a long time. Colorful "Spanish" silks ruled in these events including the straight brimmed black bolero hats festooned with the little red fluffy balls hanging from the brim's edge. But Mexicans were not part of the ceremonies. To include a group culturally representing the already significant number of "Mexican" families like ours just hadn't been done before. So, our wanting to perform with our Mexican outfits may have been the first breach in this practice in San Fernando. If that was the case, then we can assume that it didn't fit the mind-set of the organizers, and this may have been the situation that provoked the feeling that we were being snubbed. Carey McWilliams, a distinguished author already cited, referred to this regional practice as "the fantasy heritage," a fitting label to be sure.

All the same, The Santa Rosa Boys Band continued taking part in numerous civic festivals. We expanded our repertoire beyond Mexican marches to include most of the John Philip Sousa compositions like the regal "Washington Post March," the stirring "Thunderer" march, and the celebrated "Stars and Stripes Forever." We also delivered bracing renditions of Charles Zimmerman's "Anchors Aweigh," played to rousing applauses. Our repertoire was bicultural and stimulating too!

Danny remembered playing these marches in Huntington Beach as part of the Fourth of July celebrations there. I remember marching in a football stadium in Los Angeles, filled with spectators as part of a March of Dimes observance, "Turi" Chacón, a band member, reinforced my memory when he told me that we had played at the Los Angeles Coliseum and the Rams competed that day.[203] Danny summoned to memory "coming in Third Place, beating out an Air Force Band" in a musical competition in Westminster near San Pedro. According to "Turi" and my cousin, Mike Naranjo, also a band member, we even had majorettes who learned to do the appropriate twirling tricks and prancing maneuvers, including Raquel and Evangelina Bernal and Terry García. On another sun-filled day, we also marched in Santa Barbara and on another excursion in Paramount, near Comton. We appeared in many other places. I asked Danny, a retired musician at the time of this writing, what might have happened to the trophies, ribbons, and awards we earned, but he didn't know. *"No sé donde estarán,"* he replied. Probably no one was left in charge of these prizes, and the squalls of time blew them away.

What is certain in my mind is that our *profesor, don* Antonio Bañuelos, died an unsung hero. We later learned that the Santa Rosa Boys Band was only one of several Mexican youth bands he created from scratch. It's good to know he gave a sense of pride to other barrio boys as well.

Mother Gets to Sing in Public

Mother's "golden years" allowed her to celebrate by enjoying music more than ever. She loved it her entire life, and that's why we'll always remember her singing a veritable repertoire of songs with passionate enthusiasm in the last decades of her life. Her signature song was *"Amor y Lágrimas"* ("Love and Tears"), which she sang fervently to countless audiences. Other favorites came from the days of her youth like *"A la Capotín"* and *"Es Mi Hombre"* ("He's My Man"), long before the commonplace *canciónes rancheras* became popular thanks to Pedro Infante and Jorge Negrete and others.[204] *Corridos,* whose popularity was propelled by the Chicano movement in the 1970s, were never her preference.

Mom was fortunate that the opportunity to sing in public in her last years came almost literally right to her door. A music teacher from Mexico City named Violeta Quintero McHenry settled in San Fernando in the mid-1970s and proceeded to form a musical group among the members of some of the older barrio families, choosing to meet and rehearse just two blocks away from Mother's home. The ensemble of about forty musically-attuned septuagenarians and octogenarians came to be known as *Los Sueños Dorados,* the Golden Dreams, all of them survivors of the hard living in the barrio, most of them having known my parents back in the old days. It was a match made in heaven for Mother. *Maestra* McHenry either retaught the oldsters to play guitars, violins, and other stringed instruments or tutored them in the basics, but no matter how they handled their instruments, they all resonated with their beloved old songs. Just to watch and listen to them made my heart heavy with melancholy. Mom became a regularly featured octogenarian who stood up and belted out *Es Mi Hombre* with all of the proper punctuation of someone who knew what she was singing and why. Under McHenry's guidance, they sang in many locations across Southern California, giving our Mom the opportunity to sing with the group for more than fifteen years, stopping her attendance at the rehearsals only when she could no longer walk to them. Every twenty-second of November, the members of the ensemble gathered at her doorstep on Huntington Street as the sun broke on the horizon to sing *Las Mañanitas* to her, the traditional birthday song. They also sang at her gravesite when she was interred.

Mother's Love of Poetry

Mother befriended the muses of poetry to get away from it all, and we children hardly knew.[205] This is a refined way of saying that, especially after Dad's death, Mom soothed her deepest sorrows with thoughtful verse and, in this way, tried to rise above the often-bleak atmosphere of Kalisher Street where her offspring needed to be fed and clothed and redirected on a daily basis. Right under our nose, she turned to one of the guardians of inspiration to balm her soul, the muse of the meditated phrases.

It's useful to remember that among her family immigrant peers, Mother was the most avid reader. She was the only one, over the years, to read the Sunday newspaper and try to share with us ideas she found in her reading. Had we been asked whether Mother ever sat down to read, we would've replied, "Yes, she read from time to time." The fact is that we were taken aback to discover the extent to which she reached out for thoughtful texts and the rhyming word or phrase.

Yes, Mother loved to read poetry and to engage in other kinds of cultural reflections despite her own meager schooling and the absence of books and magazines in our home. She reached, instead, for the Sunday supplement of *La Opinión*, a Spanish language daily printed in Los Angeles and sold right on Kalisher Street. In this way, she tried to bridge over her often-trying-personal universe with a richer and more expansive one.

This discovery took place when I was helping my sister Soledad examine and clear out Mother's chests of drawers in her Huntington Street home after her funeral. In performing this heartbreaking task, we came upon dozens of tattered, yellowed newspaper clippings torn by hand or cut with scissors from the pages of *La Opinión*, each containing a poem. We located one batch tucked into an old envelope in one corner of one drawer and then another in another corner. These were crumpled newspaper bits, each containing a flock of emotive words. We also salvaged printed articles about cultural tidbits of her interest and perhaps most poignantly, to me at least, were the many pages in which Mom took time and effort, given her quivering aging grip, to copy a poem by hand or write the lyrics of a familiar song, friends of hers also copying a poem from somewhere or hand-duplicating song lyrics and giving them to her, she eventually placing them in the chests of drawers. I sorted them by apparent age and the poem's main idea.

The poetic topics Mom prized by deciding to copy by hand or by selecting and hand tearing to store and read on another day amounted to about a half a dozen. Almost all of them spoke about human affection: Unhappy Love, Satisfaction Having Loved, Missing Love Because It Ended Too Soon, and Forbidden Love. She also clipped poems written with a religious tone, a few patriotic ones, and a set of what I would call existentialist poems that spoke consciously about being alive, death lurking not far. A couple of clippings also revealed Mom's awareness of major Mexican poets including the first American poetess, Sor Juana Inéz de la Cruz, who wrote her widely known and subtly passionate verses in the sixteenth century.

Most of the poetry Mother cut out from the newspaper was about Missing Love Because It Ended Too Soon. The oldest, yellowiest, most dog-eared snippets seem to have been published in the late 1950s, and while Mom didn't date her clippings, I found two among the most shabby and orangey pieces on which she hand-wrote "8-24-1958;" this was nearly three years after Dad died. The poet of one of them, H. Reyna, wishes he or she could steal every sorrow and lament in the world and turn them into song. The other poet, Beatriz S. Cano, exclaims: "Don't ask me why I love you, just accept the treasure that my soul offers you."

"No Te Asomes" may be the most representative poem Mother clipped during the handful of years after my father's death. Written by Concepción C. Robles, a contributor to *La Opinión*, and translated by me, the title means "Don't Look Now," and it makes a plea to a vanished lover to overlook how depressed the speaker is.

Don't look, my love,
At my existence.
Don't look at the depths of my soul
Where only shadows and sorrows now abide.
Look even less at the chasm in my eyes.
There's no love in them now, no light;
There's no life; they dried up when you went away.[206]

On the reverse side of a colorful stationary sheet, Mom hand-copied what I am calling an existential poem. Here's an example. It is written by Amado Nervo (1870–1919), Mexico's most renowned Romantic poet.

At Peace

Close to my sundown, I bless you, life.
Because you gave me no false hope
I never suffered impossibly
Or worked without hope of reward.
And now that I have beaten my path to its end, I see,
That, truly, I was the architect of my destiny
And I know that, if indeed, I was able to extract taste, the
honey and the bitterness of things,
Then it was only because I put the honey and bitterness
into them in the first place.
Whenever I planted rose bushes,
I always harvested roses.[207]

An example of a patriotic poem that seems to have appealed to Mother is called *Patria Chica.* On ring binder-lined paper sheets bearing a handwritten inscription in the upper right hand corner, "copied 1927," with a firmer handwriting than usual, she reproduced a poem that clearly evoked nostalgia for her birthplace.

My Home Country (An evocation)
Where are you beloved land,
Handsome land, darling land?
Where are you? I fail to see me near you,
Land I love . . .
If I don't see you ever more,
Blue sky of all my hopes,
Amulet of my life,
Gospel of my life,
If I don't see you ever more
'T will be because I died on ground
Belonging to a strange land. [208]

The accidentally discovered poems my mother kept hidden in her bedroom chests of drawers, particularly the ones that lament the loss of a loved one, hastened many thoughts in my mind. Uppermost, perhaps, is the fact that they reaffirm the complexity of Mother's awareness, even when she felt most depressed. The oldest clippings not only coincided with her unhappiest time as noted in earlier chapters, but they added welcomed light as well, helping us steal a look at her most private thoughts during her darkest days. They also help us understand the wrath she exhibited. The first thing we children noticed was her anger, her hurt, and her vengefulness at having to cope with the particulars of her immediate surroundings, say, the need to prepare more corn in order to fill a tortilla order. These concerns must have struck her as a gross triviality in contrast to her despondency and loss, though sharply real for my sisters who had to fill in for what Mom didn't do. These poems tell us that when she shut herself in her bedroom, as my sister Soledad noted, she undoubtedly sank into her grief once more, feeling all alone in the world. But these shreds from *La Opinión* also tell us that she slowly nursed herself back by reaching out to the muses, turning to her poems, making contact with the world brought to her by the local newspaper.

I can imagine my mother taking a hold of herself in the solitude of her bedroom behind closed doors and gently relocating her glasses over the bridge of her nose in order to resume reading, quietly, perhaps tearfully, reciting the words of loss and betrayal written by the poets of *La Opinión* because they counseled her, assuring her that they too had known these injuries. I confess to feeling uplifted when I learned the extent to which Mom tried to elevate her mind in order to pacify her soul.

All in all, we may have been desperately poor at times, angered and frustrated at others, but our lives could be soothed by the spurts of cultural balm that came our way. These were provided by our church with its multiform rituals and the social webs and connections flowing there from and by our schools, especially the elementary school that served each and every one of us in the family, because they provided us with the skills that made these connections work and become meaningful. Music through the airwaves brought us moments of leisure in two languages and dual cultural forms including literature, however simple it might have been. Now we know too, at least, that it offered Mother an opportunity to calm herself in order to gain the strength to face up to the next ordeal.

An 'orquesta tipica' in San Fernando (ca. 1935)

The Santa Rosa Boys Band (ca. 1950)

Chapter 13

Good-bye to the First Generation

• Grandma Carlota • Uncle Pascual • Uncle Miguel • Our Dear Dad • Mom Becomes Grandma Lupe

THIS CHAPTER WRAPS up the leading characters in this book. First, it allows us to catch up with my uncles, Miguel and Pascual Naranjo. Their remembrances of the migrant trail from Mexico are well represented in Part I, but they fade away in Part II where I begin to spotlight my immediate family, specifically my parents and their arrival and settling in San Fernando.

Needless to say, my uncles underwent their own experiences, each gaining a foothold in San Fernando too, as we'll see in this chapter, but I offer only the barest essentials about them. The truth is that each of their accounts deserves the detail that I reserve here for my closer family members, but obtaining it was not possible on the same scale. Let us remember that the two Naranjo brothers were like night and day and so even the brief summaries in this chapter reflect this disparity, one being longer than the other. They were always different, like white wine versus red.

Secondly, I bid a final good-bye to Carlota, Guadalupe, and Bernabé in this chapter. And, in doing so, I summarize what all of the members of the first generation meant to us who filled the ranks of the second generation.

Lastly, I reaffirm one of the reasons for writing *We Became Mexican American:* Every family has a story worth passing down. As I've tried to show in this book, even the story of our own family, disconnected from politics or controversy, "salt of the earth," you might say, even our story offers episodes and situations that hopefully stirred the senses and evoked a feeling of commonality from you, the reader. "Look at what the Gil's did!" Or, "Look at what happened to the Gils! Something similar happened to us!" Or, "I can identify with that!" If the reader found moments in our family past that aroused feelings of sympathy or ire, then it was worth pouring over these pages.

This is another way of saying that I wish to break up the clouds of oblivion, which so frequently cast their nullifying pall on so many American families, where one generation quickly begins to overlook important facts about the preceding one. Our modern American penchant for instant information seems to impel us to become a people without a past. I don't wish this on my descendants, or anyone else's, for that matter. It is my hope that my own children and their successors may appreciate where they came from and what all was involved in having them grow up as Americans.

Grandma Carlota

Grandma Carlota, my namesake, was a woman who, at age thirty-nine, left everything behind in the mountains of western Mexico to start a new life. She did this partly because she wanted to catch up with her cross-grained son, who had gone off, north, on his own where the opportunities lay and ultimately slipped into the United States. We've seen already in chapter 3 that she grieved as a result of her own decision to leave her family and the world she knew. She might not have emigrated on her own, but we don't really know this for sure. The fact is that she became a trail blazer for the family, perhaps a reluctant one. We learned she was often sick and melancholy on the trail to America and, indeed, all of the images captured of her in our family photos expose an Indian-hued face marked by deep creases, a mouth that turns down at the ends, almost scornfully, above large dark eyes and a general expression of painful resolve.

Equally as important, if not more so, is the new kind of inner strength she revealed once she established herself in San Fernando. Very much a single woman nearly all her life, she put penny capitalism into practice and established a micro business that gave her an economic foundation for herself, one that would carry her to the end of her life. Although there must have been times when her children and grandchildren came to her aid, our family lore doesn't include one single anecdote in which she found herself economically dependent on others on an extended basis, at least, not until her last days. If we need an example of a woman who stood up by herself, she certainly fills the bill. Furthermore, her frugal living combined with endless days of hard work gave her the opportunity to share her wealth, all in relative terms, of course. She bestowed a house to each of her two sons, a generosity that gashed my mother's spirit to the very end as we've said already because she felt unappreciated as a result.

For most of her years in San Fernando, Carlota dwelled in the two-room wood-framed bedroom that my father constructed next door to her tortilla shop on Kalisher Street. She never owned nor desired, apparently, a regular house with a living room, a dining room, and so on. I remember her getting up early in the morning and spending almost all day in her *molino* or her tortilla shop, next door to our small restaurant. At the end of the day she would retire to her simple unfinished bedroom overcome with exhaustion. She took her leave of this world at the age of seventy-three when she was placed in an ambulance and taken to Los Angeles County Hospital, where she died in 1953.

Uncle Pascual

Catching Up With Pascual

The last time he was mentioned in these pages, it was 1931, and he was on his way to Mexico. He had taken a train from Fresno to Guadalajara "for only ten dollars" and stopped in Los Angeles to visit my mother, his sister, who had just given birth to my elder brother Manuel. Mom noted in her memoirs that "on the day that Manuel was forty days old, Pascual came by on his way to Mexico." He was a "*repatriado*" as discussed in chapter 8.

The reader may recall that my uncle Pascual acted as a pathfinder for my mother's side of the family. Even after the rest of the family emigrated from Mexico and caught up with him in Fresno, where he ended his role as trailblazer, he continued to play an important role in the family, Grandma consulting with him when she had to make important decisions, for example. There were many other ways in which he continued to be close to the family and why we, the young male Gils, ultimately took him on as role model of sorts, especially after our dad died. He was the first in my mother's side of the family to have befriended father and ultimately introduced him to the family including Mom, whom he married soon enough. Chapter 5 offers numerous instances when the two young bucks, Pascual and Bernabé, engaged in escapades that confirmed their chummy fellowship as immigrants in a culturally different country, a comradeship that led them to become *cuñados* or brothers-in-law, for Mexicans a very close and intimate tie indeed. The fact that Dad was raised as an orphan probably encouraged him to embrace his buddy's family openly—Grandma, Mother, and my uncle Miguel.

Pascual Returns to Mexico in 1931

My uncle decided to return to Mexico in 1931 because his job in the

California sierras had begun to fall apart much to his unhappiness. He considered himself a valued employee of the Sugar Pine Lumber Company (described in chapter 6) by dint of his steady work including being in charge of logging teams whose jobs were both risky and exciting, to say the least. He had been a willing worker for the company for many years, getting to know and work with many of its field supervisors. He made hiring recommendation to his non-Spanish-speaking bosses from the many Mexican workers he knew who were not as well connected as he was—this is how he was able to get my father a job in 1927, something he was able to do for many other Mexican workers. But "power corrupts" and so jealousies and resentments arose and the men whom he helped get jobs accused him of "rabble-rousing." He said to me, "The main reason I abandoned my job to go to Mexico was the enormous sense of duplicity that I felt when my own people, the ones I had helped, turned around and made accusations [about me] that weren't right—calumnies was what they were." He added that "In 1929, they threw me out due to the accusations of those boys . . . [So,] I went to Mexico."

His life in the ten years that he lived in Mexico echoed the life he left behind in California except for one reason. His view and understanding of the world seems to have taken a giant step that deserves mention here: he cultivated a noteworthy political sense of things, and he also acted upon it. It may have begun to sprout when he was just a fourteen-year-old lad fearing for his life as we saw in chapter 1, when the revolutionary climate of those years encouraged him to become familiar with fire arms. We may recall that he was forced to assist his boss, Don Manuel, in torturing one of his farm workers. Even though he was a mere teenager, this experience taught him a big lesson about life's inequities, especially those that befall poor folk, so it seems clear that he learned not only what life was like, working in a plantation but also about the world beyond the plantation. This contributed to his feeling impelled to run away from the land owner before he got hurt.

These early experiences seem to have prepared him to grapple with the political climate that pervaded Mexico in the 1930s after leaving California. This is the time when the pro-worker policies were buzzing everywhere in the country as a result of the Revolution of 1910 and, as we saw in chapter 3, the government administrations that arose after 1910 adopted a progressive orientation. Led by arch-liberals like Álvaro Obregón, Plutarco Elías Calles, and Lázaro Cárdenas, the Mexican government eagerly instituted reforms, which included the formation of labor unions and peasant societies. The idea was to hoist Mexico's workers and farmers into a more modern and productive society where they could have a greater say. While Pascual didn't have more than a second-grade education, he nevertheless wanted to learn and understood, at the same time, the significance of what was going in his native country and must have felt euphoric, finding himself in this kind of situation in 1931. Times had changed in his native country, and now he could do something about it.

Pascual Organizes a Strike in Mazatlán

Pascual looked for a job in Guadalajara, Mexico City, then finally in Mazatlán which he knew best. After working on several haciendas as a farm worker he found a job in a *calera* or a limekiln on the edges of Mazatlán. *Cal*—lime or quicklime—comes from limestone and is used mainly as a building material although it is also employed as a fertilizer and even as an ingredient in the cooking of corn to make *nixtamal* for tortillas as we saw already. In this hot and humid part of the country, my uncle made a name for himself.

Soon after joining the work force, he discovered that things were not in order as far as his fellow workers were concerned.

> I worked in the *calera* and found that all the workers were owed back pay by the owner. At least, sixty pesos each and the daily wage was 1.50! Imagine that!

Influenced by the political winds blowing at the time and employing his ability to influence his collaborators, he organized them into a union and soon arranged a strike. The moment of defiance arrived and instead of being met with goons armed with billy clubs as in times past, Pascual freely led the workers directly to the local police headquarters, of all places! This must have been a strategic move on his part in order to neutralize any possible repression on the part of the police. In front of his hungry and ill-shod kiln buddies, he remembered explaining to the police chief about their abuses at the hands of the *calera* owner. More importantly, he remembered the police chief saying, "Yes, I agree. We are no longer back in those days." This meant he was on their side! This is what Pascual quickly realized! Things had changed drastically from the time he was a boy in Mascota! My uncle and his coworkers must have given three loud cheers for the police commander! He wouldn't persecute them for disturbing the peace or any such thing!

My uncle knew exactly where to take the second phase of the kiln strike. He and his troupe of sixty-some men tramped to the government offices in town where labor petitions were filed.

> We hardly fit [in the office]. The man in charge came out, and I explained [to him]. "I know there is a labor law that protects us, and we want you to help us"—I had bought a brand new book about labor law and read it. I had good memory for [such] things.

The man Pascual addressed must have been another pro-revolutionary, pro-worker official. My uncle doesn't mention running into any difficulties in getting his lime kiln strike recognized by this man. It was like singing to the choir.

> From there we all went to the *mercado* and asked the food ladies to serve us all . . . we were all hungry. I made a bid to the head *mercado* lady to feed us and [proposed] that we would pay her later after we won our case . . . "Will you do it? We promise to pay you altogether! You [can] write our names down [if you want]!" The different ladies in the various stands agreed to divide us all up [among them] and feed us.

The third phase of the strike took place at the government office a handful of weeks later. This is when the owner of the lime kiln, a foreigner by the name of Mr. Meyer, showed up. He was cited to appear by the officials of the *junta de reconciliación,* and Pascual remembers he arrived with a young woman by his side who turned out to be his daughter. My uncle, who always had an eye for pretty ladies, described her as "a gorgeous thing!" In any case, Pascual reported that Mr. Meyer was lectured by the junta official for not treating his workers properly. "They're feeding you and your family with the work they do for you. Why do you treat them this way?" The official got mad at Mr. Meyer who, in the end, agreed to pay the back wages. When payday arrived, "we filled up bags with the silver coins they paid us, and [this is the way] we paid the *mercado* ladies off. They didn't pay with paper; they paid us in coin, and that's the way we paid the ladies!"

Things didn't stop there, however. Pascual was soon told that his life was in jeopardy, and so he felt obligated to leave in the middle of the night. One of his fellow workers warned him that the kiln owner had ordered his death. "They're going to come at night, and they're going to harm you!" *Te van a joder*! he was told. My uncle didn't doubt the warning one bit. The president of Mexico and his top administrators might have been worker-friendly, but that didn't mean that ordinary workers like my uncle could get away with teaching influential business owners a costly lesson.

Tutorials of this kind were paid for in blood.

Pascual Joins a Tobacco Cooperative in Tuxpan

Pascual got away and traveled north to Tuxpan, Nayarit. Through his connections, he obtained work on a large tobacco farm that had recently been expropriated by the government. The workers of this farm, known previously as La Hacienda de Los Sauces, were now organized with the help of government aides into a tobacco producer's cooperative that kept the farm bustling. Having each received a *parcela* or a patch of land, the workers now grew their own tobacco. They cut the large leaves from the tobacco bushes that were as tall as any man, hung them on long wooden rods, dried them in the kilns, and then sold them on the market. Everyone worked hard in Los Sauces, sometimes day and night, depending on the time of year. Pascual was delegated to work in the kilns where the greenish leaves turned yellowy-tan when they were cured with high heat. Despite the hot tropical weather in this region, he was put in charge of the wood burning ovens because he could read the thermometers that helped him control the temperatures to insure low sugar and high nicotine.

Having the proper savvy already demonstrated in Mazatlán, my uncle soon obtained a riverside *parcela* himself and joined the workers cooperative. Before too long, he was elected to the board of directors and found himself in a position of influence once again. The experience gained as a trusted worker with the Sugar Pine Lumber Company in the California sierras and his role in Mr. Meyer's lime kiln strike in Mazatlán led him directly into the beehive of labor politics in Tuxpan, engaging once again in decision-making affecting his fellow workers. One of his responsibilities included taking part in *acordadas* or worker-led patrols.

The word *acordada* is an antiquated term that refers to a militia used often in Mexico in the 1910s and 1920s, more like vigilante groups. An *acordada* was formed in my uncle's cooperative because the revolutionary chaos had weakened law enforcement in some localities. The situation at hand also required extra security because the tobacco lands and many others farm properties across the country had been seized by the government. Consequently, there were many powerful men who lost land this way and they retaliated with armed violence, being strongly opposed to such expropriation. Most of the time, however, the *acordada* riders were just being vigilant against any disorderly conduct on the weekends like street fights brought on by workers who imbibed too much tequila or *aguardiente*. But, in the end, the *acordada* men were armed with German bolt-action *mausers* for any eventuality and so my uncle served as a team commander or *comandante de acordada*.

While Pascual must have drawn enormous pleasure in being involved with his fellow laborers in this way, the end result was that he nearly worked himself to death in Tuxpan. Having acquired his own *parcela*, which he had to clear with an ax and a machete, he was now obliged to work it. This meant he had to fulfill his role as a farmer by planting the tobacco seedlings, raising them into proper tobacco plants, and then harvesting the leaves. He worked as a farmer during the day and as an employee at night, in charge of the ovens, often sleeping less than a handful of hours. One day, an overflowing river inundated his land patch, and so he had no choice but to start all over again, replanting in muddy ground the thousands of young bushes he lost. This is how he caught a strong dose of what he called *pulmonía* or pneumonia, the result, he claimed, of over exertion and excessive exposure to the elements. Even though he sold a pig for eighty pesos in order to hire some help, his body began to waver, aggravated by the working conditions. Wet with perspiration, he shuddered until he passed out. He remembered being told later that a doctor was dispatched to attend to him and that the medic had doubts about his prognosis. "If he's not dead by midnight, then he'll be all right," the doctor is supposed to have said. My uncle survived the night. However, once again he saw his mother in a dream, much like the fall that he had in Truckee, California, losing consciousness and having the sensation of needing to be by his mother. The *pulmonía* incident in Tuxpan drove him to change course and to return to San Fernando.

When Pascual wasn't involved with his fellow workers, he spent his leisure time in saloons, playing cards, drinking, and engaging women, particularly in Mazatlán where he had more time. A solid bachelor, it isn't too hard to presume that he cut a nervy figure among young blades in many a Mexican *cantina* and wooed a handful of young women with his calm and convincing manner. He was in his thirties when he lived in Mazatlán and Tuxpan, and so we can surmise that the ease that helped him influence his fellow workers also attracted young women. After all, how many men could claim at this time to have traveled to the United States and worked there successfully? He had certainly come a long way from the few Mexican coins that jangled in his pocket when he first landed in the port seventeen years earlier. Any backcountry yokel would be impressed, especially if Pascual could now draw a few *pesos* from his pocket to set up drinks at the bar.

This is about the time he began engaging one of the women who lived with him for many years, Salvadora. She was a native of Etzatlán, Jalisco, whom he met in Mazatlán before moving to Tuxpan. As mentioned in chapter 2, he had three long-lasting relationships, and Salva, as we used to call her, was one of them. We, the Gil children, came to know her very well when we were growing up and remember her as a fair-skinned, heavy-set woman who wore her salt-and-pepper hair long although she must have been slim and trim when they first met and probably very attractive. While they were still in Mazatlán, she asked him about a rumor she'd heard that he had killed a man in one of the red-light district bars, but Pascual reassured her this was not so. It was all scandal-mongering, he explained; he cut him up a little bit, that's all, but he deserved it. In any case, in Tuxpan, Salva helped nurse Pascual back to health after his *pulmonía*.

It's entirely possible that Pascual could have made things work for him in his home country. Even though the stated aim of the leaders who gave life to the Mexican Revolution was to bring a better life to the nations' downtrodden, its fruits didn't filter down to men like my uncle at this time. Those who did well tended to be lawyers like Luis Cervantes in Mariano Azuela's classic novel of the revolution, *Los de abajo*, who entered the fray as a medical student and survived long enough to get his medical degree and eventually prosper. But his muddy-sandaled co-revolutionary, Demetrio Macías, a campesino who didn't know exactly why he was fighting and never opened a book in his life, never survived the rebellion. In other words, peons profited little from the revolution. Had my uncle remained in Tuxpan as an *ejido* holder and a coop official willing to get into the political arena, which he seemed to be doing, he might have elevated himself to the level of the thousand and one official party gofers who, despite their low education, eked out a decent enough life, running errands for the politically-connected party lawyers and engineers. Some even became congressmen. Pascual's stubbornness might have gotten him killed too. The fact is that my uncle left all this behind and headed to Mexicali with the idea of crossing over into Southern California.

Pascual Returns to San Fernando

Grandma Carlota traveled twice to Mexicali on the United States border to see her son, Pascual. Like most parents, she always wanted all her children nearby, so she appealed to her son to quit Mexico, once and for all, and join her in San Fernando. She wanted to do whatever she could to help him get a visa to enter the United States. He claimed she told him, "I'm getting old, and I want you nearby so you can help me in my last days and bury me when the time comes." He added that "she offered to get me papers if I would care for her," which he accepted. Her offer to "get" him his "papers" meant she would sponsor his residency.

When I was about seven years, my brother Mike and I accompanied

Grandma on her second trip to Mexicali, and this is when I first met my uncle. I seem to remember he was already wearing the distinctive "toothbrush" styled moustache made famous by Charley Chaplin. He wore that kind of moustache to his dying day. Although he never had children of his own, I remember that while we were in Mexicali he struck me as a friendly but gruff kind of guy with course brown hands who laughed at my juvenile antics. He and Salva lived in a one-room adobe house near a large creek on the outskirts of that small, scorching, desert city. The only other memory I have of this moment is that my brother and I enjoyed our visit, as any boys would do, running in and out of the house, throwing rocks at trees and bushes and even the neighbor kids. My brother and I were oblivious to the more consequential nature of our visit.

Grandma ultimately succeeded in getting her son to rejoin her California family at a moment in time when he was getting ready to return to Tuxpan. The immigration process had dragged on for a year and a half but just when he had given up, his visa arrived. So, instead of heading south, he and Salva packed their meager belongings into a couple of washtubs, and using these as travel bags, they passed north through the border and then rode the rails into Los Angeles arriving in San Fernando, about 1943.

His return to the family fold must have made Grandma happy even though she didn't always show it. Why wouldn't she be happy? She now had her three children close by, once again. They may have found themselves in a foreign country but they were together, nonetheless. When my *tío* rejoined us, my family might have been harvesting crops "up north," as we've already seen, and then returned that year to live next door to Grandma on Kalisher Street, to begin operating our café. My Uncle Miguel and his even larger flock lived a few blocks away and so now Pascual would live close by as well. All was well from Grandma's perch.

His Presence Causes a Stir

Pascual's return, however, caused my mother trouble sooner rather than later. All would not be well. The idea that Grandma needed Pascual to take care of her before she died became a point of contention. Pascual undoubtedly repeated Grandma's words to our mother, and this wounded her as a result. After all, my mother had tailored her married life around Grandma over the preceding twenty years, devoting a significant amount of time and effort on her behalf in addition to freely and enthusiastically awarding her with Dad's ingenuity and labor whenever she asked for it. My elder siblings, Mary and Manuel, bitterly remembered many of these gratuitous offers of my father's handyman ability, not to mention that some of us were also required to live with Grandma so she wouldn't spend her nights alone. Yet, here was Grandma going to Pascual, the prodigal son, and saying she needed him around too. This made Mother feel affronted, to say the least. Truth be said, Grandma, who could become as grating as sandpaper, did something else regarding Pascual that would turn the knife inside Mom's heart as explained below. Were the two in conflict in these days? We won't ever know. The point is that with Pascual's return, these cross-currents of maternal and filial love grew into a bitter competition. We would hear Mother lament this situation many times.

My thick-skinned uncle Pascual, nevertheless, got down to business. It merits saying that like all the other men in our first generation, he would seldom be out of a job. He obtained work first in the orange groves, alongside many of my father's buddies. Later, he got employment in one of the few remaining olive canneries in Sylmar, a few blocks away from where my sister Soledad would live with her first husband for about twenty years. Then he would finally get a job in the construction industry. This is where he would work as a unionized construction laborer for the remainder of his life.

I remember visiting him one day while he was working at a construction site. I was attending college classes at Pierce Junior College in Woodland Hills, California, and while driving home, on the way, I stopped to say hi to him on his lunch break. Familiar with construction sites and avoiding exposed nails and other pitfalls, I climbed up to where I found him placidly munching on his soft tortilla *tacos,* washing them down with thermos coffee. I remember he always wore a hat and heavy khaki shirts and pants, no matter what the weather was, and he always holstered his ever-present hammer at the job; always ready. As we chatted about commonplace topics, one of the carpenters for whom he worked as an assistant was also enjoying his meal-break nearby with a buddy. A youngish, indistinct gringo, he threw a canteen in my uncle's direction, which sailed briefly through the air, landing on the wood-planked floor near my uncle's feet. When he launched it he yelled out, "Hey, fill it up with water!" When I saw the container hit the floor, I instantly wanted to throw it back at the lounging carpenter but resisted my impulse. You didn't communicate with anyone that way unless you disregarded that person's humanity or possessed the social ways of a lout and this gringo didn't know this. My uncle, however, rolled his eyes in my direction and, faintly raising his eyebrows, said to me, "You see how they treat me!" Here was an example of the brutish interpersonal behavior exhibited by many American males, but my uncle was already quite familiar with it, and he needed the job more than he did saving his face. So he set his food aside, got up on his feet, and walked over to the water barrel and refilled the canteen handing it to the carpenter. In the past, he had maimed more than one individual in defending himself or his interests, but here he chose to remain a submissive carpenter assistant. When my uncle's half-hour lunch was finished, I walked away under a dark cloud.

He and Salvadora lived unpretentiously but were never out of money that we could tell. My child's memory finds their house on Amboy Street, located in what used to be the lower end of the San Fernando barrio, we used to call it *la rana* because of the presence of many frogs in the evening. This, their second home, was frugally clean, furnished for the most part with unadorned wooden furniture resting on shiny linoleum, absent of any frills and trimmings. I remember Salva's kitchen as squeaky clean even though she cooked with an upright pewter kerosene stove. When they first arrived from Mexicali, they had taken a room with the perennially smashed *el chato*, one of our neighbors on Mott Street as described in chapter 12. They moved soon enough to Amboy Street, and a few years later, my uncle purchased a lot in the gravelly fields of Pacoima where he built his own very simple but sturdy home on Fillmore Street. He claimed to have earned enough money to buy Salva's mother and daughter each a house in their hometown of Etzatlán, Jalisco, taking advantage of rock-bottom property values—this being something the rest of our family didn't know. Quite willing to walk to work in the early days, he began commanding his own vehicles beginning with an old Model A Ford, which required cranking to start and a lever under the steering wheel to spark up the motor.

His relations with his sister, our Mom, and the rest of us after Grandma died in 1953 and Dad at the end of 1956, rode on a very uneven keel. Mom's relationship with him was particularly rocky at times due in part to the fact that Grandma Carlota handed him one half of the Kalisher Street property she originally purchased in 1938 before she passed away. In contrast, Mom and Dad had to purchase the other half from her, the site where we opened Gil's Café. This was the lance that Grandma threw at my mother's heart wounding her until her last days. "After all I did for her," is what Mother said so many times in pained bewilderment. She complained that he had done so little for Granma, in comparison, when he wasn't driving her to the edge of reason because of his harsh anticlerical rhetoric, her being a near fanatical Catholic. Yet, she rewarded him with a prized piece of property.

On another level, my uncle caused consternation with my sisters when they were in their nubile stage. In one of the many powwows we had in order to talk about our family past, they let me know about their long-standing feelings of repulsion they held toward him when they were growing up. It seems he tried to grope them whenever he had a chance. Whether this was done in jest or not or whether his behavior simply reflected backcountry, pre-modern ways between men and young women, from my sister's point of view, it didn't make any difference; they felt insulted and violated. That he had never had his own children wasn't an excuse either. Even my mother complained bitterly about this type of behavior at times. This was new information for me in part because I was often away and also because my sisters were reluctant to talk about it probably because of the role our *tío* Pascual played in the family. After my father's passing away, we often made it a point to include him in our clan gatherings, something that our family photo albums reveal quite openly. When his behavior became too much, one day, my younger brother, Rick, who didn't see my uncle the way my elder brothers and I saw him, confronted him head-on and laid down a line in the sand, so to speak. Rick put a stop to his grousing or saying things that offended the women in the family. My uncle Miguel didn't raise this dilemma with them, and Dad never did either.

My uncle Pascual lived out his last years on the property Grandma gave him, the same two-room house on Kalisher Street where she had slept most of her life and where I kept my bedroom with her as a pre-teenager. By this time Salvadora had long returned to Etzatlán and passed on, as did Doña Ester, his next most important woman, who helped Mother and Emily make tortillas during "our toughest years" as mentioned already. He managed to retire from the arduous jobs associated with the construction industry without major damage to his body and lived frugally, always independently, on his own, next door to us in good times and bad. His heart began to fail during the years I lived away and in 1985, after falling ill, he was taken to the hospital where he subsequently died at age eighty-five.

Uncle Miguel

The reader will remember that Chapter 7 describes my *tío* Miguel arriving in San Fernando in 1927, alongside Grandma and Juárez, her companion, while Pascual stayed on in the California sierras working for the Sugar Pine Lumber Company. Having just left Sunland, where jobs were hard to find, they moved into the *vecindad* described with assured fondness by my sister Mary in that same chapter. Miguel didn't return to Mexico like his brother, not even during the Repatriation years despite his being undocumented. At age twenty-five, he chose to remain close to his mother and sister but soon decided he would start his own life.

He met his lifelong companion shortly after his arrival in San Fernando and in doing so, the domestic orientation of his life became firmly cast. She was a pretty faced woman named Consuelo Pacheco, with dark sparkling eyes whose family had recently arrived from Purépero, Michoacán. Our grandmother knew her mother, Doña Petra, as they were neighbors in the *vecindad* and seemed to be cut from the same cloth because both hailed from Indian background and they both immigrated at a mature age alongside younger members of their family. The reader may recall that Doña Petra ministered to Juárez, Grandma's partner, by providing him with some hot soup and jello when he suffered his final agony. Both of them wrapped dark rebozos or shawls around their shoulders to stay warm as they had done in their hometowns in Mexico, and they both visited the local church daily to pray in front of one image or another of Jesus or Mary and, as such, acted as co-devotees of backcountry Mexican Catholicism.

Given the kind of chummy atmosphere at the *vecindad,* it was no surprise that Miguel would soon notice pretty Consuelo. They were similar in age, in background, and both were at an age when they were looking for a life partner, consciously or not, and so before too long, they fell in love with one another and became intertwined for life. As it turned out, Consuelo already had a daughter, named Socorro, and despite loud dissents from Grandma on this account, complaints that later turned into a spiteful, life-long snarl, my uncle seems to have dismissed her objections. Over her refusal, Miguel soon married his dark-skinned, black-haired sweetheart at the local Justice of the Peace, not being able to marry in church the way everyone would have wanted because of her previous betrothal. Grandma stamped her feet with indignation for many years but to no avail.

Defying a world of odds, Miguel and Consuelo eventually raised a large family, larger than our own. What is so singular about my uncle is that he seems to have faced the growing number of children born to him and Consuelo with perennial good humor and seldom ever complained about the economic weight the dozen children represented. Between 1931, the year the stork delivered Porfirio, their firstborn, and 1948, when Danny, the last Naranjo in this family came to this world, our cousins arrived with regularity: Raymond, then Rose Marie, followed by Patricia, Connie, Joe, Tony, Carolyn, Mike, and Richard. There were twelve altogether including Socorro.

At first, when they had only one or two children, they lived in the *vecindad* alongside my own folks for a few years and then moved to a small house on Woodworth Street about the time my folks also moved away from the *vecindad*. Eventually, my uncle transferred his growing family to one of the tiny houses on Mott Street, exactly three doors down from our house, and here they lived for about thirty years.

Raising and sustaining a family that grew to include a dozen children must have been formidable. His eldest daughter, Rose Marie, remembered that her father's earliest job, once married, was picking oranges and lemons like our dad did many times, and in fact, they may have worked side by side in the sweet smelling orchards, the two men getting along cordially, after all they had been buddies before either of them married. According to her, Miguel put the citrus harvesting job aside whenever he could and worked at the olive canning factory in Sylmar where she claims he became ill from the chemicals employed in curing the olives.

My uncle discovered he couldn't sustain his family on the agricultural harvesting jobs he performed around San Fernando, as if farm working families could ever stay in the black. Much as in our case, he found it necessary to supplement his yearly family budget by going "up north" in order to stay ahead of the bill collectors. Just as we did, the Naranjo's put all their arms to work during the summer when the children were free from school and, in this way, take advantage of the full harvest swing, laboring in the fields for longer periods than we did. Rose Marie remembers they went ten years straight during the summer.

In their childish innocence, she and her siblings thought they were going on vacation! They would eagerly pile into their vehicle and drive the full day to Fresno, where they would arrive and begin checking with one farm after another, inquiring to see if they needed any workers, especially the first year. Rose Marie recalled that they finally found "a really nice family of *americanos*," the Aratas, who owned a farm where the family was allowed to establish camp. The second summer, they returned to the same farm, and here they would come back every year. They would harvest apricots, peaches, and grapes—the Aratas operated a winery too.

Rose Marie remembered she would get busy making the beds. This meant that she would set up fruit boxes and put mattresses or other bedding material on them so they could sleep at the end of the day. She became extra handy for the Aratas because she could translate between Spanish and English and so would help out this way when questions arose among the many farm workers who could only speak Spanish. Sixty-five years later, she still laughed at herself remembering the day when a Mexican contract worker, a bracero, was presented to her as being ill and the boss's wife wanted to know what ailed him. The worker told my cousin that he had "*neumonía,*" not knowing how to say *pulmonía* (pneumonia), and pointed at his chest. Rose Marie heard *demonio*, and so she told the boss lady that he had the devil in his chest. The woman burst out laughing and so did the Mexican worker but my poor cousin remembered she could only feel her face flush red—glowing with embarrassment at making the wrong call.

When asked what her overriding memory was of those early days, Rose Marie brought to mind the words "loneliness and sadness." Her trips up north, "on vacation," opened her eyes by underscoring the enormous gap between her own family and the Aratas no matter how kind they were. She started asking herself, how could they live the way they did and "why did we live the way we did?" She soon discovered she was a "good thinker" and, in effect, began running queries inside her own head about the disconnections that kept appearing before her eyes.

> Why are my parents so wonderful and yet they're struggling to put on the table the food we eat and the *leña* (firewood) [we cook with]? We were happy being together, but we didn't get to go anywhere, [we didn't get to] do anything [that was fun]. I saw the difference by looking at the magazines. I felt a deep sadness. The only [fun] thing we had [on these trips up north] was the radio. Mother turned it on at night. They didn't even have a light to turn on! The radio played music at night, and Dad would [also] turn it on. It was so sad to me. To this day, I can't [bear to] turn on the radio at night. Oh, what my parents had to endure with us![209]

When we were growing up, we were socially close. Our cousins came first and then our friends. Because the boys enjoyed more freedom or, at least, got away with it more easily, we paired off with those who were closest in age to us. My brothers Manuel and Mike chummed with Raymond when they were teenagers, a relationship that ended when Ray went to fight in Korea only to return in a casket, a tragic episode for everyone. I remember often playing with my cousin Joe in their all-dirt yard, when I was about six or so, and when we were about twelve, he and I served as altar boys at Santa Rosa Church for several years. My brother Rick, who always felt close with Mike, Tony, and Richard, said to me one day that back in the days they frequented certain taverns in the area, he always felt more secure when his cousins also walked in the door and sat next to him. "I always felt better that way," he told me.

My aunt and uncle silently endured their penury until their children, those who survived that is, began to grow up and move away. It wasn't until the 1970s that Miguel took a job that brought some mercy on his body and on his moral self. Thanks to Rose Marie's constant vigilance over her parents and to her own grit to become somebody herself, she learned of a job opportunity that offered better working conditions for her father and a measurable but limited increase in pay. This was an affirmative action-position, working for the California Department of Transportation. As we've noted already, thanks to President Lyndon Johnson and his liberal-minded policies, state authorities were now required to open their jobs to members of racial minorities who were also poor economically. This is how my uncle became a landscaper, tending the green areas that embellish the countless Southern California freeways that crisscross each other This became my uncle's main job which he performed faithfully and diligently until his retirement. When he had to give up working because of his age, he received a modest pension and, in this way, stood out as the only member of our first generation to enjoy such compensation.

In contrast to the scanty economic condition of their earlier years, Miguel and Consuelo began to draw a measure of relaxed dignity after he retired. With the help of their surviving children, they were able to live comfortably in their own home surrounded and assisted by their offspring. It also helped that on Sundays and special holidays, Miguel could visit Guadalupe, his immigrant trail mate and sister, only three doors away.

Having the instinct of a handyman, even at the age of ninety-two, he met his demise. On a rainy day in 1995, he tried to fix a leak in the back patio roof of his house and fell head first requiring hospitalization. Everyone was stunned. This good man soon died of his injuries and was deeply mourned.

Our Dear Dad

As we've seen, Bernabé came to Southern California as an orphan teenager having left Mexico because it offered little to him. Different from Mom and her family, he was not fleeing a tyrant or an abusive taskmaster. He was putting a discontented boyhood behind him. Unhappily, his disgruntlement seems to have discouraged him from sharing details about his childhood with us, the way Mother did, and so we, his children, grew up with a minimal knowledge of his past. This circumstance led me to write "Searching for My Father's Story" found in Appendix I, which reveals my attempts at seeking more information about him and the relatives he left behind. Unfortunately, my limited discoveries add only modestly to the incomplete portrait we held of our father. The rest of our ancestors, and Mom's side, were able to choose what to share with us about their lives but not him.

Nevertheless, I can say quite plainly that his life served as a stepping stone for his children. He taught us to be good parents. He may not even have known how to write anything beyond scribbling his name with a feeble signature when he found himself obligated to sign a document, all the same my siblings and I concluded that he was a constant and loving father. This was the deduction that each of us reached independently of each other when the time came for me to begin asking my siblings questions about our years, growing up in order to write this book. This was his biggest contribution; we all agreed. He knew how it felt to be an orphan, and he didn't want us to ever feel that pain. He was forever mindful of what he missed as a child and made sure we were free of that void.

His other big lesson for us had to do with how we should conduct ourselves in the world around us. Own up to your responsibilities, he taught us, and go with what you have on hand. Use anything and everything at your disposal when having to fix or repair or build or raise something off the ground, he counseled. Do it—don't talk about what you're going to do. We learned to avoid feeling defeated because we didn't have the proper tool. Mary, who idolized her father, beamed as she remembered how he taught her how to build things, even plumbing tips including "how you put lead on water pipes." She spoke with pride, "He would teach me everything he knew, from plumbing to electricity." This is how she was able to hook up an electric line when she was a little girl in *la vecindad* so she and her friends could play after dark by the light of the hookup. He had poured himself selflessly out to her, she felt.

My eldest brother Manuel agreed on this point as well and said quite plainly as follows:

> He taught me never to back out of nothing. Be a man; do what you have to do. Get it. I couldn't get it there for a while; it took me a long time to get my shit together, but that's what he taught me. He could do anything.

"He could do anything." That was my brother's bottom line feeling about Dad. Had my brother Mike been alive when I wrote this book, he undoubtedly would have said something quite similar.

A clearly etched memory comes to me every time I'm asked what my father taught me. One day when I was in Junior High, he accompanied me to a part-time job I had. My boss wanted me to varnish a wood floor and assured me he would teach me how. I must have voiced some uncertainty about it in front of my father and so this is the moment when Dad took me aside and said, "Son, you need to learn to do whatever is necessary. Learn about everything so that you don't ever lack anything." This was his biggest lesson for me besides modeling what a constant and loving father could be.

He practiced what he preached. Looking back on these pages, we can see him, in the 1920s, attending to leaky faucets in the *vecindad* without being compensated, constructing an abode for Grandma in 1938 after she moved out of the *vecindad* to buy the Kalisher Street property, gathering building materials, no matter how flimsy they were, in order to erect a shed to protect his family from the elements on our trips to harvest fruit "up North", banging together a small restaurant in 1947 so that our family could serve rice and beans and in this way remain together and earn income at the same time, and so on. He didn't give up in 1936 after losing his left arm in an industrial accident either. Like Manuel said to me, he was a dad who gave his children the impression that "he could do anything." How wonderful!

Mom Becomes Grandma Lupe

As we saw earlier, the Sylmar Earthquake of 1971 set the motion for Mother's retirement and her move to what would become her last home. Despite all the distressing episodes of the past, she would begin to enjoy her "golden years" in this modest suburban dwelling on Huntington Street and fulfill her role as Grandma like never before. For all intents and purposes, her cottage soon filled up with frequent visits from her children and grandchildren and, ultimately, her great-grand children and in between, her friends, who would come by for a few minutes of comradeship. Visitors would always find an outdoor chair in the front garden on a sunny day and sit and chat with her under the thick bougainvilleas constantly shedding reddish blossoms on the ground.

If she didn't host visitors, she tended her garden in the front and back. These patches of suburban green grew in complexity during the thirty or so years she resided on Huntington Street because her "green thumb" combined with the fertility of the soil encouraged the twigs she snapped off from other people's shrubs, far and near, to "catch." This blunted our criticism of her harvesting habit because we couldn't deny that the pinched shoots produced lovely foliage on her property. Scarlet geraniums, egg-white calla lilies, pearl-toned camellias, ferns of various kinds, all welcomed the front-garden visitor along with the fruitful lemon tree whose fragrant blossoms scented the evening air. She turned the backyard into a small orchard that included trees like the fruit-bearing Mexican *sapote*, a mango, a pomegranate, a Mexican lemon tree (also known as Persian lemon), a fig tree, an avocado tree, etc. Many of the photos we conserve of her in those days include a multihued emerald background of trees and shrubs. Inside the house, almost every wall was covered with images, religious and profane.

The front rooms doubled as a photographic gallery festooned with family pictures. With the aid of Soledad's decorative flair, photographs of Dad and her eight children claimed the prime wall spaces of the living and dining rooms where visitors often voiced their approval. The pencil sketch that Shorty drew of Mary when she was a teenager with a pompadour hung prominently next to a color portrait of young and smooth-faced Manuel dressed in the blues and tans of an Air Force uniform. Other photos included Mike beaming proudly from a black-and-white photograph taken when he owned his waste disposal company, me in my cap and gown from Seattle University, Martha's professional portrait from the time she was working for the Sheriff's Department, Rick crying his eyes out at the age of five, Soledad dressed in a white gown when she was a year old, and Emily also as an infant dressed the same way. All visiting grandchild had the opportunity to quietly giggle upon seeing unconventional photos of their own parents up on Grandma's walls.

Religious images abounded in Grandma's house. As with nearly all Mexican women, she gave precedence to the image of Our Lady of Guadalupe above all. She possessed, at least, a dozen versions of the brown-skinned mother of Jesus so central to Mexican Catholicism. This included the traditional print representation with its dark green robe bejeweled with stars embracing her back and flowing down the sides, which stood next to a gaudy version of the same virgin that scintillated with bright colors, glittering as you moved across the room. Other versions of Mary also adorned her bedroom, like the copy of Murillo's The Immaculate Conception, *"La Inmaculada."* Mom also called her Our Lady of Sorrows, *La Virgen de los Dolores*, so popular in Spain, and the *Virgen de Los Remedios* supposedly linked to the Spanish conquest of Mexico City. Our Lady of Talpa also held a special place in Grandma's bedroom, the patroness of the small pilgrim town of Talpa, next door to Mascota, where she rode on a donkey's back as a child. The Spanish Holy Child of Atocha or *El Santo Niño de Atocha* showing his staff and drinking gourd also competed for Grandma's wall space along with other pious images like Saint Martin of Porres, one of the first Latin American mestizo saints in Christendom, and Saint Rose of Lima, considered the patroness of American Indians. The image of Jesus, primary in Protestant homes, fearlessly stood its ground on one of the walls in the guise of the Sacred Heart. She prized rosaries, and specimens of her collection could be appreciated hanging from bedposts and door knobs around the house.

Grandma Lupe lived her last years in comfort, thanks to her own thrifty prudence and to the loving support from her descendants. Her daughter Soledad and her Dutch Indonesian husband, Jan, excelled on this account because, with Mary's backup as needed, they watched over her on a daily basis until the very last days, as the rest of us came and went. After a year or so of being bedridden and fed through a tube, connected directly to her stomach, her heart stopped on her appointed day, thus closing a long and vigorous life. She was the last to exit the immigrant generation in our family. An era had closed for us too.

At her graveside, tearful and dressed in their performing costumes, strumming their guitars, her singing comrades helped bid her good-bye.

"Cruz de Madera"

Cuando al panteón ya me lleven, *No quiero llanto de nadie,* *Sólo que me estén cantando la* *canción que más me agrade,* *El luto llévenlo dentro, teñido con* *buena sangre . . .*	When you take me to the graveyard, Please don't cry for me, Just sing my favorite song And keep your sorrows in your heart . . .
Y si al correr de los años mi tumba *está abandonada* *Y aquella cruz de madera ya la* *encuentran destrozada,* *Remarquen las iniciales de aquella* *cruz olvidada, junten la tierra* *y no olviden* *Que el que muere ya no es nada.*[210]	And with the passing of time If my tomb gets neglected And my wooden cross wears out, Just rewrite my initials on that Old cross, Raise the dirt around it and don't forget That when you die you're no more.

Guadalupe at 97

Part III

The Second and Third Generations

Henry wished he'd paid more attention in English class. Until he was twelve, he had been forbidden to speak English in his own home. His father had wanted him to grow up Chinese, the way he had done. Now everything was upside down.

—Jamie Ford, *Hotel on the Corner of Bitter and Sweet* (New York: Ballantine Books, 2009), p. 122.

Chapter 14

The Second Generation

How Did We Do with Dad's advice? • How Did We Do with Mom's Concerns about Our Cultural and Religious Fulfillment? • Employment and Biographical Sketches of the Gil Children in Birth Order

HAVING STARTED A FAMILY after immigrating to America, our parents must often have told us, their children, how they wanted us to grow up. We knew they wanted us to ripen properly and become fully fledged adults even though I can't recall a time in which my parents actually sat me down and told me as much and my siblings can't either. However, all of us can recall statements or words of advice scattered over the years. For example, I recall Mom often advising us to fear God (*tengan el temor a Dios*), honor her as a parent, be good Catholics, appeal to the Virgin of Guadalupe in times of trial, and, finally, never forget our Mexican cultural roots. Dad's expectations were less sublime and more practical, on the other hand. As we've seen already, his counsel to us was to work hard and not be afraid to learn new things and, by his example, become strong and loving parents. This means that Mom was concerned about our cultural and religious fulfillment, and Dad was anxious that we stay alive in our dog-eat-dog world. From both of them this was, for all intents and purposes, our charge in filling their shoes—and fulfilling our role as members of the second generation in America.

Although the aim of the preceding pages has been to explore the life and times of our immigrant ancestors, it would be unfitting to end our story without a fuller nod to us, the Gil children. After all, some of our growing up memories are inscribed in these pages already so we can say we've been introduced already.

So, if our *viejitos* chose to immigrate to America, what can we disclose in these pages concerning the Americans they coincidentally brought into being—us? Did we follow Mom's counsel and Dad's recommendations? Did we fulfill our parents' wishes of growing up properly and becoming fully fledged adults? If so, how did we do?

In order to answer these questions, let us first address Dad's recommendations about surviving and learning to work hard and not be afraid to learn new things. Did we follow through? In order to answer this question, I asked my siblings about the jobs they had held: "Which ones meant most to you?" I asked. The specifics of their answers are molded into the employment and biographical sketches appearing in the second half of this chapter. The more important question is: "Did we follow in our parents' shoes job wise?" Stated differently, "Did we work the same way they did, being the sons and daughters of parents who earned their keep by working in agricultural jobs and by operating micro businesses like mom-and-pop grocery shops, tortilla-making shops, and small eateries?"

How Did We Do with Dad's advice?

Let's consider the men first since Dad may have aimed work-related advice more at his sons than his daughters although Mary claims to have taken deep pleasure from his teaching her about how to use tools and other practical handyman kinds of things.

It's fair to say, for us fellows, that we were all keen on surviving and getting ahead. We all identified with the importance of having a job and working hard; none of us were shirkers when it came to working. But all of us did turn our back on agricultural work once we got our occupational bearings, and the thought of opening a tortilla-making shop skipped over our head.

For example, Manuel admitted feeling good when he was in his teens about picking lemons and oranges alongside Dad but only because he wanted to be close to him, feeling good in his presence and, as it turned out, Manuel didn't work in the citrus orchards for long. He worked in the canneries because our family's first contacts at the time led to these jobs and, as we noted, he was still experimenting with the world of work. These early connections didn't last very long even though Manuel didn't study beyond ninth grade, and he didn't feel hemmed in because he lacked high school either, probably because he was the first son and his barrio peers were undoubtedly in the same situation. In fact, 67 percent of Americans did not hold a high school diploma in 1950.[211] He tried other minor jobs until a welling sense for something bigger and more advanced led him to join the air force. This is where he got the chance to see new horizons, which is to say that his military experience affected him quite positively. His occupational experimentation resumed after he returned from serving in Europe, but he eventually found his niche as a *chef de cuisine*, working in variety of principal cooking posts in Southern California and elsewhere as explained below. Manuel in effect followed his Dad's advice regarding work—not being afraid to learn new ways of working.

The rest of us men in the family followed a similar path. We too upheld the importance of being good workers, and we too turned our back on agricultural jobs and *tortillerías*. Mike and Rick, for example, directed their focus on waste collection, a vital industrial service. They did so partly as a function of their not having completed basic schooling, like Manuel. More importantly, they made their labor pay more so by combining it with their own business savvy at a time when many of our barrio buddies were finding factory jobs like working on the assembly line at the new General Motors plant in Van Nuys, California.

As disclosed below, Mike is perhaps the best example of combining business savvy with waste collection work because he carved out a distinctive middle-class lifestyle for him and his family, all based on his energetic willingness to work hard, learn the business, and then strike out on his own. And he wasn't the only one. Although from time to time, he rubbed us the wrong way on account of his gruff personality, none of us in the family can deny his achievement. He owned and operated his own rubbish company before giant corporations captured the industry in our part of the country.

The rest of us boys also combined learning on the job with business. Rick tried this approach toward the end of his work life by organizing a bathtub refinishing firm, small as it was, but it brought him a degree of financial independence. When Manuel ended his long cooking career, he and his new wife turned to retailing along the tourist byways of the Southwest in order to ease more assuredly into old age. My own experience with a small consulting and publishing business may also fit this pattern, thanks to my wife who took the lead on it.

In the end, one could almost argue that Grandma's penchant for starting up her own tortilla-making business during the Depression and our parent's perennial engagement in small businesses, including Gil's Café encouraged us to make our way through life by engaging in small business as well. My own Foreign Service work and my university career admittedly broke the mold entirely.

How did our sisters do? Were they shrinking violets content to doing woman's work at home the way Mom's aunts might have done, back in the old country? The answer is no. My sisters were also eager to get away from tortilla-making and willing to search for new horizons just like us guys. While they couldn't emulate Dad's picking citrus fruit in order to supplement family income, like Manuel did briefly, they could've worked in the tomato canneries like Mary did. Many other young women in our barrio did too, judging by a photo in our possession taken around 1940, which also reveals by the way that cannery work was not exclusive of Mexican Americans; many *gringas* worked in canning factories too. Mary, however, seems to have been anxious to get away from this line of work, and in the end, she made this shift not encountering any obstacles.

As shown below, one of Mary's earliest jobs, outside of Mom's tortilla shop, was waitressing at one of the more important soda fountain restaurants in town, a situation reminiscent of a Norman Rockwell tableau (I too followed in Mary's footsteps and bussed the soda fountain dishes). Sensing her own advancing social skills, she continued veering away from the kinds of the jobs first envisioned by our parents. For example, she worked as a sales assistant to Manny Peven, the owner of the army surplus store located on the Anglo side of the tracks, making use of her bilingual and bicultural competencies, something she also did in the pediatric nephrology assignments at the Marion Davies Center at UCLA. My big sister scaled upwardly in her work capacities, indeed. Had she been given the opportunity to obtain a good education as a real option, Mary would have seized it and found unanticipated fulfillment.

My other sisters, Marty, Sally, and Emily, were not born for cannery work either and certainly not for making tortillas. Martha carved a path quite apart from Mary by slogging all the way through high school, graduating with satisfaction, and then striking out on her own despite her health maladies and extremely difficult relations with Mother. Her sketch below reveals that she became a governess for a well-heeled Anglo family and later obtained clerical work in an insurance company and then, finally, held an important human resources job with the County of Los Angeles from which she managed to retire early due to her stubborn infirmities. If she knowingly heeded Dad's advice, he would have been proud of her because she did so superbly.

When it came time for the youngest members of the family, Sally and Emily, to take up their own jobs, agriculturally related work was entirely out of the picture. Stuffing hot cooked tomatoes in a tin can for someone else's table may have represented a temporary job for Mary as a teenager but not for my youngest sisters. When talking about work to their friends, my youngest sisters didn't use the names Sunkist or Blue Goose. Instead, they talked about hospitals and caring for the elderly and infirm. The health sector provided both of them an occupational badge of identity for many years, after which time, Sally became a Teacher's aide and Emily chose the ancient practice of chiromancy or palmistry. They too moved on, way beyond what Mother might have imagined, indeed. They were no shrinking violets.

So did we Gil children heed Dad's words of wisdom? We certainly did, all of us, the men and the women. We didn't all become teachers or engineers because our parents were unable to counsel us and guide us to that level, but our track record demonstrates that more than one of us could have stepped up had we enjoyed the right conditioning and training.

How did we do with Mom's concerns about our cultural and religious fulfillment?

Did we fear God, stay good Catholics, honor the *La Virgen*, and never forget we were *mexicanos*? Being faithful to Mom's directions about our cultural and religious fulfillments is admittedly more difficult to pin down. So the answer to this question may not be so cut and dry. Still, Mom's counsel didn't fall on deaf ears. Let's take each one of her recommendations.

Did we retain fear of God? Mother repeated this admonition to us often, even into her last days, *"Tengan temor en Dios!"* Fearing God implies believing in God. The idea appears to be rooted in the Old Testament (Deut. 6:24, at least) wherein early believers in the one God were charged on how to live a good life, and fearing God was one of the tenets.

Where did she get this notion? Even though she and other Mexican Catholics like her didn't customarily read the Bible, as most Protestants supposedly do, Mother was comforted in the understanding that hearing the Gospel in the Catholic Mass itself was sufficient along with attending Mass and taking the sacraments as directed by the priests, who mattered most in her life. One of the key ideas communicated from the pulpit, particularly during the *misiones* led by Father De Anda as discussed in chapter 12, was to fear God.

There's no doubt that had somebody asked us at the time, "Do you believe in God?" all of us Gil children would have nodded our head affirmatively, scratching it at the same time, wondering what that might mean exactly. Up to that point in our lives, we stuck close to what both Mom and Grandma taught us regarding religion, the boys less so, of course, than the girls. Dad provided us with a low-key role model on these matters. He attended Sunday Mass in his own muted way but never sermonized to us about our religious duties and rarely, if ever, addressed religious topics. Mom performed the role of the religious overseer for us, zealously. Consequently, we all grew up within the Catholic faith, pre-Vatican II as it was. We were all baptized at Santa Rosa Catholic Church, discussed in chapter 12, received the Sacrament of Confirmation, which also meant receiving a set of God parents for each rite, and nearly all of us thereafter observed the rituals required, including attending Mass on Sundays and holy days and going to confession and taking communion at least once a year. When we were *jóvenes* or youngsters, all of us attended, at least, one or more *misiones* as described in chapter 12 and vowed as instructed to renounce the devil, although Mike probably sneaked off to play snooker pool more than once, instead. Some of us even sang in the church choir for many years and I, at least, also served as an altar boy. We were dyed in the wool Catholics, you could say.

How did we do afterward? As we approached the end of our teen years, each one of us began forging our own path. We men began to slack off on our Catholic duties more quickly than the women, Mike probably occupying the most secular or most indifferent position toward the church in our larger family by the time he began raising his own children. Rick stood very close to him on this matter while Manuel and I held on to Mother's example a bit longer.

Then again, my sisters tended to favor Mother's religious orientation. On Sundays, at least, they would dress up and reach for their head veils in order to march off to church. Mary and Soledad remained close to their religious duties; Mary certainly more so than Soledad, and Martha and Emily the least. The reader may remember that Emily experienced quite a raw relationship not only with Mother but also with a Sister Katherine in Catholic school and this only served to dishearten any sense of religious devotion my sister might have nurtured, though not her sense of spirituality. Emily puts it quite clearly in chapter 12: "Mom asked me 'Who turned you against the church?' They did! They did it, all by themselves!" "They" obviously meant the priests and the nuns and Mom, most probably! Likewise, Martha's heartrending teenage battles with Mom undoubtedly cooled her commitment to Catholicism or any other form of religion. She became a secular and independent-minded young woman.

Another observation regarding our own religious or spiritual orientation is worth mentioning. Different from Mom and Dad, our marriage experiences turned out somewhat unconventional as well, far from what Mom expected. Despite the fact that we all married within the church the first time around, nearly all of us divorced at least once, Rick being the only exception. While this pattern may have reflected our being too young to wed the first time, despite any parental advice to the contrary, we children didn't think twice about breaking church rules on this matter, the Catholic Church not recognizing divorce, of course. This is why Mother felt fully outraged when Mary first stood up to reach for this option, an annulment in her case. When I asked Mary sixty-some years later about Mom's reaction, she replied, "You have no idea!" We can only imagine how our mother reacted and, to be sure, Mom continued to feel offended each time the rest of us broke our church-sanctioned marriage vows.

Did we appeal to Our Lady of Guadalupe as Mom instructed us? The answer is that even those of us who backed away from our close teenage ties to the church maintained a spiritual bond to this unique Mexican version of Jesus' mother, Mary. The history of this distinctive devotional cult combined with the religious zeal that the Guadalupe commands simply weighed too much in our hearts and psyches. Even the most secular of us children were unable to completely set aside this tradition, venerated so deeply and so personally by our ancestors. When her feast day came around on December 12, I always felt pangs in my heart, recalling earlier experiences on this date. I also remember escorting my brother Rick, indifferent about these things, to the Basilica of the Virgin of Guadalupe in Mexico City one day when we were both adults and noting the emotional power that came over him as we passed in front of her world famous image and witnessed the overwhelming veneration around us. For Mary and Sally who remained close to the barrio where we grew up staying true to the devotion of Our Lady of Guadalupe was uncomplicated because they could simply take part in the festivities organized by the church two blocks away. For those of us who moved away, December 12 always brought a wave of wistfulness and nostalgia recalling the spiritual warmth that we felt on her feast day when we were young.

All of us honored both Mom and Dad as parents, to be sure, some more than others and in differing ways. Soledad drew the highest measure when she decided to leave her own home after her children moved away and, with her husband's total support, move in with Mom in order to care for her in her last years—thirteen years, all told. The fact is that after Dad's passing, the rest of us orbited around Mom. It is entirely accurate to affirm that there was never a weekend, certainly never a Sunday, between 1955, when father died, and 2007, when Mom expired, that she spent alone by herself. This simply didn't happen, and if it did, it was unusual. One or another of us in her extended family would visit or check in to see how she was, almost on a daily basis. As stated already, the extended family would crowd into her Huntington Street home to celebrate holidays, particularly her birthday on November 22.

How did we do about not disavowing our cultural roots beyond the religious ones already mentioned above? Mother always insisted that we remain *mexicanos* to the end and that we not forget where we came from—she really meant that we should not forget where *she* came from. This helps explain the many trips she made to her hometown, Mascota, during our growing-up years and insisting that one or another of us accompany her. Dad had refused to return to Mexico as explained elsewhere in these pages but not Mom. Mary remembered that when Mother was pregnant with Soledad, she took Manuel, at age thirteen, and Martha, at age five, all the way to Mascota when getting there on the bus from Guadalajara was no easy jaunt. In these early days, it meant having to sit next to dirt farmers transporting chickens tied at their feet and roped-up cardboard boxes perched precariously overhead, while the bus waded into rivers and streams in the absence of bridges when it wasn't raising dust clouds as it bumped along rock-strewn mountain passes. Just boarding the bus proved to be perilous enough for Mom one time because she got trampled over at the door by backcountry travelers, impatient to claim their seat. The driver had to intervene, but this didn't stop Mom, of course. She returned many times with others of us in tow. Needless to say, the state of transportation and communication in Mexico improved a lot over the decades. Emily described her own expedition to Mascota with Mom in chapter 10.

Did Mother's trial-by-fire introductions to her birth region help prevent us from turning our back on our cultural origins? The answer is a qualified yes because not all of us responded in the same way. Some of us attached more importance to our roots than others, which meant that some of us preferred getting as comfortable as possible with our being American and others less so. This is a good example of how someone's cultural experience is difficult to pin down even within one single family.

We remained *mexicanos* in a variety of ways. Chapter 12 already describes our bicultural lives in that we children maintained connections to our parents' culture at the same time that we bonded with things American via radio personalities and the music around us. Not the least of this bonding was switching Spanish for English as our main language and generally taking on attitudes and styles that were American rather than Mexican.

Still, we couldn't help but make the effort to honor our Mexican roots in one way or another. We simply didn't perceive an option. We were who we were. As already mentioned, language-wise we all spoke Spanish although it wasn't quite what you could hear on the streets of Guadalajara or Mascota. Our Spanish took on a California ring to it; still, we communicated with our Mexican friends quite easily. I've mentioned already that we, the Gil boys, picked up a lot of *pachuco* slang, which horrified Mother, Mike being prone to speaking it quite regularly when she was out of ear shot. Musically, we all preferred Mexican music to American compositions—a fancy that was bolstered by our being exposed to Mexico's golden age of music and screen, as mentioned previously, featuring such great artists like Jorge Negrete, Pedro Vargas, María Félix, Pedro Infante, and Cantínflas. Enjoying these screen performers and being able to discuss them with Mother certainly must have brought her a lot of comfort.

More intimately, we Gil children favored Mexican food over American fare and homemade was the best. As mentioned in chapter 12, all of us were introduced to American cooking via the school cafeterias of our youth because Mom never cooked one single American-styled meal at home. She looked down on American food, or at least, the dishes she knew about; it just wasn't good enough. Cafeteria meals may not have been the best measure, but they were the first for us, nonetheless, since we didn't have gringo neighbors who might have shared their meals with us on occasion, and we didn't eat out as a family in our growing up years either, this being starkly different from the ubiquitous eateries that barrage American families today with their invitations to feast in their establishments. So, we didn't discover American restaurant victuals until we started going out on our own.

Did we visit our mother country? Yes. To Mother's delight, we all visited Mexico as adults. Beyond our youthful visits with her, unforgettable in many ways, some of us accompanied her as adults, given the fact that she visited numerous times. Mary and I accompanied her more than once, and others of us spent holidays there in the company of our spouses and children. I spent the most time in Mexico because of my professional work, living in various cities numerous times. I've exulted in being able to introduce Mexico personally to my own children.

So did we heed our parent's advice? It seems we did in the main even though we diverged because we all moved in different ways. My sense is that we honored Dad's words of wisdom because we ventured into unknown territory job wise, and we obtained some satisfying employment experiences, each of us according to our own abilities and circumstances, a significant claim in itself.

We paid tribute and recognition to Mother's counsel too but with some qualifications. It's fair to state that many of us drifted from the cultural-religious coordinates she set out for us. In other words, many of us children didn't practice the Catholic faith according to her desires, owing to the fact that we either became indifferent or we lapsed, the reasons for these shifts being quite complex and beyond the scope of these pages. While none of us jumped the fence to become Protestants, which would have wounded Mother grievously, one of us, at least, gave vent to his spirituality by embracing Buddhism, something that confused Mom more than anything else.

Lastly, Mother's advise about our giving due recognition to our cultural origins probably brought her a fair amount of pride. We all gave our due on this one at the same time that we all assumed our bicultural and binational identity. We were who we were and felt quite comfortable for it.

Employment and Biographical Sketches of the Gil Children in Birth Order

Mary (María de Jesús)

When she matured into a young woman, a few years after World War II, my eldest sister unveiled some social skills that made a big difference in her life. For example, she could engage people inside the barrio or outside it without any hesitation and stood ready to use her knowledge of both Spanish and English to help others. Her language skills and her social readiness served her well as did an inborn networking ability, which she used to good stead throughout her entire life. The words we've borrowed from her in the preceding pages reflect her deep sense of reliability and understanding, undoubtedly gained because she was the eldest in the family. As our senior sister and a woman who struggled to help her male partners keep their children clothed and fed for decades, she was rewarded with a humanistic wholesomeness.

Mary toiled all her life. Tasked by Mother from the beginning, she was responsible for house chores, helping out with the younger ones at the same time that she also assisted Grandma with her tortilla business by counting and wrapping tortillas, washing the tubs for cooking corn, milling, and even making and selling snow cones. She dropped out of school in ninth grade because a social straight jacket was imposed on her, so to speak. She stopped school that year because Mother was planning to travel to Mexico, and she didn't want Mary to attend school in her absence; she wanted her safe at home with Dad, and she could help Grandma too. In any case, she attended school part-time during Mother's absence and even when Mom returned from her extended visit to Jalisco. Mary, however, never returned to regular day school. She expressed her desire for staying in school, but things never worked out for her.

She began working away from home soon enough. She took a full-time job in a sewing factory and later switched to the kind of jobs that were more familiar to our family at the time: working in the various packing houses in San Fernando that relied on Mexican labor. For instance, she took a job at the Lemon Heights Association packing house near the old Mission where her brother Manuel would also work, and then she drew wages at the Blue Goose packing house on Truman Street. Grandma and Mother also worked in these noisy bustling buildings at one time or another and so we knew a lot about the work going on in those places and made friends with other folks who likewise worked in these packing houses.

As she got older, Mary began looking for other kinds of employment. This is about the time I remember going into "Kress's five and dime store" in downtown San Fernando when I was about five or so holding onto Mom's hand. As I walked on the darkly varnished squeaky wooden floorboards that released a pungent waxy aroma, trying to peer over the counters filled with exotic baubles and trinkets, I suddenly noticed my sister standing in the back. My sister appeared stylish to me in a dark top with big white lapels, perhaps a dash of lipstick color, and I remember her generous black hair folded up in a pompadour held together with a light colored sash. "She works here!" I must have said to Mom as she pulled me along. Somehow I knew that her holding a job at Kress's, a big American store, meant something special. Even at that age, I felt a dash of pride for my sister! Many decades later, Mary informed me that she was there merely applying for a job, which she didn't get.

Apparently the first job she took along these lines was her part-time waitress job at the Thrifty Drug Store in town, at the intersection of Brand Boulevard and San Fernando Road. Instead of the manual dexterity and upper body strength expected of the employees at the packing houses, at Thrifty's you needed to speak English, be sociable, look good, learn the menu, and handle money. Wages were slightly higher at Thrifty's than at the packing houses if you included tips, but you were required to put on a uniform, be presentable, and amiable to a wide mix of customers, most of them Anglos. Speaking English was never a problem for Mary and, in any case, she was a quick learner and a sociable soul, so she did well at the corner drugstore.

Her search for more meaningful jobs continued throughout the years. One of these saw her working as a sales lady at the San Fernando Army Surplus Store on Maclay Street on the other side of the tracks. The Jewish American owner hired her to give him some slack time, no doubt, but more than anything else, he wanted her to attend to the many Mexican workers who came to shop on weekends. Many of them were Braceros from the nearby camps who needed to stock up on work clothes and boots and shiny German knives; they became confident that they could rely on my sister's knowledge of Spanish and her willingness to help. She brought me in to help out when she decided to move on. She also worked as one of San Fernando's early court interpreters in cases involving speakers whose only language was Spanish, and she was quite willing to be awakened by a patrolman rudely knocking on her door before dawn, advising her that her services would be required at the court house later that morning. Soon enough, the municipal judge decided to make it easier for her to be present and on time by ordering a patrol car to transport her, no doubt, raising pangs of apprehension on the part of her barrio neighbors whenever the squad cars stopped to fetch her.

Mary's most consequential employment took place at UCLA. At age forty, she began work at the university's medical school as a filing clerk responsible for the accurate and steady filing of medical paper records in an age before digital archiving. Soon she was trained to do medical coding, which consisted then, as it does today, of "transforming narrative descriptions of diseases, injuries, and healthcare procedures into numeric or alphanumerical designations (that is, code numbers)." All this was necessary for recording and archiving the information for staff use.[212] She also did "clinical laboratory work," requiring her to supervise paternity testing and marriage certificate medical procedures, for example. And in her last years at the UCLA Marion Davies Children Center, she worked in the pediatric nephrology unit as an aide with the responsibility of preparing the documentation of child patients requiring a kidney transplant, sometimes going herself out into the field to bring them in quickly along with their parents for the critical and timely operation. She retired at age sixty-three with a desire to live alongside her husband, John, and enjoy her grandchildren.

Manuel

Manuel, my eldest brother, also quit school early. He explains it in his own words:

> I came out in the ninth grade to help my father. It was my decision to help the family. I was sixteen years old, and I got a job in construction in North Hollywood. I'd give my mother my paycheck, about eighty-five dollars a week. I also worked in the citrus packing house [that used

> to stand] on Truman [Road]; I was there for a long time. I also worked in the orchards with Dad; I even had my own [worker identification] number, and all that. My father was happy with me; I was following in his footsteps [but] he had me busting my ass! He got me a job at the Lemon Heights Association [packing house] on Mission Boulevard where my *compadre* [to be], Alberto Prado, worked. Everybody knew who I was; I was Berna's son, no one fucked around with me. I was a kid . . . My job was dumping boxes mostly. They'd arrive from the field and onto a conveyor belt. Cristina's father, Tony [who would become Manuel's father-in-law], was there. They were all good folk . . . I also worked with my mom in the tomato cannery on Brand [Street] . . . I was fourteen. [She would say,] *Ese mijo*! [Hey son!]. [I'd say,] Hi Mother!

My elder brother refers casually, in the words above, to the dilemma that he faced about 1945 when he was big enough to work. Even though we had only recently started operating Gil's Café, the family's finances were still at risk, and this contributed to his quandary regarding school vs. work. Being able bodied, should he get a job to help the family's bottom-line or should he go to school? Both he and Mary came to the realization, by the time they were teenagers, it seems, that our parents were constantly hanging by a thread, moneywise, and that they were expected to help by contributing to the family budget. To continue going to school at a time when you were physically able to work and help out became a major predicament. This contributed to his quitting and he says so. He also remembered helping out in other ways: "After Mary went away, I used to make beds, and I used to help Mom a lot."

Even so, in the days when Manuel worked in the canneries, an undeniable restlessness began accosting him, and he couldn't quite put a name on it at first. Even though he preferred to do manual labor like Dad, perform it besides him if he could, his mind tended to soar at times. "I used to go into town a lot," he said to me. "I was like a loner . . . You start digesting things that are bound to be," he said to me cryptically, which meant that he was imagining himself away from the family, doing something out of the ordinary. "I'd go to Rexall Drugs [on Maclay Boulevard and San Fernando Road] to read the magazines [which they put on display and I did it so often that] they even ran me out of there!" It seems that the magazines helped him open his mind and become attuned to the big wide world. He may have enjoyed doing ordinary manual labor, but the thoughtful and meditative mind that would mark him in his maturity was beginning to stir.

This is about the time he found an old, hand-cranked Victrola Record Player at the Goodwill Store on Celis Street, hindsight telling us he had an early yen for something out of the ordinary. Since he was already contributing money to the family budget, he asked Dad to buy it for him and he agreed. So they both walked to the store, Manuel pulling a Red Flyer Wagon. Dad purchased the music machine, and they both loaded the five-foot-high dark wooden cabinet on the red wagon and Manuel hauled it home, Dad walking alongside it to make sure it didn't tip over. My brother remembered feeling joyous being able to listen to his own music, fine music at that, a fondness for classical music that would only increase with time, Beethoven especially.

> I bought a needle for it . . . went back to the Goodwill Store and bought old Decca records [and played my music!] I was fucking singing about Kilarney and all that! [Can you believe that!] Afterward I found some classics [and played them to my enjoyment as well!].

When the packing house jobs came to an end, as they did seasonally, Manuel made a big decision all on his own. He visited a US Air Force recruiting office in town and apparently decided quickly enough. "I wanted to go see the world. I didn't want to be there [in San Fernando] anymore . . . I wanted to shift gears," he said to me.

> I remember I told my mom [about my joining the service and] she pitched a bitch. Then I talked with my father—it wasn't hard to talk to him. "I have a paper. I want you to sign because I want to join the service." [He replied,] "Ahh, you want to become a soldier?" I said yes. "And, what do you need?" Well, anyhow . . . my father said [to me], "That's what I did when I was young. I left my home and never went back!" He understood it and that was it. He and my mother signed [the form] and I took it back and they [the recruiters] engaged me real fast! I had to go to *el padre* [the local priest] to get a recommendation that I was a good boy! And one [more signature] from the police chief!

After basic training, Manuel became an air force supply specialist at the age of eighteen. Working out of Lackland Air Force Base in San Antonio, he was assigned to work with a team of supply auditors who were given the job of assessing the amount of surplus equipment the government possessed now that the war was over. In one case, at least, Manuel's team investigated multimillion dollar losses at an Arizona military installation, meaning, in his own words, that "part of it had to do with [their] having so much [*sic*] supplies they couldn't account for . . . [As a result,] a lot of guys got the hatchet, [were] discharged, or rotated elsewhere."

In the overseas phase of his military service, he was shipped to England arriving in the port of South Hampton. From there, he was assigned to Sealand in northern England near Wales where he served at a United States Air Force Base that had been supporting the celebrated American effort known as the Berlin Air Lift.[213] Manuel's role was to help manage the jet oil used by American aircraft in the airborne rescue.

On a personal level, he received an early lesson in ethnic identity issues and how complex and confounding they can be. While in England, he discovered, much to his surprise, that he had become a bloody Yank! Can you imagine that! His coming from a "Mexican" barrio in Southern California meant nothing to the local "blokes" whom he had a hard time understanding in the first place. They "talked different . . . even smelled different," and spent an awful lot of time drinking warm beer and singing as they freshened up their mugs, he noted with a grin. Manuel fondly recalled his visits to nearby Chester where he began to appreciate ancient towns; this particular one harking back to the days of the Romans. What's more, Manuel discovered that fellow Latino soldiers gathered in certain Chester pubs and so he rediscovered there, as he had discovered initially in the saloons of San Antonio, that "Mexicans" like him came in many guises including the "*manitos*" from New Mexico and the *Tejanos* from south Texas all of whom, he concluded, were a breed all their own, certainly different from California "Mexicans," to be sure. This is an introductory note on comments I make in my Afterword.

Upon his honorable discharge, Manuel returned home and groped toward a meaningful livelihood. The G.I. Bill[214] gave him the opportunity to study electronic circuitry, and this ultimately led to his opening a radio-television repair shop right in the heart of the barrio, on Kalisher Street, a few doors down from where we lived. In due course, however, he shut it down because far too many customers asked for credit pleading they couldn't pay up front. He evoked their words with bitterness, "I can't pay you right now, but at the end of the month, you'll have it." When they didn't keep their word, he'd go looking for them, and they'd hide. "They broke me, just like with my dad," he complained, harking back to the days that father likewise lost his shirt by extending too much credit. "I shut down the store and went to work as a technician for Pacific Mercury in Van Nuys," he added, but Pacific Mercury put up their shutters too soon after his arrival, and so Manuel returned to doing construction work and, in desperation, even washing dishes.

He started at the bottom of the restaurant business and worked his way to the top. This transformation took place in Anaheim, California, mostly at the Charter House Hotel located across from Disneyland. Within a ten-year span, Manuel went from dish washer to pantry cook (cold service, salads, dressings) to breakfast and lunch cook, the latter requiring "grilling mostly" but now for about three hundred to four hundred people, then with the mentoring help of a Polish chef named Frank, who supplied him with books, knives, and other cooking equipment, he became night chef preparing soups, pastas, more complicated roasting, etc., working three to four banquet rooms a night. He then took a job as the Gold and Silver Service chef at the Beverly Hills Hilton where he further perfected his French sauces and broadened his gourmet dishes. He graduated to an executive chef and worked in this capacity in several other exclusive eateries, including the Odyssey Restaurant in Granada Hills and the Cockatoo Inn in Hawthorne.

After working in other gold-plated eating houses on the West Coast like Marina Del Rey, Las Vegas, Anchorage, and Sitka, Manuel ended his thirty-year-restaurant career. It was time to be free of the pressures connected with a fast-moving kitchen and find a more quiet and meaningful life. With the help of his new wife, Pat, he devoted himself to selling merchandise to visitors touring out of the way desert towns on the edges of the Colorado River in southern Nevada. When I visited them, I observed their preference to spend quiet evening time, studying Vedanta, a Hindu philosophy, following an exhausting day, selling ladies' bags and specialty blankets to tourists.[215]

To this day Manuel speaks English and Spanish so fluidly that he can mimic Black American English and backcountry peasant Spanish without losing a beat.

Mike (Miguel)

My brother Mike, born three years after Manuel, also dropped out of school around ninth grade. Like Manuel, and different from Mary as we'll see below, he too felt he wasn't cut out to study much beyond grammar school. Of all my siblings, he must have felt the greatest discomfort sitting in a school desk by the time he reached ninth grade, trying to follow the teacher's explanation about grammar or some other theoretical topic.

"What a bore!" he must have said to himself many times! School was not his niche and many other activities hardly qualified either; for example, helping out with our family restaurant may have been more of a chore for him than anybody else in the family, Mother having to get after him more than anyone else. Like his elder brother, he didn't mind working hard, especially when his teenage body grew like a poplar tree rising on the side of a river. When he stopped growing, he stood six feet three inches, the tallest in the family spurring us to often remark, "How did you become so tall?"

As he got older, his aversion for high-blown thought increased more so, contrary to his elder brother, for example. Mike favored the practical side of life, setting his shoulder to the wheel, macho-like, especially if it meant displaying his strength and earning money at the same time. He also adopted an aggressive way of communicating, often using rough, cutting, language, off-putting his listeners' time and again, Mom and his sisters censuring him many times for this. Like the rest of us, he became bilingual in Spanish and English, more proficient in English than in Spanish, but his rough hewn Spanish was never free of *pachuco* terms and phrases which further aggravated the coarseness of his speech, yet he was able to give his English a very business-like tone when necessary. Needless to say, he forged his own path.

Mike knew enough about agricultural field work to avoid it. He may have not finished school, but he wasn't going to spend his life doing farm work either, the way we did as a family when he was a youngster. The closest he came to agricultural field work was as a *palero,* scattering chicken manure by hand with a shovel, standing on the platform of Jerry Avalos's truck as it slowly moved in between rows of lemon trees. He also sprayed insecticides into orange trees standing aboard a tank truck loaded with the chemicals, having fallen one day and broken his wrist. Mary remembers that he took advantage of his overgrown physical size to pass off as being older, and this is how he fastened onto a minor industrial job that turned into a business career.

He got hired by G. I. Rubbish, one of the many small waste-removal companies that sprang up in the valley after World War II. Young Mike was eager to test his young body against a he-man's job, so he took on the role of a "swamper" without a shrug. In those days, garbage trucks consisted of a driver's cab and a tall, heavy open metal box mounted on the rear platform designed to receive residential garbage or waste, also called a hopper. The hopper opened on top and on the side facing the curb with a vertical rectangular aperture through which trash barrels were introduced and emptied by hand. Instead of the light-weight plastic barrels of today, open-top oil drums were used in these days. They would sit on the curbs of valley homes, ready for pickup on trash day. Mike worked as the bottom swamper, whose job it was to lift with his arms a full trash barrel, weighing about eighty pounds (Manuel's guess), hoisting it up to the top "swamper," who would raise it further, empty it, and return it. This routine was done hundreds of times a day, six days a week. As a consequence, Mike must have become as strong as Charles Atlas, the famous body builder of those days. Manuel worked with him many times before embarking on his cooking career, and when they both worked as swampers, they would often compete to see who could tear a telephone directory apart with bare hands or bend a star wrench used for changing automobile tires.

Mike switched employers and went to work for United Rubbish, a trash-collection firm operating out of gritty, industrial Sun Valley near San Fernando. He again started out as a "swamper," but United Rubbish, headed by Phil Gentile, a son of Italy, purchased frontloading trucks featuring a large metal scooper that swung over the front of the truck cab, emptied itself into the trash box or hopper, and then swung back over the cab again, unfolding and ready for loading anew. A quick and eager learner, Mike soon took on the driver's job, and he also learned the streets of San Fernando Valley like the palm of his hand, confirming mentally without having to read a map, for example, that Arminta and Stagg Streets were sandwiched between Saticoy Street and Roscoe Boulevard near DeSoto Avenue. He'd rub the black, trimmed moustache under his nose and say to himself, "Yes, that's where Stagg Street is," and he'd drive in that direction and find his assigned route. I rode with him on many occasions when I'd come a-visiting, and he would take me along, pleased as can be, to show me how he worked. I observed him at work many times this way, crisscrossing the valley.

His boss, Phil, soon gave him a foreman's job because Mike learned the job better than anyone else and, what's more, he spoke Spanish. Most of Phil's employees were Mexican-born, so my brother's Spanish proved to be an asset for the company and for himself even though it was often mixed with *pachuco* words. For example, "Órale, ese, no me cabulées con tu cuento, carnal!" he said with a certain street swagger meant "OK, buddy, don't give me that line of boloney!" His Mexican-born coworkers, who probably recoiled on first exposure to this kind of lingo, would accept his patois good-naturedly enough, knowing full well it was part of sojourning in *pocho*[216] land where language communication had to differ from their own. In Rome, the Romans spoke their way, and in Los Angeles, the local "Mexicans" spoke their way too. The truth is that all of us Gil brothers used *pachuquismos* because it was part of the barrio culture that surrounded us but always best when we were out of Mother's hearing range, although Mike seemed to do so unconsciously.

In any case, my brother graduated to sales, and he successfully parlayed his knowledge of the business into a meaningful livelihood, which provided him and his family with a solid middle-class life and outlook. Despite his piqued demeanor, my brother never turned his back on his family whose members enjoyed celebrating many birthdays and other family feast days in his ample backyard, which always included a swimming pool, a worthy barbecue grill, and large quantities of beer.

When Phil Gentile lost control of his company and business, about 1971, my brother Mike organized his own waste removal firm, the Economy Disposal Company. He first began with a business partner and then on his own and, with the help of his new wife, Linda, who did payroll and bookkeeping, he built up the firm and operated it successfully for about twenty years, investing in equipment (frontloading trucks and containers) and expanding the customer base. When the tremors, known as the Northridge Earthquake of 1992, devastated the central section of the San Fernando Valley, creating mountains of debris that begged to be removed to landfills, Mike gained even more business. He had already shifted from residential service to commercial and construction waste removal, shifting to jumbo-sized containers that rolled off the back of specially accommodated trucks. So this naturally appointed windfall boosted Mike's sales but not for very long.

Mike's wife remembered that the city of Los Angeles obtained a federal grant to pay private contractors to haul earthquake debris from the city streets, instead of relying on established waste-removal companies, and this severely undercut Mike's business. His market was, in effect, taken away, forcing him to close his company as a result. We can note that the demise of Economy Disposal coincided with the approximate end of most other independent, family-owned, rubbish-removal companies in the San Fernando Valley, including the pioneering firm of G. I. Rubbish. It appears that the industry as a whole underwent a rationalization in which large enterprises swallowed smaller ones or forced them out. Thus, nationally based conglomerates like BFI and Allied Waste took over G. I. Rubbish and other valley trash haulers, and so we can state that my brother's company disappeared right along with the rest of them.[217]

Mike retired gracefully but was unable to fully enjoy his "golden years." He and his wife settled into a pleasant and sunny north valley trailer home court where he outfitted a small woodshop that took up a lot of his leisure time when he wasn't reading whodunit fiction or socializing with his fellow members of The Loyal Order of Moose, a service organization holding an active lodge in San Fernando. We celebrated one of Mom's most memorable birthday parties at the Moose Lodge. Mike contracted diabetes at age forty-four and died unexpectedly from its complications when he was seventy-three years old.

Carlos

Unlike my elder siblings, I didn't experience the need to quit school in order to help my parents with family expenses. Even though I was aware that Mary, Manuel, and Mike had relinquished their instruction beyond elementary school to help out with the family finances, I don't remember my parents asking me to do the same verbally or nonverbally. This may have been because I entered junior high in 1950, about eight years into our restaurant operation, so that the financial need for my first full-time paychecks may not have been as great as before. I may have helped matters by beginning to buy my own clothes and bear other personal expenses with a part time job at this time.

The educational path, which I followed beginning with my high school years was indeed atypical in contrast to my elder siblings. I pursued an academic track beginning in eleventh grade without any prompting from anyone that I can remember, but I do recall that eleventh grade was pivotal for me. Something drove me to graduate from San Fernando High School with the idea that I would attend college. I was treading forward blindly like most everyone else. Despite the sad scene at home, described elsewhere in these pages, I attended and graduated from Pierce Junior College in Woodland Hills, more of a cow college or an agricultural school in those days, but it suited my purposes, and it pulled me beyond high school. A special combination of circumstances led me to continue my academic studies at Seattle University, a Jesuit university, working my way through and borrowing funds at the same time. I thought I wanted to become a lawyer and so I took prelaw courses there, but I was also introduced to Latin American history courses and found I loved them; they spoke to me in a way no other courses did. As I've related in previous pages, I graduated from Seattle University in 1960 at which point I chose to go even further, being poised between law school in California and studying Latin America at Georgetown University, one of the first graduate school programs of this kind in the country. I chose the exotic route, Latin America, by attending and ultimately obtaining my master's degree in Latin American Studies from Georgetown University in Washington, DC—a city which struck me as utterly exhilarating.

The sum total of this heady training provided me with a cosmopolitan outlook as far as jobs were concerned. While studying at Georgetown, for example, I also worked as a research assistant in the Foreign Affairs Division of the Legislative Reference Service at the incomparable Library of Congress on Capitol Hill. My job was to field inquiries of a foreign or international nature for members of Congress. As a result, I became intimately familiar with the library's countless books and labyrinthine stacks. At the same time, at the university, I eagerly joined a network of youthful and promising individuals who, like me, sought to step up in the world by earning a degree from a prestigious university. These included graduate students from other American universities who came to study in the nation's capital, up and coming foreign students, and fresh staffers already working in the many US government agencies, all of them intent on working abroad in some capacity or returning to their home countries to fill special jobs waiting for them. This exciting international milieu impelled me at the age of twenty-six to join the United States Information Agency, whose job was to "tell America's story abroad" by way of its global network of binational centers.[218] This is how I came to work as a young cultural attaché in Tegucigalpa, Honduras, and later in Temuco, Chile, where my mother came to visit as part of her rejuvenation following my dad's death as I pointed out in earlier pages. On the eve of being reassigned to Cuzco, Peru, however, I decided to resign my job as a US Foreign Service Officer, a titanic decision, of course, and return to the United States with the intention of earning a PhD because I felt I needed the honing.

Returning home prematurely from Latin America ultimately led me on the path to becoming a history professor. My growing family and I moved from southern Chile to Columbus, Ohio, where I engaged a doctoral program at Ohio State University and then switched a year later to UCLA where, in due course, I obtained my PhD in History under the direction of James W. Wilkie, a lifelong mentor. This bolstered my obtaining a tenured position as a historian at the University of Washington in Seattle where I taught Modern Latin American History and, given the times, Mexican American History as well, responsibilities I endured long enough to make me want to retire in due course in order to be near my children.

In the interim, my new wife, Barbara Deane, and I opened a publishing business, which allowed us to launch *Cultural Diversity at Work*, one of the earliest trade publications concerning the importance of working intelligently with a diverse workforce in America. This also gave me a pleasant opportunity to employ my knowledge of Latin America and other developing countries to help train federal employees on improving their success when engaging foreign counterparts, especially Latin Americans. In good time I retired from that role as well.

Martha (Marta)

Martha stands out as a trooper in my mind. As we've noted in prior chapters, my dear sister suffered greatly during her teenage years under Mother's strict hand, but looking back, I can say that her difficulties with Mom didn't slow her drive one bit. She wanted to become somebody. She withstood her trials at home like a soldier in boot camp in order to continue advancing, almost entirely on her own through junior high and high school. I ought to have come to her aid, busy as I was with my own trials, but I can't recollect if I did or not, and she wasn't alive when I sat down to write these pages. If she had a mentor in school we never knew of it. Nevertheless, she wanted to reach for the stars, it seems, and was determined to ascend beyond her upbringing and be different from Mother too, without being disrespectful. We don't know of any instances in which Mother tried to place any foils on Martha's education, as she seems to have done with Mary, an absence that might indicate Mom's willingness to recognize her mistake regarding her eldest daughter's schooling. In any case, my younger sister graduated from high school the year after my father died and so it's entirely possible she may have viewed school work as a distraction from the dark atmosphere that pervaded our home in those days, just as her younger sister Emily would find solace in libraries later. All the same, Martha didn't push onto college probably because no one counseled her to do so, and my example may have seemed out of reach.

Emily reminded me that Marty, as we called her, began working outside of Mother's tortilla business in her senior high school year. Her first paid working post, probably taken after graduating from high school, seems to have been as a janitor at the new farmers' insurance office near our home, and I probably helped her obtain that job because I worked there in the same capacity the year before I left for Seattle, and I remember seeing Marty with dust mop in hand. This is about the time that she was struggling fiercely with Mother's micro-supervision and battling her first major outbreaks of psoriasis at the same time, a skin disorder that became disabling at times for her. In her search for medical attention, my sister met a dermatologist who would become an important caregiver and mentor at the same time, alongside his wife. This was Dr. Roy Hiscock and his spouse, Florence, a child psychologist.

Marty accepted a governess position inside the Hiscock home in Eagle Rock probably in exchange for dermatological care, possibly psychological attention too, given the constant skirmishing she had experienced with

Mother. Emily, who visited Marty for a week during this time, confirmed she took care of the three Hiscock children and, in the process, eagerly took lessons, it seems, on how to live with a touch of refinement, coaching no doubt received from Mrs. Hiscock, who hailed from one of the most distinguished families in America.

Appreciating a graceful stylishness in life became, in fact, one of Marty's personal emblems. She applied her newfound edification on her clothing, including texture and color, hairstyle, jewelry, home decoration, food preparation, speech and communication, and so on. She, in effect, became gentrified but didn't turn her back on us, her plebeian relatives, because she could toggle from one mode to the other in a matter of seconds, including language switching from English to Spanish and acting out her pent-up rebelliousness in comical style. I remember seeing her dancing on a table top one time, just hollering away. She made us laugh over the years at her expected disapproval of our "ruffian" ways, which most of us accepted as a fact of life and only grudgingly accepted her advice when she gave it. For example, one day she took Emily out to lunch at a distinguished establishment on La Cienaga Boulevard, noted for its prime rib and took the opportunity to instruct her younger sister on how to carry herself. Always saying, "Sit straight [and] don't bend over." Marty drilled at Emily, who could only respond with a crinkly smile. Looking back on this moment with her older sister, Emily believed she had learned to bend forward "as a result of the nun's training," referring to her odious days in Catholic school as discussed earlier, so she was thankful for her big sister's counsel. Marty found me as a piece of work too, always bemoaning my preference for simple and unassuming clothing styles. "God, Carlos, how can you wear *that*?"

Martha expanded her outlook and concentrated her search for occupations in and around central Los Angeles at the conclusion of her Hiscock period, which among other things allowed her to become accustomed to living away from her mother. In effect, she never again worked in San Fernando but did return to live near the barrio many years later as noted below. She took a job as a clerk in an insurance company for a short time and then gained employment with the County of Los Angeles. By this time her efforts at self-improvement had boosted her sense of self, all of which became more evident in her letters to me, exposing a fluid and confident writing style comparable to any college graduate in English. She acquired the habit of reading and even joined the Book of the Month Club, which supplied her with hard back copies of titles chosen by the club editors, some of which she passed on to me like Samuel Eliot Morison's classic,

The Oxford History of the American People (1965), which I apparently had an eye for because she wrote on the back page, "To my most beloved brother, finally I'm giving in, hoping you will use it to its fullest in remembrance of better days, of days gone forever."

Her clerical and organizational skills confirmed her position in the Sheriff's Department as personnel representative, a post she commanded for many years located in the old Hall of Justice building on Temple and Broadway in Los Angeles. According to a lifelong friend and workmate, Martha's job was to help people find the right job inside the Sheriff's office, recruit for new officers, help the applicants through the process, interview them, proctor their examinations, and hand the successful applicants onto the Training Bureau in Whittier for final handling.[219]

Marty remained mindful of the hurdles she had to clear to the very end. She felt proud to live as an independent woman, on her own, even if she had to battle to stay healthy. She had her good and bad moments and didn't take the good ones for granted either. In one of her letters to me, after I moved to Seattle, she wrote thus:

> Carlos, as you observed yourself, I am well and my psoriasis is a matter of a couple of lite [sic] patches . . . my skin is smooth and clear.

I sometimes cannot believe my well-being—Oh yes, I scream, rant, and fight vigorously. I no longer have any apparent problems of expressing myself. I do not believe I am happy, but I am not unhappy either. I suppose I'm just going through each day, living it with the least amount of chagrin. It's a reasonable formula at the present time . . .

I am very proud of my achievements in view of the road or trail I've left behind me. Carlos, you've seen me fall flat on my face. I'm OK. I'm making it now. Next year I will come up to Seattle; I want to see the leaves turn in the autumn. We'll see.

Marty retired early from her county job due to recurring illnesses on top of her psoriasis. Coincident with her early leave, she and her new husband, John Murillo, our Mott Street neighbor, purchased a home outside of the barrio proper but no more than a mile from Mott Street where we grew up. In their new home, in between skin treatments and other medically related therapy, she held court, so to speak, when she was still well. We all visited: we, her siblings, Mom, and other family members and friends. We spent golden moments in her home that way. When the Angel of Death began to hover around, she reordered her document files and made sure that everything was in order, right down to a T. On February 15, 1999, Mary left me a telephone message at home in Seattle, informing me that "Martha does not seem to be responding," and so I flew to her bedside. Not long after, Marty passed on to "the other dimension of time and space," as she put in an earlier letter to me.

Rick (Enrique)

My younger brother, Rick, was fourteen years old when Dad died. This means that if Rick held any memories of his father, when Dad was still reasonably well, these would have been crowded out by recollections of him at his weakest. In other words, the last five years of Dad's life coincided with Rick being between nine and fourteen years old, when Dad's health was declining fast. It's thus fair to say that he didn't experience a strong and vigorous father. He was too young to get Dad's stamp of approval, and he wasn't alive at the time of this writing either for him to answer any of my questions.

In any case, these are the thoughts that came to us, his siblings, when we looked back on our brother Rick. Manuel may have been the first to make this observation and the rest of us more or less echoed the sentiment over the years. He dropped out of school in ninth grade, coinciding more or less with Mother's blackest moments due to Dad's passing away. Rick grew rebellious as he entered teenage, cut school frequently, palled around with the wrong kids in the barrio, and got into trouble with the law early on, predictably so. Mom's ability to place a halter on him, so to speak, if she could have done such a thing, was extremely limited, given her own emotional condition at the time. His early brushes with local authorities landed him in one "honor farm" or another, and this is the unfortunate pathway that led him to young manhood, bothered by numerous gripes and disadvantages. These circumstances made it necessary for us, his elder siblings, to intervene, with Mother's acquiescence, of course.

We decided to remove him from the barrio. I was on my way to Georgetown University, in Washington DC, in the late summer of 1960, when the family decided to do something about our youngest brother. He had just spent an interlude living with Manuel and his growing family in Anaheim, as a way of providing him some male supervision in those critical days, and so the opportunity to disconnect him from his *malas compañías*, as Mother would say, meaning the wrong circles rooted in our part of San Fernando, arose with my trip. Having just graduated from Seattle University, I was driving, in those days, by myself despite having just gotten married, from the West Coast to the nation's capital for the first time in order to attend graduate school, and so we, in the family, agreed that he would help me drive. This is how he accompanied me on my first expedition across the country and how he came to live under my supervision for a handful of years.

Rick and I drove into Washington DC in my 1953 Chevrolet Bel Air sedan packed full of mostly my personal belongings. It was a memorable trip for the two of us, aided in part by the easy relationship that we developed with each other right away despite my previously long absences from him and the rest of the family. Having to survive on the road and then in a strange city knowing no one and having little cash to spare, we relied on each other, shared everything, and cooperated in getting settled in the capital city as quickly as possible. We lived in our car for a couple of weeks and then shared with a gay couple an apartment perched over a liquor store on Seventeenth Street N.W. about half an hour's walk from the White House. It was a new world for the two of us, but I had to be ready for my first day in graduate school at the beginning of fall quarter, and so we settled in quickly enough. In the three years that we lived together or near each other, Rick always honored our bond. He never defied me, nor did he break any rules that I might have laid down. He didn't pursue a vocational career that I placed in front of him but in the end, I came to feel very close to my little brother during these years, and we remained close for the rest of our lives too.

In order to stay alive and get settled quickly, we took a job together, right away. We became parking lot employees and got into the practice of wearing heavy green cotton uniforms with the letters "PMI" sewn onto the front, upper left of our jacket. Men and women who drove their automobile to the heart of the city for work or leisure would leave us their car, and we would park it in an appropriate space on the lot and return it when necessary. If we served our customers quickly and courteously, they might tip us, and so Rick almost always earned more tips than I ever did. His good looks punctuated by his twinkly brown eyes set under a mane of dark curly hair always gave him an advantage over my duskier skin, straighter hair, and muted personality. His quick smile vs. my less responsive attitude always made him the winner, which meant, among other things, that the girls always noticed him first. The parking lot where we worked was located two blocks from the White House, and so we would often imagine the older, well-dressed men who left their high quality automobiles with us as being high government executives engaged in ultra important business. "Look, Chuck," he would tell me, as he spied a certain returning customer from afar, who always dressed in a drab trench coat, "Here comes the director of the CIA, go get his Dodge! ¡Ándale, Bro! Run!" he would urge me, aware of my reluctance to do so. At the same time that I quit my parking-lot job within the first year, Rick continued working for the same company during the entire time I spent at Georgetown University. When I departed the city in order to take up my first overseas assignment, Rick stayed behind in the same job, and though I hated to leave him, I had to move on. We said good-bye at National Airport (later renamed in the memory of Ronald Reagan) as he and Victoria, his new bride, had come by to see us off, my family and me. He returned to San Fernando with his wife within a year, ready to open a new chapter in his life.

In San Fernando, he relied on his brothers, Manuel and Mike, to get him a job. They shoehorned him into the rubbish business, not unexpectedly, because this is what they knew best and where they had an "in," Manuel not yet starting his cooking career. With Rick's ample automotive experience, he became a truck driver for United Rubbish, a firm already mentioned, and with Mike's timely advice, he became a key employee, although, to tell the truth, Rick tended to resist advice from his elder brothers. He was bilingual in English and Spanish, and this made him slightly more attractive to his non-Spanish speaking bosses because non-English speaking Mexican labor was fundamental in their firm too. But while they may have expected him to help bridge any communication gaps, Rick was more likely to let the bosses figure things out for themselves. Helping them was not his thing.

Rick tended to move around, job-wise. He worked for United Rubbish as mentioned above while Mike was still working there and then for Mike himself after he separated from United and opened his own Economy Disposal. The two brothers couldn't work closely for very long. Manuel had already started his long line of cooking jobs, so he couldn't help Rick at this point, and so my little brother went off on his own, working for other waste collection companies in the valley, including G.I. Rubbish. For most of his working life, back in the valley, he remained employed by the local waste-removal industry and even purchased his own truck to try to start his own trash company, an effort that lasted only a short period of time, according to his widow.[220] She informed me that at one point, he decided to look for work in Las Vegas, but when this effort didn't pan out, he settled back into San Fernando eventually opening up a bathtub refinishing business. There were stories that he became involved with underworld circles, but none of them could be confirmed. With the assistance of one or two Mexican employees, he made the most out of this effort for about five years, a venture that became his last major shot at earning a living. In a manner reminiscent of our father, who tearfully admitted to Mom that he could no longer work, Rick too arrived at a point, where he could no longer make the effort. His poor health due to diabetes hastened this sad moment, as with my dad. Rick looked most like my Dad, in fact, with his *chinito* hair.

For all intents and purposes, he retired at the age of sixty, approximately, and settled into a sedentary life in the Kalisher Street building, where our family lived through many gloomy episodes decades earlier. Living on a shoe string budget, in a basic but tidy home kept up by his loyal spouse, Rick sought moments of enjoyment whenever and however he could in these final years even as his diabetic condition continued to diminish his ability to see and walk on his own. In his later years, he came to enjoy cooking pasta dishes, especially, and sharing them with us from time to time, celebrating his culinary ability in this way. With his ever-deferent wife by his side, who excelled with her own line of Mexican dishes, Rick also indulged his newfound interest in cultural and historical topics as presented on television like The History Channel and Discovery.

When I happened to be visiting, in his last days, the most important activity that engaged him was to come to see me. He would make the three-block excursion on foot to Mother's house on Huntington Street an exercise that consumed nearly all of his physical stamina for that day; I would return him home by automobile. Just as I can remember Rick when he was a young fellow dashing off in the Washington DC parking lot to retrieve the "CIA director's" Dodge because the important man was crossing the street and coming in our direction, I also remember him crossing the street to arrive at Mother's house in his last days. Blinded by the sun, he would wear a pair of dark wrap-around sun glasses under a wide brimmed reed hat that flapped in the hot breeze and peer anxiously in both directions before crossing Huntington Street in order to reach Mom's house. Like Mike, he also died unexpectedly from diabetes complications at the end of 2005.

Soledad (Sally)

Soledad walked a smoother pathway than any of us. Even though she was old enough to experience and bear witness to Mother's darkest days, as we've seen already, Sally reacted to them with an inner calm, her sunny cheerfulness keeping the gloom in check. She was just stamped that way from the start. Her sisters chided her for being so genial and sweet, seemingly unaffected by the waves of exasperation that roiled us from time to time. Even Emily, who was younger and closest to her in age, begrudged her for decades. Fortunately, for all of us, Sally's bighearted optimism came to the rescue when Mother's advancing years required someone to care for her. And she hardly ever complained. That was Sally.

In so far as working for a living, she was ready to do so. She had spent countless hours toiling in Mom's tortilla shop during her teen years, and so when she attained liberation through marriage, she took a job at Price Pfister located in nearby Pacoima, regarded by some as the largest foundry on the West Coast at the time. Faucets were their calling card and so my sister learned all about plating bathroom fixtures, getting acid all over her clothes and discovering that she liked the job because it exposed her to a variety of people. In the end, "It was a big change from the *tortillería*," she remembered more than anything else.

She was tired of factory employment after about three years and concluded she deserved "a better class of a job." Pat, her sister-in-law, recommended she investigate the nursing field and the possibility of wearing a uniform in a hospital—after all, she liked uniforms. Soledad didn't lose much time and soon applied at nearby Olive View, which had recently been reorganized from a tuberculosis sanatorium into an acute care hospital. "We wanted our share of the American Dream," are the words she used to explain why she felt impelled to work after three years of plating bathroom faucets. She and Javier, her first husband, had been renting a home, and with two daughters already on hand, they wanted to begin owning their own quarters like everyone else. In next to no time, she learned she was accepted as a nurse's aide and soon found herself doing the heavy lifting that the regular nurses dread. For about a year, she helped elderly patients with their bathing and toileting requirements, feeding tubercular patients who couldn't do so on their own, transporting them in wheel chairs from one end of the hospital to another, and so on. Then she headed for something "better," she said. This would be physical therapy work.

Soledad was admitted into "rehabilitation" at Olive View. As a physical therapy technician, under the supervision of physical therapists who befriended her readily, she began working with patients in the therapy gym and otherwise administering therapeutic exercises, applying hot or cold packs on affected muscles, employing ultrasound or electrical stimulation therapy, keeping a record of the various remedies employed, and so on. Seventeen years went by with a wink of an eye, so to speak, and it all came to a halt. "I slipped at work and hurt my back!" She was unable to lift anything of any consequence for a long time after that. This is the way her medical career ended, at age thirty-nine.

Her working life, however, did not cease. She tried her luck as an art-gallery saleslady in mostly Anglo Woodland Hills where one of her sons was working but found it boring mostly because the art store attracted few customers although she did learn a lot about art history. She then applied for a teacher's aide job at Dyer School in nearby Sylmar and another ten years went by quickly. She told me she loved the educational environment partly because she was required to take child development courses in college. "If it hadn't been for Algebra, I would have gotten my associate in arts degree!" she protested decades later with a touch of regret. Soledad would have been proud to own that university title. Nonetheless, she fitted right in with the first-grade teachers at Dyer School for whom she worked and, under their supervision, she helped in the instruction of the children, enjoying every minute.

At age fifty, Sally devoted herself to providing full-time care for the members of her own family. She had already rented out her own home in order to move in with Mom in 1995 to take care of her, ministering at the same time to our ailing sister, Martha, who lived nearby at this point while babysitting her third grandson, Esteban. For thirteen years, Sally cared for Mother as she grew progressively senile and finally died, her husband generously acquiescing and standing by her side. After Mother's funeral, the two were finally able to pursue their own married life in the desert communities, north of San Fernando, and care for each other in their advancing years.

Emily a.k.a "Country" (Emilia)

Emily, the youngest, grew and matured against some strong headwinds as we've seen. Mother's psychological decline and comeback occurred during Emily's late childhood and early teenage years, creating a condition that only pummeled her entry into early adulthood. She didn't marry well because Alfonso, her first husband, Mexican-born, disregarded her needs, to say the least, according to everyone in the family, and so Emily felt obliged to continue fending for herself until she met Ken, her second husband, an Anglo, who died when she was thirty years old. She met Schultzie, her third husband, a Polish American, five years later, and thus began a long and deserved reparatory phase in her life.

Like her sisters, Emily's first work experience began at home. The reader will remember that she enjoyed helping out at Mom's tortilla shop, in part, because it helped reduce her bickering with Mother, and she also enjoyed the grown-up conversations with the women who made the tortillas, whose life lessons brought her some needed perspective.

She moved on, however. Sometime during her first marriage, she obtained a job at Price Pfister, though not at the same time that her sister, Soledad, worked there. Emily remembered that in addition to manufacturing faucets, they also helped "anodize the O rings" for the Apollo space suits.[221] She clearly recalled that when "the 1969 shuttle went up, we were given time off from work" at the Panorama City plant in celebration, referring to the Apollo 11 flight that reached the moon in the summer of that year.

When the company lost the O-Ring contract, she changed her line of work and began a lengthy period of employment in health care, much like her sister, Soledad. She started out as an aide at the same Olive View Sanatorium where her sister had worked, where her job was to care for geriatric patients suffering from tuberculosis. She remembered that one of her tasks was moving the patients into a sunny spot before giving them a bath followed by lunch and then more sun in the afternoon. The work was heartbreaking because of the infirmities involved. What began to weigh her down more than anything else was the attitude of some of her fellow caregivers who in her eyes weren't sufficiently devoted to their patients and when a "sweet old man" died in her arms, she decided it was time to move on. This is about the time she met Ken, her second husband, and with her children, they all moved around the country, first to Arizona, then Illinois, and then back to the San Fernando Valley, whereupon she returned to work as a nurse's aide. Working for a temporary medical workers' bureau, she served in various hospitals and clinics in the valley and found assignments in burn units, emergency rooms, geriatric wards, and so on. Ken's death dragged her down emotionally for an extended length of time, which coincided with her need to live in small, intimate communities. This led her to Santa Fe, New Mexico, where she eventually emerged out of her own black period much as our mother had done decades earlier.

It seems that her psychological and social renewal coincided with her meeting Schultzie, the cabinet maker and lapidary, who would become her third husband. Their mutual compatibility showed up right away, and the two made a common bond that took them to one of the most relaxed communities in New Mexico where eventually Emily became known as "Country," specializing in palm readings and collecting "over a thousand" hand prints to analyze and interpret. At the time of this writing, the two of them continued to lean on each other as they explored the magnificent desert around them in search of gemstones to hone and polish at home.

The Second Generation as the Bridging Generation

By my logic we, the members of the second generation in the Gil family, acted as a bridging generation. We acted as the generational bridge between our old *viejos*, who came from Mexico and the *jóvenes*, the youngsters, members of the generation whom we seeded in America, the third generation, which we could call the anchoring generation. They helped secure "the bridge" on the forward or American edge, anchoring it, as it were, across the "water," so to speak.

Our immigrant forefathers arrived, heaped with their cultural baggage from Mexico that told them how to speak Spanish, how and what you worshiped, how to relate and communicate to others, how and why to trust someone, how to prepare food, which music to enjoy, how to dress when going out, how to treat people older than you, how to save face, and so on. We could consider all this as the cultural "anchor" on the opposite side of the "water," the Mexican side, and so we, the second generation, the "bridge," transmitted some of these values (we couldn't transfer all of them) to the third generation, who would in turn "anchor" them, so to speak, in order to transmit a hybrid share containing a larger dose of American cultural ways to their descendants. This is, of course, an elementary explanation of assimilation.

The Gil's as Mexican Americans (ca. 1957)

Chapter 15

A Glimpse at the Third Generation

The Employment Experiences of the Third Generation

BERNABÉ AND GUADALUPE generated twenty-eight grandchildren, twenty-seven alive at the time of this writing, the anchoring generation, as we just christened it above. Only a portion of them, however, came to know all the family pioneers discussed in Parts I and II of this book, but all of them did become familiar with Grandma Lupe, some more closely than others. Most of them didn't get to know my father, Bernabé, because he died so early. Only a handful remembers him for this reason, and only a slightly larger portion may be able to recall our *tíos*, Miguel and Pascual, the men who figured prominently in the early lives of those of us in the second generation. My own children and my nieces and nephews attended their funerals, and that may be their longest lasting memory of them. Furthermore, only a small portion of the third generation became an adult in the barrio that saw us grow up.

The members of the third generation range in age from forty to sixty one at the time of this writing, and it's safe to say that they escaped many or most of the experiences that befell the members of the second generation in the Gil family as described in these pages. With few exceptions, they avoided sleeping three or four to a bed like my brothers and I did when we were growing up on Mott Street, and they all missed the trips "up north" to help their parents harvest fruits and vegetables. The father of some of the boys in this generation who himself long labored in the fields under a blazing sun vowed his sons would never stoop that way, and they didn't. My children and my nephews and nieces didn't come to know the scores of Mexican immigrant workers legal and illegal as we did back in the 1950s, nor did they witness federal agents in trench coats and dark hats barging in to snatch undocumented workers, some of them friends. They didn't have to press their case to be allowed to stay in school as Mary did with her mother back in the 1940s. The fact is that their lives advanced quite differently from ours.

How different were they? This final chapter offers you, the reader, a glimpse of this third generation if only to hint at the forward movement that our family may have achieved. For this reason, my observations below parallel some of the reflections shared about the second generation, namely the degree of their assimilation into American culture. Said differently, I address the apparent cultural positioning of the members of the third generation between being Mexican and American and I also offer notes about the work they've done for their livelihood, so far, in an effort to reveal occupational progression.

So, did our descendants in the third generation become fully American about ninety years after our ancestors first crossed the border into the United States?

The answer to this subjective question perforce has to be . . . subjective. Yes, they became fully American but with some interesting reservations and stipulations. If we use language to measure a person's biculturalism or lack of it, then it's safe to say that the members of the third generation in our family became far more American than the second generation because most of them lost the use of Spanish, our mother tongue. The reader will remember that this variability also occurred to some extent in the second generation, some losing more Spanish than others.

Here are some examples regarding language. First of all, the eldest in the third generation is a woman whose bilingual and bicultural capabilities serve her superbly well at the job, the same when she visited back-country towns in Mexico in search of her father's relatives. I consider her the most "Mexican" in her generation next to one of her cousins, who also employs Spanish on the job without a hitch and, in her twenties, ran off to live in Guadalajara for a handful of months on her own. These two, among the older ones in this generation, were special that way. A small handful of members of this generation use Spanish on the job often, even when they don't fortify their Spanish competency by visiting Mexico or studying it formally, yet they manage quite well with it, nevertheless. A few others manage less well with the mother tongue but they keep on trying because they're cornered into it by virtue of the growth of Latinos in America's workforce (they find themselves having to interpret for friends or fellow work mates) but they know it's important for them as well. The rest in this generation, the majority, including the youngest, appear to feel quite comfortable in their monocultural outlook on life, speaking only English, on par with most Anglo-Americans, making little or no effort at preserving Spanish.

Why did these latter members of the anchoring or third generation let go of their Spanish and over look any observable linkages to their mother culture? The answers here, again, can be multiple and tricky to fathom. They may have been raised away from the barrio and from the extended family. The degree of Mexican-ness in their parents may have played another part but, more critically, their willingness to consciously and consistently make an effort to pass on Spanish and cultural values and practices learned from the immigrant forefathers apparently gave way to the forces of assimilation, American culture being powerful in many ways. Then, of course, we have to consider the openness and willingness of the children themselves to receive and embrace these values and practices, including their readiness to fight off peer pressure to conform to being American like everyone else. Accounting for the cultural ways of an adult, even within one family, can be challenging, indeed.

The level of personal determination to command Spanish once again and to regain knowledge about Mexican culture is also a factor for the third generation. One member, who was actually bilingual at age seven, practically lost all of her Hispanic cultural and linguistic skills by the time she was twenty, but decided to relearn her ancestor's language and did so with steely determination and now uses it in her work. A couple others have done something similar perhaps with less intensity.

These examples illustrate a "diversity" work place advantage that became available to the members of the third generation not offered to the second. By virtue of its changing demography, American society showed signs of casting off its strongly rooted ethnocentrism and finally warmed up a tad to the advantages of "cultural diversity" by the end of the twentieth century. This encouraged a willingness in some American organizations to recognize and reward bilingual capabilities that could be applied at the job, to the benefit of the organization and to the community being served, and this became an incentive to maintain the mother tongue, at least. Member of our third generation have felt this pressure.

Let's not forget a fundamental lesson here. Adult immigrants who arrive today on our shores or at our borders usually retain their cultural ways to the fullest extent possible. This is only human and it's what our ancestors did nearly ninety years ago, and it is good they did. The children of these immigrants, even those born abroad, can be expected to assimilate very quickly and become American although the process may be uneven and the factors involved may be countless, as we've seen in the case of our second generation. This willingness to maintain the old cultural ways fades with each generation.

Our family is already forming its fourth and fifth generations. These family members will most probably become plain vanilla Americans, culturally speaking, except for their bronze skin tones, and they'll be far removed from the experiences recounted in this book, the fourth generation already including members who look one hundred percent Anglo or very nearly so. They'll be part of the new America that no longer looks like the advertisments from the 1950s where blonde and blue eyed people dominated the scene. These considerations are quite relevant in our time because conservative-minded Americans complain that "foreigners" hold on to their cultural roots too long and harm our nation as a result. These people are barking up the wrong tree in part because they're unable to distinguish a Chinese immigrant and a Chinese American or a Mexican immigrant from a Mexican American. They ignore the process of assimilation. With much bias and little reason they attack newcomers for retaining their culture and language which is an unfair thing to do. They've not done their homework.

The force of assimilation is powerful in any country. This is true in the United States, given the overwhelming vigor of the English language itself, combined with the stalwart Anglo-centric world view that dominates the power centers of cultural production in the United States. The media, of course, is only a mirror to this orientation, and few Americans take these influences into account. The Spanish language media, including radio, television, and the Internet, is growing by leaps and bounds, thanks goodness, but it still stands apart at this time because it aims its information and services mostly to the immigrant generation, not the American generations.

I hope my descendants become strong-minded enough to acquire a broadened world view which is so essential to the globalized world in which we live today. I hope they embrace biculturalism or multiculturalism in some form because I want them to become part of a bulwark against the old fashioned, narrow minded mono-culturalism that dominated America when we were children. This more expansive outlook can only be gained by studying or being exposed to other cultures and languages, their parents facing the responsibility of giving them some guidance. In any case, a "brave new world" awaits them, to be sure.

The Employment Experiences of the Third Generation

As a way of extending a look at the employment experiences within the Gil family across three generations, I asked my children, nephews, and nieces to submit a statement to me, if they so chose, about their most satisfying employment experiences. Here are the testimonials of those who responded although unfortunately they don't always reveal the fullness of their occupational contributions to America:

> **(Female, sixty-one):** My favorite job was working at UCLA; those were the best twenty years of my life, not only because I worked with wonderful people within the office, but we all worked very well together like a fine-tuned machine, including the supervisors. They always pitched in to get the work done, which is called team work! No one wanted to shine more than the other; we worked as one. Even though my job title was an administrative assistant, a large part of my job was dealing with the public, which, to me, is very rewarding. It must be a gift given to me at birth. Some people do not like customer service, but that is my favorite job to do.
>
> **(Female, fifty-six):** I'd have to say that the most enjoyable job I've had is teaching exercises at the gym, spin classes. I love the way exercise makes me look and feel. I also enjoy the health and social benefits I get from it. I enjoy helping others pursue their goals too. Creating the class and the music I use gives me a challenge. I fit in well, and have a feeling of pride and accomplishment. I attribute the class to my loss of forty lbs and keeping it off! It's a lot of fun.
>
> **(Female, fifty-four):** My best job would be what I do now: Food Service Manager with LAUSD at an elementary school. I enjoy being around young children. I also enjoy the technical part of my job, using computers. We went from handwriting reports to ordering food by phone and much more, all [kitchen-related needs] going through school mail a few years ago to everything now being done by computer. Production, counting, claiming, ordering food, and identifying students are all done by computer now.

(Male, fifty-three): The most rewarding, fulfilling, and most challenging job I ever had was as a patrol deputy/training officer. I had it for four years, and I loved it! To teach these new, young, and eager deputies how to become safe, competent, and conscientious patrol deputies in this crazy, dangerous world we live in, was quite an experience. To slowly see the confidence build up in their faces over time (six-month training period) was always the best part.

(Female, fifty-three): When I first started as a bus driver at the age of twenty-one, I loved that I was paid to drive all over the city and talk to so many different kinds of people. I was outside, without really being outside. It was still a nontraditional position for a woman at that time, and I liked that. The job has had its ups and downs, but after more than thirty years, this good union job has provided my family a great living. And, after a day's work, I feel like I've actually accomplished something because many, many people got to where they needed to go because I came to work that day.

(Male, fifty-three): My best job was with the Marines. I liked to be active in physical training, shooting at the rifle range, traveling to different countries, meeting new people, see different sights. I am very proud of my service time. Sometimes it's a very lonely experience, but you take the good with the bad. Being a grandpa has been my best job lately, silly as it sounds. In some ways I get a second chance to do things I may not have done when I was raising my own family. I love to interact with my two grandkids, play catch, go camping with them, or just listen to how they see the world, from a child's eyes. My latest and longest job has been a mailman for the past thirty-one years . . . It pays the bills and meeting people along the way is good too. No job is perfect, but I'm outside on my own, doing an important task. Getting the US mail through is valuable now and in the past.

(Female, forty-nine): My best jobs have been working in

companies with a large Latino population, usually immigrants that speak very little English. I feel my strongest contributions have been helping these employees understand and maneuver the complex processes and systems within the business.

(Female, forty-eight): My best job (so far) is serving as an industrial appeals judge. This is an interesting and intellectually challenging job, and it gives me the opportunity to serve the public, which is something I have always wanted to do.

(Male, forty-eight): The most fulfilling job I've had was a patient escort at Vanderbilt University Hospital 1986–'87. This is where I wheel chaired people to and from their room, for their arrivals and their departures. I would run into people for years after who would reminisce about their stay there or about loved ones who stayed at the hospital. They were always so thankful for the friendship or the conversation held at that time.

(Female, forty-seven): My best job was the first job I had after college: working as a city code enforcement officer. The respect I received from the public and the actual "salary" was a truly rewarding experience because of how I grew up (involved with gangs). What was even more rewarding was the comradeship I came to know at that job. There were approximately 150 staff members that I came to know, and they all became "family" to me. I treasured that experience because it gave me the same kind of closeness I felt as I was growing up with my own biological family in San Fernando. I still feel as close to those people as I do to my own family. I doubt if I will ever find a better job than that one.

(Female, forty-seven): I would have to say my best job was with X Cruises where I was a revenue support agent although I was responsible for other areas too. We also created a new department, a fraud unit, within the company in which I took part.

(Male, forty-five): He worked mainly at Yosemite for seven years before becoming disabled. He got to talk to people from all over, from many nations, and this really helped him. He worked as a special events coordinator when Steve Jobs came by to get married, and so he was proud he organized special activities for this event. My son loved this job and excelled in it. (This statement was provided by his mother.)

(Male, forty-five): My best job was at X restaurant . . . It was my first real job after I had been in the restaurant business for several years and gained experience; this is where I was able to showcase all my talents as a young man: leadership, organization, and people skills; it was just a great period in my life. I met a lot of fun people, worked side by side with my cousin . . . able to see him grow into a man as well. I met my wife there; this is where I really began my fatherhood as well. Then I faced the challenge of leaving what was a great position, and a very safe one at the time, to pursue . . . a career with Y company . . . selling, marketing, and distributing food products to restaurants, healthcare, and educational facilities, lodging establishments, etc. That was quite a few years ago.

(Male, forty-four): He worked in various jobs until his aunt Martha helped straighten him out a bit by encouraging him to work as a security guard at a bank. For about five years he took various assignments from different protective agencies until the day he was shot by a bank robber, unfortunately. He then became disabled. (Statement provided by his mother.)

(Female, forty-three): My best job was being a barista. I always felt a part of the community I worked in, like I contributed to the vibe of the people in that community. They came from all walks of life, from a homeless person to the mayor or a police man to a teacher. I knew the community from its political marches to the death of a local police officer's son. It's amazing what you can learn about people by simply observing, not saying much, just being aware and staying in their presence.

(Male, forty-three): One of my favorite jobs was being a grill cook, and then I worked for a company that made special parts for the stealth bomber, where I ran the toolshed and was in charge of special tool bits that cut metal, steel, and titanium. I also worked for an art company, where I ran shipping and receiving until the company moved away. They offered me a position, but unfortunately, my dad was very ill and then passed away . . . Now I work for a company . . . where I drive a company vehicle and go everywhere: Long Beach, Los Angeles, Norwalk, Bellflower, Riverside, and so on. I love this job the best . . . Life is all good. I get to see a lot of cool places, and the money is OK, better than a lot of the others. And my boss says I'm the best driver he's ever had because I'm a kick-ass driver who takes care of business. I'm happy to be here.

(Male, forty-three): I consider my current job my most satisfying job to date. I'm in my early forties and have worked for a large phone company for over sixteen years. It provides me with a generous paycheck and insurance benefits for my family. I provide various customer-service-related tasks over the phone in an office environment. I get a great inner reward/satisfaction helping my fellow brother/sister complete their work. When I was younger, I loved the feeling I got when I was surrounded by my family every week at get-togethers. Twenty to thirty aunts, uncles, cousins, and friends of the family would congregate just because we wanted to. I get that same feeling from my office environment and the coworkers around me. My first job was special to me at a ripe age of fourteen in the summer of 1981. I was hired as a store clerk at a local mom-pop grocery store called Country Cousins. I considered the owner a father figure in my life when I had none. My parents divorced when I was eight or nine. With many people coming through that corner store, it helped me satisfy the social bug engrained in me by previous family gatherings.

(Male, forty-one): I started in the restaurant industry as a dish washer. Then I moved my way all around the kitchen, all the way up to becoming a kitchen manager. I worked for three different companies; the last one I loved to work was called X, the best in casual dining. They had the structure that I enjoyed the most. Cooking food for lots of people always made me happy. Another favorite job was working for a foam-vending company in the Los Angeles area. The reason I liked this job was that people from all over the city came to our store seeking solutions for their projects. I would recommend products and solutions and so on. I helped lots of people in the movie industry, e. g., the props departments, costumes, stunt men, and so on. . . .

(Male, forty-one): His best job was working for X department store for about twelve years. This is when he became a manager of shipping and receiving and really liked it. He became disabled when he hurt himself because he didn't use the proper equipment. (Statement provided by his mother.)

(Female, forty): She worked in many jobs, and then decided to go for it. She obtained her GED with the help of her mother-in-law and then attended Cochise College, earning an AA degree with high marks. She then decided to enroll into a six-month penal corrections course, which led her to a job with the Georgia State Prison system. She has a tenacious will. (Statement provided by her mother.)

A Word About Discrimination and Racism

Why was there Not a Word about Discrimination or Racism? • Was it a Regional Experience? • Might It have Been Institutional Racism? • Was It about Multiculturalism? • Still, We Live in an Era of Intolerance

My home town of San Fernando is no longer divided into the two worlds separated by the railroad tracks when I was a boy. It is now just one cosmos, a Latino world. In 2010, three years after my mother's death, Latinos occupied nearly the entire city area constituting about 92 percent of the municipality's population.[222]. While most Anglo residents moved away, our old barrio still stands and it no longer feels like an ethnic sanctuary. What used to be the *mexicano* commercial strips on Mission Boulevard and Kalisher Street, dependent on the barrio's Spanish speaking clientele, are now largely gone too although you can still walk past the aging buildings that used to shelter the old businesses like the smoky pool hall and our own Gil's Café. The barrio boundaries that we used to know have collapsed as well, like the limits marked by Amboy and Huntington Streets which used to signal the start of the orange groves extending southwest towards the old mission and the pasture lands that used to stretch northwest into the nearby foothills. The streets remain, of course, but the citrus trees and the fields have been replaced by nonstop housing, streets, and freeways in all directions.

The rest of what used to be our universe has changed completely too. The vegetable fields and citrus orchards that used to cover the rest of the San Fernando Valley are now taken up by smokeless factories and endless apartments and houses teeming with Latino families and the scores of

Latino businesses of one kind or another. The City of Los Angeles is now about 50% Hispanic and California itself is now approaching 40%. Different from our time, Latinos are no longer confined to agricultural work, the citrus industry having been transferred to Florida long ago. And while most Latinos still constitute a large part of the blue collar work force in the valley, engaged mostly in manufacturing and services, many Hispanics now hold positions in business, schools and colleges, government, and sports, the pattern probably being that the newer Latinos hold the less skilled jobs and the older ones like my family members commanding the more skilled jobs. At the time of this writing Latinos controlled the San Fernando City government and while the Los Angeles County Board of Supervisors wasn't controlled by Latinos, the City of Los Angeles was in fact commanded by a home grown Mexican American mayor, Antonio Villaraigosa, who grew up in one of the barrios of East Los Angeles.

The key point here is that important and progressive changes concerning Latinos are detectable, locally and across the country. And while this is not the place to analyze these changes, I believe everyone might agree that we have come a long way but still have a distance to cover.

Why was there not a word about discrimination or racism?

The careful reader may have already discovered that my ancestors didn't use the word "discrimination" in reference to Caucasians when I interviewed them, and my siblings didn't either. What's more, in my growing up years the term "racism" was rarely pronounced in our home either in Spanish or English and we didn't discuss the idea either. In other words, my old folks founded their families despite the obstinacy of their poverty without overtly blaming someone else for their troubles. I was surprised to discover this when I began reviewing these pages, encouraging me to reflect that my ancestors would have had ample reason to cast blame for their plight while they were raising us. I would have said something to someone if not my children. There was practically no acknowledgment of the exploitation of farm workers or of the vipers of ethnocentrism and racism which were considered more widespread in their days than now.

The era of Civil Rights had not yet come of age when my siblings and I were becoming adults. So, even if my parents had been sufficiently informed and politically minded, they couldn't have been emboldened to civil disobedience by men like the Reverend Martin Luther King, Jr. or a little later by Reies López Tijerina, or César Chávez. Even when these men of color did indeed initiate their historic struggles for justice and equality on behalf of the blacks in the South and the *hispanos/mexicanos* of the Southwest, Mom and Dad still didn't outwardly support their causes. They never grumbled over the dinner table, that we Gil children can recall, about the oppressive *americanos*.

You, the reader, may have noticed in these pages that when my father got into blows with his boss, in Chapter 5, my Uncle Pascual, the narrator, abstained from damning the American supervisor. It would have been a perfect moment for him to vent his wrath at Anglo oppressors but he didn't. The words wrapped in venom never came and yet he was the most anti-*gringo* member of our family in part because of his pro-worker/peasant activities in Mexico, as discussed in Chapter 13, *agrarista* and labor leaders like him often allying themselves with the Mexican Communist Party thus making them sharply anti-American. When Guadalupe, my mother, described the round up of Mexicans associated with the oft-berated Repatriation Program of the 1930s (pages 138-140), she did so more with a touch of sadness than provocation. When I pointedly asked my *tío* Pascual whether he witnessed in those days "any pressure exerted on the Mexican people to expel them," he replied that he didn't notice it. Then he added that he didn't lose his job. In other words, he put the process of expulsion in terms of having a job or not. Feeling unsatisfied with his answer I questioned him in another way. I asked, "How did the Mexican people on the train feel" or what did you hear them say as you were riding toward the border in 1931? Did they voice their anger at being kicked out when they didn't want to go? His answer was, "The Mexicans aboard were returning to Mexico on their own. There were no complaints [because] there was nothing [to keep them in the United States]...there were no jobs, no money." This is when he brought to mind, as a way of buttressing his reply, a ballad popular at the time summarizing this attitude. In other words, he didn't use this opportunity either to blame the *gringos* or their systematic subjugation of poor people.

In giving the last touches to these pages I felt required to reexamine their responses in light of these denials. After all, a significant amount of the literature that looks carefully at the experience of Chicanos or Mexican Americans, and begins to form in the late 1960s, is filtered through with an offended undertone, to say the least. The discrimination of Mexican Americans by the American populace at large and their leaders constitutes a central under-current in this literature, generally speaking, and rightfully so. Hence, did my old folks not feel this discrimination? Didn't my siblings ever feel like complaining about *gabacho* abuse? How could I explain this seeming contradiction in these pages? It wouldn't have been honest of me to put words I wanted to hear in their mouths. For me to suggest otherwise simply didn't appeal to me. Still, I had to find an explanation.

The answer seems to be that there is no contradiction. My grandmother, parents, and uncles, were born into Mexico's lowest ranks, as stated several times. And, as we've seen in these pages, they had ample experience in viewing the world from the lowest rung in society and so encountering difficulties was not unusual; nothing was going to surprise them. Condemning the Anglos and their economic system for their poverty wouldn't have occurred to them because they had suffered much more so in their homeland. Their's was a comparative understanding. They knew that their assignment in America was to crawl forward and gain ground, inch by inch, if necessary, no matter if they were condemned to live in shacks as farm workers. And, that's what my family did including my cousins, as we've seen. If my old folks were discriminated against, they didn't share their experience or feelings with us, their children. The only exception I can summon is my Uncle Pascual complaining to me when I personally witnessed behavior that disrespected him, as pointed out in Chapter 13, and even then he limited his moan to a tired handful of words: "Do you see how they treat me?" Yet, at the same time, I couldn't ignore my other uncle's words when I asked my *tío* Miguel if he felt any discrimination when he worked digging tunnels in the California sierras alongside men from other racial groups, soon after his arrival in the United States. His answer was quite clear. He replied, "I never saw any discrimination at these camp sites. I never felt that I was mistreated due to my race."

Looking over their testimony, my ancestors were willing to acknowledge meeting *gringos* who were kind and understanding. I cannot dismiss this. Mom never forgot the Stalders who owned the grape farm in LeGrand where Dad worked when he married Mom. Surrounded by farmland and few neighbors, both Mom and Mrs. Stalder, two young married women, realized they needed to cross the cultural barrier that divided them in order to enjoy a degree of human communication and so they tried to understand each other and thus became friends in the process. In the end, they went their separate ways when Mom decided to rejoin her mother in southern California but she admitted that, "the *patrones* liked us a lot." The Stalders were planning to move to Stockton and invited my parents to follow them. Stiff ethnocentrism and hard-elbowed racism may have been a common coin in America in the 1920s but it didn't circulate on the Stalder farm although mother's recognition of the economic distinctions that separated them remained clear in her mind.

The preceding pages reveal other instances when my *viejos* found Anglos who were considerate and willing to help rather than hinder. For example, there was the Pacific State Savings and Loan Company officer who talked my parents into buying our Mott Street home during the Depression because prices were low, certainly an important moment in our family past; the lawyers and real estate men who in the 1920s despite huge cultural and linguistic differences helped my grandmother buy the property on Kalisher Street which later fell into our patrimony; the same when my Mom and Dad purchased and recorded their little patch of property on Mott Street. Then there was the "nurse angel," or so I called her, who in 1941, or so, ordered my parents working in the fields, no matter their skin color, to hospitalize my sister Mary right away because she had contracted polio, and so on. Ethnocentrism and racism seems to have been absent at these critical moments and mother and my sister Mary broadly recognized this.

In a slightly different vein, there was "Negrete," the onetime Lebanese or Jewish cloth merchant or "rag peddler" who became a loan shark of sorts in our community but used his influence to help us save our home when it was up for auction. Mother always praised him for this. And let's not forget the "*chino*" who forgave our debits when Dad brought us to the brink of bankruptcy at about the time I was born. These were acts of humankind on the part of non-Mexicans which helped moderate any resentment had my forebears held it, especially mother. At the same time, she was never eager to kowtow or behave submissively in front of their status or power. My Dad and my uncles also stayed at arm's length, in this sense, my *tío* Miguel probably exhibiting the greatest degree of graciousness toward Anglos.

My siblings were likewise insensitive to any obtuse Anglo behavior when they were in the process of becoming adults. Different from our *viejos*, they worked side by side their Caucasian counterparts and got along well enough with them, able to bridge any cultural differences by simply turning on their Americaness when they needed it, speaking English and making themselves understood, at the same time that they made sure they weren't disrespected, otherwise somebody's nose would've run red. They didn't become chummy with their *gabacho* partners in the early years but they rarely groused about them and probably found more fault with fellow Mexican Americans from the barrio than anyone else, *pachucos* especially. In the 1970s, when the Chicano Movement began to spill into the streets of San Fernando with demonstrations and marches, all of my siblings maintained cool neutrality. They sympathized with the movement in the most general terms but felt repelled by the raucousness that enveloped it and weren't impressed by the local leaders or the participants many of whom they considered ne'er do wells. In contrast, I eagerly joined the local leadership groups but soon found them wanting although I did take the opportunity to learn about the movement and deepen my sympathy for its goals.

In spite of the foregoing remarks, I maintain that there is no contradiction between the views my ancestors shared with me, regarding the neutral-to-benign relations they sustained with the Anglos who crossed their paths, and the offended tone that has often resonated in the field of Chicano/Mexican American studies. How can this be?

I offer three brief explanations that may explain this apparent inconsistency. One is linked to the regional features of the Mexican American experience in the 20th century. The second considers the role of institutional discrimination and I ask whether it might have played a role in my parent's soft gloving the *americanos*. The third rests on my proposal about the silver lining my siblings and I may have perceived in the growing trend toward multiculturalism in our growing up years. Let me explain.

Was it a regional experience?

The regional explanation simply emphasizes the notion that growing up "Mexican" in southern California in the 1940s and 1950s, as we Gil's did, would have been quite different had we done so in other parts of the country where people of our cultural background also predominated, like Texas, Arizona, or New Mexico.[223]

What is clear is that when we Gil kids wanted to see an American movie at the Rennie's Theatre or the Town Theatre, both located on the Anglo side of the tracks, we could do so without restrictions as long as we were willing to pay the price of the movie ticket. Along these lines, I remember one hot summer day that my older brothers dragged me to the city's big public swimming pool at the San Fernando Ball Park and threw me into the water where I splashed anxiously alongside other brown skinned youngsters like me, plus others who were white and black.

We would not have been able to do these things in Texas. In many cases, if not most, Mexicans and Blacks were kept out of public accommodations frequented by whites. I learned while composing these notes that about the same time that I was old enough to go to movies by myself, in 1950, Aurora Orozco, a 33 year-old Mexican American woman moved with her family from Mercedes, Texas, on the Mexican border, to Cuero, east of San Antonio, where she discovered, that "Jim Crow laws were present everywhere." She also remembered that "There were signs that said 'No Blacks – No Mexicans' in doctors' offices, restaurants, hospitals, and swimming pools." Mexicans had their places assigned to them, like other people of color.

For example, at a movie house, whites occupied their own section, Mexicans another, and Blacks were shunted up to the balcony.[224] Any Mexican wanting to eat in a restaurant had to do so in the kitchen, in the back, and in the local hospital, Blacks and Mexicans were treated in the basement. She also added, "We noticed that most Mexicans who lived in Cuero felt inferior to Anglos because they didn't have any rights. They had to go to their bosses and ask for a recommendation so they could rent or buy a house, furniture, or a car." David Montejano, a leading *tejano* historian of Texas, wrote that "In the town of Ozona in West Texas....hotels were exclusively reserved for Anglo patrons until 1958...."[225] Rudy Acuña who spent his life writing ardently about Chicano history as a whole, summarized the Texas situation by observing that "Texas was a southern state with all the social, political, and intellectual limitations of the south."[226] Even officials at the Texas State Historical Association now admit, to their credit, that, "*Tejanos* formed a suspect class...and that fact led to a general aversion of them...."[227] You couldn't trust them, in other words.

Needless to say we Gil's didn't experience this kind of discrimination in San Fernando. Our experience in our home town and in southern California as a whole was more of the accommodating kind. Our experience may be helpful in exploring the regionalization of the Mexican American experience, a concept I proposed many years ago.[228] But what is more important is that this perspective sheds light on why my ancestors felt reluctant to vilify the Anglos they dealt with in California. Had we lived in Texas we might have had some bitterly laced complaints, if not discussions, at our dinner table when we were growing up.

Might it have been institutional racism?

Institutional racism is the kind of discrimination my *viejos* could have complained about but didn't. This form of racism is defined as the "institutional practice that perpetuates inequality based on racial membership....; [it] functions to reinforce white skin privilege in all facets of American life."[229] We don't have to go very far to examine an example of an "institutional practice" perpetuating "inequality." All we have to do is remember the very houses which our family occupied in the *vecindad* and on Mott Street. The reader may remember that I used the words "tiny," "matchbox," and "little" to describe them in Chapters 7 and 8, yet families of four or more were expected to live in them satisfactorily. The point is that living quarters like the *vecindad* were not erected on the *gringo* side of the tracks nor houses the size of our Mott Street home. Our dwellings were designed by architects and built by contractors who undoubtedly enjoyed the blessings of the city authorities who also overlooked unpaved streets and the absence of sidewalks and curbs for many years. *Their* neighborhoods weren't constructed to look blighted from the start. We have the testimony of the UCLA professor who studied our community in 1934 and found our barrio, on our side of the tracks as, "the most crowded and the least attractive residential district in which nearly all the Mexican population [wa]s found." Indeed! So, for our purposes, here is a clear example of an "institutional practice that perpetuates inequality based on racial membership" because this kind of lodging and the surrounding infrastructure was clearly aimed at us, the "Mexicans." Let's not forget either that Carey McWilliams reminded us that this pattern was widespread in southern California.

Unfortunately my ancestors didn't lodge a complaint about these disparities. The fact is that they couldn't have done so in any case. It seems that no one else would have been able to do so either. Unequal conditions based on race and class were barely appreciated when I was a boy in San Fernando which is another way of saying that the concept of institutional racism had not yet been defined, scholars tending to be the ones to do this usually. Consequently, the home builders who nevertheless created these unequal conditions in my home town and profited thereby could do so without critics and the officials who might have regulated them were blind to the whole situation.

I learned that the concept of institutional racism wasn't formulated and defined until 1968 when liberal minded students at Stanford University finally reasoned it out. This is the time when campuses across the country stood on the verge of rebellion over the many limitations they perceived in American society while everybody else didn't see anything of the kind. The Stanford students defined institutional racism to the best of their ability in a mimeographed pamphlet that first circulated among the campus "radicals" connected with the Mid-Peninsula Christian Ministry, this publication now considered a collector's item. Nevertheless, here are the words that these activist students chose:

> It is clear that our past thinking on race relations with its concentration on individual relation-ships and efforts to ameliorate the problems of "disadvantaged" persons has been too superficial. The problem is not merely a matter of individual bigotry; nor is it only a matter of remedial programs to "better" conditions. We are now increasingly

> aware that it is also a question of the subtle ways in which institutions function, the way in which organizational arrangements in fact exclude and discriminate against segments of the population.[230]

What all this means is that the so-called campus radicalism that began in the late 1960s brought to light many contradictions in American society and those of us who were later labeled "minorities" quickly appreciated their contribution. We can include the conceptualization of institutional racism as one of their gifts to American society. It's worth taking notice at the same time that these calls for liberal-minded change were of course pilloried by American conservatives who refused to acknowledge any limitations in the social order.[231]

Was it about multiculturalism?

Finally, I offer some comments on the subject of multiculturalism because I believe they help explain why my siblings abstained from lambasting Anglos for whatever reason. My brothers and sisters looked the other way when asked to join anti-establishment demonstrations, being less willing to pull the trigger, so to speak.

The short explanation for this is that we all felt like we belonged in America. Despite our Mexican roots, we never felt a sense of alienation that might have chipped away at our community or national loyalty even though this kind of reflection was far too sophisticated for us at the time. The reason is that we were able to engage American culture and society in a more intimate way than our parents did. This made our experience in the country which they handed to us, resulting from their migratory decisions, a more promising one. Needless to say, not living in Texas helped tremendously.

I hold that my siblings and I—the second generation—became assimilated into American society in a more straightforward manner than our old folks did not only because we were quicker to adapt than they were but also because Californians offered us a reasonably secure non-threatening environment. The people of the Golden State had long consented somehow to the peaceful coexistence of "several different cultures rather than one national culture,"[232] the comparison with Texas being helpful in this regard. And so, my siblings and I gradually came to appreciate this unofficial form of multiculturalism intuitively, even though the word and the concept were as yet barely understood. The interviews and the countless discussions I had with my parents and my brothers and sisters, complemented by my understanding of regional responses to "Mexicans," all led me to this conclusion.

By the time my siblings and I reached young adulthood we felt we could begin to claim America as our country, knowing full well that our parents had trouble with this idea. In Chapter 12, I discuss the process that we Gil kids underwent in having to blend the ways of doing things, which honored our parent's heritage yet allowed us to waddle forward somehow when engaging our playmates and classmates. As I state in those pages, in doing this we found it necessary to emulate the mannerisms and the speech patterns of youngsters more assimilated than us, if not our Anglo classmates. We stumbled forward no doubt. As explained in the chapter cited above, we didn't easily call ourselves "American" but we knew we were different from our parents. As we reflected more deeply, each in our own way, we concluded at one point or another that indeed we weren't Mexican at all. We were American—or Mexican American. We became Mexican American. Some of us did this more clearly and easily than others. For example, Mary reached this point less distinctly and with more difficulty than Martha who sharply reminded us many times that she was not a Mexican.

As stated already, my siblings did not report an insulting moment when engaging a *gabacho*. The point is that none of us Gils were directly affronted by Anglos and this helped our struggle to give ourselves a political and cultural identity. Certainly never the way Aurora Orozco described for Cuero, Texas, above or David Montejano for Ozona, Texas. We weren't denied a public accommodation and hindsight advises me that this was quite important. This was something we didn't consciously consider.

Given the tenor of all of the interviews supporting this book I have to assert that during our upbringing, instead of Jim Crow laws operating in the San Fernando Valley, a multicultural laissez faire seemed to function there. It gave us Gil kids enough leeway to become adults and engage the world outside our barrio free of personalized disrespect. This is not to say that we didn't feel apprehensive or that were didn't feel ignored, dismissed, or overlooked when we traveled beyond our ethnic quarter to go to school or to work. I recall feeling it necessary to carry a chip on my shoulder in my early twenties and I am sure that my brothers did too. Mary told me that the moment her Anglo clients or associates detected a Latino accent or a Mexican way of saying something, her skin would crawl. She felt "they would begin down-grading you in their mind, putting you into a lower category."

However, even though we weren't directly affronted on a personal basis, we ultimately had to accept that we lived in a ghetto, a southern California one. In our teen age years we came to realize more each day that our part of town was filled with folks like us who lived in dilapidated houses and were designated as the hewers of wood and drawers of water. We saw with greater clarity that our barrio embraced many youngsters who accepted dropping out of school early, getting into trouble and ending up behind bars. It's possible that the institutionalized forms of racism as defined above helped us become accustomed to this second-class citizenship, complete with the unskilled and low paying jobs that barrio men like my Dad endured. It wasn't Texas, to be sure, but our existence was cushioned by a middle-of-the-road cultural toleration, an unofficial form of low-brow multiculturalism.

This intermediate, half-hidden existence was upended by the promise of a war on poverty. The Democratic administrations of John F. Kennedy and Lyndon B. Johnson encouraged us to think ultimately that our children and grandchildren might not have to be condemned to second-class status. Rhetorically, and for political reasons, of course, these two men and their allies publicly recognized our existence, we the non-white Americans, my hindsight telling me that we were witnessing a stronger gelling of American multiculturalism as a result without our fully realizing it.[233] Our ethnic community, in effect, was recognized in this way constituting a new political gesture that met with overwhelming approval in our neck of the woods and it felt good too. President Kennedy's photograph appeared everywhere in the *barrio*, reminiscent of the popularity that Franklin D. Roosevelt enjoyed locally. I cannot remember the portrait of a single Republican politician ever setting off similar approval. The image that Robert F. Kennedy carved out for himself on March 10, 1968, by sitting beside César Chávez, the day he broke his 25-day protest fast, also took on an unparalleled significance. Even my family was impressed by this. Instances of this sort, especially in these years, help explain in my mind why my siblings and I never felt like joining something akin to the Parti Québécois, the French Canadians who advocated independence for Quebec in the 1970s. The Chicano Movement never came close to anything like this.

The Johnson administration gained more headway in our community when federal officials began trying to rectify and otherwise make up for the inequalities minority folk like us had endured with respect to voting rights (especially for Blacks), jobs, housing, education, and so on. More to the point here, the Civil Rights Act of 1964 through the EEOC nudged America farther down the path of multiculturalism not only by acknowledging the existence of "Hispanics" and other minorities but more importantly by officially banning discrimination based on "race, color, religion, or national origin" and seeking some form of redress through Affirmative Action.

We were being included, and this is the point. We became the focus of a national effort that came down all the way from the White House to shield us legally from direct forms of discrimination and institutional ones too, and we didn't have to foreswear speaking Spanish or give up any other aspect of our culture. This is not to say that bigoted Americans didn't fulminate against these rulings or that the forces of assimilation weren't busy neutralizing our Mexican cultural inheritance as already discussed, but that's beside the point. We could now begin to be ourselves yet be part of America, no one fussing about the women in our barrio wearing a *rebozo* to cover their head when going to church or walking down the street. I was conscious of how EEO policies also encouraged the formation of barrio leaders where few or none had existed before, and while their guidance might have been wanting at times, this constituted a good beginning nevertheless. It was a stimulating time. We felt like we belonged. There was hope for Brown people like us. Leaving aside the related web of politics connected to these developments and the eventual disavowal of Affirmative Action, the sum total of this experience, I believe, laid an important foundation. It encouraged my siblings and I to view our relations with Anglo Americans in a more equal and promising way. This is probably why my siblings didn't acknowledge any latent bitterness about whites when I interviewed them in order to question them about our growing up.

Still, we live in an era of intolerance

Unquestionably, many Mexican Americans and other Latinos who read these pages may deny that things are equal and promising for them. Unlike my siblings, they may consider themselves already fully engaged in criticizing and calling attention to problems of unfairness and discrimination. After all, many Latinos have been demonstrating on the streets of America while I sat writing this book. The truth is that at a national level we are presently facing the most egregious and thinly veiled expressions of racism and ethnocentrism in the United States since the time we Gil children were growing up, most of it triggered by America's need to upgrade its immigration laws.

Examples of this revived era of bigotry and intolerance are most easily appreciated in Arizona's SB 1070 also known as the "Support Our Law Enforcement and Safe Neighborhoods Act." Implemented April 23, 2010, this law currently empowers and requires local police authorities to detain anyone "reasonably" suspected of being an illegal immigrant. But who are the "illegals?" The answer is, Mexicans, mostly. Everyone knows this. So, who is more apt to *look* illegal? The answer again is as clear as looking through an eye glass: anyone who looks Mexican looks illegal and this includes a substantial percentage of Arizona's population.

Given this situation, if I were to be driving around in Phoenix and my car had a faulty brake light I could be questioned and possibly *detained* by the infamous Maricopa County sheriff or his zealous deputies in order ascertain my nationality, simply because I happen to look illegal, being the darkest of my siblings. All of my children could be exposed to police detention and interrogation for the same reason if they too were driving in this Phoenix county but not my Caucasian wife nor her blonde and blue-eyed daughter. They would be spared and so would two of my grandchildren who are as *güeros* as the day is long. The difference of course is my darker skin color and my physical appearance, and that of my children and most of my grandchildren. This law, which is now synonymous with Arizona itself, unfortunately, stands as a good example of institutional racism because "[it] functions to reinforce white skin privilege," as explained above.[234] SB 1070 demands that dark skinned folks be stopped on an Arizona highway but not white folks.

Is this a good law for America? Of course not! For these reasons SB 1070 is a racist law, pure and simple, and there is no room for racist laws in America anymore. Sooner or later it's going to be thrown into the same dust bin as Germany's odious laws against Jews, like the November 12, 1938, Decree on the Exclusion of Jews from German Economic Life which closed all Jewish-owned businesses and the expulsion of Jewish children from public schools by the Reich Ministry on November 15 of the same year.[235] SB 1070 is a step in that direction because the German laws aim directly at a racial group while Arizona veils the racial dimensions of its intentions.

This odious piece of legislation may be evaluated in one of two ways. It is either a feeble-minded legal concoction sadly reflecting the political immaturity of Arizona's top leaders or it is a carefully crafted regulation. The latter would be one that forces federal intervention to begin fending off the local effects of uncontrolled illegal immigration at the same time that it leans on Arizona's thinly veiled intolerance for people of color,[236] all at a considerable cost to individuals who look Mexican. When top government officials were hatching this law, they must have said to themselves privately that SB 1070 would weigh heavily on Arizona's Latino residents. Obviously they shrugged the thought away deciding that their Latino neighbors would simply have to bear the brunt of submitting themselves to unequal treatment. Other states have unfortunately drawn up similar legislation. For these reasons, I can claim that bigotry and racism have raised their ugly mugs once more.

Uncontrolled immigration to America in the latter part of the 20th century has indeed achieved critical proportions and some Arizonians have suffered from it, no doubt. On the other hand, adopting racist state laws that injure a portion of the population in order to force the federal government to contend with America's "broken immigration system" is simply prejudiced and unjust. The Arizona response represents an iniquitous approach unworthy of the spirit of America given us by Abraham Lincoln, and it won't solve the problem anyway. The conundrum of American immigration reform requires more profound responses than detaining brown skinned motorists, erecting walls, and beefing up border guards.

Part IV

Additional Materials

Appendix I

Searching for My Father's Story

The reader may remember that my father abandoned Mexico and met my mother in the United States. Knowing so little about him, I engaged a search for his origins, his boyhood years, why exactly did he leave, and so on. This is why I chronicle here what I gathered and how I went about my search. The exploration occurred in stages, each wrought with difficulty and frustration, a story within a story, as far as this book is concerned, about my trying to put the fragments of the puzzle together even though some of the pieces continued to be missing in the end. So here I share this information and how I struggled to give perspective to the scraps I found. Reviewing these stages of my growing comprehension encouraged me to lay out the following segments in the order that they actually occurred.

What We Knew Initially about Dad

We knew that my father, Bernabé, was born in Chavinda, Michoacán, and that he was raised by two aunts named Elodia (eh-LOH-dee-aah) and Manuela. We understood him to be an only child, an orphan, and that his boyhood was an unhappy one, so that he ran away when he was a teenager, leaving for the United States and giving up any contact with the remnants of his family. A studio photograph of the two aunts, probably taken in the early 1900s, hung in my mother's house for many decades, and it shows two women in their thirties, more or less, each wearing straight black hair pulled behind their heads. They stand beside a wicker chair framed in dark glossy wood, dressed in black or charcoal-colored, ankle-length gowns with broad lapels. The slightly taller woman rests her outstretched left arm on the other's shoulder as they both gaze placidly toward one side of the photographer's camera. They don't look like the daughters of *peones* even though they appear dark of skin as most farm workers in Mexico. Instead, they look like two well-dressed city women of that time, provincially prim. At the bottom of the photograph, Mom wrote, "Aunts who raised Berna." When I scrutinized this photograph, I said to myself, "Mom's relatives living on the Hacienda Santa Rosa wouldn't have had the wherewithal to dress in this manner, much less take a studio photo."

It seems that my father's mother died when he was only three years old and that he also lost his father in a construction accident when he was twelve. This, in any case, is what my brother Manuel learned at age thirteen when he visited Chavinda in the company of my mother in 1944. In a telephone call sixty-two years later, he told me he remembered meeting Elodia, "a dark-skinned single lady in her forties," who said that Dad's mother died when he was three years old and that his father died when Dad was twelve—that "a beam fell on him." These bald facts must have been driven deeply into my brother's memory because he dredged them up with some intensity without pause, revealing information about Dad that he hadn't thought about in a long time. I took notes of my brother's remembrances and set them aside and did not discover them again until I was trying to compose this chapter four years later. As it turned out, the notes fit in quite well.

The precipitating event causing my father to leave everything and everyone remained a blank for us, his descendents. If he shared this information with Mother, we'll never know now. She spoke many times about a man closely associated with his aunts, perhaps a relative, who scrutinized what young Bernabé ate and how much. This apparently made my father feel resentful and unwanted. When his resentment overflowed, he went away, young as he was. We were left to assume that his aunts were uncaring and that the same thing could be said about the unidentified male connected to them.

Our family lore repeated the story that he boarded a train crammed-full with soldiers traveling north toward the United States border where a lot of the fighting in connection with the Mexican Revolution of 1910 was taking place. We were told that Dad asked a soldier, accompanied by his wife and child, all riding atop one of the box cars, if he would allow him to travel with them, feigning as a family member, otherwise he feared he would be prevented from riding the train. The soldier assented, and this is the way young Bernabé travelled all the way to the United States border, more than a thousand miles away, employing a ruse that both of my uncles also made use of. When they reached the international boundary, Dad crossed into the United States, about 1917. He most probably entered the United States without proper documentation. My uncle Pascual remembered he met my father in Fresno in 1919. Writing this book made me realize how much better it would've been adding Dad's words and perspective.

It wasn't until I was sixty-nine years of age that I put other parts of my life aside, including my teaching career, and finally set foot in Dad's hometown to begin gathering some information.

Searching for Clues in Chavinda

I traveled to Chavinda in February 2006, anxious to learn something about my dad's origins. From the nearest city, Zamora, a busy agricultural hub, I boarded a bus with a sign in the front window that read "Chavinda" and rode over the rolling landscape toward my father's hometown where I had visited a couple of times before but was unable to investigate at the time. The well-paved, two-lane road took me past worn-down volcano tops, reflecting patches of green that gave way to the yellowish browns and tans that come with the dry season—it wouldn't rain until June. The sturdy bus picked up and dropped off passengers along the twenty-or-so-mile length as we drove past fields of corn, wheat, strawberries, and new plantations of spiky blue-green *agave,* the general name given to the pointy, waist-high plant that produces tequila. First produced in neighboring Jalisco, local farmers were banking the agave would grow well here as well. We passed many vendors who displayed their wares out by the roadside, including soda pop, translucent jelly cast in molds, stalks of sugarcane framing doorways in lazy angles, hand-woven baskets resting on the ground, and colorful pottery stacked six feet high. I was engaged in one of my favorite pastimes—traveling through the countryside of Michoacán, which has always struck me as pastorally sublime.[237]

My father's hometown in west central Mexico lies slightly south-east of Lake of Chapala and near the Chavinda River that flows down from a bluff called the Cerro de Patambán. On any given day, the town's small open-air market is crammed with foodstuffs and on this day a few significant displays of pottery or textiles were apparent. I thought to myself that farther south nearly every town displays its pottery and other artisan crafts by the highway but not in Chavinda—too far away from the road.

It seems that with enough sons and daughters of Chavinda moving away and returning periodically, the town fathers decided to build an elegant white stucco archway that greets them on their return. The archway greeted me and my fellow bus riders at about midday as our bus driver steered our heavy vehicle away from the main highway and onto a side road to carry us under the welcoming archway emblazoned with the words, *Bienvenidos a Chavinda.* Had we not turned off the main road, the highway would have taken us to Jiquilpan, the birthplace of Mexico's most famous president, Lázaro Cárdenas, and then on to busy Sahuayo.

The bus left me on the edge of town, and so I walked in the direction of a modest church steeple that I could see over the roof tops where I expected to find the town center. As I strolled in the bright February sun, through narrow streets separating white-washed residential walls, I paused to look through wrought-iron grills to gaze momentarily at some striking patio interiors. Different from Mascota where the old cobble-stone streets still reign supreme, here the narrow road surfaces are all cemented over. The church steeple did indeed look down on the main plaza where I found a bench and sat awhile to enjoy the scene and prepare a mental plan. Rustic-looking men, wearing whitish "rice" hats adorned with a short tassel hanging from the back brim, watched me from the corner of their eye as they chatted amiably with each other. They looked like Mexican retirees—they might have been Braceros in their younger years, I said to myself.

I decided my first target would be the Civil Registry office, the local government office of public records,[238] usually near the main plaza. After a few inquiries, I entered the cramped second-floor office of the Registro Civil, jam-packed with old-style register books. The smell of aging paper was strong and the absence of computers (and computerized records) was quite noticeable. I asked the man in charge, a *Licenciado* (a title denoting a university degree) named Antonio Valencia, well-dressed, in his forties, that a search be done of my father's birth. I knew from experience this was a customary request of anyone working in the Registro Civil. Cheerlessly, *Licenciado* Valencia, complied; I learned he was a judge appointed by the state. Sitting three feet away from him, I saw him walk over to some shelves crammed with old-style register books and return with two or three of them. He then thumbed through them, old hand-filled pages similar to the ones I had perused for scores of months in Mascota, years ago. He scanned the yellowing pages with his eye, moistening his thumb several tunes to gain greater page-turning friction, and became increasingly glum as he came to the end of the volumes that corresponded with our search parameters. Alas, there was no trace, no record. He explained with a careful mixture of formality and courtesy that in those days many individuals were inscribed at the local church but not at the government office. "Yes, I know that too," I said to myself.

Thanking him for his efforts, I then ambled to the church office on the other side of the plaza. Chavinda is a small community of about ten thousand inhabitants[239] and it holds only one single church, a Catholic house of worship named for the Virgin of Guadalupe. Like most Catholic churches in Mexico, it includes an office that administers an archive of handwritten registers filled with information about baptisms and funerals, usually older than those held by the civilian-controlled offices of public records like Valencia's. Mexico's strict separation of church and state produced two record-keeping systems. Once inside the office, I asked a pert and efficient young lady with sweet dark eyes to look for my father's baptismal record. She took what looked to me like expert notes and began searching in her old-style register volumes, she located the birth certificate within minutes!

Handing me the document, I saw that it stated that the men who originally filled out the baptismal certificate declared that my father was born July 23, 1899. This coincided with what we already knew about my father's birth date and so this confirmation stirred my heart—I was on the right track! After paying a modest fee, the winsome young clerk slipped the one-page credential she had filled out into a plastic holder embossed with the name of the church and bid me farewell with a disarming smile. I walked out of her office in a slight daze.

Sitting outside in the sunny plaza, I scrutinized the document more carefully. I noticed that the baptismal certificate was certified by the diocese of Zamora and that it made several other statements of fact: namely, that (a) my father was a legitimate son; (b) his full name was José Bernabé Gil Negrete; (c) his father's name was Benedicto Gil; (d) his mother's was Librada Negrete; (e) the witnesses of the baptism, Eugenio García and María Jesús Valencia, declared themselves as my father's godparents, (f) they baptized Bernabé three days after his birth, and (g) that the baptismal entry is recorded on page 156 of Book 9 of the church's baptismal books. From my work in Mascota, many years earlier, I knew that Chavinda might hold other archives like the criminal files belonging to the local court of first instance, or state tax records, but not a newspaper archive. Dad didn't live here as an adult, and so he didn't have the opportunity to cause the creation of documents in these archives like in buying or selling land or leaving post-mortem assets for disposal. It appeared, then, that my father's documentary trail stopped here. But I didn't feel quite so bad. I had the nearest thing to my father's birth record, and it became one of my most important findings on this trip.

My next step was to begin talking to selected local town folks, thanks to a list of names I compiled before traveling to Chavinda. With the help of Internet tools like Google, many Chavinda natives, or their descendents living in the United States, discovered my online article about my wanting to do investigation in my father's native town—their town.[240] They wrote friendly and encouraging notes to me about the possibility of having ancestors in common and in the same hometown to boot. More often than not, they provided me with local references to help me along.[241] Jose Antonio González Maciel from Salinas, California, also known as "Peps," is a good stand-in for these helpful *chavindeños;* he sent me numerous e-mail messages generously providing me with names of his Gil relatives in Chavinda. They might be able to help you, he wrote.

What these e-mail messages told me, in the end, was that Chavinda was filled with Gils, a new discovery for me. So when I began knocking on doors I found many Gil families but no one who could recognize a Benedicto in their up-line of relatives, my grandfather, my father's father. The men and women with my surname who answered the knock showed an interest once I revealed my whole name and then sympathized with me when they couldn't recognize the names of my grandparents or my father. Yes, all agreed, many sons of Chavinda left for the United States in the early 1900s, like my father had done, and many had not returned. It was not unusual. And if Benedicto belonged to one of the poorer Gil families in town, back at the beginning of the twentieth century, surely no one could remember him now—nearly a century later. The poor don't leave much of a paper trail, I reminded myself, as I walked away glumly. I also asked the Civil Registry official to look up Benedicto's death, but Valencia couldn't find that either.

Reviewing my situation, I concluded that my meager documentary findings laid down several facts. They confirmed Dad's parents' names just as we had preserved them in our family lore. They also confirmed his birth year, although his exact birth date (July 23, 1899) did not match the information entered on his death certificate—not surprising since the certificate revealed that I, at age 19, was the one who gave the information to the hospital officials in the first place, I having since forgotten everything about that day!

As I sat in the plaza reflecting on my modest results, it dawned on me that I was overlooking my father's mother's side of the family entirely, the Negretes! After all, her name, my father's mother's name, Librada Negrete, was written quite clearly on the baptismal certificate I held in my hands. And, I woke up to the fact that my mother and sisters in San Fernando already enjoyed a certain rapport with the part of the Negrete clan that resided in Fillmore, California, near San Fernando, something I personally had not fully appreciated mostly because I hadn't lived there for many decades. I also ignored the specific links the Negrete's claimed with my father and also felt my mother and my sisters didn't quite understand the connection either, the word "cousin" having been used to describe the relationship, we thought loosely but we didn't know anything for sure. What's worse is that the most knowledgeable informant about these matters, my uncle Francisco Negrete García (*tío* Pancho),[242] had died a few years before—all this to explain why I hadn't pursued the Negrete angle. As I slowly gathered my wits, sitting in the sunny plaza, I stirred myself into a new realization.

The Negrete's represented my maternal grandmother's descendents[243] and a portion of them resided nearby! Rancho Palmira, my memory cells yelled out at me! Some of them lived in Rancho Palmira only a few miles from where I sat enjoying the Michoacán sun! So I went looking for them right away.

Rediscovering Dad's Relatives on His Mother's Side

I hired one of the few taxicabs available in Chavinda. The driver, who didn't question me when I told him where I wanted to go, sped us to Rancho Palmira, a farming community about twenty minutes outside of the town. I was confident I would find some of the Negrete folk there. On the way over, I refreshed my memory about my *tío* Pancho, recalling that I came to know him in my teenage years as a jolly, rustic fellow who visited us from time to time, always dressed in heavy khakis work clothes, perhaps trimmed with a Levis jacket, and work boots. He spoke with the enthusiasm of a backcountry farmer making us chuckle from time to time, especially when he made fun, from his old-fashioned, rural point of view, of some our modern gadgets or ways of doing things. He reminded us often that Dad was his *primo* by way of the elders in his family, but somehow this didn't percolate deeply enough into my memory nor that of my siblings. In any case, *tío* Pancho had always maintained Rancho Palmira as his nesting place, a claim that echoed in my mind as we approached the farm settlement.[244]

Palmira, as they say locally, is a fragment of one of several haciendas that dominated this northern part of Michoacán, I learned after doing some research. As in other parts of Mexico, much of the arable land was granted in the 1500s by the king of Spain to aristocrats of various sorts, but the owners had completely changed in this area by the late 1890s, and the sizes of the once-extensive haciendas had also changed considerably too. The plantations had become smaller and consequently more numerous and now they included ranchos (agricultural units smaller than haciendas) as in the case of the Hacienda Las Cruces, the Rancho El Varal,[245] and the Hacienda San Juan Sin Agua also known as Hacienda San Juan Palmira. The old name suggests a farm with insufficient irrigation and, indeed, there is enough local lore about the canals that were dug connecting the hacienda to a nearby river.

The man considered by my Negrete cousins as the patriarch of the family, Pedro Negrete, born ca. 1870, arrived at the old Hacienda San Juan Sin Agua about 1895 with his wife Catarina Sotelo in tow. His grandson, my *tío* Pancho, believed he was an expert in the cultivation of tobacco but spent much of his energy directing ditch diggers or *paleros* who ultimately brought water to the hacienda by opening up a canal to the nearby river.[246] Whenever I spoke with the Negrete men about their family past, they often referred to their male ancestors as *paleros.*

The reader will remember that the Revolution of 1910 led to the break-up of the old hacienda system [247] so, just as we saw in Mascota, the Hacienda San Juan Sin Agua was likewise divided into smaller pieces, and one of these chunks became known as Rancho Palmira. The Negretes received land parcels when the hacienda was distributed in much the same way as some of our ancestors did on Mother's side from the Hacienda de Galope in Mascota as I've pointed out in chapter 1, other plantations across the face of Mexico suffering a similar fate.

I arrived in Rancho Palmira and found a pleasant community of small landholders living in Mexican country houses protected by variety of shade trees stretching their branches out over cobblestone streets. Because the residents of Rancho Palmira all knew each other, I didn't have to look too far in order to begin locating my kin. This is how I found myself face-to-face with my relatives on my grandmother's side. They slowly congregated under the cooling shade of a spreading bougainvillea with happy curiosity and began offering me their hands to shake and greeting me by name. "So you're Carlos!" Needless to say I began to feel at home very quickly, especially after they offered me some delicious tacos filled with beans and hot sauce.

On the day of my visit, in 2006, the Negrete clan was headed by Gonzalo Negrete, approximately eighty years old at the time, well-built, and very much a dignified, graying patriarch, now passed away. He was my *tío* Francisco's younger brother. This network of families included the following surviving brothers and sisters: María Luisa, Catalina, Elías, Ignacio, Javier, and Esperanza, all in their sixties and seventies when I visited. Gonzalo also watched over his own extensive family mostly younger folk living in the United States spread over three states—California, Washington, and South Carolina. Although he and his siblings held down the small *ejido* farms that help make up Rancho Palmira, he and his brothers became braceros in the 1950s and traveled to the United States in order to earn extra money by helping bring in American agricultural harvests.[248]

The bracero experience changed their lives in a hundred ways. Not only did they earn extra income that was surely welcomed, it also gave them a cosmopolitan view of the world. They came to know American farmers who trusted their work, and they learned how to travel back and forth across the US-Mexico border. They also learned about the unparalleled opportunities available for younger people in the United States. The bottom-line is that their relations with the American communities in which they worked, provided them an international perspective about the prospects of life, and this was transmitted to the younger Negretes. This helps explain why most of the younger ones in this clan continue to live in the United States. My relatives in Palmira gave me the impression of being more cosmopolitan in their world view than the relatives we left behind in the Mascotan highlands who never emigrated.

Long before visiting Chavinda, when our mother Guadalupe was still alive, I attended one of the Negrete clan reunions in Fillmore, California, this being one of the American cities where they landed and stayed. I counted about twenty-seven youngsters, all descendents of the old folks who I later met in Palmira as I describe above. The youngsters that day were playing soccer as part of a program of organized family festivities, and they were all wearing blue T-shirts emblazoned with silk-printed photographs of their grandparents, my *tío* Pancho, deceased by that time, and my aunt María Refugio (Cuca) Contreras. The two *viejos* represented part of the vanguard immigrants of the Negrete clan who started out from Rancho Palmira.

One contrast between the Gil's and the Negrete's is that while Francisco Negrete Sotelo ventured to California in the 1920s, as the first Negrete wave, and sought out and visited with my father (his cousin on his mother's side), he returned to Michoacán whereas my father did not. The reader may remember that my mother cautioned that "This was the cousin who often suggested that he [my father] return home." As we've seen, Dad was disillusioned with the aunts who raised him and chose never to return, and he probably said so to Francisco, who, in turn, might have replied, "Forget all that, cousin, go back anyway," or he might have said to Dad, "Go back and visit them, at least." But my dad didn't, and so he stayed in California and founded our family.

Another contrast involves receiving Mexican farmland. The second wave of Negrete pathfinders (Francisco, Elías, Ignacio, and Javier), those who worked in the United States after Francisco Negrete Sotelo returned, did, indeed, found a family in California too but not until the 1950s. They worked in the United States in the 1940s and then returned home to Michoacán to take advantage of the revolutionary dole discussed earlier, an *ejido* farm, each receiving a portion of the old hacienda where their elders had worked as *paleros*. It was supposed to provide each of them with economic hope along with opportunities to make it work.

They may have, in fact, returned to Mexico for this very reason whereas my parents left Mexico before any land parcels were distributed in this manner. This may have been yet another reason why Dad never considered returning to Mexico. There was nothing to go back for. As we've seen, Mom and Dad hung on even during the Depression with the hope of finding economic stability in California and perhaps a measure of prosperity.

A final contrast between our family and our cousins, the Negrete's, is that they were willing to celebrate a personal holiday in Fillmore in a truly traditional manner whereas we never went that far. According to my sister Mary, who was invited for the celebration, in January 2008, someone in the family decided to surprise my *tia* Cuca, *tío* Pancho's widow, on her birthday with a half a dozen or so *cohetes*. These are traditionally crafted fire crackers tied to a wooden shaft that fly into the air once they're ignited and explode with an earsplitting bang, leaving puffs of smoke and shredded paper to flutter away—a touch of New Year's fireworks for a birthday. This is done all over Mexico to this day, even in big cities. In Fillmore, the Negrete boys shot their *cohetes* into the California afternoon, just as if they were having a birthday party in Rancho Palmira. The explosions undoubtedly startled the Fillmore police department probably sending them scrambling for their cruisers.[249]

It seems that the continued ties the Negretes enjoyed with their old folks back home in Michoacán inspired this kind of party surprise. We, the Gils lost those ties; we never sent celebratory rockets into the sky, and it never occurred to us!

Finally Discovering Dad's Relatives on His Father's Side

Upon my return home from visiting the Negretes, I continued to work on this book and once again experienced the frustration of having such limited information about Dad. It felt like I had met up with a brick wall when I needed to get around it to the other side. As a result, I forced myself to go back to my notes and reread, among other things, the remarks I had written thirty years earlier of a conversation I had with my *tío* Pancho. He came to visit my mother on an April day in 1978 when I happened to be visiting. Consequently, he and I talked about my father and I made annotations which sat in my files for decades, my uncle passing away in the interim. I overlooked these notes because I was concentrating on the main interviews leading to my writing of Part I and so my hand-scribbled notes and comments of my conversation with my *tío* continued to sit in my files for another three years.

When I finally dug them out, after returning from Rancho Palmira, and scrutinized them anew, my uncle's remarks yelled out at me: "Your father has cousins including Epifanio, Lupe, Esther, and one whom you [the author] best resemble, Avelino," he said to me during that April visit. I still remember the rustic sound of his Michoacán Spanish. He informed me that "they were small merchants and they resided in Ario Santa Monica, now Ario de Rayón."[250]

His recommendations and clues could not have been any clearer! I had not visited Ario de Rayón all this time! What a numbskull! So I packed my bags as soon as I could and returned to the Chavinda region, this time travelling in the company of my sister, Soledad. We arrived in Zamora and the old but comfortable Hotel Fénix became our headquarters. The next day after our arrival, we headed to Ario de Rayón, a small township rooted just a few miles from both Chavinda and Rancho Palmira.

My sister and I prepared for our visit; she is fluent in Spanish, so it was good to have her along. We searched for and made a record of the Gils listed in the telephone pages for Ario. Our aim was to hunt them down and talk with all of them in an effort to find a relative. If my *tío* Pancho knew what he was talking about, we were bound to find someone, I thought.

In a rented automobile, we obtained directions and soon drove the ten or so miles from Zamora past its sleazy outskirts and into sugar cane fields and other lush agricultural plantations. We parked our car in the shade of a small and lovely town square of Ario de Rayón. Our next step was to locate the mayor's office or city hall because, I surmised, someone there would help us get a bearing on the street names identified in the telephone list we compiled as there were no clearly visible street signs. We found the *municipio* offices right away and walked inside to be greeted by a pleasant young woman clerk who reacted positively when we explained our purpose. She immediately said, "Yes, there are some Gils who run a store two blocks up the main street. You can begin your search with them." And with her hand she pointed us in that direction.

In the rising heat of the bright morning, Soledad and I ambled up the sidewalk. We stepped along with some trepidation because business signs in Mexican small towns don't stand out as they do in the United States, but soon we crossed the threshold of what looked like a small general store. Standing amid rolls of wire and farm implements, our eyes focused on a man standing behind the counter, attending to some customers. I said to him that we were looking for a family of Gils who included an Epifanio in their family tree and could he help us in any way? Attending to his customers and talking to me at the same time, I thought he reacted somewhat askance at our proposition but, nonetheless, in between words to his shopper he told us to walk another block up the street and seek out a *papelería* or paper products shop with a big open door where we would find his sister, Eloisa. He said that she would be willing to talk with us. Soledad remembered that he identified himself as Roberto Gil and that his response was more positive and friendlier than I recalled and that he referred us to his sister because she was the one who held all of the family information, not him.

Back on the street, scratching my head a little because I couldn't quite fully comprehend why the shop owner answered in this fashion, we found a *papelería* with a big open door. Entering, we asked a young woman clerk for Eloisa and very soon, a middle-aged woman of medium height appeared, asking us how she might help us. Gray-haired, of middle complexion, with large dark eyes, wearing a rayon-like flower-print dress, she spoke casually in a high-pitched voice—*¿En que les puedo servir*? Taking the lead, I introduced us briefly by name and pulled out copies of two photographs I had brought along and handed them to her. One my mother had preserved for about seventy years, showing the aunts who raised my father as described above. The other was a photo I took in 1970 or thereabouts of a woman named Esther who was supposed to be one of my father's relatives; my mother and I visited her either in Chavinda or Ario de Rayón. I said, "Do you recognize the women in these pictures?" Somewhat taken aback and with mounting scrutiny, Eloisa inspected the photographs and then glanced at us to get a better look. She then exclaimed, "Yes, these are my aunts, Elodia and Manuela! And this other one is my aunt Esther!" Her words rang out with a slight edginess as if to say, why would you be carrying these photographs?

My sister felt that she reacted cautiously at first. She remembered that Eloisa first replied with some reserve to our brief explanation of who we were and why we might be standing at her shop door and, secondly, with confused trepidation after examining the photos for the first time. Sally remembered that Eloisa started out by explaining that she was in the middle of taking inventory because the school term was about to begin, and that she was in the middle of calling in some orders to her vendors. I don't really know what kind of reaction I expected, but I said to myself, "She certainly is an active business woman, that's for sure." And so I quickly replied that we could return at a better time. Instead of letting us walk away, she asked us to give her a while to call in her orders and that, in the meantime, we could visit with her niece who owned a mom-and-pop grocery shop right across the street. Perhaps we could return in short order.

We did as she suggested and received a warm welcome from her niece, a pleasant woman in her late thirties, who chatted with us from behind her store counter cluttered with various and sundry food packages. She too felt obligated to converse with us while attending to customers who needed to purchase a package of milk, or cigarettes, or make a telephone call using her cell phone, and so on. I said to myself, "Boy, these Gils are merchants indeed!"

Eloisa soon retrieved us. We walked back across the street to her store, but instead of entering the paper shop, she led us to another door nearby that opened up into her own home. My sister and I strode in and discovered a well-furnished home, whose corners and hallways served as storage areas for paper merchandise stacked high in boxes. She asked us to excuse the apparent jumble by exclaiming, "I run a business, and my house is not as tidy as it ought to be." And after ordering some beverages for us from her niece, the young woman clerk we met earlier in the store, Eloisa cleared piles of paper and booklets off her sturdy dining room table and bid us to sit.

We discussed our families in a friendly and animated tone. In our case, we painted a more detailed picture of our family, our mother, and who our father had been, including the limited details we commanded about his emigrating to California. I also showed her yet another photograph; this one of my dad when he was about thirty years old, standing and holding Mary in his arms, noticing also that his likeness didn't evoke a response from her. She, in turn, asked us to examine some photographs of herself and her father, Epifanio, who worked in the United States as a bracero at one time, a claim that she punctuated by showing us a government identification card he received at the time. She delighted in sharing what she knew about Ario de Rayón and made an attempt at explaining why her family had moved there from Chavinda. She then placed Elodia, Manuela, and Esther in a larger family context. Soledad and I greeted the details of these relationships with heightened interest. In the process, I quizzed her about her family enough to sketch out a rough family tree.

However, she had never heard of my father or of his father Benedicto, and so this gap separating the threads of our family left my sister and I quite puzzled. Eloisa might have felt our bewilderment. We had uncovered some obvious connections between our two families, but the critical links were still missing. When I began to feel that we had probed our subject sufficiently for a first round, we said our good-byes, promising to do some follow-up. Soledad and I returned to the United States the next day.

Three months later, I returned to Ario de Rayón, but this time I traveled in the company of my wife, Barbara Deane, of Anglo-Irish descent, who speaks Spanish fluently. Knowing we were arriving, this time Eloisa arranged enough time to spend with us and, in fact, we conversed for about six hours. Our enlivened discussion included not only introducing my wife into the picture and dwelling briefly about her American origins, it also allowed me to follow up and clarify my understanding of who-was-who on her side of the Gil family. Having brought a typed draft of the family tree I had fashioned at home, we spent some time making final amendments to it on her dining room table and in the course of our deliberations she proudly handed me a document.

"I did some searching on my own," she said, "and I found your grandfather Benedicto's baptismal certificate!" Taking a moment to let my mind catch up with what she was saying, I inspected the document and suddenly realized what she was telling me. Here was my grandfather's baptismal certificate, Dad's father, Benedicto. It also identified his parents' names: Bernabé Gil and María Trinidad Salceda. This is how we learned that my father was named for his grandfather! Eloisa pointed out too that her grandfather's mother's surname was Salcedo, spelled with an "a" at the end, instead of an "o." She rationalized that someone had changed the spelling from an "a" to an "o" at one point or another, intentionally or not, but affirmed that she held no doubt that these names fitted into her family tree—this helped us connect more missing links.

In other words, Eloisa's search in the local records yielded archival proof that we had common ancestors. Her relatives belonged to us as well. She confirmed this connection by producing my grandfather Benedicto's baptismal certificate, which she handed to me on our second visit with a measure of pride and in this way confirmed that Benedicto and Epifanio, her grandfather, shared the same parents, Bernabe Gil and Maria Trinidad Salceda. They were brothers. Now we had a solid family link, first because Eloisa visually recognized in the photos of I shared with her the aunts who raised my father and now she also recognized Benedicto's relationship to her grandfather as demonstrated by his baptismal certificate.

So Epifanio, senior, was Benedicto's elder brother, and hence my father's uncle. Unable to locate a birth document for Epifanio, I estimated he was born ca. 1851 because Eloisa remembers he died in 1949 when she believed him to be about ninety-eight years old.

Visitors arrived while my wife and I tried to keep track of the conversation. Several of her nieces turned up as well, most of them in their twenties or thirties, and after we had all introduced ourselves we gathered around the dining room table and enjoyed a hearty homemade dinner washed down with various kinds of carbonated beverages. In the course of our tête-à-tête, we exchanged more personal stories, and Barbara and I also learned that two of Eloisa's nephews had crossed the border into the United States, probably without documents, and were living near San Fernando and working somewhere in greater Los Angeles. All this time I had been searching for my father's relatives on his father's side and fretting about not finding them, yet his descendents were residing nearby, owing to the tugs and pulls of Mexican immigration into the United States!

Taking a Fresh Look at Dad's Early Life and Surroundings

Here I weave together the various threads of the information I gathered about father in an effort to fill in the huge gaps that always eluded us. These strands include the strained memories that nourished our family lore as summarized at the top of this chapter to which I added the clues and hunches gleaned when I began pressing my siblings to rekindle their memory further. My own searching in libraries and in archives, both paper and digital, supplemented the emerging vision enhanced by the statements made by our newly discovered cousins, the Negretes in Rancho Palmira, and Eloisa Gil in Ario de Rayón. This intertwining of inklings, memory, and knowledge affords us the widest possible understanding of Dad's life before he left his Michoacán home, never to return.

When my dad came to this world in 1899, the countryside surrounding his hometown was already a bountiful agricultural region. The large haciendas that originally claimed the rolling landscape in the 1700s had already begun to break up into smaller more functional farms, as stated earlier. His uncles on his mother's side, as we've already learned, were already working as *paleros*, ditch diggers who had the task of improving the local farmland by bringing river water to San Juan Sin Agua, and there may have been other laborers doing the same thing for other farms, irrigating the more arid properties in order to boost wheat and corn production. Even before Dad was born, there was already enough produce to merit building and running a small rail line that ran right through town and linked up with a bigger railroad track to the north, as we'll see below, thus allowing local farm products to reach bigger markets. My sister and I walked along the rail line when we visited.

Early in my investigation, I began gathering the sense that my dad's relatives were not *peones* like my mother's relatives. They may have been surrounded by peasants, but they did not count themselves among them. I've written already that my mother's relatives were all "salt of the earth" farm workers who lived on a hacienda in the early 1900s and were indebted to the owner in a way that limited their possibilities. This social and economic dependence, which I sketch out in chapter 1 and the consequent close relationship to farm work that my mother claimed, seems not to have applied to Dad's relatives.

This initial understanding contributed largely to my hunch about Dad's *pueblerino* or small town background. Living in a small town, he and his extended family were a step or two removed from serf like conditions, and this may help explain why his aunts, who took the studio photo described above, give the appearance of belonging to Mexico's budding middle class in the early 1900s. All seems to point to the fact that Dad belonged to a family that lived in town, instead of on a farm, and the men in his family, including his father, may have hired out to do casual work but not farm work necessarily. This is why I maintain that they were *pueblerinos* or small town folk at the start of the twentieth century in Mexico, and their lives did not depend on the whims of a single farm owner—all this I deducted before I discovered Eloisa, my cousin.

On the face of it, and contrary to our family lore, my father didn't lack for relatives when he was a child. My own digging[251] in the Mormon digital archives uncovered his grandparents, Bernabé Gil and Maria Trinidad Salceda, confirming the information Eloisa exposed when she went searching for Benedicto's birth certificate, likewise revealing that my father was named after his grandfather. I also discovered that Bernabé senior and María Trinidad brought eight children to this world, at least, from the mid—to late-1800s. Epifanio was the firstborn in 1851, approximately, and according to the Mormon archives, he was followed by seven other children: José Seferino de Jesús, Melquiades Silvestre, José Juan Bautista de Jesús, Juan José Germán de Jesús, José Benedicto de Jesús (my grandfather), Manuela, and finally Elodia, approximately in that order. The reader will note the clear biblical-Christian ring to some of these names except for Epifanio, Manuela, and Elodia and chances are that their certificates as yet unobtainable may contain compound Christian combinations as well, probably reflecting a strong Christian faith. In any case, my father could claim four uncles and two aunts in his extended family—his father's brothers and sisters.

Eloisa not only helped me validate my *pueblerino* hunch about my father's family in Mexico, but she also indirectly unveiled someone who seems to have had an important impact on my father—Epifanio Gil Salcedo, her grandfather and Dad's eldest uncle, Bernabé Gil senior's oldest son. When I asked her to tell me about her family, her grandfather came to mind first and foremost. He could read and write and keep books for the owner of the hacienda where he worked, she asserted, referring to the Hacienda San Juan Palmira, also known as San Juan Sin Agua. (This tells me too that my father's ancestors also came from Palmira and, hence, why Benedicto married Librada—they lived on the same hacienda.)

The fact that Epifanio could read and write and was good with numbers set him apart from everyone else in those days. He may have been poor economically but gave evidence of using his mind in order to survive, instead of his physical labor, and everyone respected that. Filled with pride, Eloisa reminded me, "He was in charge of payroll on the hacienda." And the second most cherished memory was that "he had beautiful handwriting." "How did he learn to read and write?" I asked. She conjectured that, back in the days, before the revolution, he learned from the teachers who were assigned to work in certain haciendas. He was Eloisa's most important ancestor and had, in effect, set down a model of self-improvement for his descendents, or so it seems.

I also concluded there was a more direct connection to my father. Namely, that Epifanio was the person who made my Dad uneasy when he was a boy and may have been the main reason why he fled, to end up in the United States. I arrived at this conclusion because Dad's story to us is that he remembered two aunts, Manuela and Elodia, plus a man who scrutinized what he ate and how much, and this made my father, who had already lost both parents, feel unwanted.

Here are the reasons for this conjecture. Epifanio worked as an administrative employee on the Hacienda San Juan Palmira "in charge of payroll" at the same time that he also lived on the farm property as Eloisa stated. The local records obtained through the Mormon genealogical service tell us that he had several siblings although we don't know anything about them or why they failed to cast an imprint on Eloisa's memory. She does, however, retain in her memory that Epifanio moved to Ario, a handful of miles away, about a year or two before Dad was born or about 1898. Whatever may have been the reasons for moving, his granddaughter learned that he opened up a grocery store and engaged in retail business for the rest of his life, a situation that gave him the wherewithal to build a *patrimonio* or asset base, allowing him to keep a house for his unmarried younger sisters in nearby Chavinda where my dad lived as an orphan.

Eloisa described Epifanio as visiting his sisters periodically. Since they lived as spinsters in a small provincial Mexican town, where no other male would enter their home except family, specifically their elder brother, Epifanio, and my dad as a boy, I concluded Epifanio was the one who kept an eye on my father after he began living with his aunts, following his father Benedicto's demise when he lost his life in a building accident "because a beam fell on him." Dad's mother died when he was an infant, so after losing his father, Dad began living in Chavinda with his spinster aunts although he may have known them well already, assuming Benedicto asked them to babysit long before he lost his life. Epifanio was probably about sixty years old when my father became an orphan. His other brothers seem to have disappeared by this time for reasons that no one knows.

I imagined him as a sober and dutiful man of medium height, tending toward a light-skin complexion, instead of a mestizo bronze. It's likely he favored English/American-style cuts of clothing rather than the quasi-Spanish cuts of a Mexican *ranchero*, a man oriented toward the urban world.

Epifanio's human qualities most probably contributed to Dad's unhappiness and his ultimate departure. He seems to have possessed a stern and morose personality that frowned on social exchange as we learned above when his granddaughter Eloisa informed us that he was *muy reservado*. This means that he wasn't open to carrying on a conversation or listening to the views of others; he was probably an introvert. This introversion must have contributed to her not knowing about my grandfather, Benedicto, something she admitted to me from the start, and much less about my father. She didn't know about Melquiades Silvestre nor about Juan José Germán, the other uncles turned up in the Mormon archives. This blind-sidedness may have been the result of Eloisa's grandfather setting down a norm within the family about not probing the past and not talking about family matters. If this was so, he was indeed *muy reservado*.

Eloisa commanded knowledge about present-day family relationships. This is why her brother, Roberto, the general store owner, told us to see her, not him. With her guidance I was able to fashion the first draft of a family tree when I first visited with my sister Soledad but nothing about family ties before her father was born. At one point in our visits, she conceded not knowing her grandfather's mother's name until we arrived and began asking questions. The bible-sounding names of some of Epifanio's other brothers were new to her as well. She knew about but never met her uncle Jose (José Seferino de Jesús) who lived in nearby Santiago Tangamandapio but not about his compound Christian name although she did meet his children, she mentioned.

The bafflement that I felt when my sister Soledad and I said good-bye to Eloisa at the conclusion of our visit is thus explained. Our cousin had positively identified the women in the photographs that my family preserved for several decades and which I showed her when we first met, but she could not remember my father's father and much less know my own father.

The main reason seems to be that old Epifanio had said little about his past to Eloisa before he died. It's entirely possible too that he may have faced some tough moments in his life, and this may have soured him. After all, he became a man during Mexico's most difficult decades, an arduous and costly time of nation-building according to the history books. The Mexican government changed countless times as a result of violence during Epifanio's first thirty years of life. It sounds like he may have been a pious man too and thus felt impacted by the tumultuous years in which the government fought against the Catholic Church in the late 1920s when he was in his late 70s. In these political contests, he may have known local priests who died in the fracas or lost friends, if not family members. Missed opportunities connected to these difficult years may have also impacted him negatively. He may have left the hacienda for these reasons, and his siblings may have died or moved away as a result of the political storms. All this may have had a depressing effect on him so that his granddaughter remembered him as *muy reservado*.

Another factor explaining the knowledge-gaps in the family's past is simply that my cousin Eloisa was just too young to have taken advantage of her grandfather's fading memory. She was eighteen years old when he died, and so even if she had already developed an interest in keeping track of the relatives in her family, to the extent that her brother Roberto identified her as "the one who knew about the family's past," it would have been too late to learn anything of value, especially if Epifanio became senile in his final years and communicated even less than when his mind was still whole. In other words, her own youthfulness probably prevented her from probing his mind at the proper moment and her siblings may not have had a mind for such things.

There's also the matter of Dad's aunt, Elodia—also Eloisa's aunt. She was a crusty country lady according to Eloisa. She was the younger of Epifanio's two sisters, who were obligated on the basis of family ties to care for my father when he became an orphan. Manuela and Elodia were young when Dad's father died. Elodia's temperament may have contributed to my father's disaffection because Eloisa described her as blunt-spoken and reluctant to accept her neighbor's shortcomings. "My father didn't like the way she expressed herself," my cousin told me. "Her speech was rustic, she wasn't very educated [for that matter], and she was quite direct," she added. Eloisa recalled one day when her grandfather took her to visit her aunts in Chavinda and he needed some water. He asked Elodia the location of the water bucket to which she curtly responded, "C'mon, you're not a fifteen-year-old kid!" He should have known where it was. Sometimes she would apologize for her brusqueness or just plain make people laugh at the way she spoke, but that's the way she was, my cousin explained. "Manuela, on the other hand, was a finer sort of person, more prudent; Elodia was the opposite," she clarified.

My father's behavior as a boy may have been a factor too. He probably didn't remember his mother at all because she is said to have died when he was three. But the question arises, did his mother's absence cause behavioral problems for the adults who supervised him beginning with his own father? We don't know how Dad's mother died and so any speculation about how that might have affected him appears even more contrived. A more realistic question is how his father's death might have wounded him. Losing his father, on top of his mother's absence, must have had some sort of impact on him. His behavior would necessarily have been effected by such a loss. Even though children, in early-1900s, in a town like Chavinda, most probably hid their emotions more than children in our time, Dad must have felt a loss and, in his eyes, his aunts and his morose uncle might not have shown enough appreciation for what he was feeling.

We can now conjecture young Bernabé's departure from Chavinda to some extent. He must have hopped a ride on one of the flat-bed rail cars that rattled by every day or every other day, transporting sugarcane and other farm products out of the Chavinda area. His aunts must have reacted angrily about his absence at first, but after a week or more of not hearing from their nephew, who they might have considered troublesome, they may have begun feeling regretful and bewildered. They must have informed Epifanio the first night he was gone, but by the end of the first week or two, they all must have sensed that young Bernabé had taken a decisive step. Did they reflect on why he might have run away? Manuela may have blamed Eloisa for being hard on the boy, especially if she scolded the teenager once too many. My brother Manuel, named after Manuela, reminded us in chapter 8 that Dad held special regard for her. "He loved her," he said, Eloisa confirming that she was the compassionate one. We'll never know the answers to these questions, but Epifanio may have reacted more guardedly as he had surely known many young men and even young women get separated from their loved ones by past upheavals. So here was his own nephew, Benedicto's boy, grabbing the wolf by the ears. "More fodder for those cannons in these times of revolution," he might have mused with the skepticism of a life's veteran. The fact is that my father walked away and never returned.

Bernabe's aunts in Chavinda, Manuela and Elodia (ca. 1923)

Appendix II:

The Gil Family Tree
(a partial view)

On Our Father's Side of the Family:

Bernabe Gil (b. 1831? - d. 1900?) + Maria Trinidad Salcedo (b. ? - d.?): they had 8 children including Benedicto.
Benedicto Gil (b. 1878 - d. 1912?) + Librada Negrete (b. 1892? - d.?): they had only one child:
Bernabe Gil (b. 1899 - d.1955) see below

On Our Mother's Side of the Family:

Carlota Hernandez (b.1880 - d.1953) + C. Naranjo (b? - d.?) + C. Brambila (b.? -d. ?) + F. Juarez (b.1866 - d.1931?):
Carlota had 3 children:
Pascual N. (b.1900 - d.1985) + Salvadora (b.? - d.?) + Ester (b.? - d.?): no children
Miguel N. (b.1902 - d.1995) + Consuelo P. (b.1905 - d.2001): they had 12 children
(our Naranjo cousins)
Guadalupe B. (b.1905 - d.2007)+ Bernabe Gil: they had the 8 children below:

1st Gen.	2d Gen.	3d Gen.	4th Gen.
Bernabe Gil + Guadalupe Brambila			
	Mary G. (b.1928 -) + I. Aguirre + J. Valdez		
		Irene A. (m.)	Veronica
			Marcelo
		Johnnie V. (m.)	John
			Amanda
		Bernie V. (dv.)	Celina
			Bernabe J.
			Noemi
			Jacqueline
		Alfonso V. (dv.)	0 children
		Angel V. (s.)	0 children
	Manuel G. (b.1931 -) + C. Mendez + Pat G.		
		Cecilia G. (m.)	Rosalinda
			Jessica
		Maria E. G. (m.)	Joel
			Myndel
			Donovan

1st Gen.	2d Gen.	3d Gen.	4th Gen.
		Susie G. (m.)	Timothy
			Rachel
			Anna
		Mario G. (dv.)	0 children
	Mike G. (b. 1934 - d.2007) + Pat W. + Linda P.		
		Chris G. (d.)	0 children
		Linda G. (m.)	0 children
		Mike G. (m.)	Michael Brandon
		Cindy G. (m.)	Tanya
			Tony
	Carlos G. (b.1937 -) + R. Ruiz + L. Pompeo + B. Deane		
		Jennie G. (m.)	Daniel
			Carla
		Rachel G. (m.)	Ruben
			David
			Christian
		Anamaria (m.)	Matthew (bm.)
			Joshua (bm.)
		Carlos G. (dv.)	Kaila (bm.)
			Sydnee
			Zachary
		Chadley S. (bm.,s.)	0 children
		Julia S. (bm., m.)	Cesar
			Solana
	Martha G. (b.1939 - d. 1999) + S.A. Polanco + J. Nunez + J. Murillo		
		0 children	
	Rick G. (b.1942 - d.2007) + V. Escalante		
		Nancy G. (dv.)	Valerie Vanessa
		Leon G. (m.)	Leon Anthony
			Monique
			Brandon Lee
	Sally G. (b.1944) + J. Cruz + J. Ruitenbach		
		Rebecca C.	Vanessa
			Joy
			Christopher
			Anthony
		Betty C. (dv.)	Vincent
		Ruben C. (m.)	See Julia S.
		Steve C. (m.)	Esteban
			Ezra
	Emily G. (b.1946) + A. Gomez + K. Countryman + R. Schultz		
		Kirin L. C. (s.)	0 children
		Raymond G. (s.)	0 children
		Kathy C. (m.)	Christopher (a.)
			Ashley
			Katie
		James C. (m.)	James Jr.
			Tanysha
			Patricia
			Jaimie
			Patrick

Spouses are not shown for 3rd or 4th generations

b.=birth d.=death s.=single m.=married dv.=divorced bm.=by marriage a.=adopted

Appendix III:

The Boys And One Girl in the Santa Rosa Band
(ca. 1950)

Row 7				John Hernandez "El Ocho"		David Vaiz "El Puya"	Joe Espinosa "Little Joe"	Bobby Gamboa
Row 6	Carlos Gil "El Charly"					Bobbie Ruiz		Manuel Vaiz
Row 5	Albert Garcia		Arturo Chacon "El Turi"		Tony Melendrez	Danny Franco "El Cuate"	Freddie Aguilera	
Row 4	Johnny Ramirez		Manuel Munoz	Jimmie Villegas	Louis Baraja "Barajitas"	Charlie Meza	Tony Garcia	Danny Rosales
Row 3	Richard Durazo	Joe Ruiz	Ruben Herrera		Roy Lopez		Augie Lerma	Henry Landin
Row 2	Anita Hernandez		Louis Vaiz	Eddie Cardona "El Dagwood"	Raymond Lerma "El Monchi"	Mike Naranjo	Enrique Gil	Tony Naranjo
Bottom Row		Augie Maldonado	Roger Pedraza	Ray Lopez	**Profesor Antonio Banuelos**	George Bernal "El Coki"	Michael Garcia	Freddie Perez

My gratitude to Danny Rosales for providing me the names of my old band buddies.

Appendix IV:

The Sources

Primary Sources

Interviews and Manuscripts

Chacón, Arturo ("El Turi"). Telephone conversation in English and Spanish, May 23, 2011.

Countryman, Emilia (Emily) Gil. Telephone interview in English and Spanish recorded digitally, April 9–11, 2009, and multiple other dates.

Emanuel, Victoria ("Vy"). Telephone interview in English, June 12, 2011.

Gil, Guadalupe. "Pues Acerca del Modo de Mantenerse, [Adición A]." [ca. 1985] This is a transcription in Spanish made by the author of a hand written manuscript also in Spanish, two typewritten copies, 9 pp. each.

Gil, Guadalupe. "Recuerdos de mi niñez, como en el año 1916." [ca. 1985] This is a manuscript in Spanish, hand written on both sides of lined paper, pp. 14, transcribed by the author in Spanish with two typewritten copies, 6 pp. each.

Gil, Guadalupe. "Recuerdos ho memorias." [March 31, 1992] This is a manuscript in Spanish hand written on both sides of lined notebook paper, 15 pp, transcribed by the author in Spanish with four machine printed copies titled "Borrador #1, Recuerdos de Guadalupe B.Gil," two 17 pp., one spiral bound ("Recuerdos de Guadalupe Gil: Typed from the original hand-written manuscript by Carlos B. Gil"), another 7 pp., and the third 4 pp.

Gil, Guadalupe. "Recuerdos. Vivíamos en la acienda Sta. Rosa. Llo nací el 22 de Nov. 1905." [Julio 15, 1997] This is a manuscript in Spanish hand written on both sides of line notebook paper, bound by hand with crocheting thread, pp. 22.

Gil, Guadalupe. [Untitled] typewritten transcription by author in Spanish that begins on page 7 with the words, "Yo no tenía mucha ropa...," pp. 7-32.

Gil, Manuel. Interviews in English and Spanish with Manuel Gil recorded digitally on November 22, 2008, in Golden Shores Nevada; also by telephone digitally, September 10, 2009, and multiple other conversations.

Gil, Victoria. Telephone interview in Spanish, June 29, 2011.

Landín, Manuel J. Telephone interview in English, March 20, 2007.

Naranjo, Miguel. Interviews recorded in Spanish on tape by the author beginning May 3, 1978, San Fernando, California.

Naranjo, Mike. Telephone interview in English, April 26, 2011.

Naranjo, Pascual. Interviews in Spanish recorded on tape by the author beginning, May 2, 1978.

Naranjo Thigpen, Rose Marie. Telephone interview in English, November 23, 2010, and on multiple other dates.

Negrete García, Francisco. Author interviewed him in Spanish with the aid of paper notes, April 30, 1978, San Fernando, California.

Peña, Rosendo. Interview notes in Spanish, handwritten by the author beginning August 3, 1973.

Rosales, Danny. Telephone interview in English, May 9, 2011.

Ruitenbach, Soledad (Sally) Gil. Interview in English and Spanish, recorded digitally, September 10, 2009, Kenmore, Washington, and multiple conversations on other dates.

Valdez, Mary Gil de. Interview in English and Spanish, recorded on tape by the author May 1978, in San Fernando, California, and multiple conversations on other dates.

Valenzuela, Alfonso. Email correspondence, May 24, 2012.

Other Primary Sources

The Arizona Republic.

Cabrera, Luis. *Diccionario de Aztequismos* (Mexico: Ediciones Oasis, 1974).

Diccionario Porrúa. Historia, Biografía, y Geografía de México (Mexico City: Editorial Porrúa, 1995). 6ª edición.

Gale Encyclopedia of Medicine (Detroit: Gale, 1999). Vol. 5. *Institutional Racism and the Social Work Profession. A Call to Action. National Association of Social Workers, 2007.* http://www.socialworkers.org/diversity/institutionalracism.pdf.

IRPP, Reg Civ Data, Mascota field notes taken by author in 1970s.

Loomis, Derward P. 'Dode,' (comp. and author), *San Fernando Retrospective: The First Fifty Years* (San Fernando, California: San Fernando Heritage, 1985).

Los Angeles Times.

National Archives and Records Administration (NARA); Washington D.C.; Naturalization Index Cards of the U.S. District Court for the Southern District of California, Central Division (Los Angeles), 1915-1976.

Mormon Digital Archives, Family Search Internet, www.familysearch.org.

New York Times.

Passel, Jeffrey and D'Vera Cohn. 'Unauthorized Immigrant Population: National and State Trends, 2010,' February 1, 2011. *The Pew Hispanic Center.* http://www.pewhispanic.org/2011/02/01/appendix-a-additional-figures-and-tables/.

Photo Album Arranged by Soledad Gil Ruitenbach for Carlos Gil in the possession of the author.

Pictographic Map of San Fernando created by the Sanford Map Company, 1918, held at the California State University at Northridge, Map Center, Geography Department.

Report of the Conservation Commission of the State of California, January 1, 1913 (Sacramento: Friend William Richardson, Superintendent of State Printing, 1912).

Robinson, W. W. *San Fernando Valley: A Calendar of Events* (Seattle: The Shorey Bookstore, 1968), First Edition of Facsimile Reprint Ltd to 100 copies February 1968. Reproduction of 1938 publication, SJS #171.

Sanborn 1923 Land Use Map held by the Community Development Office of the City of San Fernando, California. Updated in 1951.

Santa Rosa de Lima. 50th Anniversary. 1925–1975, a pictorial directory containing a thumbnail history of the Santa Rosa de Lima Church. N. p., n. d.

Santos, Robert L. *A Bibliography of Early California and Neighboring Territory Through 1846: An Era of Exploration, Missions, Presidios, Ranchos, and Indians. Supplement One, 1990–2001* (Turlock California: Alley-Cass Publications, 2002).

US Census Bureau. *Educational Attainment. A Half-Century of Learning: Historical Census Statistics on Educational Attainment in the United States, 1940 to 2000: Detailed Tables.* http://www.census.gov/hhes/socdemo/education/data/census/half-century/introduction.html.

US Department of Commerce, Bureau of the Census, *Fourteenth Census of the United States Taken in 1920,* Vol. I, Population, 1920 (Washington, DC: Government Printing Office, 1921).

US Department of Commerce, Bureau of the Census. *Fifteenth Census of the United States: 1930. Population. Volume I. Number and Distribution of Inhabitants* (US Government Printing Office, 1931).

US Department of Labor, Immigration Service, Mexican Border District, M1769 Index and *Manifests of Alien Arrivals at Nogales, Arizona, 1905–1952.*

Vida del Valle de San Fernando, Vol. 4, No. 194, December 2, 1937. The author possesses pages 1-2, 5-6, possibly the only extant copy of this weekly barrio newspaper that listed offices at 1433 Kewen Street and a publisher named Carlos de Silva and an administrator named E. N. Landín who succeeded De Silva.

Wikipedia, The Free Encyclopedia.

Secondary Sources

Abel, Emily K. 'From Exclusion to Expulsion: Mexicans and Tuberculosis Control in Los Angeles, 1914–1940,' *Bull. Hist. Med*, 77 (2003), pp. 823–849.

A Cultural History of the United States through the 1930s (San Diego: Lucent Books, Inc., Petra Press, 1999).

Acuña, Rodolfo. *Occupied America: A History of Chicanos* (New York: Longman, 2000).

Arredondo, Gabriela F. *Mexican Chicago: Race, Identity, and Nat*ion (Urbana: University of Illinois, 2008), Statute of Liberty-Ellis Island Centennial Series.

Bailey, David C. *Viva Cristo Rey! The Cristero Rebellion and the Church–State Conflict in Mexico* (Austin: University of Texas, 1974).

Beckett, Wendy. *Sister Wendy's Book of Muses* (New York: Harry N. Abrams, Inc., 2000).

Berger, John A. *The Franciscan Missions of California* (New York: G. P. Putnam, 1948).

Better, Sherry. *Institutional Racism, A Primer on Theory and Strategies for Social Change*, Second Edition (Lanham MD: Rowman and Littlefield, 2008).

Cabrera, Luis. *Diccionario de Aztequismos* (Mexico: Ediciones Oasis, 1974).

Camacho, Loyo, Martha Beatriz. *Joaquín Amaro y el proceso de institucionalización del ejército mexicano, 1917-1931* (Mexico City: Universidad Nacional Autónoma de México, 2004).

Chase, J. Smeaton. "Through the Valley by Horseback," in Jorgenson (ed.), p. 115, reprinted from *California Coast Trails*, 1913.

Clark, Victor S. 'Mexican Labor in the United States,' *Bulletin of the Bureau of Labor, No. 78* (Washington DC: 1908).

Danzones del Porfiriato y la Revolución, a CD issued by the Dirección General de Culturas Populares, AMEF T-44-03, PECD-367.

Frias Armenta, Martha et al., "Determinants of Harsh Parenting in Mexico," *Journal of Abnormal Child Psychology* (April 1988).

Galarza, Ernesto. *Farmworkers and Agribusiness in California, 1947–1960* (Notre Dame: University of Notre Dame Press, 1977).

Gamboa, Erasmo. *Mexican Labor and World War II: Braceros in the Pacific Northwest, 1942-1947* (Seattle: University of Washington, 2000).

García, Jerry. *Mexicans in North Central Washington* (Charleston SC: Arcadia Publishing, 2007), Images of America.

García, John R. et al. *Mexicans in the Mid West* (Tucson: University of Arizona, 1989).

García, Matt. *A World of Its Own: Race, Labor, and Citrus in the Making of Greater Los Angeles, 1900–1970* (Chapel Hill: The University of North Carolina Press, 2001).

Gil, Carlos B. *The Many Faces of the Mexican American People: an essay concerning Chicano character* (Seattle: Centro de Estudios Chicanos, University of Washington, 1982).

Gil, Carlos B. *Life in Provincial Mexico: National and Regional History Seen From Mascota, Jalisco, 1867–1972* (Los Angeles: UCLA Latin American Center Publications, 1983).

Gil, Carlos B. *Mascota, 1867–1972*, translation of *Life in Provincial Mexico* (Guadalajara: Gobierno de Jalisco, Secretaría General Unidad Editorial, 1988).

Gonzalez, Gilbert G. *Labor and Community: Mexican Citrus Worker Villages in a Southern California County, 1900–1950* (Urbana: University of Illinois Press, 1994). Statue of Liberty-Ellis Island Centennial Series.

Grindle, Merilee S. *Bureaucrats, Politicians, and Peasants in Mexico: A Case Study in Public Policy* (Berkeley: University of California, 1977).

Griswold del Castillo, Richard, and Arnoldo De León. *North to Aztlán, A History of Mexican Americans in the United States* (New York: Twayne Publishers, 1996).

Gunther, Francis A. (ed.) *Residue Reviews* (New York: Springer-Verlag New York Inc., 1969).

Historia de Jalisco. Tomo I. Desde los tiempos prehistóricos hasta el siglo xvii (Guadalajara: Gobierno de Jalisco, Secretaría General Unidad Editorial), 1980.

Huntington, Samuel P. *Who Are We? The Challenges to America's National Identity* (New York: Simon & Schuster, 2004).

Jamieson, David and Julie O'Mara. *Managing Workforce 2000* (San Francisco: Jossey Bass, 1991).

Johnston, Hank. *Rails to Minarets: The Story of the Sugar Pine Lumber Compa-*

ny (Corona del Mar: Trans-Anglo Books, 1930).

Jorgenson, Lawrence C. (ed.) *The San Fernando Valley: Past and Present* (Los Angeles: Pacific Rim Research, 1982).

Kennedy, Diana. *The Art of Mexican Cooking: Traditional Mexican Cooking for Aficionados* (New York: Bantam Books, 1989).

La Botz, Dan. *César Chávez and La Causa* (New York: Pearson Longman, 2006).

Loden, Marilyn and Judy B. Rosner. *Workforce America! Managing Employee Diversity as a Vital Resource* (Homewood Illinois: Business One Irwin, 1991).

Lewis, Oscar. *Five Families: Mexican Case Studies in the Culture of Poverty* (New York: Basic Books, Inc., 1959).

Loomis, Derward P. "Dode" (comp. and author). *San Fernando Retrospective: The First Fifty Years* (San Fernando, California: San Fernando Heritage, 1985).

López Sánchez, Sergio. *El Teatro Angela Peralta de Mazatlán: Del Desahucio a la Resurrección* (Mazatlán: Ayuntamiento de Mazatlán, 2004).

McArthur, Judith N. and Harold L. Smith. *Texas Through Women's Eyes. The Twentieth Century Experience* (Austin: University of Texas, 2010).

McWilliams, Carey. *Factories in the Field: The Story of Migratory Farm Labor in California* (Boston: Little, Brown and Company, 1939).

McWilliams, Carey. *North from Mexico: The Spanish Speaking People of the United States* (New York: Greenwood Press, Publishers, 1968), reprinted from 1948 edition.

Meister, Dick and Anne Loftis, *A Long Time Coming: The Struggle to Unionize America's Farm Workers* (New York: Macmillan Publishing Co. Inc., 1977).

Montejano, David. *Anglos and Mexicans in the Making of Texas, 1836–1986* (Austin, TX: U. of Texas Press, 1987).

Morison, Samuel Eliot. *The Oxford History of the American People* (New York: Oxford University Press, 1965).

Murray, C.C.V.I., M.A. Sister Mary John. *A Socio-Cultural Study of 118 Mexican Families Living in a Low Rent Public Housing Project in San Antonio,* Texas (Washington DC: The Catholic University of America, 1954). Arno Press (reprinted), 1976.

Pletcher, David M. *Rails, Mines, and Progress: Seven American Promoters in Mexico, 1867–1911* (Ithaca: Cornell University Press, 1958).

Sánchez, George J. *Becoming Mexican American: Ethnicity, Culture, and Identity in Chicano Los Angeles, 1900–1945* (New York: Oxford University, 1993).

Schroeder, O.P., Rev. J. H. *Canons and Decrees of the Council of Trent*. English Translation (Rockford, Illinois: Tan Books and Publishers Inc., 1978).
Sierra, Justo. *The Political Evolution of the Mexican People* (Austin: University of Texas Press, 1969).
Sierra Rubio, Andrés. *La hacienda del valle de Chavinda en el tiempo y el espacio. Tenencia de la tierra y problemática social, 1528–1778*. Coordinación de Apoyo Municipal, Gobierno de Michoacán. Información Monográfica Municipal, 1986).
Smart, Allen. *Viva Juárez!* (London: Eyre and Spottiswoode, 1964).
Steinbeck, John. *The Grapes of Wrath* (New York: The Viking Press, 1958).
Tannenbaum, Frank. *Mexico: The Struggle for Peace and Bread* (New York: Knopf, 1956).
Tax, Sol. *Penny Capitalism: A Guatemalan Economy* (Washington, DC: US Government Printing Office, 1953).
Terkel, Studs. *Hard Times: An Oral History of the Great Depression* (New York: Pantheon Books, 1970).
Thomas, Evan. *Robert Kennedy: His Life* (New York: Simon and Schuster, 2002).
Walton, John. *Western Times and Water Wars: State, Culture, and Rebellion in California* (Berkeley: University of California Press, Centennial Book, 1992).
Wecter, Dixon. *The Age of the Great Depression, 1929–1941* (New York: The Macmillan Company, 1948).
Wollenberg, Charles. 'Working on El Traque: The Pacific Electric Strike of 1903,' in Norris Hundley, Jr., ed. *The Chicano* (Santa Barbara: Clio Books, 1975).
Zierer, Clifford M. 'The Citrus Fruit Industry of the Los Angeles Basin,' *Economic Geography*, Vol. 10, No. 1 (January 1934):pp. 53–73.
Zierer, Clifford M. 'San Fernando—A Type of Southern California Town,' *Annals of the Association of American Geographers*, Vol. XXIV, No. 1 (March 1934), pp. 1–28.

Other Internet Websites (the URL's are withheld here due to their inconstancy):

Academia de Apellidos, La (Barcelona)
Agricultural Research Center. US Department of Agriculture. Arid Lands Publications
Allina Hospitals and Clinics, Sister Kenny Rehabilitation Institute
American Health Information Management Association

Burton Cotton Gin and Museum, Burton, Texas, The
Catholic Answers
Central Pacific Railroad Photographic History Museum Seventy-Five Years of Progress. An Historical Sketch of the Southern Pacific 1869–1944
City of Nogales, Sonora
Connecting Circles of Influence
"Institutional Racism in American Society: A Primer."
MedlinePlus, A Service of the U.S .National Library of Medicine and the National Institutes of Health
MentalHelp.net, Allan Schwartz, PhD., Weblog
Mexico and Language, Open your Ojos
Mormon Digital Archives, Family Search Internet
MSW Management, The Journal for Municipal Solid Waste Professionals
National Propane Gas Association
San Fernando Valley Historical Society
"Teaching with Documents: The Civil Rights Act of 1964 and the Equal Employment Opportunity Commission," National Archives
Texas State Historical Association
U.S. Census Bureau. Educational Attainment. A Half-Century of Learning: Historical Census Statistics on Educational Attainment in the United States, 1940 to 2000: Detailed Tables
United States Holocaust Memorial Museum
Where Are They Now? LARadio.com
WordNet

Glossary

Barrio	This is a term that refers to a neighborhood or an urban district where Mexican-origin inhabitants predominate, found more often in the Southwest of the United States.
Bracero Program	An agricultural guest worker program (1942–1964) resulting from agreements between the United States and Mexico aimed at importing Mexican contract laborers. The original intentions were to replace American farm workers needed for military industrial production with Mexican agricultural workers and this proved to be very beneficial.
Cabecera	This is the term given to a Mexican city that governs and administers the surrounding rural areas with administrative and other governmental services similar to a US county seat.
Campesino (a)	An agricultural worker.
Chicano(a)	This word was used widely in the Southwest from the 1960s through the 1980s as a self-referent ("I am a Chicano") by Mexican Americans who felt engaged by the Chicano Movement and consequently considered themselves politically minded and committed to advance *la causa* or fighting for equality.
Cholo (s)	A derogatory term used in South America as late as the nineteenth century to refer to a dark-skinned worker, the word transfering to Spanish California. It was also used in the Southwest in the 1980s to refer to poor, young Latino men.
Compa	Short form of *compadre.*
Compadre	The word used to refer to the relationship between the

father of a child baptized within the Catholic Church and the man who serves as the godfather. Literally, it means cofather. Also *comadre* for a woman. *Padrino/ Madrina* are the terms used to refer to the relationship between the coparents and the baptized child who is referred to as an *ahijado (a)*. The concept, applied to other sacraments in the church, such as confirmation or matrimony, is rooted in the culture of the Catholic Church over many centuries.

Don/doña — Deference titles in Mexico added to a person's given name when he/she enjoys an elevated status usually resulting from wealth or some other distinction, noble lineage in the old days. An older person is offered respect in this way too. Don Alfonso or Doña María.

Ejido — The name given to small farms in Mexico that once formed part of a larger plantation partitioned by the government as a result of the Mexican Revolution of 1910. The farmer who received an *ejido* was referred to as an *ejidatario*. Legislation in the 1980s substantially weakened the concept.

Family lore — Stories considered true oral tales about a family's history.

Gringo (a) — This is a Mexican term that refers to an American. The word can be merely descriptive (for someone who looks white) but it may also be pejorative, depending on the speaker and the context. In this book it is used without malice as a synonym for Anglo, American, *americano*, or someone who is white. *Gabacho* was also a synonym employed by Mexican Americans especially in the 1940s and 1950s.

Hacienda — A Mexican term for a large plantation or farm. The revolutionary governments in Mexico sought to crush the hacienda system.

Indios de pata rajada

This phrase literally means "Indians with cracked feet." It remains a widely known verbal thrust used in Mexico to put down a poor person of dark skin. In the old days, there were Indians who wore sandals in part because they made them and those who didn't, and these were presumably worse off. Walking barefoot apparently produced cracked skin on the bottom of the feet. *Pata* is used to refer to the foot of an animal instead of *pié* employed to refer to a human foot, so the use of word *pata* in itself simply doubled the insult. Mexicans do not use "Native American" or any such euphemism.

Masa — Dough, wheat or corn.

Mestizo (a) — This term refers to a person of Indian and Spanish ancestry, a racial blend that occurs over one or more generations. The term "half breed" is not used in Latin America.

Metate — A rectangularly shaped stone carved from volcanic rock like a small bed with short legs used to grind corn. The *metates* in our *tortillerias* measured about 12 inches wide by 16 inches long by 8 inches high, imported from Mexico.

Nixtamal — An Aztec-rooted word that refers to the cooked corn kernels which are ground into *masa* for making *tortillas* or *tamales*.

Novena — A term that refers to a series of nine prayer sessions, usually the rosary, on behalf of someone recently deceased.

Pachuco (a) — A word that refers to a young Mexican American in the 1940s in the Southwest who dressed extravagantly (zoot suits) in order to reinforce his/her antiauthoritarian mind-set and simply wanted to be different. Pachucos learned to speak a dialect called *caló*. Many Mexican Americans considered them delinquents.

Padrino — See *Compadre* above.

Peón (es) — In Mexico it means an unskilled worker, even today. In older times when industrial jobs were few, most workers toiled in agriculture and this is why the term became synonymous with agricultural workers. A *peón acasillado* refers to the hacienda worker before the Revolution of 1910 who lived on the property and worked exclusively for the owner or administrator, many *peones* being tied to the land owner through debt.

Posadas — A Mexican folk reenactment of the traditional search by Mary and Joseph for an inn, accompanied by traditional songs for the occasion.

Strip mall	An open-area suburban shopping center popular in the United States in the early 2000's whose stores are arranged in a row facing a major arterial.
Tortillera	A woman who makes tortillas by hand.
Tortillería	A place where tortillas are made and sold. A tortilla factory.
Vecindad	A neighborhood, more often applied to a tenement neighborhood. In this book it refers to the tiny apartments that were ubiquitous in Southern California providing housing for Mexican workers and their families.
Viejos	Old people, literally. *Viejitos* means little old people. Both are used as endearing form to refer to our ancestors, our forefathers.
Wetbacks	The term "wetback" was used in the latter half of the twentieth century in the Southwest to refer to Mexicans who entered the United States without documents. It may have been a Texan invention because the Rio Grande River serves as an international boundary only in Texas.

Index

A

acordada, 271
Acuña, Rodolfo, 137-138
Adams, Rick, 184
agraristas, 23-24
aguador, 37
Alvarado, Lydio, 125
Álvarez, Basilio, 155
Alvis, Elmer, 59
Amado (Arizona), 34
Amaro, (Col.) Joaquín, 32-33
Angulo, María, 56
Anne Bolyn, 234
artists, American, 248-249
artists, Mexican, 248, 250-251
Asians in our barrio, 120
(Audelo), *Doña* Ester, 226
Audelo, *Don* José, 226
Ávalos, Jerry, 175, 305

B

Bakersfield (California), 41, 72, 103
Bañuelos, *Profesor* Antonio, 253-254, 257, 263, 375
Bermúdez, Pedro, 6-7
Bernal, Evangelina 257
Bernal, Raquel, 257
Black Thursday, 135
bootleggers, 103
Bracero Program, 172
Braceros, 172-176
Brambila, Concepción, 14, 20-21, 47

C

cabecera, 8
Californios, 118
Calles, President Plutaro Elías, 231, 233, 268
Campos, Luis, 82, 93
Cano, Beatriz S. (poetess), 260
Cantwell, Bishop John, 228
Cárdenas, Benjamín, 165
Cárdenas, President Lázaro, 139n131, 354
Cárdenas, Luis, 407n102
carrancistas, 32
Carranza, President Venustiano, 24
Carrasco, General, 56
Carrillo, Leo, 259
Cedillo, Gen. Saturnino, 409n131
Celestina (a member of Cleofas' family), 102
Central Café, 227
Chacón, Arturo ("Turi"), 257
Chávez, César, 161, 336, 345
Chavinda (Michoacán), 353-356, 420n237
cholo, 118, 238
Civil Rights Act of 1964, 345
Cleofas (one of Pascual's significant partners), 42, 94, 101-102, 106
Codino, Genaro (composer), 416n202
Conchita (Guadalupe's best friend), 59-60
Contreras, María del Refugio ("Cuca"), 359, 361
(Countryman), Ken (Emily's second husband), 319
Cristero Revolt, 231
Cruz, Javier, 192-193

Cruz, Sor Juana Inez de la, 259
cultural and religious fulfillment, our, 290-298

D

Daughters of Mary/Las Hijas de María, 231
DDT, 132
DeAnda, Padre Andrés, 234, 293
Deane, Barbara, 309, 364
DeLeón, Arnoldo, 137, 178
Díaz, President Porfirio, 11-12, 23
discrimination, 335-348
Doña Lupe (merchant), 226
Don Casimiro (merchant), 226

E

Eaton, Fred, 126
Economy Disposal Company, 307
ejidos, 23-24
El Gordo/Everardo, 236
El Judío (merchant), 226-227
Elías, Laurie, 243
Elías, *Doña* Lugarda, 230
El Rialto Café, 227
enganchados, 69
Ernestine (*Don* José Audelo's daughter), 226
Escalante, Victoria, 198
Espinosa, Petra, 124, 230

F

Father Kino, 68
Father López, 192
Felipa (Carlota's grandniece), 27
Fernández, Esther (movie actress), 398n10
Fernández, Jesús, 398n10
First Methodist Church, 116
fogoneros, 56
Followers of Our Lady of Guadalupe/Las Guadalupanas, 231
Fresno (California), 42, 92

G

Galarza, Ernesto, 161
galletas, 32
García brothers, 226
García, Terry, 257
garroteros, 55
Gasca, Tomás, 232
Gentile, Phil, 306-307
GI Rubbish Company, 305, 307, 315
Gil, Bernabé (great grandfather), 364
Gil, Bernabé (Dad), xvi, 281-283
  Bakersfield (California), in, 103-105
  constructing Carlota's tortilla shop, 148
  death of, 182-184
  during the Great Depression, 104, 142-144
  entering the United States, 43
  going to work up north with the family, 161-170
  losing his arm, 150-156
  marrying Guadalupe, 95-96
  opening a restaurant, 171-173
  setting up a grocery store, 151-152
  teaming up with Pascual, 90-92
  what he taught us, 281-283
  working as a *piscador*, 134-135
  working at the Sugar Pine Lumber Co., 105
Gil, Carlos B. (author), 308-309
  birth of, 157
  during the Sylmar earthquake, 198
  going to grammar school, 240
  graduating from college, 189
  in the Santa Rosa Boys Band, 252-257
  Life in Provincial Mexico, 15
  on his family going to work "up north," 161-170
  on his mother's compulsiveness, 210-216
  on Mott Street, 158-160
  on the relationship between Guadalupe and Bernabé, 209-211
  on the role of movies in their lives, 249-250
  on the role of music in their lives, 250-252
  on the role of radio in their lives, 247-248
  on running a business, 291
  on the third generation of Gil's, 323-326

tracing Bernabé's lineage, 353-371
watching his father work as a *piscador*, 134-135
Gil, Elodia, 351, 362, 366, 369-371
Gil, Eloisa, 362-365
Gil, Emilia/Emily (sister), xvii, 318-319
birth of, 158
experiences in Gil's Café, 177
getting married, 197, 319
going to school, 241-244
on Bernabé getting sick, 180-181
on Guadalupe's grief over Bernabé's death, 186
on Guadalupe's grief over Carlota's death, 179-180
on her relationship with her mother, 191-192, 194-197
Gil, Enrique/Rick (brother), 158, 164, 166-167, 180, 198, 241, 252, 291, 313-316
Gil, Epifanio, 361, 364, 366-370
Gil, Guadalupe B. (Mom), xv-xvi, 283-285
at Sugar Pine Lumber Co. Camp #9, 106-108
borrowing money to save our home, 154
buying a house, 144
death of, 285
during the Great Depression, 104-105, 135-136
first days in California, 79-80
immigrating to the United States, 79
her home on Huntington Street, 283-284
in the *vecindad*, 121-125
in Mazatlán (Sinaloa), 56-59
in Puerto Vallarta (Jalisco), 48-52
leaving Mazatlán, 60-61
life in Mexico, 20-22
love for poetry, 258-262
marrying Bernabé, 95-96
on Bernabé running a grocery store, 153
on Carlota's death, 179-180
on the Mexican Revolution, 22-23
on Pascual's letters from the United States, 45
opening a restaurant, 171-172
planning to leave for the United States, 46-47
relationship with Jesús López, 93-94
retirement of, 197-200, 285-286
running a tortilla shop, 186-187
singing in public, 257-258
working as a cotton picker, 79-80
writing her memoirs, 398n8
Gil, José Benedicto de Jesús (grandfather), 356, 364, 366, 373
Gil, José Juan Bautista de Jesús, 366
Gil, José Seferino de Jesús, 366
Gil, Juan José Germán de Jesús, 366
Gil, Manuel (brother), xvii, 300-304
birth of, 157
going to school, 239
in the *vecindad*, 122
on Bernabé losing his arm, 150-156
on Bernabé's death, 184
on the relationship between Guadalupe and Bernabé, 206-207
traveling "up north" to work with the family, 164, 166
Gil, Manuela, 351, 362-363, 366, 370-371
Gil, Marta/Martha (sister), 163, 166, 179, 192, 210
Gil, Melquiades Silvestre, 366
Gil, Miguel/Mike (brother), 144, 157, 163-165, 185, 239, 293, 304-308
Gil, Roberto, 362, 368
going "up north," 161-170
González, Gilbert G., 126-127
González, Manuel, 174
González, Miguel, 174
González, Pablo J., 248
González Maciel, José Antonio ("Peps"), 356
Grapes of Wrath, The (John Steinbeck), 163
Great Depression, the, 103, 131, 135, 137
Great Society program, 183
Griswold del Castillo, Richard, 137, 178
Guerrero, Esperanza, 193
Guzmán, *Don* Ponciano, 9

H

Haag, Bob, 106
Hacienda San Juan Sin Agua, 358
Hacienda Santa Rosa, 2-6
Hawk Ranch, 116

Hernández, Carlota (grandmother), xiv-xv, 266-267
as an active member of the Santa Rosa Church, 230-232
as a source of trouble between Guadalupe and Bernabé, 217-220
buying real estate, 147-148
death of, 178-179
immigrating to the United States, 79-81
in Mazatlán (Sinaloa), 57-59
in Puerto Vallarta (Jalisco), 49-52
in Sunland (California), 96-97
leaving the Hacienda Santa Rosa, 48-49
leaving Mazatlán, 60
life in Mexico, 9-15
on Guadalupe's marriage to Bernabé, 96
on Juárez's death, 144-145
registering the birth of, 6-7
setting up a tortilla shop, 148-150
Hernández, Estanislao, 10, 17, 21, 27
Hernández, Francisco, 4-6
Hernández, Johnny, 142
Hernández, Rafaela, 10
Hernández, Sabino, 10
Hernández, Soledad, 10
Hernández, Sotero, 10
Hiscock, Florence, 310-311
Hiscock, Dr. Roy, 310-311
Hoover, President Herbert, 132, 136-137
Hoyos, Rodolfo, 248
Hubbard house, 116
Huntington, Collis, 36

I

Infante, Pedro, see Artists, Mexican
institutional racism, 341-343

J

Jim Crow in Texas, 340
Johnson, President Lyndon B., 183, 345
Johnston, Hank, 106-107
Juárez, Florencio, 81

K

Kalisher Street, 225-228
KELW (radio station), 248
Kennedy, Atty. General Robert F., 162, 345
Kennedy, Diana, 5
Kennedy, President John F., 345
KFWB (radio station), 248
King Jr., Rev. Martin Luther, 336
KMPC (radio station), 248
Knuff, Rev. Justin E., 189
KWKW (radio station), 248

L

La India Market, 226
La Mexicana Market, 226
Landeros, Chuy, 224
Landín, Eusebio, 181, 226
Landín, Manuel J., 415n186
Landín's grocery store, 226
Landín's *Vida del Valle de San Fernando* (newspaper), 226
La Opinión (newspaper), 21, 258-262
La Perla Market, 227
Lara, Sofía, 94-95
Lay Catholic organizations in San Fernando identified, 231
Lázaro (Miguel's guide for getting around), 70-74
Life in Provincial Mexico by Carlos B. Gil, 15
López Adobe, 116
López, Catalina, 116
López, Conrado, 147-148
López, Gerónimo, 116
López, Jesús, 92-93
Los Jiménez (Jalisco), 15-16, 22
Los Sueños Dorados, 258
Luján, Ermelinda, 135, 230

M

Maclay, Charles (Sen.), 115, 117-119
Madero, President Francisco, 23
malathion, 132
marriage, 13
Martínez Café, 227
Mascota in the 1800's, 7-9
Mazatlán (Sinaloa)
in 1914, 29-30
in 1919, 52, 56-59

McHenry, Violeta Quintero, 258
McWilliams, Carey, 118-119, 122, 160-162, 257
Medicaid, 183
Medicare, 183
Méndez, Cristina, 193
Merino, *Don* Manuel, 3-4, 14, 20, 24-26, 85
Merino, *Doña* Victoria, 3-4
Mexican Revolution, 22-24, 271-273, 352
Mexican rules of behavior, 213-216
misión at Santa Rosa Church, the, 233-235
Mott Street neighborhood, 223-224
Mozos, Rev. Sebastián, 253
Mulholland, William, 126
multiculturalism, 343-346

N

Najar, Juan, 230
Naranjo, Cecilio, 15-16, 21-22
(Naranjo), Consuelo, 278
Naranjo, Miguel, , xv, 277-281
  arriving in San Fernando (California), 113
  crossing into the United States, 64, 67-68
  death of, 281
  going "up north" with his family, 279-281
  in Fresno, California, 74-79
  in Mazatlán (Sinaloa), 56-59
  in Puerto Vallarta (Jalisco), 18, 50
  in Sunland (California), 101-102
  leaving Mazatlán, 59-62
  on Mott Street, 225
  on Pascual's letters from the United States, 45-46
  planning to leave for the United States, 46-47
  reuniting with Pascual, 79
  traveling with Lázaro, 70-74
  working as a *piscador*, 136
  working in the mine, 76-78
  working on the railroad in Mazatlán, 53-56
  working on the railroad in the United States, 69
Naranjo, Mike, 257
Naranjo, Pascual, xv, 267-277
  addicted to gambling, 41-42
  attacked by Yaqui Indians, 31-32
  birth of, 15
  crossing into the United States, 34-36
  death of, 277
  in Hermosillo (Sonora), 32-34
  in Mazatlán (Sinaloa), 29-31
  in Puerto Vallarta (Jalisco), 27-28
  in Sunland (California), 101
  in Tuxpan (Nayarit), 271-273
  learning to drink at an early age, 15
  living with his father, 15-16
  organizing a strike in Mazatlán, 271-273
  returning to Mexico as a *repatriado*, 138-140, 268
  returning to San Fernando (California), 273, 277
  reuniting with Miguel, 79
  teaming up with Bernabé, 102-104
  working at the Sugar Pine Lumber Co., 105-106
  working on the railroad, 36-43
Naranjo Thigpen, Rose Marie, 278-280
Negrete (money lender), 155
Negrete, Jorge, See Artists, Mexican
Negrete, Librada, 355-356
Negrete, Pedro, 358
Negrete García, Francisco ("Tío Pancho"), 357-358
Negrete García, Gonzalo, 358
Negrete Sotelo, Francisco, 107, 360, 404n62
Nervo, Amado (poet), 260
Newhall (California), 71
nixtamal, 141, 148, 387
Nogales (Sonora), 1-2, 62-63
Nogales (Arizona), 1-2, 33, 63, 67-68

O

Obregón, President Álvaro, 60, 268
Oblate Fathers, 228-229
Ontario (California) in 1922, 85
Operation Wetback, 178
Ortega, Agustín, 139
Ortega, Lola, 230
orquestas típicas, 251

P

Pacheco, Consuelo, 278, 281
Pacheco, Petrita, 125, 145, 229
(Pacheco), Margarita, 230
pachuco, 184
Pacific States Savings and Loan Company, 143-144, 157
Padillas (members of the Santa Rosa Catholic Church), 230
Palafox, Rev. Salvador, 20
Panadería Las Palmas, 226
Partido Sinarquista, 232
pasaleña, 56
Paxton Ranch, 116
Peña, Aurelio, 11, 251
Peña, Lupe, 11, 251
Peña, Pilar, 398n10
Peña, Rosendo, 398n10
Peña, Trinidad, 398n10
penny capitalism, 141-142
peones acasillados, 3-4
petición de mano, 192
Peven, Manny, 292
Pico, Andrés, 117, 406n81-82
Pico, Pío, 406n82
Pius XI (Pope), 228
Plata, César, 414n180
pocho, 306, 417n216
poems in Guadalupe's life, 259-262
Ponce, Leonides ("Güicho"), 12, 14, 46, 48, 64
Ponce, Nepomucena, 5-6, 9
Portolá, Gaspar de, 114
(Powers), Linda (Mike's second wife), 307
Prado, Alberto, 124, 301
Presidio de Tubac, 68
Presley, Elvis, See Artists, American
Prohibition era, 103
Puerto Las Peñas, 2
Puerto Vallarta, 3, 7,18, 27-28, 48-52, 190

R

racism, not a word about, 335-340, 346-348
railroads in the United States, 36-37
Ramos, María, 190
Ramos, Rafael, 28
rana, la 227
Rancho Palmira, 358-359
Rayón, Ignacio López, 421n250
regional patterns of the Chicano experience, 340-341
Rennie's Theatre, 340
renganche, 37
repatriado, 138, 267
Repatriation Program, 137-140
Reyna, H. (poet), 260
Robinson, W.W., 115
Robles, Concepción C. (poetess), 260
Roosevelt, President Franklin Delano, 136
Rosales, Danny, 256-257
Rosario (Pascual's first significant partner), 35-41
Ruitenbach, Soledad/Sally Gil (sister), xvii, 316-319
  at Guadalupe's deathbed, 285
  attending Carlos's college graduation, 188-189
  birth of, 158
  getting married, 192-193
  going to school, 244-245
  on Bernabés's getting sick, 182-183
  on Bernabé's losing his arm, 156
  on Guadalupe's friend, Virginia, 188
  on Guadalupe's grief over Bernabé's death, 186
  marrying Javier Cruz, 193
  tracing Bernabé's lineage, 361-362, 364
  working in the tortilla shop, 193-194, 198
Ruiz, Rosemary, 193
Ruiz, Vicki, 414n180

S

Salceda, María Trinidad, 364, 366
Saldaña, María, 143
Salinas, Elena, 247-249
Salvadora (one of Pascual's significant partners), 35, 276
Sánchez, Prof. George J., 140, 247, 401n41
San Fernando (California), 113-121, 125-127
at the present time, 335

San Fernando Hotel, 116
San Fernando Mission, 114-115
Santarín, Susana, 58
Santa Rosa Boys Band, 252-257
Santa Rosa Catholic Church, 228-229
Santiago, Rev. J. Jesús, 399n18
Santiago, Pedro, 58, 92, 96, 102
Santo Domingo (Jalisco), 15, 21
Sarabia's tavern, 227
SB 1070 (Support Our Law Enforcement and Safe Neighborhoods Act), 347
scapular, 415n189
Schultzie (Raymond L. P. Schultz, Emily's third husband), 319
Sevilla family, 226
Sierra, Arsenia, 145
sinarquistas, 232
Sister Katherine, 243-244, 294
Sister Kenny Method (for Polio), 167
Society of the Perpetual Light/La Vela Perpétua, 231
soldaderas, 32
songs cited
  A la capotín, 257
  Alejandra, 251
  Amor y lágrimas, 257
  Barrio viejo, 110, 404n63
  Cruz de madera, 285
  Cuatro milpas/Cuatro llantas, 135, 408n120
  Dónde estás corazón?, 251
  Es mi hombre!, 258
  Jesusita en Chihuahua, 251
  Juárez, 251
  La embarcación, 61, 401n37
  Júrame, 251, 416n198
  Me he de comer esa tuna!, 250, 416n197
Sotelo, Caterina, 358
Sousa, John Phillip, 257
sports, organized, 245
Steinbeck, John, 163
Stalders, the, 96
Sugar Pine Lumber Company (SPL), 105-106, 139, 173
Sunland-Tujunga (California), 101-102
Sylmar earthquake, 198

T

teachers in our lives, 235-246
teenagers' brain development, 414n181
Texas discrimination against Blacks and Mexicans, 340
Tijerina, Reies López, 336
Tomatlán (Jalisco), 18, 190
Town Theatre, 340
Tuberculosis in the orchards, 132-133
Tucson (Arizona), 68-69
Tumacacori Missions, 68

U

"Up north," see Going "up north"

V

Valdez, John, 193
Valdez, María de Jesús/Mary Gil (sister), xvii, 298-300
  contracting Polio, 167
  getting to know Gil Café patrons, 173-177
  going to school, 236-238
  going to work "up north" with the family, 163-169
  on Bernabé's death, 183
  on Bernabé's getting sick, 182
  on Guadalupe controlling her children, 209-210
  on the Gil Café years, 208
  on the menu at Gil's Café, 173
  on the relationship between Guadalupe and Bernabé, 206-207
  on work, 292
Valdez, Rev. Ignacio, 399n18
Valencia, Lic. Antonio, 354
(Vásquez), Leonardo (Felipa's son), 27
vecindad, la, 121-123
Villa, Pancho, 23-24, 31-33
Virginia (Guadalupe's friend), 188

W

Wall Street Crash of 1929, 135
Wallace, Pat, 193
Wilkie, Prof. James W., xiv, 309
Wittinghill, Dick, 248

Wright, Francis Mario "Bud," 116

Z

Zapata, Emiliano, 49
Zierer, Clifford M., 115, 118, 126, 158, 404n67, 408n107

End Notes

Introduction

1 In Spanish, Gil is pronounced "hheeel," but most of us in the family accepted the English pronunciation with a hard G. The surname Gil is traceable to northern Spain at the time of the wars against the Moors; nevertheless, our family never embraced any related heraldic icons nor did any one pursue any Iberian connections. See information on the surname in, *La Academia de Apellidos* (Barcelona), http://www.surnames.org/empresa.htm, accessed May 26, 2011.

2 In the Mexican manner, which employs first name(s) + patronymic + matronymic, their names would be as follows:
Carlota Hernández Ponce
Guadalupe Brambila Hernández de Gil
Bernabé Gil Negrete
Pascual Naranjo Hernández
Miguel Naranjo Hernández

3 Three siblings died before I could interview them: Miguel (Mike), Enrique (Rick), and Marta (Martha).

Chapter 1 - Peasants One and All

4 The Hacienda Santa Rosa is one of the many plantations that are included in a study I did of this region. This research was poured into my doctoral thesis later rewritten into *Life in Provincial Mexico: National and Regional History Seen from Mascota, Jalisco, 1867–1972.* (Los Angeles: UCLA Latin American Center Publications, 1983). See the Spanish translation, *Mascota, 1867–1972.* (Guadalajara: Gobierno de Jalisco, Secretaría General Unidad Editorial, 1988).

5 Kennedy, Diana. *The Art of Mexican Cooking: Traditional Mexican Cooking for Aficionados* (New York: Bantam Books, 1989), p. 3. Kennedy built her career by living in Mexico's back country in the 1960s and observing and capturing invaluable details about food preparation in the traditional Mexican style.

6 Acta de Nacimiento, 1880, entry of September 25, 1880, in the Registro Civil de Mascota, Jalisco.

7 Aztec or any other central Mexican Indian cultural connections were weak in Jalisco. See a discussion of the cultural evolution of Indian cultures in Jalisco in *Historia de Jalisco. Tomo I. Desde los tiempos prehistóricos hasta el signo xvii* (Guadalajara: Gobierno de Jalisco, Secretaría General Unidad Editorial), 1980, pp. 124-126.

8 Despite the fact that Guadalupe Gil attended primary school for about two years only, she dedicated herself in her last decades to recording her memoirs by hand with clear determination—she made sure I came into their possession. Her grammar and punctuation is all her own and her spelling reveals limited schooling. This did not stop her from recording her memories because she wrote three documents with similar information. Her memory observed a defined sequence of events which can be appreciated in each of the three manuscripts. I remember many of these same stories and situations from many years of their being repeated to me and my siblings. It is possible she forgot she had written the first or the second manuscript when she started up the third. I entitled each one by employing the first word or string of words she wrote. Thus she wrote "Pues Acerca del Modo de Mantenerse," to which I added 'Adición A,'" "Recuerdos de mi niñez, como en el año 1916," and "Recuerdos." Any words or thoughts attributed to her are taken from these primary sources unless otherwise noted. See more details in the bibliography.

9 The cause of her death was recorded as *reumas* or rheumatism. I recorded this fact in handwritten field notes I made in the 1970s based on the local Registro Civil ("I RPP, Reg Civ Data"). Registered causes of death were highly inaccurate in the nineteenth century. See "Reported Causes of Death" in my *Life in Provincial Mexico*, pp. 88–89.

10 Soledad was Rosendo Peña's mother. He was my ninety-year old uncle who still rode about fifteen miles from his *ejido* farm into Mascota every Sunday on an old mule to visit his daughter, Pilar, when I lived there. He was married to Trinidad Peña, and they lived in the ex-Hacienda Galope. The hacienda had been owned by Jesús Fernández, reputedly the father of the famous screen star of the 1950s, Esther Fernández. Pilar would give Rosendo sugar, salt, and other staples to take back to his *ejido* with him. I interviewed Rosendo in 1972 and talked with him many times in those days.

11 *Life in Provincial Mexico.* There are many other history books written about this vibrant and controversial period in Mexican history.

12 Guadalupe Gil, "Pues Acerca del Modo de Mantenerse, 'Adición A:'" handwritten manuscript, 5pp.

13 Ibid.

14 Lau is an abbreviation of Estanislao, a Gothic-origin name. Aunt (or *Tía*) Lau was Carlota's older sister.

15 Naranjo, Pascual. Interviews recorded on tape by the author beginning August 19, 1974, San Fernando, California. Any words or thoughts attributed to him are taken from this interview unless otherwise noted.

16 Naranjo, Miguel. Interviews recorded on tape by the author beginning May 3,

1978, San Fernando, California. Any words or thoughts attributed to him are taken from this interview unless otherwise noted.

17 Secretaría de Economía, Dirección General de Estadística, *Estadísticas sociales del Porfiriato, 1877–1910* (México: 1956), p. 10.

18 Mother obtained two typed copies of her birth record in 1967, one dated October 31 and the other December 5. The first copy was copied out of the register in typewritten form by Rev. Ignacio Valdez and the second copy was by Rev. J. Jesús Santiago. Both copies are in the possession of the author.

19 James W. Wilkie and Edna Monzón de Wilkie's *Mexico visto en el siglo XX: Entrevistas de historia oral* (Mexico City: Instituto Mexicano de Investigaciones Económicas, 1969).

20 See an early discussion of *ejidos* in Frank Tannenbaum's *Mexico: The Struggle for Peace and Bread* (New York: Knopf, 1956). Also see Gil's *Life in Provincial Mexico*, pp. 151–154.

21 The official party later known as the PRI (Partido Revolucionario Institucional) organized the nation's peasants into voting blocs that were managed by party leaders. While the regime established government agencies charged with assisting *ejidatarios*, corruption and mismanagement hobbled the results. See for example, Merilee S. Grindle's *Bureaucrats, Politicians, and Peasants in Mexico: A Case Study in Public Policy* (Berkeley: University of California, 1977).

22 See David C. Bailey's *Viva Cristo Rey! The Cristero Rebellion and the Church–State Conflict in Mexico* (Austin: University of Texas, 1974).

Chapter 2 - The Young Rebel Goes North

23 Diccionario Porrúa. *Historia, Biografía, y Geografía de México* (Mexico City: Editorial Porrúa, 1995).

24 See for example the map on p. 60 in Sergio López Sánchez's *El Teatro Angela Peralta de Mazatlán: Del Desahucio a la Resurrección* (Mazatlán: Ayuntamiento de Mazatlán, 2004).

25 Venustiano Carranza served as the unifying leader of several armed groups that rebelled against the Díaz government and later against Pancho Villa and Emiliano Zapata. He became president of Mexico in 1917.

26 Loyo Camacho, Martha Beatriz. *Joaquín Amaro y el proceso de institucionalización del ejército mexicano, 1917-1931* (Mexico City: Universidad Nacional Autónoma de México, 2004, p. 22.

27 These were terms used by the rank and file. *Galleta* is the feminine version of *gallo* or rooster. An aggressive man may be called a *gallo*. *Soldadera* is a feminine twist to the Spanish word for soldier, *soldado*.

28 *New York Times*, January 9, 1921 ("Seek to Grow Guayule: Domestication of Wild Rubber Plant Expected to Cut Prices."). Agricultural Research Center. US Department of Agriculture. Arid Lands Publications, http://query.nytimes.com/gst/abstract.html?res=9A03E5DE153CE533A2575AC0A9679C946095D6CF, October 2006. At the time of this writing, guayule was also being tested as a possible source for latex to make gloves and for biofuel.

29 Orsí, Richard J. *Sunset Limited: The Southern Pacific Railroad and the Development of the West, 1850–1930* (Berkeley: University of California Press, 2005), p. 33.

30 These are the controversial findings of one of the earliest observers of Mexican Americans in the United States; Victor S. Clark, "Mexican Labor in the United States," *Bulletin of the Bureau of Labor, No. 78* (Washington DC: 1908); pp. 466–521 as quoted in Charles Wollenberg, "Working on El Traque: The Pacific Electric Strike of 1903," in Norris Hundley Jr. (ed.), *The Chicano* (Santa Barbara: Clio Books, 1975), p. 99.

31 Wollenberg, p. 99.

32 In 1920, the number was actually 576,673. See Department of Commerce, Bureau of the Census, *Fourteenth Census of the United States Taken in 1920, Vol. I, Population, 1920* (Washington, DC: Government Printing Office, 1921), p. 82.

33 Central Pacific Railroad Photographic History Museum Seventy-Five Years of Progress. An Historical Sketch of the Southern Pacific 1869–1944 [with Historical Map of Southern Pacific's Rail Lines] by Erle Heath Editor, *The Southern Pacific Bulletin* (Transcribed and annotated by Bruce C. Cooper) http://cprr.org/Museum/SP_1869-1944/index.html#Map, accessed November 30, 2011.

34 Orsí, p. 27.

Chapter 3 - The Family Follows

35 A roundhouse is a building used by railroad companies for servicing locomotives. It is a large circular or semicircular structure that surrounds or stands adjacent to turntables allowing a locomotive to be turned around, thus avoiding reverse motion. Buildings contained a variety of shops that facilitated the maintenance and repairs. The first roundhouses were built in England and were introduced to Mexico by American railroad builders. Most US roundhouses have been torn down. *Wikipedia*, the free encyclopedia, accessed April 19, 2007. See also David M. Pletcher, *Rails, Mines, and Progress: Seven American Promoters in Mexico, 1867–1911* (Ithaca: Cornell University Press, 1958).

36 This photograph dated by my mother as 1925 is the second earliest the family possesses of her. The photo album, created by Soledad, is in the possession of the author.

37 *La Embarcación* is a traditional Mexican song that bids good-bye; the composition is anonymous.

38 This sounds like a rustic version of the brassy musical ensembles known in the early 1970s as *bandas sinaloenses* or musical bands from the state of Sinaloa. I enjoyed them immensely in my early visits to Mazatlán. The instruments and sounds are obviously of German origin, but the lyrics and music are uniquely northern Mexican or *norteño*. The sound, later known simply as *banda* music, became wildly popular in the areas of the United States overtaken by Mexican immigration in the early 2000s.

39 Suárez Barnet, Alberto. Nogales. *Crecimiento en población de Nogales, Sonora*, an interactive population graph hosted on the city of Nogales website. http://www.municipiodenogales.org/castellano/sociedad/poblacion.htm, accessed December 1, 2011.

Chapter 4 - Arriving in the United States

40 Manifests 814 and 815, Serial 36, Lines 22–23, US Department of Labor, Immigration Service, Mexican Border District, M1769 Index and Manifests of Alien Arrivals at Nogales, Arizona, 1905–1952. Series 2; August 23, 1922–January 17, 1923, Roll 36.

41 *Plazita* is the diminutive of plaza, meaning a small town square. Most Hispanic communities are laid out around a central square which itself is surrounded by the most important civic institutions, including the local church. A town's most important social interactions customarily take place in the plaza, and so Miguel's decision to reconnoiter things at the local plaza simply represented an extension of what he learned as a child in Mascota. In the United States, plazas may be best appreciated in places like Santa Fe, New Mexico, Los Angeles, and Tucson. George J. Sánchez's keen eye for microcultural behavior informs the reader that "single male Mexican migrants through the 1920s" utilized the *plazita* in Los Angeles as "the most important area of introduction to the city" in his *Becoming Mexican American*, p. 135.

42 "Gringo" is a Mexican word for an American. It is employed in this work as a descriptive term which is normally the case although it may be used pejoratively at times by Mexicans who hold a grudge.

43 A "tramp" is a person who rides the train without permission, usually in open boxcars. The word was used widely during the Great Depression and later.

44 My uncle was correct regarding the El Tigre silver mine in the general vicinity of

Cananea near the US border. El Rosario mine in fact lies near Mazatlán, Sinaloa.

45 "Yes! The sack was approx. 12 ft. long for an adult male—a "good" picker could pick 350 pounds a day—four to five sacks full!" *The Burton Cotton Gin and Museum*, Burton, Texas. http://www.cottonginmuseum.org/Museum.htm, accessed December 15, 2011.

Chapter 5 - The First Years in the United States

46 *Cuña* is short for *cuñado* or brother-in-law, a term that may border on the insolent when used between fast friends. It can also be used to denote a close friendship, implying that the friendship is as close as a brother-in-law relationship. Yet, my uncle hadn't met my mother at this point in time.

47 The ill-fated but highly endowed Sugar Pine Lumber Company began opening land in the California sierras east of Fresno in early 1922 for the purpose of laying down railroad tracks to begin harvesting the bountiful stands of sugar pine in the mountains above Wishon. Hank Johnston, *Rails to Minarets: The Story of the Sugar Pine Lumber Company* (Corona del Mar: Trans-Anglo Books, 1930), p. 22.

48 Pascual may have misspoken when he identified pasture land—opening jobs like these as far south as Fillmore, California, which is near Ventura. He may have been referring to job sites closer to Fresno.

49 Jesús is a common man's name in Mexico. It is pronounced "Hay-soos."

50 *Seguí de novia con Jesús.* The word *novia* suggests a relationship stronger than boyfriend–girlfriend.

51 "*. . . Y que ya nos ibamos a presentar en la iglesia . . .*" When I was a boy, it was customary at our Catholic Church for the *novios* (a man and a woman promising to marry each other) to present themselves before a priest so he could announce their intentions to wed at Mass, and if anyone objected, the matter could be investigated. This is known as announcing the *amonestaciones* or the wedding banns. The Catholic Church confirmed this practice as early as 1563 but removed it in 1983. See "Banns of Marriage," *Wikipedia,* http://en.wikipedia.org/wiki/Banns_of_marriage, accessed April, 26, 2012.

52 Her handwritten memoirs state that when Miguel traveled to Fresno to consult with his mother and sister about Jesús López, Bernabé accompanied her brother, and this is when my mother first met my father. In one of my interviews with Mother, she said she met him when she went with Miguel to Le Grand to get over her unhappy experience with Jesús.

53 Guadalupe's memory is nearly correct. They obtained a marriage license in Fresno on September 15, 1923. The actual civil marriage between Bernabé Gil and Guada-

lupe Brambila was recorded in the same city but on November 11, 1923. See State of California, County of Fresno, "Marriage License" in original parchment, dated as already indicated, "Filed for Record and Recorded" for the county by George Doyle on November 26, 1923. Bernabé was 24, but his age is recorded as 21. Guadalupe was 17 (two months shy of 18), but her age is recorded as 19.

54 The Eighteenth Amendment to the US Constitution was passed in 1919, making the manufacture, transportation, sales, and consumption of liquor illegal, punishable by federal law. A rural Protestant-backed movement helped pass this amendment which lasted on the books until 1933 although it was probably very difficult to enforce uniformly. See "Bootlegging and Other Sports" in Samuel Eliot Morison's *The Oxford History of the American People* (New York: Oxford University Press, 1965), pp. 899–904.

55 See for example, *Los Angeles Times*, December 17, 1927, and December 14, 1928.

Chapter 6 - Shuttling Between Sunland and the Logging Camp

56 Sánchez, George J. *Becoming Mexican American: Ethnicity, Culture, and Identity in Chicano Los Angeles, 1900–1945* (New York: Oxford University, 1993), p. 210.

57 Arthur Fleming, Robert Gillis, and Elmer Cox. See Johnston, p. 12.

58 Johnston, p. 97.

59 Johnston, p. 86.

60 The Sugar Pine Lumber Company built a central camp large enough to serve as a small city for "lumberjacks, railroad, construction, and service people in its mountain logging operation." It included principal civic buildings, dormitories, guest houses, the "cookhouse" or dining hall with a capacity of 448 people, a camp school, and so on.

61 Wishon, California, a community named after an important developer of this region, A. G. Wishon. See Johnston, p. 22.

62 Probably Francisco Negrete Sotelo, Bernabé's maternal uncle or his mother's younger brother. Guadalupe called him a cousin, not realizing the relationship.

63 . . . Old barrio, my old barrio,
I enjoyed you when I was young,
Where I'd run about barefoot
In the midst of all my friends . . .
. . . They'd say we were poor,
But I never ever felt it.

I was happy in my world,
In that barrio that I loved.
[Author's translation]

Chapter 7 - Settling in San Fernando

64 A mission in Spanish California in the 1700s served several purposes. In tandem with military leaders, it served the king of Spain as an imperial outpost where Spanish friars conducted the religious instruction of the local Indian natives while simultaneously directing farming operations and organizing religious observances. They also taught the natives Spanish manual arts and presided over the spiritual life of the slow-growing secular communities like Los Angeles and San Gabriel. The Spanish Crown ordered the building of the Misión de San Fernando in 1797. See John A. Berger, *The Franciscan Missions of California* (New York: G. P. Putnam, 1948).

65 See W. W. Robinson. *San Fernando Valley: A Calendar of Events* (Seattle: The Shorey Bookstore, 1968), First Edition of Facsimile Reprint Ltd. to 100 copies, February 1968, p.3, if it were paginated.

66 The mission was named to commemorate *el rey* Fernando, King Ferdinand, a thirteenth-century monarch, who was canonized by the Catholic Church because he ousted the Moors from the city of Córdoba.

67 Clifford M. Zierer affirms that "The town was named for the valley in which it lay—," "San Fernando—A Type of Southern California Town," *Annals of the Association of American Geographers,* XXIV:1 (March 1934): 15.

68 This is the term that Zierer employs for the area near Griffith Park. See Zierer, Vol. 2, p. 8.

69 "Land for Sale. "1,000 Acres in the Town of San Fernando—" in Derward P. "Dode" Loomis (comp. and author), *San Fernando Retrospective: The First Fifty Years* (San Fernando, California: San Fernando Heritage, 1985), p. 20. Sen. Charles Maclay is considered one of the founders of San Fernando, 21. He represented a Northern California district in the state legislature in his earlier years. A Pennsylvanian minister and ex-vigilante in San Francisco, he was one of the two first Anglo-Americans to acquire land in the San Fernando vicinity. His granddaughter claimed he named the streets of San Fernando in honor of many of his friends: "O'Melveny Street, for a young Los Angeles attorney, Pico Street for Don Andrés Pico, Celis Street for De Celis, the original purchaser of the rancho, and Workman and Coronel Streets for former Los Angeles mayors." Loomis, p. 23.

70 Robinson, p. 20, if it were paginated.

71 The term *Anglo* here is used to refer to Americans of non-Hispanic descent.

72 Zierer, pp. 4–5.

73 Elva Meline, "Historical Sites of the San Fernando Valley," in Jorgenson (ed.), p. 99.

74 This home belonged to "Col." Henry C. Hubbard, a Vermonter who became an important local figure. Loomis, p. 28.

75 Loomis, p. 30.

76 Loomis, pp. 82–83.

77 San Fernando reported 7,567 in the 1930 census. US Department of Commerce, Bureau of the Census. *Fifteenth Census of the United States: 1930. Population. Volume I. Number and Distribution of Inhabitants.* (US Government Printing Office, 1931), p. 128.

78 I employ the term *Hispano* to refer to someone claiming Spanish and/or Spanish-Mexican heritage. The term is an umbrella word like *Latino*, a widely used term to refer to Americans of Latin American descent at the time of this writing, but Hispano possesses a historical dimension useful for the period under consideration here which the terms *Latino* and *Chicano* do not.

79 Californios is the name given by historians to the Spanish-speaking residents who remained in California after it passed from Mexico to the United States at the conclusion of the Mexican American War (1848). In my view, Californios and Tejanos, represent subcategories of Hispanos. Both were Spanish-Mexican, culturally speaking, and became US citizens by virtue of the treaty that concluded the hostilities, the Treaty of Guadalupe Hidalgo. See a discussion of Californios in Carey McWilliams's *North from Mexico: The Spanish-Speaking People of the United States* (New York: Greenwood Press Publishers New York, 1968), pp. 88–94.

80 As opposed to Baja California.

81 The Pico family is Gen. Andrés Pico's relatives. As the Mexican commander of the California forces, he capitulated to Lt. Col. John C. Fremont; he was also Pio Pico's brother, the last Mexican governor of California. See some brief notes about some of the local Californio families in Elva Meline's "Historical Sites of the San Fernando Valley," in Jorgenson (ed.), pp. 92–108.

82 Harrington, Marie. "Andrés Pico Adobe," *San Fernando Valley Historical Society* website, www.sfvhs.com/AndresPicoAdobe2.htm, accessed October 27, 2009. Text is borrowed from the society's *The Branding Iron*, December 1976, No. 124, 1977.

83 Loomis, p. 35.

84 Carey McWilliams, pp. 89–90. The word *cholo* has also been used to refer to poor Indian workers in the Andean nations since the 1600s. It came to be employed by young Latinos in California in the 1980s as well.

85 Zierer, p. 24.

86 Zierer claims that 7,500 inhabitants lived in San Fernando in 1933–34.

87 See many early photographs of Anglo-American homes in Loomis. See also the pictographic map of San Fernando created by The Sanford Map Company, 1918, held at the California State University at Northridge, Map Center, Geography Department.

88 McWilliams, p. 217.

89 Zierer, p. 11.

90 See Table I in Zierer, 13.

91 Gonzalez, Gilbert G. *Labor and Community: Mexican Citrus Worker Villages in a Southern California County, 1900–1950* (Urbana: University of Illinois, 1994).

92 Pronounced "el hahdee."

93 "Sanborn 1923 Land Use Maps," held by the Community Development Office of the City of San Fernando, California. The large pictographic map book was updated in 1951, supposedly.

94 *Santa Rosa de Lima. 50th Anniversary. 1925–1975*, issued as a pictorial directory (n.p., n.d.).

95 The word refers to a residential cluster, smaller than a barrio. The term is popular in Mexican cities.

96 In 2010, the *vecindad* building revealed seven units and two bathrooms, the latter most probably reconverted from one or two of the old units. The toilets in 1927 were reported as outdoor pit toilets.

97 McWilliams, p. 223.

98 See Emma Lazarus' poem "The New Colossus," inscribed on the Statue of Liberty.

99 Mike (Miguel), my brother, was the third-born child.

100 Valdez, Mary Gil de. Interview recorded on tape by the author May 1978, and multiple conversations on other dates, San Fernando, California. Manuel, Mary's brother, agrees about which units we occupied: "We lived at the end, the first one,"

he told me, adding that "my grandma and Juarez were in the next one."

101 The bonfires attracted outsiders undoubtedly. On at least one occasion, a family surnamed Herrera from Calexico was driving "up north" to work in the agricultural fields and having entered our barrio and driving past the vecindad they saw the people gathered around an evening fire; they stopped for a respite. They became lifelong friends of our family. Francisca, the mother, wrote poetry. I became a godfather to one of the Herrera boys. Conversation with paper notes with Mary Gil Valdez, April 7, 2008.

102 Mary, my sister, insists that the Cárdenas' in our past were related to the famous Mexican president Lázaro Cárdenas. Luis Cárdenas was Mary's baptismal godfather, and he and his brother Manuel were cousins to President Cárdenas. Conversation with paper notes with Mary Gil Valdez, April 7, 2008.

103 Department of Commerce. Bureau of the Census. Fifteenth Census of the United States: 1930. Population Schedule. Sheet No. 66A.

104 State officials reported in 1912 that large properties in the San Fernando Valley were in the process of being allotted into smaller portions. For example, "the Lankershim and Van Nuys Ranches were now being sold in tracts of 5–20 acres." In San Fernando, where "the Maclay Rancho Water Company and the Mission Land and Water Company" controlled large acreages, individual holdings approximated 10–40 acres. Near Burbank, landholdings varied from 20 to 80 acres, and in Glendale, 5–10 acres. *Report of the Conservation Commission of the State of California, January 1, 1913* (Sacramento: Friend William Richardson, Superintendent of State Printing, 1912).

105 J. Smeaton Chase, "Through the Valley by Horseback," in Jorgenson (ed.), p. 115. This is a reprint from *California Coast Trails*, 1913.

106 See John Walton's *Western Times and Water Wars: State, Culture, and Rebellion in California* (Berkeley: University of California Press, 1992), A Centennial Book. See also a review of these issues in Lawrence C. Jorgensen, "Subdivision and Subdividers" in Jorgenson (ed.), pp. 136–153.

107 Zierer, "The Citrus Industry of the Los Angeles Basin," *Economic Geography* 10:1 (January 1934), p. 57.

108 Gonzalez, p. 6.

109 Gonzalez, p.20.

Chapter 8 - Life Becomes Ever More Challenging

110 "Few realize that up until 1930, *all* Protestant denominations agreed with the Cath-

olic Church's teaching condemning contraception as sinful," in *Catholic Answers*, a website supporting the teachings of the Catholic Church, http://www.catholic.com/library/Birth_Control.asp.

111 Gunther, Francis A. (ed.) *Residue Reviews* (New York: Springer-Verlag New York Inc., 1969), p. 2.

112 Gunther, p. 102.

113 Mite killers.

114 For example, Gonzalez and Matt Garcia's *A World of Its Own: Race, Labor, and Citrus in the Making of Greater Los Angeles, 1900–1970* (Chapel Hill: The University of North Carolina Press, 2001).

115 *Gale Encyclopedia of Medicine* (Detroit: Gale, 1999), Vol. 5, p. 2932.

116 Abel, Emily K. "From Exclusion to Expulsion: Mexicans and Tuberculosis Control in Los Angeles, 1914–1940," *Bulletin of the History of Medicine* (2003) 77:830. The sanatorium became the Olive View Veteran's Hospital many decades later. Both my sisters, Soledad and Emily, worked there as a physical therapy aides.

117 See a 1927 sheet that appears to have been added as the last page of the 1923 Sanborn pictographic map book.

118 "Mexicans in California: Report of Governor CC. Young's Fact-Finding Committee" reprinted in Manuel P. Servín (ed.). *An Awakened Minority: The Mexican Americans*, Second Edition (Beverly Hills: Glencoe Press, 1974), pp. 64–79.

119 González, p. 29.

120 *Cuatro Milpas*, a popular *canción ranchera* written in three/four time was composed in the 1930s by Belisario de Jesús García, a native of Nuevo León.

121 Paul Webbink, "The Course of Unemployment" in Shannon, pp. 6–7.

122 There is ample literature on the Great Depression. See for example, Studs Terkel, *Hard Times: An Oral History of the Great Depression* (New York: Pantheon Books, 1970), David A. Shannan, (ed.), *The Great Depression* (Englewood Cliffs: Prentice-Hall, 1960), and Dixon Wecter, *The Age of the Great Depression, 1929–1941* (New York: The Macmillan Company, 1948).

123 Griswold del Castillo and De León, p. 87.

124 Acuña, Rodolfo. *Occupied America: A History of Chicanos* (New York: Longman, 2000), p. 222.

125 Acuña, ibid.

126 Griswold del Castillo and De León, ibid.

127 Letter to me dated January 11, 1978.

128 Manuel Gil, my brother.

129 *Repatriado* or repatriate is someone who accepted the offer to leave the United States at this time.

130 Agents of the Immigration and Naturalization Service or immigration officers.

131 The minister of agriculture under President Cárdenas, the controversial Gen. Saturnino Cedillo, visited Los Angeles in the first days of December 1935 for the purpose of publicizing government efforts to open up agricultural communities near Tijuana and Ensenada, Baja California, for Mexican repatriates. Eréndira was not mentioned in this report. He took advantage of his visit by spending several days as a tourist in Hollywood too. See *Los Angeles Times*, December 1, 1935.

132 A ballad.

133 Adios, California, Adios.
Adios tierra de ilusiones,
Ya me voy pa'l terrenzo
Y ahi te dejo tus millones.

134 Sánchez, p. 220.

135 Telephone conference with Mary Valdez, Manuel Gil, Soledad Gil Ruitenbach, and Emily Countryman, June 27, 2008.

136 The term was first coined by Sol Tax in *Penny Capitalism: A Guatemalan Economy* (Washington, DC: US Government Printing Office, 1953).

137 This excerpt from Guadalupe's memoirs and interviews deserves two comments. One is Bernabé's birthday. His certificate of baptism announces he was born three days after his baptism, July 26, 1899. His death certificate records his birth date as June 11.

138 *Bogue* (pronounced bohgay) is the Spanish corruption of buggy or a children's carriage—an old-fashioned baby stroller.

139 *Nixtamal* is an Aztec word used commonly in Spanish to refer to corn kernels already cooked in limewater prior to grinding into dough or masa. See Luis Cabrera, *Diccionario de Aztequismos* (Mexico: Ediciones Oasis, 1974), p. 99.

140 Propane gas was just beginning to be bottled in the US. See National Propane Gas Association website accessed February, 18, 2009, http://www.npga.org/i4a/pages/index.cfm? pageid=634.

141 A vessel made of volcanic stone used for grinding corn in accordance to pre-Hispanic practices.

142 Guadalupe uses the name Pacific Savings and Loan Company. A March 27, 1939, story ("Rescue Operation") in *Time* magazine refers to Pacific States as "the largest building and loan company in the US." It also reports that Robert Stewart Odell, chief owner, employed a complicated financial stratagem to gain full ownership of his company by reducing tenant rental fees by 20%.

143 Telephone conference with Mary Valdez, Manuel Gil, Soledad Gil Ruitenbach, and Emily Countryman, June 27, 2008.

144 Elsewhere in her autobiographical notes Guadalupe writes, "*La casita nos costó cién dólares y pagabamos diez por mes.*" (The little house cost us one hundred dollars, and we paid ten a month).

145 Buyer Instructions for Use in Pacific States Savings and Loan Company Escrows Only, n.d.; Deed. Pacific States Savings and Loan Company dated November 8, 1934; and Policy of Title Insurance, Title Guarantee and Trust Company dated December 14, 1934 (4 pp).

146 Petra Press, *A Cultural History of the United States through the 1930s* (San Diego: Lucent Books, Inc., 1999), p. 25. The editors of Petra Press assert that only 3% of American families were able to claim ownership of their homes in 1935.

147 He was registered as a woman, Florencia Juárez, probably as a result of funeral parlor clerks being unfamiliar with non-English names.

148 Gil, Manuel. Interview with Manuel Gil recorded digitally on November 22, 2008, in Golden Shores, Nevada.

149 "Flood Control Projects Cited," *Los Angeles Times*, September 25, 1926.

150 "Flood Prevention Work Assumes Great Proportions," *Los Angeles Times*, January 11, 1925.

151 *Vida del Valle de San Fernando* Vol. 4 No. 194 (December 2, 1937).

Chapter 9 - We Stumble Forward

152 Ibid.

153 *Cuando se aliviaba [de dar nacimiento] ya los pollos estaban listos para cocerlos.*

154 During World War II, Americans were encouraged to use their backyards to grow their own vegetables in a "Victory Garden."

155 McWilliams, pp. 224–225.

156 McWilliams, p. 172. McWilliams stands as an early and foremost advocate of social and political responsibility in California in addition to writing one of the earliest histories of Mexican Americans.

157 Tejanos (Teh-haanous) is the Spanish term for Texans of Mexican descent.

158 See his short discussion of the idea that California cities fed marginal urban workers into the agricultural migrant worker stream in Ernesto Galarza's *Farmworkers and Agribusiness in California, 1947–1960* (Notre Dame: University of Notre Dame Press, 1977), p. 6.

159 La Botz, Dan. *César Chávez and La Causa* (New York: Pearson Longman, 2006), p. 8.

160 McWilliams, Carey. *Factories in the Field: The Story of Migratory Farm Labor in California* (Boston: Little, Brown and Company, 1939). See also Dick Meister and Anne Loftis, *A Long Time Coming: The Struggle to Unionize America's Farm Workers* (New York: Macmillan Publishing Co. Inc., 1977).

161 Robert Kennedy served as the attorney general of the United States under his brother's administration, John F. Kennedy, 1961–1964. See Evan Thomas, *Robert Kennedy: His Life* (New York: Simon and Schuster, 2002).

162 "Anglo-Americans begin extending segregation to Mexican Americans after the Texas Revolution as a social custom. Tejanos formed a suspect class during and after the revolution, and that fact led to a general aversion of them . . . See "Segregation" in the *Texas State Historical Association* website. http://www.tshaonline.org/handbook/online/articles/pks01, accessed January 1, 2012. "In the town of Ozona in West Texas . . . hotels were exclusively reserved for Anglo patrons until 1958 . . ." in Montejano, David. *Anglos and Mexicans in the Making of Texas, 1836–1986* (Austin, TX: U. of Texas Press, 1987), p. 285.

163 John Steinbeck. *The Grapes of Wrath* (New York: The Viking Press, 1958), p. 147.

164 Our family lore included the phrase, *se le cayó la mollera* in reference to Rick's situation when he was an infant. The fontanelle is the soft spot that infants have on top of their head formed by the space separating the bony plates that remain soft and pliable at birth but ultimately harden and fuse together. Doctors believe that dehydration and/or malnutrition can delay the filling in of the space and the consequent disappearance of the *mollera*. See "Fontanelles-sunken," *MedlinePlus,*

A Service of the U.S .National Library of Medicine and the National Institutes of Health, www.nlm.nih.gov/medlineplus, accessed October 2, 2008. Medical note updated by Rachel A. Lewis, MD, FAAP, Columbia University.

165 See "Polio and Post-Polio Syndrome," in *MedlinePlus*.

166 "History of Poliomyelitis," in *Wikipedia*, http://en.wikipedia.org/wiki/History_of_poliomyelitis, accessed December 2, 2011.

167 See "History," *Allina Hospitals and Clinics, Sister Kenny Rehabilitation Institute* website, www.allina.com/ahs/ski.nsf/page/history. Sister Kenny was an Australian nurse, not a nun, who approached polio in an unconventional way. Her work led to the creation of an institute in Minneapolis.

168 Manuel could not recall any details about Mary's polio condition.

169 Rheumatic fever is an inflammatory disease that strikes youngsters. Mary remembers being taken to the Los Angeles County Hospital, where at one point a doctor wheeled her into a medical class and presented her as a case study to watchful interns.

170 The "survival of the fittest" is a term first used, reputedly, by Herbert Spencer in 1866, when he offered it as the socio-economic equivalent of Charles Darwin's "natural selection," namely the "preservation of favorite races in the struggle for life." In other words, farmers who own land will survive more easily than the farm workers they hire and for whom they fail to adequately shelter during their agricultural employment. See "Survival of the fittest," in the *Wikipedia*, http://en.wikipedia.org/wiki/Survival_of_the_fittest, accessed on May 3, 2012.

Chapter 10 - Our Toughest Years

171 The Bracero Program represents a treaty-approved system to place Mexican "guest workers" on American farms. It was launched during World War II between the United States and Mexico in order to replace rural workers absorbed into military industrial production. It began in 1943 and ended in 1965. See Richard Griswold del Castillo and Arnoldo De León, *North to Aztlán, A History of Mexican Americans in the United States* (New York: Twayne Publishers, 1996), pp. 104–109.

172 Our music vendor dressed in overalls and came by regularly, armed with the latest popular Mexican recordings. He would split the jukebox earnings with us and gift the old records to us—78's and later 45's. Some of these became the foundation of my record collection.

173 He was a young, slender, green-eyed *güero* with a noticeable hawk nose, who seemed to be allergic to work of any kind. My brothers and I gave him this moniker because his greetings never varied: "*¿Y 'tos que*? (*¿Y entonces que pasa*?). As these words greeted us, he would swagger and sway as he swept his right hand slightly across his chest while snapping his fingers, stifling a chuckle at the same time.

174 The word *pachuco* refers to a Mexican or Mexican-American Zoot-Zooter, a young man dressed in an extravagant style of the 1940s. "The first *pachucos* in San Fernando were known as *Tarzanes*, young urban toughs from Mexico City who arrived with the first waves of country bumpkin *braceros*." Mary Gil Valdez, telephone interview, October 30, 2008. She believes the *Tarzanes* were the prototypes to the native-born *pachucos*. The *tarzanes* did not last long in San Fernando because they were soon crowded out by the local *pachucos*, according to my sister.

175 Griswold del Castillo and De León, pp. 105–106.

176 "Diabetes is the number one cause of acquired blindness." People with diabetes are 60 percent more likely to develop cataracts according to the American Optometric Association website. http://www.aoa.org/x6814.xml.

177 President Lyndon B. Johnson, a Democrat from Texas, pursued its passage as part of his agenda for a Great Society in 1965.

178 Dad's Certificate of Death identifies uremia as the condition leading directly to his death. The attending doctor concluded that his *diabetes mellitus* had grown unabated for about eight years and his kidneys were no longer functioning properly; they no longer filtered bodily impurities from his blood.

179 National Archives and Records Administration (NARA); Washington D.C.; Naturalization Index Cards of the U.S. District Court for the Southern District of California, Central Division (Los Angeles), 1915-1976 (M1525) Microfilm Series M1525,

Roll 51. No. 7983811.

180 I thank Cesar Plata for helpfully confirming and summarizing my thoughts on this topic. I found his contribution in his "Historical Perspective on a Traditional Mexican Wedding" submitted as a term project for Professor Vicki Ruiz, University of California. See http://www.muybueno.net/articles/mexicanwedding2.html, a website organized by *info*BayArea.com ~ *Connecting* Circles of Influence, accessed August 12, 2010.

Chapter 11 - Looking Back at Our Toughest Years

181 "A study done in the psychology department at Temple University in Philadelphia shows the results of research on the adolescent brain and behavior. The parts of the brain responsible for impulse control, delayed gratification and good judgment are not fully developed until adulthood is reached at around twenty years of age. This may help explain why teenagers engage in risky behavior." Allan Schwartz, "Teenagers, Their Brains Are Different," *MentalHelp.net*, Allan Schwartz, PhD., Weblog, Posted by Allan N. Schwartz, LCSW, PhD, on Wed, May 2, 2007.

182 "Teenage girls are strictly forbidden to walk home from school with boys . . . [in one case in San Antonio in the 1950s a young mother remembered,] 'I could never go out at night—had to sit at home and embroider . . . Sometimes I was let go to a show on Sunday afternoons but always had to be home by five o'clock . . . I couldn't belong to any group at school which admitted both boys and girls . . . I was always treated very cruelly by my father. I was never allowed to have any friends, either boys or girls.'" Murray, CCVI, MA, Sister Mary John. *A Socio-Cultural Study of 118 Mexican Families Living in a Low-Rent Public Housing Project in San Antonio*, Texas (Washington DC: The Catholic University of America, 1954, reprinted by Arno Press, 1976), pp. 48–50.

183 Here are two examples of the many books on the subject of cross-cultural communication: David Jamieson and Julie O'Mara, *Managing Workforce 2000* (San Francisco: Jossey Bass, 1991) and Marilyn Loden and Judy B. Rosner, *Workforce America! Managing Employee Diversity as a Vital Resource* (Homewood Illinois: Business One Irwin, 1991).

184 Frias Armenta, Martha et al., "Determinants of Harsh Parenting in Mexico," *Journal of Abnormal Child Psychology* (April 1988), p. 1.

Chapter 12 - Connecting and Celebrating

185 ". . . [N]o one, relying on his own judgment shall, in matters of faith and morals... distorting the Holy Scriptures in accordance with his own conceptions, presume to interpret them...." Rev. H. J. Schroeder, O.P., *Canons and Decrees of the Council of Trent*. English Translation (Rockford, Illinois: Tan Books and Publishers Inc., 1978), pp. 18-19. These are words attributed to a Council of Trent decree (ca. 1550) that

discouraged Catholics to interpret the Bible on their own.

186 My information gathering led me to talk on the telephone on March 20, 2007, with Manuel J. Landín, Eusebio's eldest son. He confirmed my impression that his father was an educated man from a "big city" He was born in Topeka, Kansas, from Mexican railroad workers living there, and he graduated from a high school there. Manuel also stated that Eusebio bought *La Vida* from a man by the name of Carlos de Silva and published from about 1945 to 1955.

187 "Missionary Oblates of Mary Immaculate," *Wikipedia*, http://en.wikipedia.org/wiki/Missionary_Oblates_of_Mary_Immaculate, accessed on January 2011.

188 "[T]he evangelization of the Canadian West and of British Columbia was the almost exclusive work of the Oblate Fathers . . . ," *New Advent. Catholic Encyclopedia*, http://www.newadvent.org/cathen/, accessed January 2, 2011.

189 Scapulars date back to Europe in the 1600s, at least. The ones for lay people are made up of two badge-sized religious images, often blessed by a priest, one for the front and one for the back, worn next to your skin inside your clothes. Favorite images are the Sacred Heart, for example, Grandma's favorite icon. They serve as reminders of the wearer's dedication to the meaning of that image, fealty to the Sacred Heart of Jesus, for example. See "Scapular," *Wikipedia*, http://en.wikipedia.org/wiki/Scapular, accessed May 7, 2012.

190 *Santa Rosa de Lima. 50th Anniversary. 1925–1975*, issued as a pictorial directory (n.p., n.d.).

191 Sánchez, p. 182.

192 KWKW, one of the radio stations that carried Elena Salinas' broadcasts, claims to be the first radio station broadcasting in Spanish in the Los Angeles area. See Sánchez, p. 183.

193 Sánchez, p. 183.

194 Where Are They Now? LARadio.com by Don Barrett, http://www.laradio.com, accessed March 5, 2011.

195 These were the top five songs in April 1953 according to *Billboard*.

196 "The Shadow," *Wikipedia, The Free Encyclopedia*, http://en.wikipedia.org/wiki/The_Shadow, accessed March 8, 2011.

197 "I'll eat that prickly pear," a song written with double-meaning lyrics made popular by Jorge Negrete, the main character in a 1945 movie by the same name directed by Miguel Zacarías.

198 "Swear to me [you'll remember me]," written ca. 1926, made famous by the leading Mexican tenor of that time, José Mojica.

199 Written by Quirino Mendoza y Cortés ca. 1916, see *Wikipedia*, http://en.wikipedia.org/wiki/Jesusita_en_Chihuahua. See examples in *Danzones del Porfiriato y la Revolución*, a CD issued by the Dirección General de Culturas Populares, AMEF T-44-03, PECD-367.

200 See "The Federal TRIO Programs" in *Wikipedia*, http://en.wikipedia.org/wiki/TRIO_%28program%29, accessed on April 29, 2011.

201 See a Spanish description in *Wikipedia*, http://es.wikipedia.org/wiki/Solfeo#V.C3.A9ase_tambi.C3.A9n, accessed on April 28, 2011.

202 Genaro Codino (1852–1901), a native of Zacatecas, is the accredited composer of *La Marcha de Zacatecas*, considered Mexico's second national anthem. See "Marcha de Zacatecas," *Wikipedia*, http://en.wikipedia.org/wiki/Marcha_de_Zacatecas, accessed on April 29, 2011.

203 "Turi" was one of the boys in the band. Telephone conversation with Arturo (Turi) Chacón, May 23, 2011. Telephone conversation with Mike Naranjo, Telephone interview, April 26, 2011.

204 *"A la Capotín"* appears to be loved by people all over the Hispanic world. *"Es Mi Hombre"* was made famous by the Spanish singer and actress, Sara Montiel. Selena, the *tejana* singer who ended tragically helped popularize *"Amor y Lágrimas."*

205 A muse was a goddess in Greek literature, which represented the arts and sciences; for example, there was a muse of poetry, another of song, another of history, and so on. See Wendy Beckett, *Sister Wendy's Book of Muses* (New York: Harry N. Abrams, Inc., 2000).

206 No te asomes, amor
A mi existencia.
No te asomes al abismo de mi alma
Donde hay sombras y dolor unicamente.
No te asomes mucho menos
Al abismo de mis ojos.
En ellos no hay amor ya, ni luz,
Ni vida, se secaron de llorar tu ausencia.

207 Translation by Cruz Rodriguez (cruton) in *Mexico and Language, Open your Ojos*, http://holayadios.wordpress.com/author/cruton/, accessed April 15, 2011.

208 Patria Chica (Evocación)
¿Donde estás tierra querida,
Suelo hermoso, tierra amada?

¿Donde estás que no me miro junto
A ti, querida Patria . . .
Si no vuelvo a verte ya
Cielo azul de mi esperanza,
Amuleto de mi vida,
Evangelio de mi infancia;
Si no vuelvo a verte ya
[Será] porque muero en otro suelo
De otra tierra muy extraña.

Chapter 13 - Goodbye to the First Generation

209 Rose Marie Naranjo Thigpen, Telephone interview, April 26, 2011.

210 Lyrics of "*Cruz de Madera*," recorded by Los Huracanes del Norte.

Chapter 14 - The Second Generation

211 *Table 1, "Percent of the Population 25 Years and Over with a High School Diploma or Higher by Sex and Age, for the United States: 1940 to 2000,"* U.S. Census Bureau. Educational Attainment. A Half-Century of Learning: Historical Census Statistics on Educational Attainment in the United States, 1940 to 2000: Detailed Tables. *http://www.census.gov/hhes/socdemo/education/data/census/half-century/introduction.html, accessed on January 19, 2012.*

212 American Health Information Management Association, website, http://www.ahima.org/coding/, accessed May 18, 2011.

213 In one of the earliest chapters of the Cold War, the United States and its World War II allies rescued West Berlin from Soviet control in 1949 by supplying its people with needed food and fuel, a maneuver known as the Berlin Airlift, not expected by the Soviets.

214 The G.I. Bill (officially titled Servicemen's Readjustment Act of 1944) provided college or vocational education for returning World War II veterans. See *Wikipedia, the Free Encyclopedia*, accessed on May 24, 2011, http://en.wikipedia.org/wiki/G.I._Bill.

215 A Hindu "philosophical tradition concerned with the self-realization by which one understands the ultimate nature of reality." See *Wikipedia, the Free Encyclopedia*, http://en.wikipedia.org/wiki/Advaita, accessed June 6, 2011.

216 *Pocho* is used by Mexicans to refer to Mexican-origin Americans who speak a bastardized form of Spanish or no Spanish at all; it is usually a pejorative term. *Pocho* land is the United States.

217 The writing was on the wall when the out-of-state firm, Browning Ferris Indus-

tries (BFI), began soliciting bids in the city of Moorpark. It was now competing with companies like G. I. Rubbish and Economy Disposal, eventually putting them out of business or buying them outright, see *The Los Angeles Times*, April 19, 1995. See also "A Brief History of Solid Waste Management in the U.S., 1950-2000," in *MSW Management, The Journal for Municipal Solid Waste Professionals,* website, http://www.mswmanagement.com/july-august-2000/history-solid-waste.aspx, accessed June 1, 2011.

218 The Ronald Reagan administration shut down the United States Information Agency and the binational centers slowly withered.

219 Telephone interview with Victoria C. Emanuel, June 12, 2011.

220 Telephone interview with Victoria Gil, June 29, 2011.

221 Price Pfister specialized in manufacturing faucets and valves. "Anodizing . . . increases corrosion resistance and wear resistance and provides better adhesion for paint primers and glues than bare metal." See "Pfister (firm)," in *Wikipedia, The Free Encyclopedia,* http://en.wikipedia.org/wiki/Pfister_%28firm%29, accessed July 25, 2011, and "Sokol Space Suit" on the Canadian educational science website, http://www.science24.org/show/Sokol_space_suit, accessed July 25, 2011, Science 24.

Afterword

222 "San Fernando, California," in *The Wikipedia*, http://en.wikipedia.org/wiki/San_Fernando,_California, accessed January 9, 2012. The percentage cited is drawn from the US Census Bureau.

223 And, in other places too. Recent contributions to Mexican American Studies now provide us with an understanding of Mexican Americans living and working in other parts of the country like Washington State, Kansas and Chicago, Illinois, for example, all of which simply adds to my regional hypothesis. See, García, John R. et al. *Mexicans in the Mid West* (Tucson: University of Arizona, 1989); Arredondo, Gabriela F. *Mexican Chicago: Race, Identity, and Nat*ion (Urbana: University of Illinois, 2008), Statute of Liberty-Ellis Island Centennial Series; Gamboa, Erasmo. *Mexican Labor and World War II: Braceros in the Pacific Northwest, 1942-1947* (Seattle: University of Washington, 2000); and García, Jerry. *Mexicans in North Central Washington* (Charleston SC: Arcadia Publishing, 2007), Images of America.

224 McArthur, Judith N. and Harold L. Smith. *Texas Through Women's Eyes. The Twentieth Century Experience* (Austin: University of Texas, 2010), p. 177. Social historians of Texas are well served with this important volume.

225 Montejano,David. *Anglos and Mexicans in the Making of Texas, 1836-1986* (U. of Texas Press, 1987), p. 285.

226 *Occupied America. A History of Chicanos*, 4th ed. (New York:Longman, 2000), p. 258.

227 The Texas State Historical Association website states that "Anglo-Americans begin extending segregation to Mexican Americans after the Texas Revolution as a social custom." http://www.tshaonline.org/handbook/online/articles/pks01 accessed January 1, 2012.

228 *The Many Faces of the Mexican American People: an essay concerning Chicano character* (Seattle: Centro de Estudios Chicanos, University of Washington, 1982).

229 Better, Sherry. *Institutional Racism, A Primer on Theory and Strategies for Social Change*, Second Edition (Lanham MD: Rowman and Littlefield, 2008), p. 10-11.

230 "Institutional Racism in American Society: A Primer." http://profiles.nlm.nih.gov/ps/access/BBGDQM.ocr, accessed on March 21, 2012.

231 For example see "Deconstructing America: The Rise of Subnational Identities," in Samuel P. Huntington, *Who Are We? The Challenges to America's National Identity* (New York: Simon & Schuster, 2004), pp.

232 Multiculturalism is "the doctrine that several different cultures (rather than one national culture) can coexist peacefully and equitably in a single country)." I thank Princeton University's WordNet for this simple but effective definition, http://wordnet.princeton.edu/, accessed March 25, 2012.

233 Affirmative Action legislation offered Hispanics, Blacks and other groups "protection" from unfair discrimination under the EEOC (Equal Employment Opportunity Commission) created by Title VII of the Civil Rights Act of 1964. See "Teaching with Documents: The Civil Rights Act of 1964 and the Equal Employment Opportunity Commission," National Archives, http://www.archives.gov/education/lessons/civil-rights-act/, accessed on May 13, 2012.

234 Alfonso Valenzuela, one of the author's correspondents in Tucson undoubtedly represents the feelings of many Arizona Latinos who feel endangered by the spirit behind SB1070. He wrote these words to me: "In my humble opinion, our community in Tucson and by extension, other areas along the U.S.-Mexico Border like Douglas, Pirtleville, Nogales, Arizona and Phoenix are facing 'blatant racism.' There is enough evidence that indicates or points to a well-orchestrated scheme to disenfranchise anyone who looks Mexican."

235 See "Examples of Antisemitic Legislation, 1933-1939," *United States Holocaust Memorial Museum*, http://www.ushmm.org/wlc/en/article.php?ModuleId=10007459, accessed May 15, 2012.

236 The Arizona Legislature banned ethnic studies courses fearing they promote "the overthrow of the American government." See *The Arizona Republic*, January 1,

2011.

Appendix I - Searching for My Father's Origins

237 The history of Chavinda dates from the sixteenth century, at least. According to one investigator, it is located on an old pre-Hispanic route connecting the ancient network of Tarascan or Purépeche communities in the south with the northern Chichimeca lands, including Jalisco—it may have been a frontier town during the Spanish colonial period. The earliest documentary mention of Chavinda occurs in *La Tasación de Ortega* (1528), a report about land disputes aired before the Spanish colonial government. In the sixteenth century, the town of Chavinda was surrounded by the original land grants, in the form of haciendas, given to the first twenty families that founded nearby Zamora-Jacona soon after the conquest of central Mexico by Hernán Cortés. None of these properties were held by a Gil. See Andrés Sierra Rubio, *La hacienda del valle de Chavinda en el tiempo y el espacio. Tenencia de la tierra y problemática social, 1528–1778*. Coordinación de Apoyo Municipal, Gobierno de Michoacán. Información Monográfica Municipal, 1986.

238 Oficina del Registro Civil. This office was directed by Lic. Antonio Valencia, a judge (*juez*) assigned by the state government. He made a special effort to look through his prized but well-worn registry books and found nothing. There are no copies of these old handwritten books and there are no Xerox copying services either despite the fact that the office stays busy with many requests for typed transcriptions of the records.

239 "*Enclopédia de los Municípios de México. Michoacán. Chavinda.*" http://www.e-local.gob.mx/work/templates/enciclo/michoacan/mpios/16023a.htm, accessed January 21, 2012.

240 I visited Chavinda in the company of my mother ca. 1970, but I lacked the frame of mind to investigate my father's origins. Possessing the right frame of mind in May 2002, returning in my own car from Mexico City, I was unable to get out and walk around because I had sprained an ankle that very morning. This rendered me unable to get out of my vehicle much less do anything else. Traveling alone and beset by pain and not having a set of crutches, I had to leave my father's hometown quite reluctantly. I wrote a short piece about my frustrating experience published on the Internet entitled, "I Couldn't Walk in My Father's Hometown."

241 One of these very helpful *chavindeños* living in the United States was Lupita Gil, wife of Antonio Maciel, Los Angeles residents. Before immigrating to Los Angeles, Antonio worked for a municipal administration in Chavinda headed by one Alfredo Gil.

242 He was a nephew of Francisco Negrete Sotelo who visited Bernabé in 1926. The Negrete family has a lot of Franciscos.

243 This Negrete family seems to have little or no connection with a Mexican singer who became internationally popular in the 1950s by the name of Jorge Negrete.

244 The elders of the Negrete family believed they originated elsewhere. Gonzalo (b. 1926?–2008?) told me they arrived in Palmira from Piedras Negras, Coahuila, in the late 1920s. My *tío* Pancho, his older brother (b. 1922–d. 1995?) offered that his grandfather, Pedro, moved to Palmira from San Juan Amangacutiro, Michoacán, in the 1890s, although the latter place name does not appear in the *Diccionario Porrúa*. They all agree their ancestors were agricultural workers, and Pedro was a supervisor in the digging of irrigation canals in the Palmira area. Francisco Negrete García Interview, with paper notes, April 30, 1978, San Fernando, CA.

245 Sierra Rubio, pp. 40–41.

246 The hacienda was owned by Antonio Méndez Bernal, according to Francisco Negrete García.

247 See "A Time of Revolution," chapter 1.

248 See chapter 10 for a discussion of the Bracero Program.

249 Telephone conversation with Mary Gil Valdez on January 14, 2008, Mary attending the birthday feast.

250 Negrete García, Francisco. Interview recorded with paper notes, April 30, 1978, San Fernando, CA. The name of the town was changed from Ario de Santa Monica to Arios de Rayón as part of the federal government's attempt to glorify Mexican heroes. The "Rayón" here probably refers to Ignacio López Rayón, a fighter for Mexican independence from Spain.

251 Mormon Digital Archives, Family Search Internet, www.familysearch.org.

CPSIA information can be obtained
at www.ICGtesting.com
Printed in the USA
FSHW021829230319
56626FS